"Drs. Parker-Bell and Osborn provide readers with a meticulously organized book that promotes art therapy and career counseling collaborations. This book is timely and inspiring for practitioners wishing to creatively engage students or clients in career exploration."

Patricia D. Isis, *PhD, LMHC-QS, ATR-BC, ATCS, certified mindful self-compassion teacher*

"Many of us have clients who get stuck in the logical side of the brain when considering careers. Art therapy interventions have the power to push them into the creative side where inspiration lives. This book explores many career theories through the lens of art and creativity."

Lisa Severy, *PhD, NCDA, certified career counselor*

"This book is a definite YES for career counseling courses and will be a wonderful resource for both practitioners and students. A shining example of interdisciplinary collaboration, this remarkable synthesis of career counseling and art therapy will aid clients to visualize their career path, goals, and obstacles more clearly."

Gail Rule, *MEd, ATR-BC, LPC-S, LICDC-S, professor at Ursuline College*

Art Therapy and Career Counseling

Art Therapy and Career Counseling is a comprehensive career development guide that offers creative approaches for understanding, assessing, and supporting ethical career development strategies.

This book expands on traditional approaches by adding a robust art therapy lens to topics such as career development theories, relational approaches, career resource identification, multicultural concerns, and ethical practices. Additionally, research and practice findings of art therapists, counselors, psychologists, educators, and students are utilized as sources for career-centered art-based strategies.

Art therapy educators, art therapists, counselors, and psychologists will appreciate creative approaches to teaching and applying career development through the lifespan.

Barbara Parker-Bell, ATR-BC, is the director of Art Therapy Programs at Florida State University. She is a Fulbright scholar and the former president of the Art Therapy Credentials Board.

Debra Osborn, NCC, is a professor and past president of both the National and Florida Career Development Associations, and fellow of NCDA and the American Counseling Association.

Art Therapy and Career Counseling

Creative Strategies for Career Development
Across the Lifespan

Barbara Parker-Bell and Debra Osborn

Routledge
Taylor & Francis Group

NEW YORK AND LONDON

Designed cover image by Sena Karatas Ozturk

First published 2023
by Routledge
605 Third Avenue, New York, NY 10158

and by Routledge
4 Park Square, Milton Park, Abingdon, Oxon, OX14 4RN

Routledge is an imprint of the Taylor & Francis Group, an informa business

© 2023 Taylor & Francis

The right of Barbara Parker-Bell and Debra Osborn to be identified as authors of this work has been asserted in accordance with sections 77 and 78 of the Copyright, Designs and Patents Act 1988.

Library of Congress Cataloging-in-Publication Data
Names: Parker-Bell, Barbara (Barbara Faye), author. | Osborn, Debra S., 1968- author.
Title: Art therapy & career counseling : creative strategies for career development across the lifespan / Barbara Parker-Bell, Debra Osborn.
Description: New York, NY : Routledge, 2023. | Includes bibliographical references and index.
Identifiers: LCCN 2022034083 (print) | LCCN 2022034084 (ebook) | ISBN 9780367476687 (hardback) | ISBN 9780367476656 (paperback) | ISBN 9781003035756 (ebook)
Subjects: LCSH: Vocational guidance–Vocational guidance–United States. | Art therapy–Vocational guidance–United States. | Vocational guidance–Methodology.
Classification: LCC HF5382.5.U5 P34 2023 (print) | LCC HF5382.5.U5 (ebook) | DDC 331.7020973–dc23/eng/20221128
LC record available at https://lccn.loc.gov/2022034083
LC ebook record available at https://lccn.loc.gov/2022034084

ISBN: 978-0-367-47668-7 (hbk)
ISBN: 978-0-367-47665-6 (pbk)
ISBN: 978-1-003-03575-6 (ebk)

DOI: 10.4324/9781003035756

Typeset in Baskerville
by KnowledgeWorks Global Ltd.

Contents

Acknowledgments

From Barbara

The process of co-creating this book has been exhilarating, rewarding, and sometimes daunting as we navigated associated pandemic challenges in addition to "normal" day-to-day work tasks and life activities. Therefore, I am tremendously grateful to those who helped to support this labor of love during the past few years. First, I extend my greatest appreciation and respect to my co-author, Deb Osborn, for her depth of knowledge, spirit of adventure, and patience with some of my "creative" ways of approaching book ideas and tasks. I value the rich and wonderful collaborations and blossoming friendship that we have shared. Second, I thank the FSU Art Therapy Program graduate assistants who contributed to the development of the book in so many ways. These students include Sarah Bell, Megan Buzby, Madi Forgione, Jennifer Suarez, and Kayla Walker. Thank you for your art explorations and artworks, scholarly resource investigations, and the animated brainstorming discussions which helped me grapple with book content and student learning perspectives. Importantly, I must also provide thanks to the art therapy students who participated in Career Development and Art Therapy classes during the past years, where many of the included art processes were tested and refined. Witnessing your creativity and learning processes inspired the idea of this book. Finally, I extend thanks to my family members who actively cheered me on, participated in career related discussions, and offered perspectives on career concepts through creative expressions (thank you, Wilson). And to my husband, Rich Daniels, who has patiently waited for my answer to be yes to the question, "Are you ready for a road trip?" Thanks a million times over, and yes, let's hit the road!

From Deb

For someone with a Holland code of ASI, perhaps it was just a matter of time that my path would lead to co-authoring a book on art therapy and career counseling. Or that on this path I would happen upon so many creative wonderful people, including my dear friend and co-author, Barbara Parker-Bell, our colleague who introduced us, Dave Gussak, or my animator/artist/author husband, Keith Osborn. I am so grateful to each one of these inspiring artists who see possibilities that aren't evident to anyone else, who are willing to try new things without fear – and more importantly, who encourage others to do the same. Barbara, I am so grateful for your insight, humor, creativity, and wisdom – our talks are often the highlight of my day. I also appreciate my cognitive information processing theorist/researcher friends and colleagues: Jim Sampson, Gary Peterson, Janet Lenz, Bob Reardon, Seth Hayden, Emily Bullock-Yowell, Casey Dozier, and the rest of the CIP crew who tolerate and even encourage that "A" side of me. Finally, a shout out to my family – my mother, Dr. Verna Norris who helped tremendously with the "C" task of alphabetizing author names for the index; my dad, Bob Norris, who teased me about burning down the house while I worked on chapters by scented candlelight but also encouraged me to keep with it; and my daughters, Sarah and Savannah, who inspire me daily with their individual passions and talents – I can't wait to see what happens next in your lives. And Keith, I am most grateful for you. You challenge me to look beyond the obvious, to search for beauty when it's hard to find, to delight in the uncommon, to risk taking roads less traveled. Thank you for walking beside me each step of the way.

1   Introduction

Art Therapy and Career Counseling: Harnessing Creative Strategies to Promote Career Exploration, Career Satisfaction, and Mental Health

This chapter serves as the introduction to the art therapy and career counseling fields, beginning with painting a picture of the two separate fields from their history to the present, including their specific unique attributes while also highlighting where they can partner to help a practitioner enhance a client's understanding of themselves, their options, their career satisfaction, and their mental health needs.

Introduction

Legacy. History. Roots. Where we come from. Having an idea of one's background, family history, and experiences serves as a reminder that no person is an island, in this current period of time, with no connections to the past or the future. The same is true with the professional fields of art therapy and career counseling. Understanding from whence the professions came, appreciating how each period of time impacted the development of these fields, ultimately leads to the question of "Where are the professions heading?" What impact will today's emphases in the field have on tomorrow's concerns and cures? For what will the profession be known?

Before delving into the respective histories of art therapy and career counseling, take a minute and think about the projections you have for your prospective field. At the end of your life, or even 10 or 20 years from now, if you were to see an advertisement for your profession on a billboard or online, what would you like the headline to be, as well as the main comments? In Figure 1.1, create the content for a billboard for the profession's future focus.

After completing the billboard, evaluate from your perspective how the profession is doing towards meeting that goal. What steps or changes need to occur in order for the profession to move forward? What might prohibit or slow this progression? By the end of the chapter, a clearer picture should emerge of where the fields are now and the factors that impacted their development, as well as the current trajectory moving forward. Given that readers of this book have an interest in art therapy, career counseling, and hopefully, both, we hope that readers will feel empowered to take practical steps towards making the envisioned future a reality.

Foundations of Art Therapy

Important Historical Impacts

The field of art therapy is still considered a relatively young mental health profession, although its foundation is built upon the long history of humanity's use of the arts for healing, community building, communication, and personal expression and reflection.

DOI: 10.4324/9781003035756-1

Figure 1.1 Blank Billboard

For the purposes of this book, historical frameworks pertaining to the development of art therapy as a mental health discipline will predominantly center on occurrences in the United States. It is important to recognize, however, that the practice of art therapy occurs globally, with variations in methods, professional status, educational standards, and training occurring according to each country's social and historical framework, their conceptual and practical structures for understanding and promoting mental health, and cultural traditions and preferences for arts engagement. Additionally, it is important to acknowledge that this history will be brief and therefore incomplete. Therefore, I invite readers who have an interest in the development of art therapy in the United States or in other regions, to explore this rich history further. Figure 1.2 captures some of the major art therapy influences and milestones in the US.

The 1940s–1950s: Psychodynamic Origins and Art of the Mentally Ill

Art therapist and art therapy educator Maxine Junge (1994, 2010, 2016) has compiled many of the available histories of the art therapy profession in the United States. According to Junge (2016) and those before her (Ulman, Kramer, & Kwiatkowska, 1978), the origins of art therapy in the United States began with work of Margaret Naumburg in the 1940s. Naumburg's practices were informed by Freudian and Jungian principles of

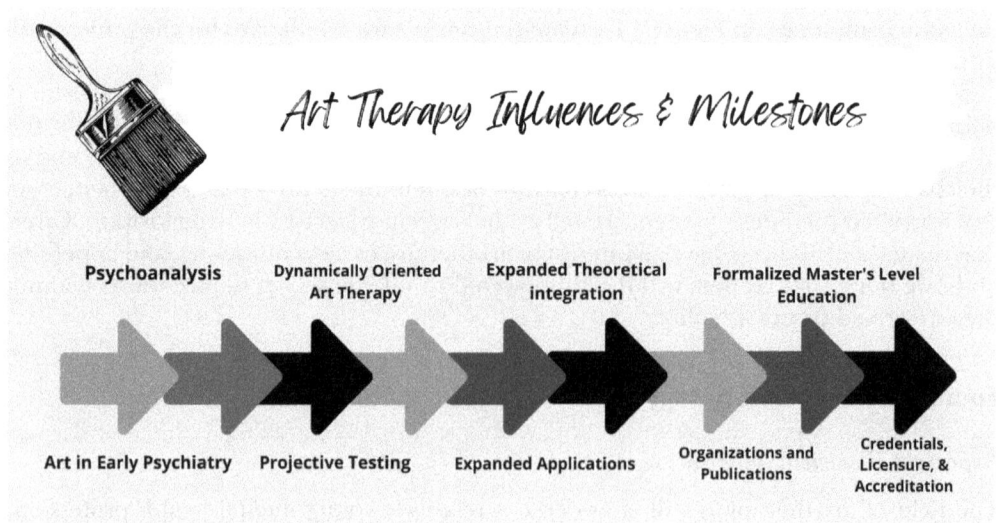

Figure 1.2 Art Therapy Influences and Milestones

psychoanalysis and entailed clients' engagement in spontaneous artmaking that revealed unconscious processes. Naumburg described art as symbolic speech and the type of psychotherapy she conducted dynamically oriented art therapy (Naumburg, 1987). Her aims for art therapy focused on promoting insight and resolving conflicts through the exploration of revealed unconscious material and deemphasized the focus on creating aesthetically pleasing or finalized works of art.

In the later 1950s, Edith Kramer was also influenced by Freudian principles but saw the roles and practices of art therapists somewhat differently (Ulman, Kramer, & Kwiatkowska, 1978). She worked predominantly with children and described the role of the art therapist as a combination of artist, art teacher, and therapist whose aim was to provide clients with symbolic artistic experiences that brought unconscious materials closer to the surface so that conflicts could be contained and integrated via creative acts and production. Kramer's approach has been informally termed "art as therapy" as less emphasis was placed on facilitating verbal association and insight. In contemporary art therapy, art psychotherapy and art as therapy are not dichotomous positions, but are approaches that are often intertwined based on client developmental factors and needs.

Psychiatrists working with people institutionalized for mental illness also became fascinated with the power of visual arts for understanding patients' inner experiences and began studying artworks created by patients. For example, with support of psychiatrists in the 1940s, British artist Edward Adamson established a studio environment within the psychiatric institution, providing patients with their own easel and materials for drawing and painting (Hogan, 2000). Patients who were participating or scheduled to participate in psychotherapy that may have difficulty expressing feelings were referred to the studio (Hogan, 2000). Visual productions were collected and reviewed and kept by psychiatrists as client case notes. Similarly, psychiatrists in the United States enlisted the talents of artists to reach their clients. Mary Huntoon in the 1940s and Don Jones in the 1950s provided art instruction and psychotherapy to patients at sites affiliated with Menninger's Clinic in Kansas (Junge, 2016). Their efforts inspired other psychiatrists, such as Pedro Corrons, to cultivate arts-based programs in other psychiatric institutions and regions of the US (Junge, 2016).

Projective Testing

During this time period, psychiatrists and psychologists began to incorporate visual phenomena and artmaking into projective testing. For example, the Rorschach test examiners offer a series of inkblots, and clients are asked what they see, and later how they see it. Patterns of associations and methods for identifying items within the blots were used to identify personality constructs and presence of mood disorders, psychosis, and more (Exner, 2003). Other projective tests, such as Draw-a-Person (Machover, 1952), the House-Tree-Person (Buck, 1948; Hammer, 1969), and the Kinetic Family Drawing (Burns, 1982), were designed to provide psychologists with visual data and verbal reflections that could be analyzed to assess developmental progress, self-concept, personality constructs, and family system relational dynamics. These projective tests pre-dated the art therapy profession but have influenced art therapy assessment design and implementation in subsequent years. Contemporary art therapy assessments incorporate observation of artistic processes and responses to material and the therapist, consideration of the art's formal qualities and graphic indicators, as well as client associations elicited through writing or verbal reflection. See Chapter 4 for more information on art therapy assessment applications and approaches.

1960s and Beyond: Expanding Theoretical Frameworks and Practical Applications

In the 1960s and following decades, a significant expansion of influential people, places, and ideas contributed to the further development of art therapy in the United States. For example, artist and early art therapist, Hanna Kwiatkowska worked with clients and their families at the National Institute for Health in the 1960s and early 1970s. She developed family art evaluations and research which stimulated the integration of art therapy into family systems work (Kwiatkowska, 1973). Kwiatkowska's work demonstrated the value of providing interactive creative tasks to families in order to reveal interactional patterns and themes. Other emerging practitioners integrated art-based processes into humanistic approaches inspired by Gestalt frameworks (Rhyne, 1973) and creative arts approaches using art, music, and movement to support clients' expression and self-actualization (McNiff, 1981; Rogers, 2001). In the 1970s, cognitive behavioral therapy (CBT) concepts began to appear in art therapy literature and art therapists such as Rosal (2016) who incorporated practices into art therapy work with children experiencing behavioral issues. Additionally, the inclusion of spiritual dimensions within art therapy has been embraced by some art therapists, as artmaking can be cultivated as a contemplative process that generates well-being (Franklin, 2016). Given the advent of these approaches, and a list of other approaches too long to mention, art therapy practices designed to address a variety of treatment goals extended beyond psychiatric institutions into other settings such as schools, retirement homes, addiction treatment centers, community counseling centers, community-based studios, museums, and prisons.

Recognizing Diverse Perspectives and Contributions

Early histories of art therapy in the United States frequently overlooked contributions of art therapists of color (Stepney, 2019). In her writings, Stepney called attention to the significant contributions of several individuals including African American art therapy professionals Georgette Powell and Cliff Joseph. In 2008, Powell received the American Art Therapy Association Pioneer Award for "enduring effect on the field of art therapy" and the importance of her contributions to the profession (Stepney, 2019, p. 116). Her work in art therapy began in the 1960s after years of accomplishments as an artist and community activist. She studied art therapy with pioneering art therapists Edith Kramer and Elinor Ulman and founded community-based programs for older adults and youth which included art therapy and education services. During her professional work, Powell mentored art therapy students of color and advocated for effort to engage minority groups in professional preparation as art therapists. Unfortunately, underrepresentation of minority groups within the field of art therapy is still a contemporary concern.

   Cliff Joseph was trained as an illustrator and commercial artist, but his art therapy origins stemmed from his experiences growing up in Panama and Harlem, and were further influenced by the social political contexts of the 1964 Civil Rights Act. Consequently, Joseph viewed arts engagement as a means to activate personal and systemic change (Stepney, 2019). In the late 1960s and 1970s, Joseph's art therapy engagement amplified the importance of group art therapy processes as he facilitated mural groups within psychiatric settings. Following these early art therapy experiences, Joseph accepted faculty and organizational leadership roles within educational and professional organizations. Importantly, Joseph articulated the consequences of economic, racial, and systemic oppression on psychological processes and called for these concerns to be addressed within and outside of the art therapy profession. His work foreshadowed contemporary attention on unjust systemic dynamics and its impact on mental health and equitable access to career opportunities.

Puerto Rican American art therapist Wayne Ramirez began his engagement with art therapy in the 1960s and has since served as an art therapy practitioner, educator, grant writer, organizational leader, mentor, and designer and administrator of arts-based programs (Potash & Ramirez, 2013). One of many areas of Ramirez contributions to art therapy include his development of accessible art programs within special education settings and his advocacy for students with learning and physical disabilities. Of particular relevance to this book is Ramirez's management of vocational and transitional services for students with disabilities in the US Virgin Islands.

Unfortunately, so many art therapists who have significantly contributed to the development of therapy are not mentioned in this chapter. I encourage readers to engage in a more thorough exploration of art therapy history, theory, applications, and practices with close attention to contributors of a variety of backgrounds and cultural experiences. Additionally, art therapy contributions related to career development and art therapy topics will be featured within subsequent chapters.

From Mentorship to Formalized Education

Many of the pioneers of art therapy began their journey towards a professional identity as an art therapist via multiple paths and experiences related to art training, personal engagement in psychoanalysis or other forms of personal growth exploration, studies in related fields, peer mentorship, or psychiatrists' invitations to apply their knowledge and skill sets in mental health service environments (Junge & Wadeson, 2006). It was not until 1969 that the first graduate level art therapy training program was founded. Currently, more than 35 art therapy master's programs exist and follow rigorous educational standards. Programs that meet these standards may achieve approval status by the American Art Therapy Association Educational Program Approval Board (EPAB) or accreditation status from the Commission on Accreditation of Allied Health Education Programs (CAAHEP).

Journals

Scholarly journals serve an important role in disseminating information regarding emerging and well-developed professional fields. In 1961, the first journal in the United States dedicated to art therapy was *The Bulletin of Art Therapy* developed by art therapist Elinor Ulman (Junge, 2010). The journal's name changed to the *American Journal of Art Therapy* in 1970 and continued to publish scholarly works until 2002 (Junge, 2016). Following the establishment of the American Art Therapy Association, *Art Therapy: The Journal of the American Art Therapy Association* was also established and has provided scholarly art therapy to the public for over 30 years. Other important journals related to the art therapy field include: *The Arts in Psychotherapy*, the *Canadian Journal of Art Therapy*, and the *International Journal of Therapy*, formerly known as *Inscape*.

Organizations

As interest and practice throughout the United States expanded, professional organizations formed to support exchanges of ideas, to formalize conceptualizations of art therapy education, establish ethical principles and practice, and to foster recognition and research. Three related organizations will be described here.

The American Art Therapy Association (AATA), was formed in 1969 by those aspiring to form art therapy as a distinct profession (Junge, 2010). Junge notes that the establishment of the organization was not without some controversy, as some key art therapy figures did not endorse separating from psychiatric organizations which emphasized art and diagnostics, while others wished to separate in order to further develop art therapy as a form of treatment. Over 50 years later, AATA has developed into an active membership and advocacy organization that contributes to the recognition and advancement of the art therapy field on state and national levels.

The Art Therapy Credentials Board (ATCB) is a certified credentialing organization whose mission is to "protect the public by promoting the competent and ethical practice of art therapy through the credentialing of art therapy professionals" (ATCB, 2022). The ATCB evaluates art therapists' competencies through registration processes, the Art Therapy Board Certification Examination (ATBCE), and the facilitation of credential renewal processes that require professionals to engage in continuing education for maintenance of professional skills. Additionally, the ATCB, has established the Code of Ethics, Conduct and Disciplinary Procedures and addresses violations of the code.

The International Expressive Arts Therapy Association (IEATA), established in 1994, supports "expressive arts therapists, artists, educators, consultants and others using integrative, multimodal arts processes for personal and community growth and transformation" (IEATA, 2022a). IEATA provides an international network for expressive arts therapists and provides registration processes to promote professional excellence and ethical standards in the field of expressive therapies.

Current Definitions Relevant to Art Therapy

As this book is designed for art therapists, counselors, and career practitioners, additional terms will be provided additional clarity regarding the field of art therapy.

> *Art as Therapy*: "In art as therapy, where the goal is *sublimation* through the creative process, there is usually less discussion and more emphasis on helping the patient to create a finished and satisfying product" (Rubin, 2016, p. 30).
>
> *Art Psychotherapy*: "In art psychotherapy, where the goal is *uncovering and insight*, there is generally less emphasis on the product, and more interviewing about the art, as well as an attempt to help the individual to relate it to" themself (Rubin, 2016, p. 30).
>
> *Art Therapists*: "Art therapists are master-level clinicians who work with people of all ages across a broad spectrum of practice. Guided by ethical standards and scope of practice, their education and supervised training prepares them for culturally proficient work with diverse populations in a variety of settings. Honoring individuals' values and beliefs, art therapists work with people who are challenged with medical and mental health problems, as well as individuals seeking emotional, creative, and spiritual growth" (American Art Therapy Association, 2022)
>
> *Art Therapy*: "Art therapy is an integrative mental health and human services profession that enriches the lives of individuals, families, and communities through active art-making, creative processes, applied psychological theory, and human experience within a psychotherapeutic relationship" (American Art Therapy Association, 2022)
>
> *Art Therapy Certified Supervisor (ATCS)*: The ATCS credential "is designed for ATR-BCs who have acquired specific training and skills in clinical supervision. Working with an ATCS ensures that current art therapy students and early-career practitioners receive the best art therapy clinical supervision available." (Art Therapy Credentials Board, 2022).
>
> *Board Certified Art Therapist*: "The Board Certified Art Therapist (ATR-BC) is the highest-level art therapy credential. ATR-BCs pass a national examination, demonstrating comprehensive knowledge of the theories and clinical skills used in art therapy. All board-certified art therapists (ATR-BC) are required to recertify their board

certification every five years through the completion of 100 continuing education credits or successful passage of the ATCBE national examination" (Art Therapy Credentials Board, 2022).

Creative Arts Therapies: "Creative Arts Therapies is an umbrella term for healthcare professions that use the creative and expressive process of art making to improve and enhance the psychological and social well-being of individuals of all ages and health conditions. Creative arts therapies use the relationship between the client and therapist and among clients in group or dyadic therapy in the context of the creative-expressive process as a dynamic and vital force for growth and change" (Shafir et al., 2020).

Expressive Arts: "The expressive arts combine the visual arts, movement, drama, music, writing and other creative processes to foster deep personal growth and community development. ... By integrating the arts processes and allowing one to flow into another, we gain access to our inner resources for healing, clarity, illumination and creativity" (International Expressive Arts Therapy Association, 2022a).

Expressive Therapies Continuum: "A means to classify how clients interact with art media or other experiential activities in order to process information and form images" organizing media interactions developmentally from simple to complex including kinesthetic, sensory, perceptual, affective, cognitive, symbolic and creative levels (Hinz, 2020, p. 4).

Media Dimension Variables: Classification of art media use in regard to the variables of complexity, structure, and media properties. Materials' properties and associated tasks may be classified as high complexity or low complexity related to the number of steps necessary for completion of the task; unstructured or structured, related to prescribed or open-ended material use; and the fluid or resistive nature of the medium, which occurs on a continuum. (Graves-Alcorn & Kagin, 2017). Materials that resist easy manipulation have been reported to provoke thought-oriented experiences and fluid materials elicit more emotional responses (Hinz, 2016).

Provisional Registered Art Therapist (ATR-Provisional): "is the credential that ensures an art therapist meets established educational standards, with successful completion of advanced specific graduate-level education in art therapy, and is practicing art therapy under an approved supervisor" (Art Therapy Credentials Board, 2022).

Registered Art Therapist: "The Registered Art Therapist (ATR) is the credential that ensures an art therapist meets established standards, with successful completion of advanced specific graduate-level education in art therapy and supervised post-graduate art therapy experience" (Art Therapy Credentials Board, 2022).

Registered Expressive Art Therapist (REAT): "A Registered Expressive Arts Therapist (REAT) is someone who combines multiple forms of the creative arts (drama, movement, visual arts, music, writing, etc.) in counseling, psychotherapy or in other forms of interdisciplinary mental health professions to address behavioral and mental health challenges or stressors with individuals or groups. A REAT offers a multimodal/ intermodal approach or method and integrates the creative arts using more than one art form in their work with clients. These professionals received the REAT status from the International Expressive Arts Therapy Association, indicating they met all necessary requirements, including thorough training, education and supervised experience in expressive arts therapy to ensure that clients and individuals receiving this method and approach receive safe, beneficial and high quality treatment" (International Expressive Arts Therapy Assocation, 2022b).

Sublimation: "When successful, conflicted impulses are 'tamed' (neutralized) by being channeled into artwork" (Rubin, 2016, p. 28).

Visual Expression in Art Therapy: "The use of art media to express internal images, feelings, thoughts, and sensations in a concrete form and the visual feedback of these

Figure 1.3 Art Therapy Synthesis

products. Visual expressions produce a tangible, permanent record of the images that do not undergo changes and/or distractions through later recall from memory" (Lusebrink, 1990, pp. 9–10).

Putting It All Together, Visually

To end this section of the chapter, it seems fitting to provide an image that weaves together many elements of art therapy that cannot be fully expressed in written narratives, lists of terms, or diagrams. How do we define art therapy and communicate the spirit of the healing power of art therapy practices? The artwork of graduate art therapy student, Jennifer Suarez, shown in Figure 1.3 achieves this goal. She states, "While working on this, I considered the numerous directions art therapy can go and what it can accomplish." With an artist's paintbrush, the art therapist connects ideas related to psychotherapy, emotional regulation, interpersonal relationships, neuroscience, self-awareness, personal growth, and more.

Foundations of Career Counseling

It can be argued that the foundations of career counseling can be seen in the earliest philosophies, with such mantras as "know thyself" (from the ancient Greek oracle at Delphi) as self-knowledge is seen by most career theorists as a key and necessary component for making career decisions. In this section, we'll highlight key developments in history that shaped the field and practice of career counseling.

Important Historical Impacts

Industrial Revolution and Social Reform

Several societal events have shaped the field of career counseling. One of the most noticeable impacts on the emergence of career development was the rise of industrialism and the resulting industrial revolution. It was from the crowded sweatshops, and the focus being on the machine rather than the individual, that a spirit of reform would emerge, one that would focus on the individual and their specific abilities.

Among social reformers, one man rose to the top, and is known as the father of vocational guidance. He wrote several books on social reform movements such as women's suffrage, taxation, and education for all. In addition to being an activist, he also worked in various fields, as a teacher of history, math, and French in public schools; a railroad engineer; a law professor; and an academic dean. That man was Frank Parsons. With a passion for helping immigrants and under-educated individuals find work, he created, delivered, and lectured on a simple practical approach that serves as the basis of many of today's career theories. In a nutshell, a person would consider their abilities, as well as the requirements of available opportunities, and use "true reasoning" to figure out the best match.

In his posthumously published 1909 book, *Choosing a Vocation*, Parsons provided details on how to help individuals do just that. Some of his advice included choosing a vocation that best matches "abilities and enthusiasms" (p. 3), "get[ting] your friends to help you form true judgments about yourself" (p. 6), and gaining a variety of experiences as a way to "bring true interests and aptitudes into clear relief" (p. 12). He also had some advice for what not to do, including: don't jump from job to job, unless it is clear the move is advantageous, and avoid "drifting" into jobs, haphazardly (p. 4). From its earliest days, social justice was at the heart of career counseling. This idea of making a career choice was so important, in his words, second only to that of choosing a spouse, that Parsons would often share this sentiment in classes or organizations:

> If you had a million dollars to invest, you would be very careful about it; you would study methods of investment, and get expert counsel and advice from those familiar with such things, and would try to invest your money so it would be safe and pay you good dividends. Your life is worth more than a million dollars to you. You would not sell it for that. And you are investing it day by day and week by week. Are you studying the different methods of investment open to you, and taking counsel to help you decide just what investment you had better make in order to get the best returns upon your capital?
>
> (Parsons, 1909, p. 14)

Wars and the Measurement Movement

With World War I, the military needed to be able to quickly – and more importantly, accurately – place 1.5 million service members into jobs that they were capable of doing. Thus, a push for valid career assessments occurred. With World War II, and the need to again classify personnel, testing was utilized, albeit there was more of an emphasis on maximizing personal potential. This focus on testing with both wars coincided nicely with Parsons' theory, although, it may have led to an overuse of formalized assessment for job placement, and to an ongoing struggle career practitioners have today in terms of the public's perception, and even the perception of other mental health practitioners. This misperception is that career counseling is nothing more than a matching system, which, with today's technology, could be easily managed through comparing test results with occupational databases.

The war also had an unintended consequence of opening the world of work to women, who in their husbands' absences stepped in to fill positions once occupied by men. Thus, would begin the long struggle with glass ceilings, equal pay for equal work, and other benefits and protections for women in the workplace. Other groups would continue to fight this battle as well, with disparities in pay and opportunity still being felt today.

Following the war, veterans needed to segue back into civilian life, and in order to best take advantage of military funds towards education, and to find suitable civilian career paths, "separation programs" emphasizing vocational guidance were created by the Veterans Administration. With the influx of individuals enrolling in the universities, career counseling and testing merged even more to help direct students towards majors/fields of study in which they might be more successful. The creation of the National Defense Education Act, which was enacted in 1958 provided funding to all US educational institutions to support students in fields of science, math, and engineering. This was greatly influenced by the USSR's launch of Sputnik and public sentiment that US schools were inferior.

Role of Government

Government has always played a significant role with respect to work and career development. The creation of the Department of Labor in 1913 led to tools still being used today, such as the Occupational Outlook Handbook (bls.gov/ocohome) and O*NET (online.onet.org), and the National (and state) Occupational Information Coordinating Committees (established in 1976, now defunct). The Civilian Conservation Corps was created by Roosevelt in 1933 as a response to the depression to provide training and work opportunities for unemployed youth. In 1946, the George–Barden Vocational Education Act provided money for school counselor preparation. At the time, half of the counselor preparation programs were at the undergraduate level. This act led to the United States Office of Education Director to create the policy that counselor education must be graduate education. Counselor education programs at the time had at least one course emphasizing career development, and career development remains a key area of training today. In 1958, the National Defense Education Act provided funding for counselor education programs and stipends for graduate students in counselor education, and resulted in an exponential growth of these programs.

With respect to career development in schools, in 1917, the Smith–Hughes Act was the first federal funding authorized for career education, establishing vocational education training for secondary schools, while the Carl Perkins Act of 2006 provides major federal funding to states to improve high school and post-high school career and technical programs in schools. Other examples of career-related laws that foster the relationship between education and career are GEAR-UP (ed.gov/gearup) and the 1994 School-to-Work Opportunities Act, both of which focus on helping students make the transition from school to work or post-secondary education and training. All states have departments of labor, and many still sponsor career information delivery systems that provide their state residents with free occupational information and computerized career tools such as matching interests with occupations.

The Sixties

The sixties were a turbulent time for our nation in terms of both collective and individual identity. Questions such as "Who am I?" and "Why am I here?" and "Is corporate America the best way to go career-wise?" and environmental/societal conscientiousness gave rise to values inventories as well as career education. As part of this career education, the National Career Development Guidelines were created, with an emphasis on three domains: personal/social development, educational achievement and lifelong learning, and career management for childhood through adulthood. Sub-goals and specific strategies, examples of which are provided in Chapter 7, were implemented in schools across the nation.

The Seventies to the Present Day

The seventies saw a continued focus on career assessments, but in the eighties, new measures focusing on career beliefs, decision-making styles, career indecision, and self-esteem began to emerge. Career infusion, or imbedding career development topics into teacher lesson plans for all subjects, became more commonplace. The field's focus continued to shift from placing individuals into work to personal agency, or teaching individuals to locate and use resources to meet their own career needs and find work, rather than relying on an external party to do so. Computer-assisted career guidance systems also clearly moved the individual into the driving seat, as they were able to change lists of occupational options based on the priorities they entered. As the Internet continued to develop, and individuals became more skilled in navigating it, personal agency in finding, evaluating, and applying information from a variety of sources also increased. Although, with this new-found information source, practitioners also found their role shifting from being the holder of information to becoming an educator of how to inform clients of where and how to use information effectively.

Theories across the Decades

Theories about careers/life and decision-making have existed from our earliest philosophers. Socrates said, "An unexamined life is not worth living" (BrainyQuote, n.d.a); and Plato said, "A good decision is based on knowledge," "Man – a being in search of meaning," and "Hardly any human being is capable of pursuing two professions or two arts rightly" (BrainyQuote, n.d.b). Other well-known theorists, psychologists, and others have offered ideas about career decision-making. For example, Freud (1930) reflected on the significant impact that work has on the libido, stating:

> Laying stress upon importance of work has a greater effect than any other technique of living in the direction of bonding the individual more closely to reality; in his work he is at least securely attached to a part of reality, the human community. … And yet as a path to happiness, work is not valued very highly by men. They do not run after it as they do after other opportunities for gratification. The great majority work only when forced by necessity, and this natural human aversion to work gives rise to the most difficult social problems.
>
> (p. 34)

Figure 1.4 provides a basic timeline of career theories. In terms of theorists and theories devoted to career counseling, the first emerged with Frank Parsons in 1908 and focused on making a career commitment based upon true reasoning that matched knowledge of self with conditions of success of available occupations. The next major thrust of theories occurred in 1950, known as the developmental theories, which explored how career development occurred across the lifespan. In the 1960s, one of the most researched theories of all time, John Holland's RIASEC theory was introduced. The seventies showed an emphasis on applying social and learning theories to career development, while the eighties focused on adjustment between individuals and their options. The nineties found an emphasis on cognition, planning, and storytelling, and following that, an emphasis on constructionism occurred. With just over a hundred years passing from the official beginning of formalized career theories, many of the earliest theories are still in play today, being researched and applied to career counseling. Common to all of these theories is the quest to understand how elements of

Integrative Life
Planning,
Narrative,
Krumboltz   Cognitive
Developmental   Social   Information
(Ginzberg, Roe,   Learning   Processing,
Parsons   Super)   Theory   Happenstance

(1908)(1940s)(1950s)(1960s)(1970s)(1980s)(1990s)(2000s)

Lewin   Holland   Social   Career
Change   RIASEC   Cognitive;   Construction,
Management   theory   Circumscription   Life Design;
                                            & Compromise;   Systems Theory
                                            Work   of Career Development;
                                            Adjustment   Chaos Theory;
                                            Theory   Psychology of Working

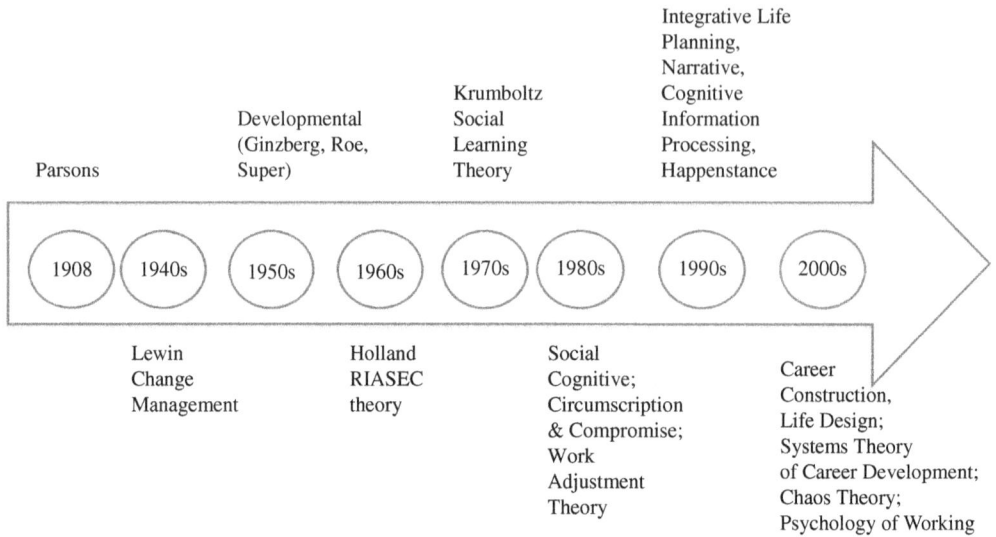

Figure 1.4 Timeline of Major Career Development Events

self and society impact career decisions. Issues of the day (e.g., economic depression, marginalization of different groups, technological advances) play a role in the focus of the application of theory, but the common features persist. Some criticisms of current theories are that they were created by mostly White males who may not have been sensitive to career development factors and pressures outside of that demographic. Many theories have been researched with respect to varying groups to enhance understanding of the applicability of theory.

Professional Associations

Career development and counseling has had a professional association since 1913, when the National Vocational Guidance Association (NVGA) was founded. Interestingly, that was also the year that the United States Department of Labor was formed. Now officially called the National Career Development Association (NCDA), this organization has helped establish career counseling as a profession, with ethical guidelines to express expected behaviors of career development professionals, advocacy for career development at the federal level, ongoing professional development trainings, and resources for practitioners, theorists, and researchers.

   The original mission of the NVGA, developed in 1913, was "The objects of this association shall be to promote intercourse between those who are interested in vocational guidance; to give stronger and more general impulse and more systematic direction to the study and practice of vocational guidance; to establish a center or centers for the distribution of information concerning the study and practice of vocational guidance; and to cooperate with the public school and other agencies in the furtherance of these objects" (Feller, 2014). Since that time, the focus has sharpened to support those who work specifically in career development. According to its website, the mission of NCDA is to provide "professional development, publications, standards, and advocacy to practitioners and educators who inspire and empower individuals to achieve their career and life goals" (NCDA website, December 2021).

Current Definitions Relevant to Career Counseling

Several terms related to the provision of career services exist, and are often used interchangeably. The definitions below attempt to differentiate among the terms, highlighting unique aspects.

Career: "Time extended working out of a purposeful life pattern through work undertaken by the person" (Reardon et al., 2000, p. 6), including the "positions involved in vocations, occupations, and jobs as well as to related activities associated with an individual's lifetime work" (Zunker, 2016, p. 7).

Career Change: "a shift from one job family to another" (Lent & Brown, 2020, p. 9).

Career Coach: According to the International Coaching Federation, key foci include: demonstrating ethical practice, embodying a coaching mindset (e.g., are client-centered and flexible), co-creating a client–coach relationship, communication skills, and cultivating learning and growth (https://coachingfederation.org/core-competencies). While there are no educational/training or licensure/certification requirements, credentials are available which can increase confidence in service quality.

Career Coaching: Focusing specifically on career-related goals such as enhancing one's job search, coaching in general has been defined as, "An action-oriented partnership that … concentrates on where you are today and how you can reach your goals" (Cole, 2000, p. 95). Coaching (in general) is defined as "partnering in a thought-provoking and creative process that inspires a person to maximize their personal and professional potential. The process of coaching often unlocks previously untapped sources of imagination, productivity and leadership" (https://experiencecoaching.com/?utm_source=ICF&utm_medium=direct-link&utm_campaign=icf-to-ec).

Career Counseling: In addition to the activities included in the definition for career planning, career counseling provides the opportunity for a deeper level of involvement with the client, based on the establishment of a professional counseling relationship and the potential for assisting clients with career and personal development concerns beyond those included in career planning (NCDA, 2015, p. 3).

Career Counselor: "a professional (or a student who is a career counselor-in-training) with an advanced degree (master's or doctoral level) in counselor education, counseling psychology or closely related counseling degree, engaged in a career counseling practice or other career counseling-related services. Career counselors fulfill many roles and responsibilities such as career counselor educators, researchers, supervisors, practitioners, and consultants" (NCDA, 2015, p. 26).

Career Decisions: "include choices individuals make about occupations, education, training and employment" (Sampson et al., 2004).

Career Development: "A process that encompasses much of the lifespan – one that begins in childhood …; continues into adulthood via the progression of one's career behavior (e.g., entry into and adjustment to work over time); and may culminate with the transition into, and adjustment to, retirement" (Lent & Brown, 2020, p. 11).

Career Education: "formal school-based programs, often at the middle and high school levels, aimed at introducing students to the world of work, assessment of career-relevant personal attributes and exploration of career options that may fit one's attributes" (Lent & Brown, 2020, p. 16).

Career Guidance: "encompasses all components of services and activities in educational institutions, agencies, and other organizations that offer counseling and career-related programs. It is a counselor-coordinated effort designed to facilitate career development through a variety of professional services that foster each client's ability and desire to manage their own career development" (Zunker, 2016, p. 7).

Career Intervention: "any treatment or effort intended to enhance an individual's career development or to enable the person to make better career-related decisions" (Spokane, 1991, p. 22).

Career Planning: Career planning services "include an active provision of information designed to help a client with a specific need, such as review of a resumé; assistance in networking strategies; identification of occupations based on values, interests, skills, prior work experience, and/or other characteristics; support in the job-seeking process; and assessment by means of paper-based and/or online inventories of interest, abilities, personality, work-related values" (NCDA, 2015, p. 3).

Job: "a specific work position held over a defined period of time" (Lent & Brown, 2020, p. 9).

Occupation: "A group of similar jobs found in different industries or organizations" (Reardon et al., 2000, p. 8). "Occupations exist in the economy and have existed in history even when no man, woman, or child is engaged in them. Occupations, trades, and professions exist independently of any person" (Herr et al., 2004, p. 44).

Position: "a group of tasks performed by one person in an organization; a unit of work with a recurring or continuous set of tasks. A task is a unit of job behavior with a beginning point and an ending point performed in a matter of hours rather than days" (Reardon et al., 2000, p. 8).

Vocation: "an occupation or profession to which one is particularly suited, especially one involving a sense of mission or calling" (https://dictionary.apa.org/vocation).

Work: "the domain of life in which people provide services or create goods, typically (though not always) on a paid basis" (Lent & Brown, 2020, p. 9), "that produces something of value for oneself or others" (Reardon et al., 2000, p. 7).

Key Components and Interventions

Many of the components of career counseling mirror that of more generic or personal counseling. The ethics followed by career counselors reflect those of the broad counseling field as outlined by the American Counseling Association (2014). Similarities can be seen in defining the counseling relationship, use of evidence-based and culturally sensitive practices and interventions, confidentiality, working within boundaries of competence, focus on wellness and improving clients' lives, and using theory to guide practice.

Career practitioners specifically address concerns related to career decision-making, and use a variety of interventions (e.g., assessments, information, cognitive restructuring for negative career beliefs, decision-making guides) to support clients in their career concerns. According to Lent and Brown, three main foci of career counselors include assisting clients in making and enacting a career decision, adjusting to career-related decisions and managing their career, and navigating career/life transitions. Approaches can be standardized (e.g., the *Career Thoughts Inventory Workbook*, Sampson et al., 1996) or non-standardized (e.g., card sorts, Osborn et al., 2016). These interventions may focus on helping individuals clarify and prioritize information about themselves that they would like to apply to their career concern, pointing to resources and information about the options under consideration, identifying and strategizing to address barriers to implementing career choice, as well as career-planning and goal-setting activities.

Types of Questions Career Counselors Help People Answer

Career counselors help people answer questions specific to career decision-making, career problem-solving, and job searching. Common questions include:

- What am I good at, and what occupations might best fit my skills?
- What type of occupations best match my values (e.g., making a difference)?

- How do I find out the starting salary for an occupation?
- What occupations are going to be in demand in the future?
- How do I change careers?
- How do I know what I should study to prepare me for my career?
- How do I access the hidden job market?
- How do I get a job if I have no work experience?
- Should I (and if so, how should I) disclose about my disability?
- What should I do if I feel like I'm being discriminated against at work but I'm worried about keeping my job/future promotions?
- How do I plan for the future when it seems so unstable?
- Can you critique my résumé?
- How can I best prepare for interviews?
- How can I help my child best prepare for their career future?
- How do I figure out what I want to do for work?

These are just a sample of questions that career practitioners field every day, and are often more complex than they seem at face value. Often, as a practitioner tries to clarify what information is needed, other questions will arise. For example, if a person is trying to identify options as related to skills, and they then respond with a statement such as, "I'm not good at anything," the session may shift to focus on potential mental health concerns. Or, when talking about job search, the client may reveal that there are some restrictions due to a partner's job or the need to stay local for caretaking responsibilities, which in turn, might reveal additional issues to be explored. Ultimately, the goal of career counseling is to help equip the client with the information and support they need to make an informed decision, and so focused questions are asked to increase the likelihood of this occurring.

Future Trends in Art Therapy and Career Counseling

While it's difficult to project what the future may hold, especially as both fields of art therapy and career counseling are just over a century old, the current trends seem to suggest some likely trajectories.

Digital Arts Media

The use of digital media in art therapy contexts has expanded exponentially since early advocates (Parker-Bell, 1999) encouraged art therapist exploration and potential adoption in therapeutic practice. Orr (2016) addressed digital media limitations that include confidentiality and security concerns, failures of technology that cause loss of artwork or connections, and notes that digital art media may not be suitable for all clients. Yet, Orr also asserted that available digital media arts options have applications and possibilities that are only limited by user imagination. Hinz (2020) noted that art therapists' criticisms have related to the lack of sensory exploration involved in digital works which may be seen as less emotionally engaging, yet these same considerations may extend use and support independence for others who may experience fine motor challenges, for example. It is also noteworthy that youth and young adults have grown up as "digital natives" and may have more comfort with digital media than traditional art media (Carlton, 2014). When choosing digital media as an option for client artmaking, it is important that practitioners have competency with the media and apply it with ethical understanding of its advantages and limitations, as is the case with traditional arts media (Carlton, 2014; Hinz, 2020; Orr, 2016).

Integration from Various Fields

First, just as the title of this book intimates, integration from various fields (e.g., sociology, education, psychology, engineering) is likely to increase. For example, recent publications and presentations on career development have focused on trauma (Kim & Smith, 2021), mental health (Sampaio et al., 2021), and physical health/illness (Bouchard & Nauta, 2021).

Impact of Technology

Another area of continued emphasis is likely to be increased and more nuanced use of technology, both to enhance service delivery and to expand it. COVID-19 had and continues to have a tremendous impact on work, learning, and how people go about working (Osborn et al., 2022). One of these impacts has been the exponential influx of technology, with real-time online meetings via platforms such as Zoom, to working and learning from a distance. Occupations and positions that had previously minimal technological skills listed as necessary (e.g., counseling) shifted for online service delivery. Practitioners and clients had to shift in how services and interventions were delivered, and it is likely that moving post-pandemic there will still be preferences for some type of online delivery.

Neuroscience-Informed Art Therapy

Interdisciplinary efforts among creative arts therapy and neuroscience professionals have stimulated rich dialogues regarding the neurological processes involved in art therapy experiences. Through current technologies of neuroimaging and Mobile Brain/Body Imaging (MoBI), researchers have examined what is happening in a person's brain as they physically engage with materials, respond to imagery, and engaged in series of processes that constitute creativity (King, 2018). For example, neuroaesthetics researchers have provided art therapists with increased information regarding how aesthetic experiences are processed in the brain and how reward systems are activated via exposure to aesthetic and creative experiences. With increased research and knowledge of the how art therapy engagement works, art therapists will be able to fine-tune approaches to client considerations and needs; expand evidence of the effectiveness of art therapy interventions for a variety of populations; and answer questions regarding creativity's role in enhancing well-being and career success (Kaufman, 2022; Madden, 2022; Vartanian, 2022).

Emphasis on Cultural Sensitivity, Humility, and Inclusivity

The past couple of years have seen a renewed awareness of the experiences of culturally marginalized groups in education, work, and opportunities. Many professional organizations are recognizing a need for training to increase cultural sensitivity and humility. Theories and interventions are being reviewed to evaluate their applicability to and appropriateness for use with people from different backgrounds. NCDA's website includes multiple training opportunities to help practitioners identify attitudes, beliefs, and actions that might negatively affect clients, such as micro-aggressions. Researchers are trying to attend to the gaps by focusing research efforts on diverse groups so as to better understand how different social identities might interface with a career concern. This recent awareness in the profession is likely to continue.

Social Justice Awareness and Advocacy

In addition to increased awareness and humility related to cultural groups' experiences, helping professionals including art therapists and career counselors have increasingly considered their roles as advocates and activists for social justice (Brown & Baraka, 2021;

Gipson, 2015; Lee, Smith, & Henry, 2013). Inside and outside of professional offices, practitioners are called to "become an active voice and conduit for change in the social/political domain of the public arena" (Lee, Smith, & Henry, 2013, p. 78). Consequently, today's art therapists and career counselors are called to recognize and name inequities, empower clients to address unjust social systems, and apply communications skills towards policy and legislative change efforts that facilitate environments conducive to mental health and equitable access to career opportunities.

Art Therapy and Career Counseling: An Argument for Collaboration

Deb's Story

As a career development/vocational psychology/career counseling professor at a Research 1 institution, one might think that my (Deb) primary Holland codes (covered in Chapter 2) are Social and Investigative. While both of these are in my top three, the Artistic code is my primary type. Throughout my career of education, research, counseling, and supervision, I have always been drawn to and most energized by creative approaches to these tasks. Even with interpreting standard assessment results, or in designing rigorous research, critiquing résumés, or teaching common elements of career theory, I have always pursued how to accomplish these tasks from "the road less traveled." Choosing the unconventional route has consistently proven to be incredibly satisfying in my career. That being said, I have not always understood, and therefore have not appreciated the power that some of the artistic/creative approaches potentially have. Partnering with an art therapy professor (Barb) in teaching and research has deepened my appreciation for these techniques, and also raised an awareness of my lack of knowledge of art therapy principles (such as how choice of medium relates to risk), while increasing my commitment to learn more so that I can continue to ethically integrate art and creativity into my practice.

Barbara's Story

As an art therapist and art therapy educator that holds a doctorate in clinical psychology, I have experienced a long history of embracing interdisciplinary efforts and integrating ideas and practices from various disciplines. I grew up in family that embraced the arts and encouraged me when my talents and interests led me to pursuing a Bachelor of Fine Arts in drawing and painting. Following my graduation, I was fortunate to find employment in arts-related settings such as a frame shop, and a gallery/art auction house, while I painted and exhibited my work. Through these experiences, I learned more about myself. I discovered that I yearned to work more closely with people and recalled a guest lecture I had heard during undergraduate days about art therapy. Over 40 years later, I still recall this "happenstance" experience and the content of the lecture which addressed the significance of clients' first artworks created within art therapy sessions. This snapshot of experience stimulated my research into art therapy and training requirements. I pursued a Master's of Arts in Expressive Therapies at Lesley College (now University) where interdisciplinary or intermodal work combining art, music, movement, and psychodrama processes was valued, in service of the client.

Leaping forward several years, after engagement in art therapy practice and experience with supervising early career professionals, I embraced an offered opportunity to become an art therapy educator, and still later, I pursued a doctorate in clinical psychology. During this period, personal experiences and curiosity guided me to research professional dementia caregivers' experiences. I wondered, how do nurses with longevity in long-term care settings remain motivated and satisfied with such work over time? What types of experiences (including creative, social, and spiritual activities) were used

Figure 1.5 Author Collaboration Expressing Art Therapy and Career Counseling Integration

to sustain them? Looking back, my dissertation choice revealed an underlying interest in career selection and satisfaction. Further opportunities in my clinical practice, allowed me to work with clients whose career concerns were intertwined with their aims for well-being and optimal life functioning. Career development and satisfaction topics continued to capture my interest.

When I became affiliated with Florida State University, I seized an opportunity to teach a career development course for art therapy students. Subsequently, I engaged in reviews of literature and consultations with FSU Career Center professionals and planned to infuse art therapy practices within the course as much as possible. However, I discovered a gap in available materials specific to art therapy and career counseling. Thankfully, I was introduced to Deb, who shared my passion for building upon creative work that has been incorporated and accomplished by art therapy and career professionals. It is my hope that readers of this book expand their exposure to both career development and art therapy professions and all the amazing theories and applications that can enhance career-related self-knowledge, options knowledge, decision-making processes, agency, and meaningful engagement in work which contributes to quality of life throughout the lifespan.

Together, Dr. Osborn and I hope this text sparks your curiosity and ongoing commitment to proactively addressing career concerns with competency, creativity, and care!

To represent our collaborative spirit we provide you with Figure 1.5, a co-created image of creative energy, art, and career focus.

Discussion Questions and Activities

1 How does the billboard you completed in Figure 1.1 compare to the projections laid out in the chapter? Do your projections seem realistic? What might have to happen to increase the likelihood of that desired future? What could get in the way? What role might you play in shaping the field?
2 See Table 1.1 for a sample comparison of the world's activities and their impact on career development between the decades of the 1860s and 1870s. Choosing any two decades, create and complete a similar table. What does the comparison of decades reveal about common and unique impacts?

Table 1.1 Sample Decade Analysis

	Major happenings	Impact on career development	Advertisement from that period	Any work-related music? (if so, what?)	Anything else?	URLs used?
1860s	Abolition of slavery; Civil War was fought; assassination of President Lincoln; First Transcontinental Railroad was built; gold discovered in Wyoming and Montana; typewriter was invented; first wave of women's suffrage began; and greenbacks (first national paper money) were created.	Western settlement; the discovery of gold; the completion of the Transcontinental Railroad and the Civil War popularized professions such as mining, cattle and sheep ranching, being a cowboy, and serving in the military for men; with the men away at war, women were homemakers, while some turned to military nursing and teaching.	Celebration of the completion of the First Transcontinental Railroad: http://en.wikipedia.org/wiki/File:69workmen.jpg	"When Johnny Comes Marching Home Again": www.civilwar.org/education/history/on-the-homefront/culture/music/when-johnny-comes-marching-home-again/when-johnny-comes-marching.html	Bicycles became a craze; political satire was popular; skiing was popular; Milton Bradley began making games; Thanksgiving Day was established; "the wild west" was coined and referred to the unorganized settled areas of the Western US; the Salvation Army was established; and the Periodic Table was developed.	Kingwood College Library: http://kclibrary.lonestar.edu/19thcentury1860.htm Civil War Preservation Trust: www.civilwar.org/education/history/on-the-homefront/culture/music/when-johnny-comes-marching-home-again/when-johnny-comes-marching.html Wikipedia: http://en.wikipedia.org/wiki/1860s
1870s	The Fifteenth Amendment was ratified in 1870 giving African Americans the right to vote in elections; the Naturalization Act of 1870 restricted all immigration into the US to only "white persons and persons of African descent"; construction of Brooklyn Bridge begins; John D. Rockefeller incorporates Standard Oil; Virginia rejoins US; Texas becomes last confederate state readmitted to Union; Congress creates Department of Justice; phonograph patented by Thomas Edison.	Women entered the manual and manufacturing labor force, Great Railroad Strike in 1877, when railworkers across the nation went on strike in response to a 10-percent pay cut by owners, Esther Morris appointed 1st female judge, The 1870 census used only four primary classifications for its occupational statistics: Agriculture, Professional and Personal Services, Trade and Transportation, Mechanical, and Mixing Industries, 1870 Census was the first to count child labor.	Cadbury's Cocoa Women's fashion Iron & Steel Company	Popular music was mostly concerned with military and political events in this time period. Some popular types of music included gospel, folk, mother goose, and opera. Jolly factory boy The Factory Children's Prayer Eight hour strike	Donkey first used as symbol of Democratic Party; soda fountain patented; Charles Dickens dies; Christmas is declared federal holiday in US.	Goldin, Claudia. (1980). The work and wages of single women, 1870–1920. *Journal of Economic History, 40*(1), 81–88: http://dash.harvard.edu/bitstream/handle/1/2643864/Golding_WorkWages.pdf?sequence=2 Thinkquest.org: http://library.thinkquest.org/20619/Chinese.html Wikipedia: http://en.wikipedia.org/wiki/History_of_the_United_States_(1865–1918) Brainy History: www.brainyhistory.com/years/1870.html 1870 Census: www.1930census.com/1870_the_year_in_history.php History Link: www.historylink.org/index.cfm?DisplayPage=output.cfm&file_id=9466 http://kclibrary.lonestar.edu/music-1.html

3 Locate art related to career and work. What emotions are captured? What is the artist trying to convey? If you were to create artwork to capture your current perceptions of work, what might it look like? What materials would you use? What emotion and message would you hope to convey?

4 If you were to depict your career journey thus far with a single line, what type of line would that be (thick, thin, wavy, straight, curvy, long, multidirectional, monotone, multicolored, staccato, short, etc.)? How might your experiences and perceptions of career journeys influence how you might work with others regarding their career development?

5 Think of the different practicum or internship sites you have had or expect to experience. What type of career development issues might be relevant to that setting, and how might those issues come up for people who are served?

6 What are some other issues that you believe career and art therapy practitioners should be addressing, given today's culture and context?

7 Considering the collaborative art in Figure 1.5, how might you envision art therapy and career counseling integrating? What would that look like?

References

American Art Therapy Association. (2022). About art therapy. https://arttherapy.org/about-art-therapy/

American Counseling Association. (2014). ACA code of ethics. www.counseling.org/resources/aca-code-of-ethics.pdf

Art Therapy Credentials Board. (2022). About the credentials. www.atcb.org/about-the-credentials/

Bouchard, L. M., & Nauta, M. M. (2021). Associations of health symptoms and perceptions with work volition. *Career Development Quarterly, 69*(2), 165–177. https://doi-org.proxy.lib.fsu.edu/10.1002/cdq.12257

BrainyQuote. (n.d.a). BrainyQuote.com. Retrieved January 1, 2022, from BrainyQuote.com website: www.brainyquote.com/quotes/socrates_101168

BrainyQuote. (n.d.b). BrainyQuote.com. Retrieved January 1, 2022, from BrainyQuote.com website: www.brainyquote.com/quotes/plato_105918

Brown, E. M., & Baraka, M. (2021). Teaching career counseling as a pathway for justice and advocacy work. *Counselor Education and Supervision, 61*, 47–54. https://doi.org/10.1002/cea.12224

Buck, J. N. (1948). The H-T-P test. *Journal of Clinical Psychology, 4*, 151–159.

Burns, R. C. (1982). *Self-growth in families: Kinetic Family Drawings (K-F-D) research and application*. Brunner Mazel.

Carlton, N. R. (2014). Digital culture and art therapy. *The Arts in Psychotherapy, 41*(1), 41–45. https://doi.org/10.1016/j.aip.2013.11.006

Cole, W. (2000, October 16). The un-therapists. *Time*, 95.

Exner, Jr., J. E. (2003). *The Rorschach: A comprehensive system*. Vol. 1: *Basic foundations and principles of interpretation* (4th ed.). John Wiley & Sons.

Feller, R. (2014). The first conference of the National Vocational Guidance Association: Roots of the National Career Development Association #2. Retrieved from www.ncda.org/aws/NCDA/pt/sd/news_article/70380/_PARENT/layout_details_cc/false

Franklin, M. (2016). Essence, art & therapy: A transpersonal view. In D. Gussak & M. Rosal (Eds.), *The Wiley handbook of art therapy* (pp. 99–111). John Wiley & Sons.

Freud, S. (1930). Civilization and its discontents. *The Standard Edition of the Complete Psychological Works of Sigmund Freud*, Vol. 21 (pp. 57–146). Hogarth Press.

Gipson, L. R. (2015). Is cultural competence enough? Deepening social justice pedagogy in art therapy. *Art Therapy: Journal of the American Art Therapy Association, 32*(3), 142–145.

Graves-Alcorn, S., & Kagin, C. (2017). *Implementing the Expressive Therapies Continuum: A guide for clinical practice*. Routledge

Hammer, E. F. (1969). Hierarchical organization of personality and the H-T-P, achromatic and chromatic. In J. N. Buck & E. F. Hammer (Eds.), *Advances in House-Tree-Person techniques: Variations and applications* (pp. 417–447). Western Psychological Services.

Herr, E. L., Cramer, S. H., & Niles, S. G. (2004). *Career guidance and counseling through the lifespan* (6th ed.). Pearson Education.

Hinz, L. D. (2016). Media considerations in art therapy: Directions for future research. In D. Gussak & M. Rosal (Eds.), *The Wiley handbook of art therapy* (pp. 135–143). John Wiley & Sons.

Hinz, L. D. (2020). *Expressive Therapies Continuum: A framework for using art in therapy* (2nd ed.). Routledge.

Hogan, S. (2000). British art therapy pioneer Edward Adamson: A non-interventionist approach. *History of Psychiatry, 11,* 259–271. https://doi-org.proxy.lib.fsu.edu/10.1177/0957154X0001104302

International Expressive Arts Therapy Association. (2022a). What are the expressive arts? www.ieata.org/who-we-are

International Expressive Arts Therapy Association. (2022b). What is REAT? www.ieata.org/what-is-reat

Junge, M. B. (1994). *A history of art therapy in the United States.* American Art Therapy Association.

Junge, M. B. (2010). *The modern history of art therapy in the United States.* Charles C. Thomas.

Junge, M. B. (2016). History of art therapy. In D. Gussak & M. Rosal (Eds.), *The Wiley handbook of art therapy* (pp. 7–16). John Wiley & Sons.

Junge, M. B., & Wadeson, H. (2006). *Architects of art therapy: Memoirs and life stories.* Charles C. Thomas.

Kaufman, J. C. (2022). Creativity and mental illness: So many studies, so many scattered conclusions. In J. A. Plucker (Ed.), *Creativity and innovation theory, research, and practice* (pp. 83–88). Routledge.

Kim, J., & Smith, C. K. (2021). Traumatic experiences and female university students' career adaptability. *Career Development Quarterly, 69*(3), 263–277. https://doi-org.proxy.lib.fsu.edu/10.1002/cdq.12272

King, J. (2018). Summary of twenty-first century great conversations in art, neuroscience, and related therapeutics. *Frontiers in Psychology, 9*: 1428. https://doi.org/10.3389/fpsyg.2018.01428

Kwiatkowska, H. Y. (1973). *Family therapy and evaluation through art.* Charles C. Thomas.

Lee, M. A., Smith, T. J., & Henry, R. G. (2013). Power politics: Advocacy to activism in social justice counseling. *Journal for Social Action in Counseling and Psychology, 5*(3), 70–94.

Lent, R. W. & Brown, S. D. (2020). Career development and counseling: An introduction. In S. D. Brown & R. W. Lent (Eds.), *Career Development and counseling: Putting theory and research to work* (pp. 1–30). Cengage.

Lusebrink, V. B. (1990). *Imagery and visual expression in art therapy.* Plenum Press.

Machover, K. (1952). *Personality projection in the drawing of the human figure.* Charles. C. Thomas.

Madden, R. (2022). What teachers should know about creativity in business. In J. A. Plucker (Ed.), *Creativity and innovation theory, research, and practice* (pp. 295–304). Routledge.

McNiff, S. (1981). *The arts and psychotherapy.* Charles C. Thomas.

National Career Development Association. (2015). NCDA code of ethics. www.ncda.org/aws/NCDA/asset_manager/get_file/3395

Naumburg, M. (1987). *Dynamically oriented art therapy: Its principles and practice.* Magnolia Street Publishers.

Orr, P. (2016). Art therapy and digital media. In D. Gussak & M. Rosal (Eds.), *The Wiley handbook of art therapy* (pp. 188–197). John Wiley & Sons.

Osborn, D. S., Kronholz, J. F., & Finklea, J. T. (2016). Card sorts. In M. McMahon & M. Watson (Eds.), *Career assessment: Qualitative approaches* (pp. 81–88). Sense Publishing. Retrieved from www.sensepublishers.com/catalogs/bookseries/career-development-series/career-assessment/

Osborn, D. S., Hayden, S. W. C., Reid Marks, L., et al. (2022). Career practitioners' response to career development concerns in the time of COVID-19. *Career Development Quarterly, 70*(1), 52–66. doi:http://dx.doi.org/10.1002/cdq.12283

Parker-Bell, B. (1999). Embracing a future with computers and art therapy. *Art Therapy: Journal of the American Art Therapy Association, 16*(4), 180–185.

Parsons, F. (1909). *Choosing a vocation*. Garrett Park Press.

Potash, J. S. & Ramirez, W. A. (2013). Broadening history, expanding possibilities: Contributions of Wayne Ramirez to art therapy. *Art Therapy: Journal of the American Art Therapy Association, 30*(4), 169–176. https://doi.org/10.1080/07421656.2014.847084

Reardon, R., Lenz, J., Sampson, J., & Peterson, G. (2000). *Career development and planning: A comprehensive approach*. Brooks-Cole/Wadsworth.

Rhyne, J. (1973). *The Gestalt art experience*. Brooks Cole Publishing.

Rogers, N. (2001). Person centered expressive arts therapy. In J. Rubin (Ed.), *Approaches to art therapy: Theory and technique* (2nd ed., pp. 163–177). Brunner Routledge.

Rosal, M. (2016). Cognitive-behavioral art therapy revisited. In D. Gussak & M. Rosal (Eds.), *The Wiley handbook of art therapy* (pp. 68–76). John Wiley & Sons.

Rubin, J. (2016). Psychoanalytic art therapy. In D. Gussak & M. Rosal (Eds.), *The Wiley handbook of art therapy* (pp. 26–36). John Wiley & Sons.

Sampaio, C., Cardoso, P., Rossier, J., & Savickas, M. L. (2021). Attending to clients' psychological needs during career construction counseling. *Career Development Quarterly, 69*(2), 96–113. https://doi-org.proxy.lib.fsu.edu/10.1002/cdq.12252

Sampson, J. P., Jr., Peterson, G. W., Lenz, J. G., et al. (1996). *Career Thoughts Inventory workbook*. Psychological Assessment Resources.

Sampson, J. P., Jr., Reardon, R. C., Peterson, G. W., & Lenz, J. G. (2004). *Career counseling and services: A cognitive information processing approach*. Brooks/Cole.

Shafir, T., Orkibi, H., Baker, F. A., et al. (2020). Editorial: The state of the art in creative arts therapies. *Frontiers in Psychology, 11*(68). https://doi.org/10.3389/fpsyg.2020.00068

Spokane, A. R. (1991). *Career intervention*. Prentice Hall.

Stepney, S. A. (2019). Visionary architects of color in art therapy: Georgette Powell, Cliff Joseph, Lucille Venture, and Charles Anderson. *Art Therapy: Journal of the American Art Therapy Association, 36*(3), 115–121. https://doi.org/10.1080/07421656.2019.1649545

Ulman, E., Kramer, E., & Kwiatkowska, H. (1978). *Art therapy in the United States*. Art Therapy Publications.

Vartanian, O. (2022). Neuroscience of creativity. In J.A. Plucker (Ed.), *Creativity and innovation theory, research, and practice* (pp. 89–96). Routledge.

Zunker, V. (2016). *Career counseling: A holistic approach*, 9th ed. Cengage.

2 Main Theories of Career Counseling and the Integration of Art Therapy Theories and Practices

In this chapter, we begin with outlining what constitutes a theory. Then, key components of major theories and models for each field will be presented, providing a lens for understanding a client's concerns and identifying interventions. Attention will be given to how each theory includes cultural considerations, examples of theory-based interventions, and the research supporting each. In the final section of this chapter, we will provide a rationale for and give examples of how art therapy and career counseling theories and practice can be integrated to enhance service delivery.

What Constitutes a Theory?

According to NCDA (2013), operating from a theoretical base is considered "essential" when providing career counseling. Theories are everywhere. A quick scan of textbooks and articles will easily identify over 20 career development "theories." While anyone can call an idea a theory, a reliable theory is one that is based on empirical research and a body of evidence. In addition, researchers and scholars (e.g., Brown, 2002; Sharf, 2013) have identified several indicators of good or reputable theory. These elements are represented in Table 2.1.

We used the criteria in Table 2.1 to determine which theories would be covered in this chapter, and encourage the reader to consider these aspects when determining which theory they will utilize in practice.

The Role of Theory in Practice

Theory serves as a map from which to understand a client's path and to guide interventions (Krumboltz & Nichols, 1990). The theory the practitioner chooses will inform what questions you ask (and don't ask), the reason for asking them, how you conceptualize a client's career concern and subsequent goals, the interventions that are chosen, and how next steps are determined. Using a theory to guide the session helps organize what is being done, the purpose for which it is being done, and the timing of interventions. For example, a counselor using cognitive information processing theory might start with having a client identify the gap between where they are now with their career concern (e.g., undecided) and where they want to be (e.g., decided), while a counselor using Super's developmental approach might try to identify in which career development stage a person currently is. Interventions and next steps would depend on the client's answers to those questions.

Often, when asked what theory a person uses, they will respond "eclectic," which means they combine elements from two or more theories to inform how they conceptualize a client's concerns and determine interventions. It could mean that they vary their theoretical

DOI: 10.4324/9781003035756-2

Table 2.1 Evaluating career theories

Criterion	Definition
Comprehensiveness	A theory must be comprehensive in completely explaining the problem in question, which includes describing the construct in how it developed in the past, may present in the moment, and what might occur in the future.
Consistency	A theory's assumptions, propositions, hypotheses, etc., must hold together logically.
Parsimony or simplicity	A theory should be explained with minimal complexity, and a limited number of concepts, and contain few assumptions.
Preciseness and clarity	A theory must be explicit, clear, and free from ambiguity in its propositions, theorems, and hypotheses. These must be precise enough to enable measurement and testing.
Operationality	Operationality is the extent to which a theory can be reduced to procedures for testing its propositions. Its concepts and hypotheses must be precise enough to be measurable and able to be tested.
Falsifiability	A theory must make claims and hypotheses that are clear enough that they can be tested and possibly refuted.
Empirical validity, verifiability, or testability	A theory should be supported by tests and experiments that confirm its validity and the validity of its hypotheses and predictions, for general and diverse populations.
Utility/practicality	A theory should be useful, in its definitions and predictions, whether in research or in its application to practice.
Importance, fruitfulness and generativity	A theory should be valuable to its field, and should demonstrate longevity through its ongoing generation of research.

approach within or between sessions with a single client, or that they decide on a theory to apply depending upon each client's situation. Overlap among the theories can lead to a desire to simplify by consolidating the common elements. While on the surface, this may seem to be a practical approach, consider the previous section in which we described what constitutes a theory. Theories come about as a result of research. Based on research, elements of a given theory are confirmed, changed, or removed. Using a buffet table approach, where elements from different theories are mixed and matched, is questionable, in that a non-validated approach is being used to help clients make life decisions. In addition, changing approaches can be confusing to the client, like when you are following directions to a location and suddenly are re-directed. That being said, most career interventions, resources, and assessments can be used with any theory. For example, the Self-Directed Search (Holland & Messer, 2013) directly corresponds with Holland's RIASEC theory (1997), and can also be used to build the self-knowledge domain as described in cognitive information processing theory (Sampson et al., 2004, 2020); and the RIASEC themes are often explored in narrative approaches (Savickas, 2018), among others. As a practitioner, if you can tie your intervention back to the theory you are using, you can reduce the likelihood of confusing your clients.

Classification of Career Theories

Career theories have been classified in a number of ways to help practitioners make sense of the vast number that exist. One classification consisted of trait–factor/person–environment correspondence, developmental, and learning theories. More recently, career theories have been grouped into either modern or postmodern categories. What separates the two categories is the emphasis on individual versus collective, reason versus relativism, stability versus fluidity in identity, objectivity versus subjectivity, discovery versus

Table 2.2 Comparison of modern and postmodern career theories

	Modern	*Postmodern*
Main focus in career conversation	Individual	Collective
Determining possible career paths	Reason	Relativism
Career factors (traits, aptitudes, interests, values, skills)	Stable	Fluid
Identifying career paths	Connecting career factors with occupational requirements	Identifying possible future careers through narratives
Career assessments	Objective; standardized (often) instruments	Subjective; non-standardized (often) approaches
Occupational identity	Discovery	Creation
Career session design	Planful	Emergent

creation of occupational identity, and planful versus emergent session design. Table 2.2 shows a breakdown of these two philosophies.

Thus, someone operating from a modern career theory would focus on the career needs from an individualistic point of view, likely guiding the conversation in a rational manner to identify career-related traits and linking those to possible career options. Career sessions might follow a fairly prescribed approach of intake, exploring the career concern, and then outlining steps and planning sessions to address the career concern such as identifying interventions like an interest inventory or reviewing career information. A practitioner operating from a postmodern approach would likely begin in a similar way of exploring the career concern, but would spend more time exploring the context of the concern, including intersectionality of the client's identities (cultural, religious, familial, societal) with a less direct approach of identifying the client's career factors through assessments, but leaning on client stories.

A main issue, however, is that theorists' and authors' categorizations of career theories into these two groups varies. Social constructivist and narrative career theories, by their very name, would automatically be in the postmodern group. Career theories that focus on identifying or clarifying specific individual characteristics would likely be classified as modern. This divide, while aiding in classification, in practicality is superficial at best, as the similarities between the two approaches exceed the differences. Both aim to help individuals make an informed career decision, both utilize assessments, and both emphasize conversation with the client. No career theory utilizes a "test and tell" approach, where a client takes a "test," and is "told" to follow or avoid careers based on the results. No career assessment yields a "best" career option; they provide multiple options, which then requires the client to engage in a decision-making process. Career practitioners from both the modern and postmodern camps will likely use standardized and non-standardized career assessments as the situation demands.

In reality, most clients will not ask if you are using a modern or postmodern theoretical approach. These classifications are of more use for students of career theory to organize and simplify the various theories that exist. In our case, we will examine career theories through the lens of developmental, person–environment congruence, learning and cognitive theories, and narrative categories. Given that all theories recognize that individuals' career concerns and situations differ across the lifespan, and that career interventions that are appropriate for an adult might not be as appropriate for a child, we will begin with developmental career theories. But first, we present a career counseling case. At the end of each theoretical section, comments about how a career practitioner might conceptualize and work with Bill will be described.

Box 2.1

The Case of Bill

Bill: The Case of the Downsized Father

Bill is a 39 year old and has a bachelor's degree in political science. Bill has most recently been employed as a regional senior sales executive with a well-known national consumer product corporation based in Georgia. He worked for the same company since he was 24. He lives with his partner, Patricia, and their two children (aged 8 and 11) in their home on the outskirts of the city. They purchased their home shortly after they were married and they put a great deal into what Bill calls their "dream house." Bill presents himself in dress and manner as a well-educated professional. He comments about the importance of appearances especially in his field and at his level.

Recently, Bill's company reorganized and his position was eliminated, resulting in his termination. his company provided Bill with 6 months of severance pay with benefits and has underwritten the cost of outplacement career counseling. During his 15 years with this company, Bill worked his way up from sales associate to sales office coordinator to regional director in a small region to his present position as regional director of the Northeast. He has been working out of the New York office for over the past 4 years and has had to travel a great deal to the South to be with his family and maintain his home. He does most of his traveling on weekends and occasionally adds a day of vacation to the 2-day weekend to extend his time with his family. Bill states that he prefers living in the South but would consider jobs in the Northeast if necessary. Bill's partner is able to be flexible about the location of her job.

Bill worries about the impact of his termination on his family and how his friends will perceive him. Being successful and supporting his family has motivated Bill to work hard and strive for promotion. He says, "I believe in giving my all to the job and being rewarded fairly for my efforts." He admits that he just fell into his first job with this company and has never really explored any other jobs, nor has he ever had to conduct a job search. Bill felt sure that he would never be without a position with this company as long as he was a loyal and productive employee. Bill's spouse is supportive, but does not want to be the sole financial provider for the family.

Although Bill expressed anger over his termination, he wants to move on as quickly as possible. He states that there is no time to waste because he may be losing out to younger job seekers. He approaches the task of finding a new position as an unwelcome hurdle in his career plan. Because of his inexperience as a job seeker, Bill feels at a loss as to what he should do and where he should begin searching.

Currently, Bill puts a lot of time into projects around the house. He enjoys improving the property that he feels he has neglected during the past 4 years. He admits that he may as well get the home ready for the market in case it has to be sold. He is not pleased with this prospect but feels helpless due to his current situation. Other than caring for the home, Bill has lessened his involvement in social activities, and this concerns his spouse. He really does not feel comfortable around the "employed" right now and states that he feels embarrassed about his termination.

Bill is determined to use the outplacement career counseling provided by his company. He feels that they owe him that much. He hopes to get something out of the experience, but has no idea what to expect. Bill wants to replace what he has lost in his career as quickly as possible. Because he enjoys sales, he would like to find a similar position, but is willing to make some adjustments if necessary.

Developmental Career Theories

Developmental career theories focus on how a person's career develops over the lifespan. As with any developmental theory, a key element is that of stages, with accompanying tasks, which should be attained by a generally accepted age. It is accepted by most that ages are relative and time-constrained. In the 1950s, most people sought work or further education immediately following high school, whereas today, many delay their starting a career by taking a gap year or extending their education. By understanding which stage a person is in, a practitioner can determine whether the person is at a developmentally appropriate stage, and also focus interventions that are relevant to that stage. Developmental theories tend to be more descriptive than focusing on the process of making a career decision.

Ginzberg

Eli Ginzberg (Ginzberg et al., 1951) was one of the first developmental career theorists. He identified three stages, including fantasy (before age 11), tentative (11–17), and realistic (17–adult). During the fantasy stage, individuals "try on" different career roles through play, and eventually that play orientation transforms to a work orientation as they transition to the tentative stage, and begin to clarify what they like and do not like, what different types of work require, and what career options might be good fits for them. Everything comes together in the realistic stage, where interest, clarified values, and patterns or themes start to crystallize. This realistic stage involves three mini stages: exploration, where options are narrowed down to two or three; crystallization, in which a tentative decision of a general career field or pseudo-crystallization occurs; and specification, when the person acts on their first choice by either pursuing employment or training specific to that option.

Circumscription and Compromise

Linda Gottfredson's theory of circumscription and compromise (1981) focused on how occupational aspirations form. These stages are important in that Gottfredson believed an individual narrowed or circumscribed their career options on the basis of interests, sex type (how traditionally female/male a person believes an occupation is), and prestige level. According to her theory, each person creates a "zone of acceptable alternatives" based on their preferences and tolerance levels for each of these three areas and their perception of how closely occupations match their self-image. For example, someone who wants to be in a career field that focuses on helping people has a "tolerable level" or boundary that, if exceeded (i.e., it offers too little or too much helping of others), will become unacceptable. While one might argue that any career ultimately helps people, each individual person will place limits on what that looks like. One person might believe that working with animals inadvertently helps individuals and is satisfied with that level of helping, while another might desire helping someone directly through a career field like nursing or teaching. The process of circumscription is related to four developmental stages in which one's career identity forms. According to Gottfredson, individuals orient to size and power from ages three to five, with very concrete thought process. From age six to eight, we become aware of sex roles; from age nine to thirteen, we focus on social valuation, who we are in that context, and develop prestige preferences, and from age 14 on, are focused on our internal, unique self. It is in this final stage that introspective thinking leads to the development of occupational aspirations.

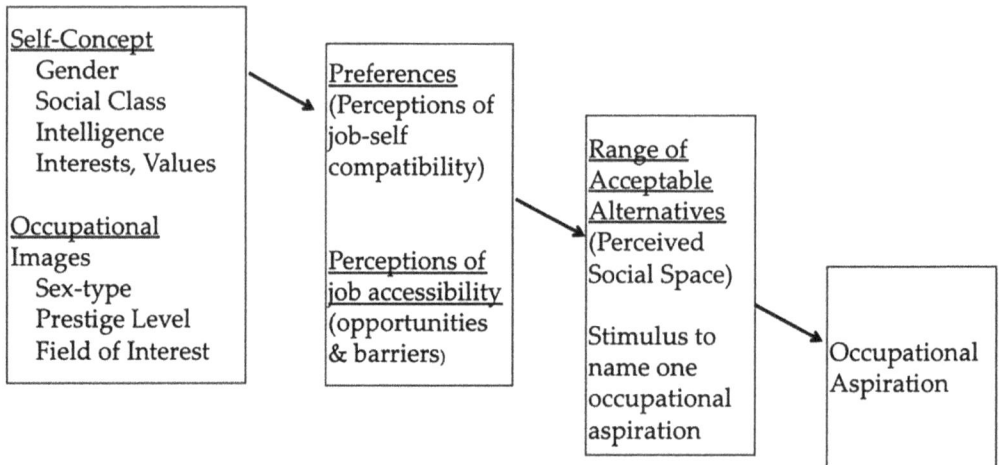

Figure 2.1 Diagram of Components of Gottfredson's Career Theory

While circumscription addresses development, compromise reflects implementation. When compromise is required, Gottfredson proposed that we are most willing to compromise field of work/interests first then prestige, and lastly, on sex type, as sex type is most closely associated with our core identity as it was developed earliest. Figure 2.1 demonstrates how Gottfredson's concepts are related and lead to identifying occupational aspiration.

Lifespan/Life-Stage

Donald Super (1990) believed career development was a lifelong process that occurred over five stages of the lifespan, during which our self-concept is constantly shaped. His theory includes 14 propositions, some of which reflect more of the person–environment congruence theories (e.g., people differ, every occupation requires specific skills). More central to the developmental aspect of his theory are tenets that interests and skills change over time, that this development can be guided, and the process of career development is one of developing and implementing occupational self-concepts. Learning theory, which occurs through the interaction between self and the environment, is the cement that helps develop and consolidate self-concept. Super also introduced the construct of career maturity, when a person takes responsibility for and makes informed career decisions.

Figure 2.2 shows the five different life stages, starting with growth and ending with decline or disengagement, along with the different roles he says people play, at different levels of intensity, over the lifespan. During the Growth stage, people learn about their interests and skills, and then examine how those fit in the world of work in the Exploration stage, where tentative occupational choices are made. During the Establishment stage, people narrow down their options and settle into a vocational identity. Maintenance is the stage where the person attempts to stay current, relevant, and productive in their chosen field, and during the final stage, one looks to retirement and starts the process of disengaging from their work and considering their legacy, or how they will transition what they are doing to the people who are continuing the work. Super believed the goal of counseling should be to help clients see an accurate picture of themselves and their life roles, and it might also include coaching, educating, restructuring, and mentoring.

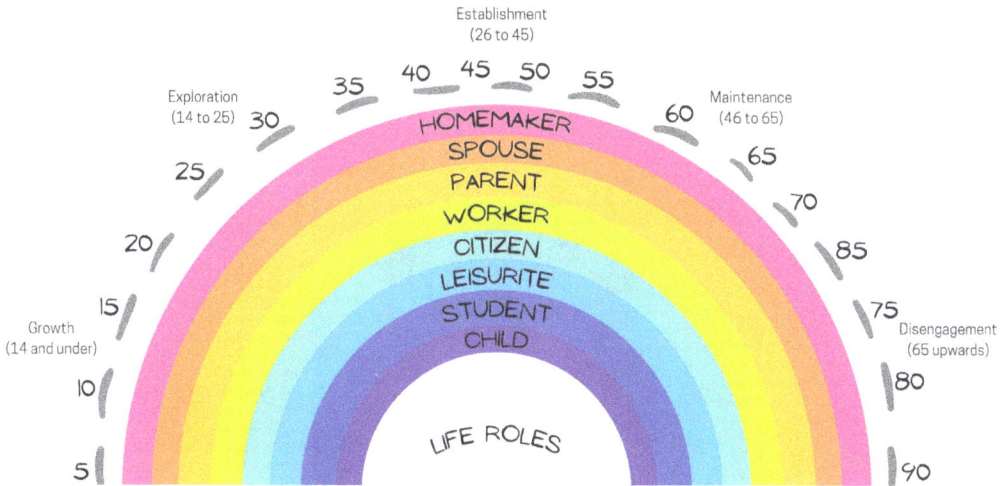

Establishment (26 to 45)

Exploration (14 to 25)

Maintenance (46 to 65)

HOMEMAKER
SPOUSE
PARENT
WORKER
CITIZEN
LEISURITE
STUDENT
CHILD

Growth (14 and under)

Disengagement (65 upwards)

LIFE ROLES

Figure 2.2 From D. E. Super. (1980). A life-span, life-space approach to career development. Journal of Vocational Behavior, 16(3), 282–298. Copyright © 1980 by Elsevier; all rights reserved.

Reflections on the Case Study of Bill: Developmental Considerations

Operating from a developmental perspective, a practitioner will want to first determine in which stage Bill is located, and how close he is to moving to the next stage. Given that Bill just "fell into" his first job without much consideration and decided to stay there, it might be recommended that he recycle back through earlier stages and engage in the relevant tasks for each. For example, according to Ginzberg et al. (1951), while Bill appears to be in the realistic stage, he might want to explore the fantasy stage, consider boyhood dreams that he put off and explore those options. Gottfredson (1981) might encourage Bill to consider how he circumscribed his zone of acceptable alternatives at each stage of his development. Someone operating from this theory might observe that Bill's social space seems very narrow, and seek to re-examine those boundaries of tolerance, and determine how flexible those are. Gottfredson might also encourage him to consider the compromises he's made thus far, as well as the compromises his partner has made, both in the past and looking towards the future.

According to Super's (1990) theory, Bill should be at the maintenance stage, and yet that has been interrupted by the sudden job loss. He sounds like he would like to continue maintaining his career as a salesperson, but given that he has only been with one company, may need to do some work to establish himself, especially if he will be selling different products to different customers. Someone operating from Super's theory might have him complete his life rainbow, and examine how he feels about the roles he's played, is currently playing, and anticipates or prefers to play in the future. It might also be useful to compare his rainbow to his partner's. Both Super and Gottfredson would seek to understand Bill's self-concept, and to help him identify compatible options.

Art therapy inspired by Super's theory

Bill may benefit from art therapy interventions designed to explore career lifespan concepts. For example, Bill could be provided the opportunity to create an accordion book to further explore his career lifespan rainbow. The name accordion book comes from his type of book's resemblance to the musical accordion's bellows. This type of book consists of a continuously folded sheet of paper connected to two boards that serve as book covers

Figure 2.3 Sample Accordion Book

at both ends of the paper. Each page can be viewed separately, but when the paper is unfolded, all of the pages can be viewed at simultaneously.

Given Bill's interest in completing home projects, Bill may be receptive to creating and assembling his lifespan book. In the career counseling art therapy context, the working process of book making could be characterized as a metaphor for Bill's active role in constructing and considering his career development story. Bill would be invited to make choices about materials such as papers used for the covers as well as the central section of the book. Bill's choices could reflect aesthetic preferences and or represent particular associations with the career lifespan story.

Within the book, one or two pages could be designated to represent each career lifespan stage: growth, exploration, establishment, maintenance, and disengagement. To fill the pages, Bill would be invited to select magazine images or phrases to represent his roles and experiences of past, current, and imagined future stages of development. The process of selecting items for each page would stimulate reflection regarding his experiences and clarify associations with his career development processes. Each stage and set of pages could be considered within the art therapist/career counselor relationship via quiet joint attention, empathetic appreciation, and/or lively discussion. When finished, Bill would be invited to expand the accordion book so that all the pages and lifespan stages could be seen simultaneously and collectively. Working to view the lifespan story as a whole would provide visual stimulus for identifying reoccurring themes or contrasting interests and goals. A sample accordion book is shown in Figure 2.3.

Person–Environment Congruence Theories

Person–environment congruence theories examine how personal traits interact with the demands of the work environment. Frank Parsons, also known as the father of vocational psychology, is also credited with the straightforward three-pronged approach to career decision-making. At its core, trait–factor career theory required knowledge of one's skills and aptitudes, knowledge of "conditions of success" for specific occupations, and "true reasoning" to put the two together.

Frank Parsons (Basic Trait–Factor)

Parsons was most concerned with helping immigrants find work, so his approach was very practical in nature, aiming to determine what a person could do, and using his knowledge of what jobs were available in the Boston area and what was required to be successful in those jobs, he would work with the client to create a list of reasonable alternatives. While this approach seems simple on the surface, the list of intake questions Parsons used was exhaustive, ranging from how a person shook hands, whether they slept with the window opened or closed, and what exhibits they would be most interested in seeing at the World's Fair. His questions are listed in chapter two of his book, *Choosing a Vocation* (1909).

Theory of Work Adjustment

The theory of work adjustment (TWA; Dawis & Lofquist) and person–environment correspondence theory focused on the relationship between a person and their work environment, predicting likelihood of staying employed in a specific job. They viewed this outcome through the lens of the individual and the employer. Consider the diagram in Figure 2.4 that demonstrates the theory.

Following the arrows on the left half, an individual has needs that they expect work to fulfill. These might be a certain level of salary, flexibility, upward mobility, stability, collaboration, and so forth. Every job has potential reinforcers, which may or may not match the needs of the individual. For example, a job might require a great deal of travel, or multiple team projects. Depending on the individual, those "benefits" may or may not be positive. If an individual's primary needs that they expect work to meet are met by the job, they are likely to stay, or in TWA terms, achieve tenure at the job. If not, they are likely to quit.

The arrows on the right half more specifically address Parsons' theory. A person has specific skills that match or do not match with the demands of the job. If they match,

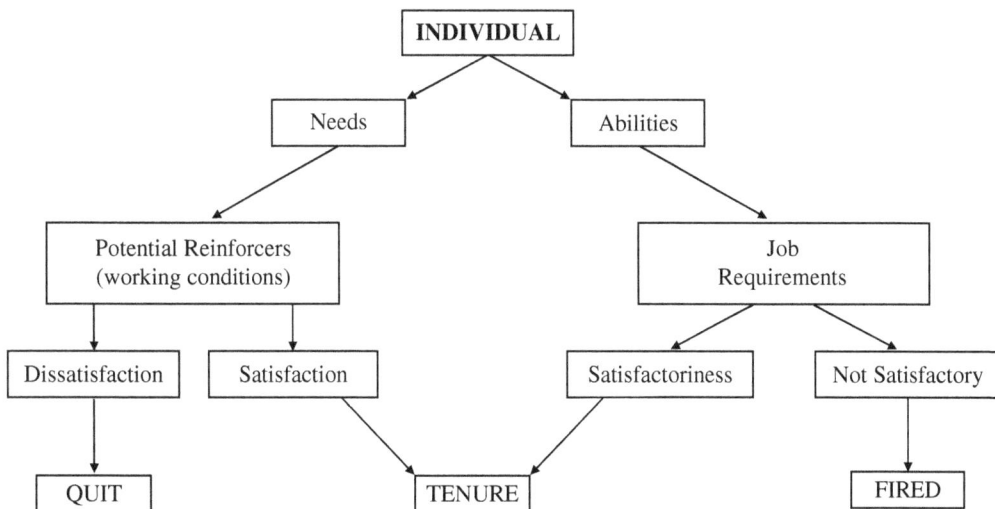

Figure 2.4 Diagram of PEC Theory

they will likely perform satisfactorily, and achieve tenure on the job; if not, they will not be able to perform the job demands and likely be fired. The correspondence of this theory is what happens between the final outcomes. Instead of just quitting, a person might talk with their employer about what reinforcers would be more positive for them, to see if that might be negotiated. Instead of losing an otherwise valuable employee, an employer might decide to invest in either training or relocation to a different job.

Values-Based Holistic Model of Career and Life-Role Choices

Brown (1996) espoused that the most important element in making a career decision is the consideration of one's most highly prioritized work values. These might include salary, prestige, engaging in enjoyable work, upward mobility and so forth. He encouraged practitioners to consider the degree to which a client's values stemmed from an individualistic or collectivist background. One of the tenets of his theory is that occupational tenure, or staying in a job, greatly depends on the match between the cultural and work values of the individual, their colleagues, and their supervisors.

RIASEC Theory (John Holland)

One of the most enduring career development theories is John Holland's RIASEC theory (1997). Holland sought to answer three questions with his theory: (1) what leads to satisfaction, involvement and success at work?, (2) what contributes to stability?, and (3) what works with helping people make career decisions? During his work with the army as a classification interviewer, he noticed that there were typically six types of career interests or personalities, and said there were similarly six "environments" in which a person might find themselves, including work, leisure, academic majors, and so forth. He believed that individuals were happiest and likely to be most successful when they were in an environment that matched their primary type. The six types include: Realistic (hands-on, outdoors, sports, mechanical), Investigative (problem-solving, ideas, scientific, research), Artistic (creative, expressive), Social (helping, teaching, nurturing), Enterprising (leadership, sales, managing, directing), and Conventional (data, math, organizational), and are presented in relationship to each other through the shape of a hexagon, shown in Figure 2.5.

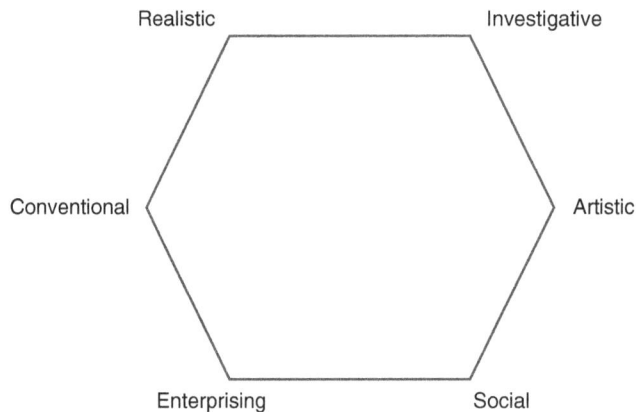

Figure 2.5 Sample RIASEC Hexagon

Four key assumptions underlay RIASEC theory:

- There are six distinct types of interests, and most people have a primary type.
- There are six distinct types of environments.
- We search for environments that allow us to express our main types.
- Our behavior is determined by the interactions between our primary type and the environment in which we find ourselves.

Represented in a hexagon, the six types begin in the top left corner and proceed clockwise, never changing in order. Holland stated that types that were adjacent (e.g., R is adjacent with I and C) had the most in common or the highest *consistency*. Those with higher consistency were more likely to have higher vocational identity, defined as how clear and consistent one's interests, values, and goals are, as opposed to those with lower vocational identity (e.g., someone whose primary type is R and their second type is S). How well a person's type fits with their environment is referred to as *congruence*. A person with a primary type of Artistic that is in an Artistic environment (work, field of study, etc.), would have high congruence – and is likely to be satisfied with that environment, as opposed to being in a low congruence match, such as an accounting position. RIASEC theory recognizes that a person may have more than one primary type, and states that how well-differentiated a person is between their types is also indicative of their vocational identity.

Practically speaking, helping someone identify career options with high consistency and low differentiation between their first two types (e.g., Artistic and Social) is easier than someone with low consistency and low differentiation (e.g., Artistic and Conventional). In the first case, career options that are creative and involve helping others would be identified. In the latter, career options would need to involve both creativity and predictability. It is not impossible to find career options for the latter case (e.g., technical writer involves both A and C interests), but a career practitioner might want to encourage the client to consider focusing on one type at work, and another in their leisure time. RIASEC theory has generated hundreds of research articles and is still generating research today, along with multiple assessments, the most well-known being the Self-Directed Search (SDS), which identifies how a person scores across the six different types and generates options based on those scores. Of note, a key reason Holland developed the SDS was from his frustration with other inventories that required mailing in the protocols, waiting for their return, and relying on interpretation from a counselor. He firmly believed that the majority of people could take an inventory, score it, and interpret it themselves, thus the name.

Reflections on the Case Study of Bill: Person–Environment Congruence Considerations

Person–environment correspondence theorists would focus on the degree to which Bill's characteristics fit with the environments he is considering. Bill was fired due to external reasons, not because of a lack of fit between his traits and job requirements. From these perspectives, if Bill wants to identify other options, he should further explore his traits, occupations that utilize his strongest traits, and the conditions of success for the occupations that seem most appealing. If his skills are impressive for sales (as evidenced by job interviews), he needs to write a résumé that demonstrates those skills and search for companies that offer positions that utilize his strongest skills. If he wants to explore options, he should take one of the assessments and follow up as indicated in the section entitled "problem."

TWA would observe that this past position was satisfying to Bill and also satisfactory in terms of Bill's performance. Going forward, Bill needs to find a position that will utilize his skills and meet his needs. Bill needs to re-evaluate his needs. Fifteen years have passed, so it is likely that his and his family's needs have changed at least to some degree. Following this exploration, he needs to search for positions that would match his priorities and his abilities. Brown's model would suggest that a key value of Bill's is loyalty. He was loyal to the company, but the company betrayed him by not sharing that same value. Based on this model, other values should be explored, and questions identified for Bill to research when interviewing with companies. For example, he might want to examine how long individuals stay at a certain company, and how promotions happen. RIASEC theory would see congruence between his interests, skills, and environments, e.g., Enterprising. Based on this theory, Bill needs to develop a job search approach that is also congruent with his interests, skills, and personality. For example, a job search strategy that leans heavily on networking skills will likely be satisfying and effective for Bill. If he wants to expand his options, he should take the Self-Directed Search to identify other job titles that might be satisfying.

Art Therapy Intervention Inspired by Holland's RIASEC Theory

After learning and discussing the outcomes of his Self-Directed Search, an art therapist/career counselor may invite Bill to further his self-knowledge of person–work environment fit through a creative engagement called: RIASEC Collage and Self-Symbol Exploration: Where Do I Fit? Bill would be provided seven 8″ × 11″ blank pages, color papers, tissue

Figure 2.6 RIASEC Collage

paper, magazine, images, scissors, ruler, pencils, glue sticks, and our diluted glue, as well as a blank figure cut-out or photo cut-out or self-symbol (to be mounted on cardstock) as well as reference materials and descriptions of the six types – Realistic (hands-on, outdoors, sports, mechanical), Investigative (problem-solving, ideas, scientific, research), Artistic (creative, expressive), Social (helping, teaching, nurturing), Enterprising (leadership, sales, managing, directing), and Conventional (data, math, organizational) – would be provided as a reference. Bill would be invited to create a series of collages or environments that reflect his associations, thoughts, and feelings regarding the career type and its related activities and possible occupations.

Once these were complete, the figure would be placed on each artwork and Bill would be invited to identify his symbolic experiences of "being in" the different career environments. A sample of Bill's collage is seen in Figure 2.6. The career counselor/art therapist would observe and note reactions and narratives that may arise during this process. Next, Bill would be offered an opportunity to take the individual images and combine them into one ideal work/occupation environment using as much or as little of each artwork as he wished. Upon viewing the final image, Bill would be encouraged to step back and review the components of the work, and reflect on the portions of types that he both selected and discarded. Tapping on deepened self-knowledge, Bill could refine his ideas about occupational options, and other means to add type components to his broader life-picture.

Learning and Cognitive Theories

The third set of theories share common threads of learning and the environment, and also attending to how cognitions impact the career decision-making process.

Cognitive Information Processing Theory (CIP)

CIP theory (Sampson et al., 2020; Sampson et al., 2004) is based in cognitive and learning theories, and seeks to help individuals make effective career decisions. As a learning approach, CIP espouses that individuals can learn how to apply an effective decision-making process, not only for the current concern, but for future career concerns. Four key components of the theory include the pyramid of information processing domains which identifies the essential elements of making a career decision, the CASVE Cycle (a recommended career decision-making model), a career decision-making readiness model that considers capability and complexity an individual is experiencing at the time of the decision, and a differentiated approach to career service delivery.

The pyramid of information processing, pictured in Figure 2.7, includes the domains of knowledge, decision-making, and executive processing. As a foundation of decision-making, the knowledge domain consists of self and options knowledge. At the apex is the executive processing domain, which is how a person perceives they are managing the process of making a career decision, or metacognitions about the process. These thoughts, also known as self-talk, can be helpful or unhelpful, true or untrue, and impact the areas beneath. Examples of this include believing one isn't good at anything, or there are too many or too few options available, or that they always make bad decisions. Thus, if negative thoughts emerge in conversations with a client, a practitioner should point these out, examine the underlying belief, and encourage cognitive reframing. Unchecked, these beliefs may affect how a person engages in career activities such as completing an assessment, exploring career information, or committing to a choice.

In the center of the pyramid is the CASVE (pronounced cuh-SAH-vee) Cycle, shown in Figure 2.8. One starts and begins at Communication, and examining internal and

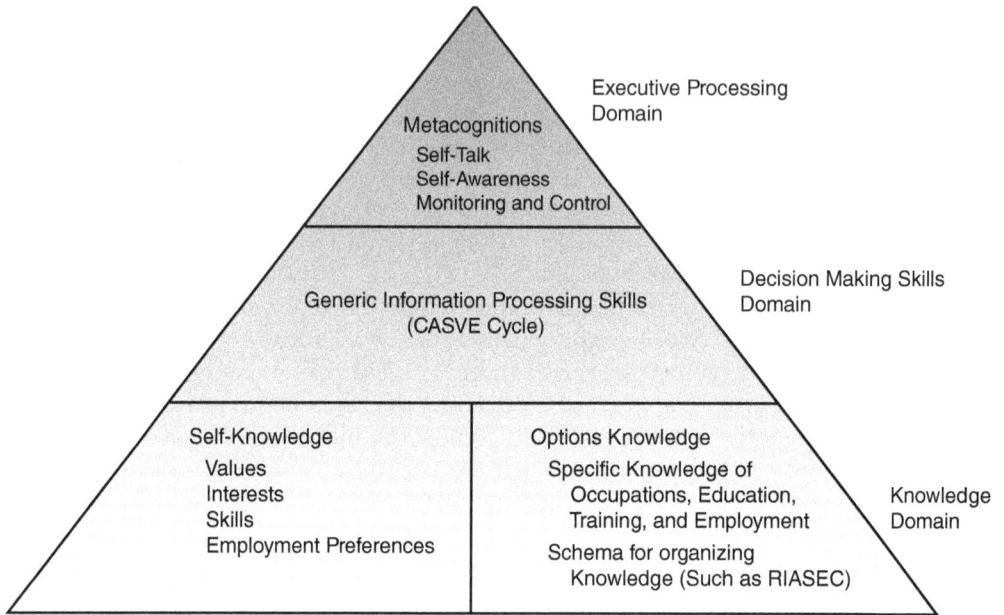

Figure 2.7 Practitioner Version of the Pyramid of Information Processing Domains.

Note: Adapted from Career counseling and services: A cognitive information processing approach (p. 20), by J. P. Sampson, R. C. Reardon, G. W. Peterson, and J. G. Lenz, Copyright 2004 by Brooks/Cole with copyright transferred to J. P. Sampson, R. C. Reardon, G. W. Peterson, and J. G. Lenz. Adapted with permission.

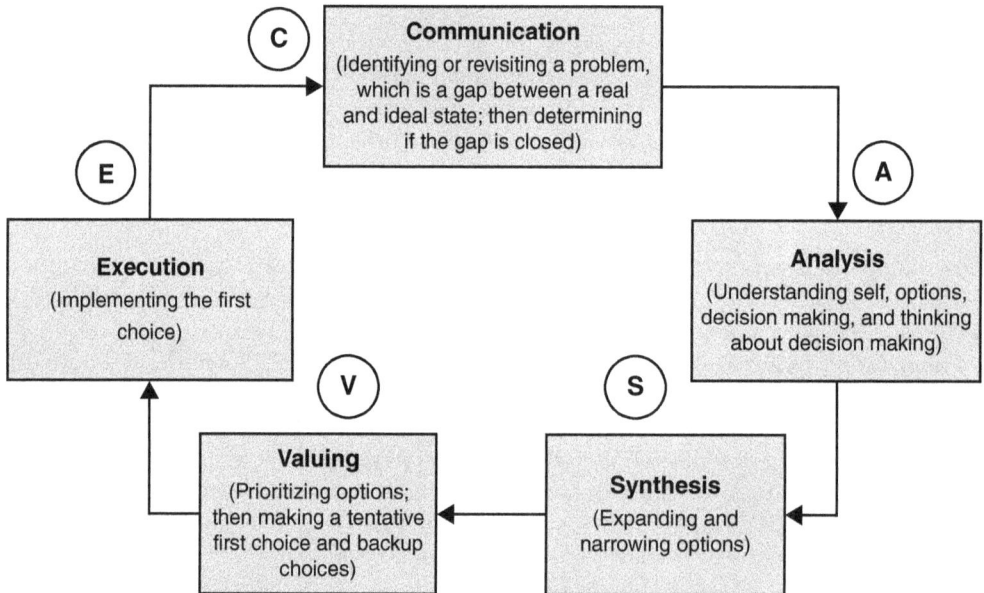

Figure 2.8 Practitioner Version of the CASVE Cycle.

Note: Adapted from Career counseling and services: A cognitive information processing approach (p. 26), by J. P. Sampson, R. C. Reardon, G. W. Peterson, and J. G. Lenz, Copyright 2004 by Brooks/Cole with copyright transferred to J. P. Sampson, R. C. Reardon, G. W. Peterson, and J. G. Lenz. Adapted with permission.

external cues that a decision needs to be made or has been successfully made (C-revisited). Once a gap between the real (i.e., where I am with my decision) and the ideal (i.e., where I want to be) has been expressed, the person moves to analysis of themselves and their options. A career assessment may aid at this point in the process, which supports synthesis of these two areas by elaborating on or expanding options, and then followed by crystallization, in which the person narrows their list to three to five possibilities. In Valuing, a person explores these options more closely, considering the benefits and drawbacks of each option to themselves, their significant others, their family, community and so forth, ultimately identifying a first choice with a backup. In Execution, they try out the first choice to determine fit, and then return to Communication to determine if the gap has been closed or if they need to repeat any steps.

CIP also identifies three types of individual career readiness to engage in career problem-solving and decision-making. Career readiness is based on two factors, capability and complexity. Capability is internal to the individual, and includes strengths and weaknesses such as motivation, mental health or illness, awareness of emotions, willingness to honestly reflect on self and options, and assuming personal responsibility for decision-making. Complexity is external to the person and includes factors such as familial, economic, and social pressures that impact a person's decision positively or negatively. Someone with low career readiness would have high complexity and low capability, and would benefit most from an individual, case-managed approach. Someone with high career readiness would have low complexity and high capability, and most likely benefit from a self-directed approach, with less frequent or intensive support. Those with moderate career readiness have either high complexity and high capability or low complexity and low capability. These individuals can benefit most from a brief staff-assisted approach, where they can alternate working with a practitioner to establish goals and strategies with working by themselves to achieve the goals. This differentiated model is a way to best allocate resources, so that those with the least need for support still have those needs met, while clients with the greatest needs have access to the most time-intensive and often most limited resource (i.e., individual counseling). Research and handouts on CIP theory can be found here: https://career.fsu.edu/tech-center/resources.

Social Cognitive Career Theory (SCCT)

SCCT (Lent, 2020) emphasizes personal agency and overcoming barriers. The career decision-making process follows this pattern:

> self-efficacy/outcome expectations → career-related interests → personal goals → performance experiences → outcomes of performance experiences (good or bad) → career decision

Self-efficacy beliefs, outcome expectations, and goals are the building blocks of SCCT.

Self-efficacy is influenced and shaped by social aspects of gender, race, and ethnicity, as well as personal experiences. SCCT has an interest model, a choice model, and a performance model. Interests develop as shown in the figure above from self-efficacy and outcome expectations. The social aspect of this theory comes from what the environment provides, such as exposure to different activities, learning opportunities, as well as the degree to which engagement in these activities is reinforced by others. Interests solidify as a person gains competence in an activity and the person values the activity and outcomes related to it. The choice model reflects the educational or training and occupational intentions a person has committed to pursuing. This choice is influenced by social supports or barriers such as finances, geographical location, cultural values and other environmental influences. The performance model addresses how successful one is once they have implemented their choice. SCCT posits that self-efficacy and outcome expectations impact the goals individuals set for themselves, and those with higher self-efficacy and outcome expectations will likely perform better and persist over the long term as opposed to those with lower levels. Having unsubstantiated levels of self-efficacy can also be negative, as this may cause a person to set unrealistic goals, fail in achieving them, and result in poorer self-efficacy and outcome expectations.

Learning Theory of Career Counseling (LTCC) and Happenstance Learning Theory.

John Krumboltz designed both LTCC and happenstance learning theory (HLT). The learning theory in LTCC can best be described as a social learning approach to career decision-making, with an emphasis on how feedback received from the environment shapes how we perceive ourselves and the world of work, and, ultimately, the occupations we choose. Numerous cognitive processes, interactions with the environment, and inherited characteristics and traits influence the career development process, which comprises four key components. First, we each have specific genetic endowments and special abilities that may provide opportunities or barriers. Second, we must consider environmental conditions and events. Third, are learning experiences which may be either instrumental or associative and act as reinforcers or non-reinforcers of the activity engaged in, a person's perception of their skills, and other cognitive processes. Instrumental learning experiences are direct experiences that the person has, and receives feedback from, while associative experiences are those where a person learns through observation, and subsequently experiences either a positive or negative reaction. Fourth, we apply task approach skills, which we learn early in our development, such as problem-solving, specific work habits, and how we respond emotionally and cognitively.

All of these culminate in generalizations we make about ourselves and the world of work, coping strategies, career decision-making, and how we enter a career. Sometimes, cognitions are faulty or problematic, and in these cases, practitioners are urged to probe the cognitions for underlying assumptions, explore alternative explanations, and engage the client in cognitive restructuring (e.g., "Perhaps you are not a bad decision-maker, but bad outcomes happen when you are pressured to make a decision quickly and without enough information"). Because career decision-making is seen as a skill that can be learned, a career practitioner is encouraged to use learning experiences with a client along with behavioral counseling techniques; focus not only on existing skills, but on expanding interests and skills; prepare clients for the changing world of work; and focus on more than just making a career choice.

Happenstance learning theory (HLT; Krumboltz, 2009) has its roots in LTCC, and emphasizes an active engagement in the environment by the clients to increase knowledge about self and options. HLT argues against traditional career theories by stating that career indecision is rational and desirable, given the uncertainty of the world. Also, instead of trying to minimize chance events occurring through careful planning, HLT states that clients should be taught how to create unplanned chance events. Five skills are required to do this: curiosity, persistence, optimism, flexibility, and risk-taking. Practically speaking, career practitioners can encourage clients to create chance events by being curious, acting when unexpected opportunities arise, and engaging with others in ways that will increase the likelihood of beneficial chance events occurring. For example, a person may decide to join a committee or go to a party that is outside their comfort zone in order to meet new people and learn of opportunities. HLT argues that every event is an opportunity for learning about self and options. The five steps of HLT include normalizing happenstance (i.e., showing how a person's actions contributed to unplanned events in their lives), transforming curiosity into learning and exploration opportunities, teaching clients to create positive chance events, teaching clients to over-come blocks to action, and advocating open-mindedness.

Reflections on the Case Study of Bill: Learning and Cognitive Considerations

Career theories in the learning and cognition categories will focus primarily on how and what Bill has learned about himself and his options, and how that learning has impacted his thinking. There may be some dysfunctional thinking, as evidenced by feelings of embarrassment, concerns of younger workers getting the jump on him, not sure about how to get started. Identify and begin reframing negative thoughts, paying close attention to depressive or anxious speech that might suggest more pressing mental health issues. He might also have poor self-efficacy beliefs, and need to acknowledge and then explore the barriers he is expressing, to determine if they are real or perceived, and brainstorm ways to overcome these. For example, discrimination is real, but not all employers will discriminate.

Cognitive restructuring is recommended for these beliefs that are impeding his pro-gress. CIP would ask Bill to talk about each stage of the pyramid and try to locate where he is in the CASVE Cycle. While he may say that he wants to be in execution, it may be helpful to walk through each stage, so that he has a backup plan and is clearer about his self and options knowledge. CIP would also examine his current capability and the com-plexities that complicate his current concern. SCCT would suggest that Bill set new goals, engage in new performance behaviors, and create new success stories. LTCC would likely see that Bill's genetic endowments and abilities seem appropriate for his career choice, but that he needs help developing his task approach skills. Bill might be encouraged to look at sample résumés, perhaps read some books (to increase associative learning) that have personal examples of self-marketing and job search. HLT might conceptualize Bill as trying to move past this uncomfortable feeling too quickly. Instead, he should be encouraged to embrace this time as an opportunity to explore all of his options. He should explore what he curious about, and what excites him at this point in life. In addi-tion, encourage the client to take reasonable risks when exploring new options. When else will he have this chance to really try things out? All of the theories in this section would encourage exploration and restructuring of Bill's faulty beliefs that might not only impact the way he sees his options, but the way he engages in the job search.

CBAT Approaches to Supporting Positive Career Outcomes

Cognitive behavioral art therapy (CBAT) methods are well suited to SCCT and CIP approaches to career counseling. Rosal (2018) asserted "that imagery has been found to have a profound impact on the individual and can be used therapeutically to change per-spectives, constructs, and behavior" (p. 89). Using imagery to capture automatic thoughts about career or career decision-making would be an active and visual way to begin exploring layers of Bill's thoughts regarding this transitional period in his career. The art therapist/ career counselor can introduce the process by asking Bill to create an image that reflects his career status at this time. In this case, a moderately fluid medium such as use of a traditional watercolor set or a set of soft pastels would be preferable, so there is some challenge with control while at the same time the medium does not feel out of control. Once the image was created, the therapist could use traditional CBT downward-arrow

Socratic questioning techniques to reveal and explore automatic thoughts and conditional and core beliefs about themselves (Beck, 2011) and in relationship to careers. Questions could include, "As you reflect on this image what thoughts come to mind? If that thought is true, what does that mean to you? Where do these ideas come from?" The therapist would prompt another artwork that would invite Bill to explore/reflect these ideas and sources of his beliefs. Follow-up questions may include: Are these core beliefs accurate today? What would happen if those beliefs changed? The therapist could invite Bill to create a final image that reflected the possibilities he may experience with his career transition if the beliefs that may have been getting in the way of his career exploration and decision-making could change.

Alternatively, a related upward-arrow questioning technique associated with a positive cognitive behavioral therapy approach (Bannink, 2014) could be combined with art processes. Consequently, positive attributes and associations would be the focus of imagery prompts and questions. According to the broaden-and-build theory, positive emotions lead to increased thought/action repertoires and then to increased flexibility, resilience, and positive relational and health outcomes (Garland, 2010). In the case of Bill, positive career outcomes would be identified as a goal, and Bill would be encouraged to identify available resources, incidents that reflect his positive efforts and experiences, and optimal solutions to the career dilemma he is experiencing. Images that could be suggested include a portrait of his strengths and resources, an image of things that were working well for him at his past job, and an image of his optimum career solution.

Narrative Frameworks and Approaches

Narrative frameworks and approaches focus on clients' telling of stories in which they place themselves as the main character as a way to discover themes, identify possible career interests, and then develop narratives about the future, in this case, related to career. Another key component of narrative approaches is the use of metaphors. Life Design Counseling (Savickas, 2005, 2012, 2015), and the Systems Theory Framework of Career Development (McMahon, Patton, & Watson, 2015; Patton & McMahon, 2018) are examples of these approaches.

Life Design Counseling (LDC)

LDC (Savickas 2012; 2015) practically applies career construction theory, with a goal of having clients able to purposely design and clearly articulate an identity that is stable, albeit adaptable, which in turn allows them to address their career concerns. Career adaptability is a key concept within LDC, defined as "a psychosocial construct that denotes an individual's readiness and resources for coping with current and imminent vocational development tasks, occupational transitions, and personal traumas" (Savickas, 2005, p. 51). Four components of career adaptability include the "4 Cs": concern about the future, control over self and environment, curiosity about alternative settings and roles, and confidence in implementing one's life design. LDC interventions generally have four steps, in which a client constructs their current view of self, de-constructs (with a counselor) stories that are interfering with a person's ability to see options or an accurate view of self, reconstruction (by the counselor) of a new story from the client's stories, and then sharing that macro-story with the client who determines its accuracy and offers edits. A final step is using the macro-story as a springboard for developing a future-oriented story, and then detailing action steps. My Career Story (Savickas & Hartung, 2012), and the Career Construction Interview (Savickas, 2018) were developed to accompany this theory.

Systems Theory Framework of Career Development (STF)

STF (McMahon, Patton, & Watson, 2015; Patton & McMahon, 2018) seeks to acknowledge and integrate contributions of all career theories, as demonstrated through the narrative exploration of the individual system, as well as the social and environmental-societal system. This framework also considers the systems of the counselor, and the interaction of the client and counselor. The counselor ends up becoming an influencer on the individual, and vice versa. Figure 2.9 demonstrates the elements and their relationship to each other in the career counseling process. At the center of the figure is the individual system, which includes multiple influences. Three main systems that are considered include interpersonal (e.g., gender, race, personality, sexuality), social (e.g., membership in different groups such as family and work), and environmental/social (e.g., workplace policies, socioeconomic variables, and historical oppression). Each system is outlined by dotted lines to show that it is open and can influence (and be influenced by) factors outside of its boundaries. Discussion of the systems within the context of time (past, present, and future) recognizes that the past influences present, and the future is influenced by both the past

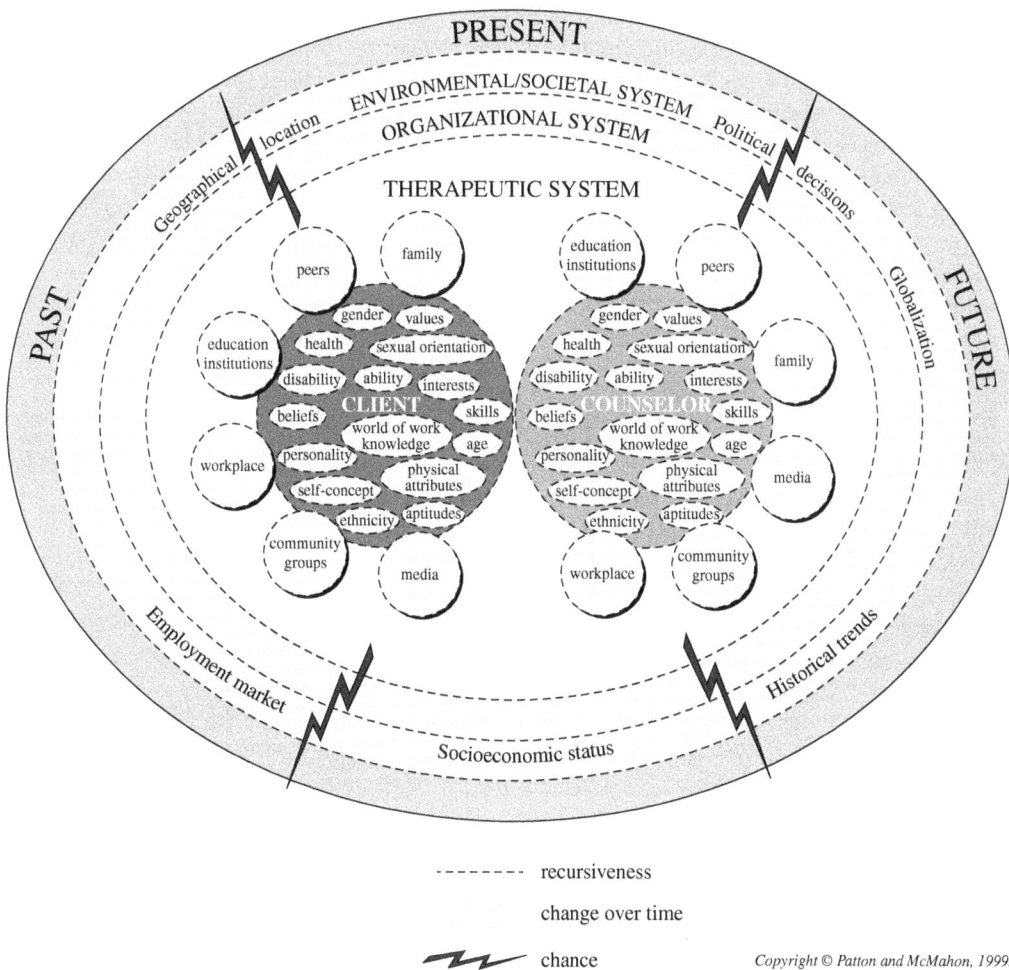

Figure 2.9 Career Systems Interview Model. Copyright @Patton and McMahon, 1999. Reprinted with author permission

and present. In addition, these interactions among the systems are dynamic and recursive. The flash symbols acknowledge that chance events occur that impact our decisions.

Career Systems Interview (McIlveen, 2015), My System of Career Influences (McMahon, Watson, & Patton, 2015), and My Career Chapter (McIlveen, 2015) are qualitative assessments aimed to focus conversations around the client and their context. STF utilizes a storytelling approach (McMahon & Watson, 2013), which includes constructs of encouraging clients to be reflective throughout the process (reflection), to make connections with their systems of influence as they share their stories (connectedness), to describe how these influences impact their story (meaning-making), to see themes and patterns across the stories (learning), and to determine to be more active in constructing their future career stories (agency). Throughout the process is an emphasis on the client narrating about their systems of influence from past to present and culminating in co-constructing the future and next steps. In addition, practitioners are encouraged to implement interventions across all levels of the system, instead of just with the individual system.

Reflections on the Case Study of Bill: Narrative Framework Considerations

Narrative approaches will focus on having Bill share stories about himself, within the larger contexts of his environments and time. LDC would want Bill to talk about his current view of himself, addressing the 4 Cs of career adaptability. A practitioner would work with Bill to look for missed opportunities or alternative endings to stories that might be blocking his ability to see options. Together, the practitioner and Bill would co-create the upcoming possible chapters of Bill's story and identify next steps. From the STF, this job loss has likely had an impact on various aspects of all of the systems in Bill's life. Having him narrate this impact on the various systems, and the impacts the various systems are having in response would be recommended. In addition, the counselor would encourage multiple stories from the past to the present day in the hopes of discovering potential themes. The final step would be working with Bill to co-construct desired future chapters and outlining next steps.

Art and the Narrative Approach

One creative way for art therapists and counselors to invite narrative storytelling, is to utilize comic strip structures to explore and rehearse varied career story outcomes. Art therapists and counselors (Lucas-Falk & Moon, 2010; McCreight, 2018; Mulholland, 2004; Parker-Bell, 2011) have offered these familiar narrative structures to clients so that they may tell their stories, explore ways of coping with stressful situations, and envision new journeys. Comic structures present many helpful elements and attributes in this regard. Mulholland noted that creating and identifying with a cartoon character can provide a person with a constructive means to release negative feelings they are experiencing. Additionally, cartoon formats provide a containing structure for narratives. For example, the square frames of the comics provide visual boundaries for clients' issues or concerns and can potentially promote a feeling of more control. McCreight asserted that client engagement in creating comic strip stories also helps clients externalize their concerns and reduce overidentification with their issues. Overidentification with issues may manifest as clients perceiving themselves *as* the problem versus seeing a problem as something separate to be addressed and managed.

A comic strip approach to telling a career story has much in common with Taylor and Savickas's (2016) pictorial narratives process aimed at cultivating reflection and meaningful dialogues between client and counselor regarding the career concern. In their described pictorial narrative process, clients were provided paper of undefined size and colored pencils and were asked to draw an image of their career problems, followed by an

Figure 2.10 Bill's Career Event Comic. This comic strip was generated at http://www.MakeBeliefs
    Comix.com. Used by permission of author and site creator Bill Zimmerman

image of their preferred career outcome images. After these were explored, clients were
also encouraged to create baby steps images to identify the incremental actions that will
lead to their optimum outcomes. This series of artworks could be created in a series of
sessions. In contrast to a comic structure for career stories, these pictorial narratives are
less structured in their artistic format. Free-form drawings do not provide the containing
square frames, thought bubbles, and narrative boxes that may ease some of the discomfort associated with more open-ended drawing processes.

Currently, many creative ways to facilitate comic creation exist. These methods include
art therapist/counselor provision of pre-made story boards or comic structures for clients
to fill with their own drawings and narratives, or digital comic templates that can be
found on computer software or tablet, or phone apps such as Comic Life (Plasq, 2021).
These programs support uploading of images or photographs into cartoon frames and
provide many options for designing text balloons to amplify expression. Additionally,
comic creation websites such as Make Belief Comix (Zimmerman, 2021) do not require
purchase of software and provide templates, characters, and props that can be sized
and placed in the comic frames. When considering a digital program to offer a client,
it is important to preview available features to ensure cultural inclusivity and age appropriateness. For example, Make Belief Comix templates and characters appear to be
designed with school-aged children and young adults in mind. Therefore, some adults
may not relate as well to available cartoon options. However, Make Belief Comix provides
multiple language options. Creators can write comic text in Arabic, French, Hebrew,
Spanish, Russian, and more. The comic in Figure 2.10, created with Make Belief Comix,
shows how Bill might utilize comic structures to externalize and explore his career experience and concerns.

Of course, a narrative approach to art therapy and career counseling is not restricted
to the use of comics structures. Clients can create symbols and metaphors for their
career problems with a variety of materials, and these symbolic references can be utilized
as means of externalizing the problem and stimulating storytelling and problem-solving. Conner (2017) noted art practices enhanced clients' access to thoughts and feelings. Once created, representations can be named or titled, and then further explored
through narrative inquiry and subsequent artmaking.

Other Career Theories

This chapter did not cover every career theory that has existed or is currently popular. Some theories, such as chaos theory (Bright & Pryor, 2012) and transition theory

(Schlossberg, 1984; Schlossberg, Waters, & Goodman, 1995) will be covered in future chapters. Other theories that are not current today but did have an impact on current theories include theories that emphasized the impact of relationships with parents on subsequent choices (Bordin, Nachmann, & Segal, 1963; Roe & Lunneborg, 1990); decision-making models (Tiedeman & Miller-Tiedeman, 1984); sociological and economical approaches (Blau et al., 1956); and integrative life planning (Hansen, 2011). In evaluating these and emerging career theorists, practitioners are encouraged to use the criteria at the beginning of the chapter to determine the validity of and appropriateness for the specific theory for their population.

Role of Culture and Individual Differences in Career Theory

Culturally sensitive counselors and therapists recognize the power and potential that a client's unique culture, experiences, and "diverse abilities" provide. While many career theories above do not explicitly describe or predict how these attributes impact the career decision-making and problem-solving process, they do provide space for this discussion to occur, whether as a part of understanding self-knowledge, evaluating costs and benefits to self and family, or how personal and family beliefs impact the career decision-making process. The psychology of working framework (Blustein, 2013; Duffy et al., 2016) was designed partially to complement existing theories by "more directly highlighting the role that social class, privilege, and freedom of choice play in career selection and fulfillment" (Duffy et al., 2016, p. 127). This theory will be explored in greater detail in the chapter on diversity and career development.

Regardless of which career theory a career practitioner chooses, they should research how efficacious the career theory they are using is with their specific client group. If research on using a specific career theory or aspects of that theory on a specific group does not exist, this does not mean that the theory should not be used with that population. Perhaps there are specific types of assessments or interventions that are atheoretical in nature but have been found to help that specific group build competency or knowledge in a given area, such as decision-making or self-knowledge. For example, self-knowledge is a common component of career theories. Gaining a thorough understanding of how a person views themselves beyond values, interests, and skills, to include exploration of other identities they may hold will aid in understanding their unique attributes, perspectives, strengths, and supports, and also help the counselor become more culturally sensitive and effective. They might be less likely, for example, to emphasize evaluating options with respect to their individual needs and desires if the client has indicated that their decision is dependent upon the impact and feedback from family.

Summary

Career theories serve to provide a map for understanding how clients have come to their current career concern, as well as a lens for viewing the surrounding areas that might be impacting their current concern, and a focal point for where they hope to be when the career problem is solved. Theories identify key areas to home in on that will provide context, and suggest steps to helping the client make progress towards solving their career problem. Practitioners should explore whether a theory has been designed for, used with, or researched about the population or career concern specific to the client, and seek supervision when using a theory for the first time.

Discussion Questions and Activities

1 Choose a theory from each of the main categories and identify counseling questions specific to each theory. What commonalities do you find? What unique aspects of each do you see?

2 Locate a toy, or a picture of a toy, or a symbol or memento of something you spent a lot of time playing with as a child. How would you describe the item? What stories do you have about how you played with it? What is it about this object that is so memorable and special to you? What do these stories/memories reveal about your interests, values, etc.? How did your experiences with this item influence your opinion of career possibilities? Do you see any evidence of this in your life and the options you are considering today or for your future?

3 Create a rainbow that portrays the different intensities of the roles you've played previously, currently, and you anticipate playing in the future. You can use bright colors to indicate positive feelings, dark to reflect negative feelings, and pale to reflect neutral feelings. How do these different roles interact and influence each other, and your overall career goals?

4 What compromises have you had to make through the years with respect to your career and life? What were those like? What doors opened and closed as a result? What do the compromises reveal about your primary values?

5 How might you adjust your career interventions based on a client's preferred Holland type? Consider your own primary type, and how that plays out in the therapy you provide, interventions you prefer. How might you need to adjust for a client whose primary type was the opposite of yours?

6 What are some art directives for challenging negative or dysfunctional career beliefs?

References

Bannink, F. P. (2014). Positive CBT: From reducing distress to building success, *Journal of Contemporary Psychotherapy, 44*, 1–8.

Beck, J. S. (2011). *Cognitive behavioral therapy: Basics and beyond.* Guilford Press

Blau, P. M., Gustad, J. W., Jessor, R., Pames, R. C. W. (1956). Occupational choice: A conceptual framework. *Industrial & Labor Relations Review, 9*(1), 531–543. https://doi.org/10.1177/001979395600900401

Blustein, D. L. (2013). The psychology of working: A new perspective for a new era. In D. L. Blustein (Ed.), *Oxford handbooks online.* https://doi.org/10.1093/oxfordhb/9780199758791.013.0001

Bordin, E. S., Nachmann, B., & Segal, S. J. (1963). An articulated framework for vocational development. *Journal of Counseling Psychology, 10*, 107–116.

Bright, J., & Pryor, R. (2012). The chaos theory of careers in career education. *Journal of the National Institute for Career Education and Counseling, 28*, 10–20.

Brown, D. (1996). A values-based, holistic model of career and life-role decision making. In D. Brown, L. Brooks, & Associates (Eds.), *Career choice and development* (3rd ed., pp. 337–332). Jossey-Bass.

Brown, D. (2002). Introduction to theories of career choice and development. In D. Brown & Associates (Eds.), *Career choice and development* (4th ed., pp. 3–23). Jossey-Bass.

Conner, S. (2017). Externalizing problems using art in a group setting for substance use treatment. *Journal of Family Psychotherapy, 28*(2), 187–192. https://dx.doi.org/10.1080/08975353.2017.1288995

Duffy, R. D., Blustein, D. L., Diemer, M. A., & Autin, K. L. (2016). The psychology of working theory. *Journal of Counseling Psychology, 63*(2), 127–148. https://doi.org/10.1037/cou0000140

Garland, E. L. (2010). Upward spirals of positive emotions counter downward spirals of negativity: Insights from the broaden-and-build theory and affective neuroscience on the treatment of emotion dysfunctions and deficits in psychopathology. *Clinical Psychology Review, 30*, 849–864.

Ginzberg, E. Ginsburg, S. W., Axelrad, S., & Herma, J. L. (1951). *Occupational choice: An approach to a general theory.* Columbia University Press.

Gottfredson, L. (1981). Circumscription and compromise: A developmental theory of occupational aspirations. *Journal of Counseling Psychology, 28,* 545–579.

Hansen, S. S. (2011). Integrative life planning; A holistic approach. *Journal of Employment Counseling, 48*(4), 167–169. https://doi.org/10.1002/j.2161-1920.2011.tb01105.x

Holland, J. L. (1997). *Making vocational choices: A theory of vocational personalities and work environments.* PAR.

Holland, J. L., & Messer, M. A. (2013). *Self-Directed Search (SDS) assessment booklet: A guide to educational and career planning.* PAR.

Krumboltz, J. D. (2009). The happenstance learning theory. *Journal of Career Assessment, 17*(2), 135–154. https://doi.org/10.1177/1069072708328861

Krumboltz, J. D., & Nichols, C. W. (1990). Integrating the social learning theory of career decision making. In W. B. Walsh & S. H. Osipow (Eds.), *Career counseling: Contemporary topics in vocational psychology* (pp. 159–192). Routledge.

Lent, R. W. (2020). Career development and counseling: A social cognitive framework. In S. D. Brown, & R. W. Lent (Eds.), *Career development and counseling: Putting theories and research to work* (pp. 129–164). Wiley & Sons.

Lucas-Falk, K. & Moon, C. (2010). Comic books, connection, and the artist identity, in C. Moon, (Ed.), *Materials & media in art therapy: Critical understandings of diverse artistic vocabularies,* pp. 231–256, Routledge.

McCreight, D. (2018, February). Creating comics with clients. *Counseling Today,* 37–41.

McIlveen, P. (2015). My Career Chapter and the Career Systems Interview. In M. McMahon & M. Watson (Eds.), *Career assessment: Qualitative approaches* (pp. 123–128). Sense Publishers.

McMahon, M., Patton, W., & Watson, M. (2015). My System of Career Influences. In M. McMahon & M. Watson (Eds.), *Career assessment: Qualitative approaches* (pp. 169–177). Sense Publishers. https://doi.org/10.1007/978-94-6300-034-5_20

McMahon, M., & Watson, M. (2013). Story telling: Crafting identities. *British Journal of Guidance and Counselling, 41,* 277–286.

McMahon, M., Watson, M., & Patton, W. (2015). The Systems Theory Framework of Career Development: Applications to career counselling and career assessment. *Australian Journal of Career Development, 23*(3), 148–156.

Mulholland, M. J. (2004). Comics as art therapy. *Art Therapy: Journal of the American Art Therapy Association, 12*(1), 42–43, https://doi.org/10.1080/07421656.2004.10129317

National Career Development Association. (2013). *The career counseling casebook: A resource for students, practitioners, and counselor educators.* Author.

Parker-Bell, B. (2011). Art therapy with children and adolescents: Inspiring creativity and growth. In C. L. Norton (Ed.). *Innovative interventions in child and adolescent mental health,* pp. 18–35. Routledge.

Parsons, F. (1909). *Choosing a vocation.* Houghton Mifflin.

Patton, W., & McMahon, M. (2018). The systems theory framework of career development. In J. P. Sampson et al. (Eds.), *Integrating theory, research, and practice in vocational psychology: Current status and future directions* (pp. 50–61). Florida State University.

Plasq. (2021). *Comic Life.* https://plasq.com/apps/comiclife/macwin/

Roe, A., & Lunneborg, P. W. (1990). Personality development and career choice. In D. Brown & L. Brooks (Eds.), *Career choice and development: Applying contemporary theories to practice* (2nd ed., pp. 68–101). Jossey-Bass.

Rosal, M. (2018). *Cognitive-behavioral art therapy: From behaviorism to the third wave.* Routledge.

Sampson, J. P., Osborn, D. S., Bullock-Yowell, E., et al. (2020). *An introduction to CIP theory, research, and practice* (Technical Report No. 62). Florida State University, Center for the Study of Technology in Counseling and Career Development. Retrieved from http://fsu.digital.flvc.org/islandora/object/fsu%3A749259

Sampson, J. P., Jr., Reardon, R. C., Peterson, G. W., & Lenz, J. G. (2004). *Career counseling and services: A cognitive information processing approach.* Brooks/Cole.

Savickas, M. L. (2005). The theory and practice of career construction. In S. D. Brown & R. W. Lent (Eds.), *Career development and counseling: Putting theory and research to work* (pp. 42–70). John Wiley.

Savickas, M. L. (2012). Life design: A paradigm for career intervention in the 21st century. *Journal of Counseling and Development, 90*, 13–19. https://doi.org/10.1016/j.jvb.2009.04.004

Savickas, M. L. (2015). *Life-design counseling manual.* Retrieved from http://vocopher.com/LifeDesign/LifeDesign.pdf

Savickas, M. L. (2018). *Career counseling.* APA Books.

Savickas, M. L., & Hartung, P. J. (2012). *My career story: An autobiographical workbook for life-career success.* Retrieved from www.vocopher.com/CSI/CCI_workbook.pdf

Schlossberg, N. K. (1984). *Counseling adults in transitions.* Springer.

Schlossberg, N. K., Waters, E., & Goodman, J. (1995). *Counseling adults in transition.* Springer.

Sharf, R. S. (2013). *Applying career development theory to counseling* (6th ed.). Brooks Cole.

Super, D. E. (1990). A life-span, life-space approach to career development. In D. Brown, L. Brooks, & Associates (Eds.), *Career choice and development* (2nd ed., pp. 197–261). Jossey-Bass.

Taylor, J. M., & Savickas, S. (2016). Narrative career counseling: My Career Story and pictorial narratives. *Journal of Vocational Behavior, 97*, 68–77.

Tiedeman, D. V., & Miller-Tiedeman, A. L. (1984). Career decision making: An individualistic perspective. In D. Brown, L. Brooks, & Associates (Eds.), *Career choice and development: Applying contemporary theories to practice* (pp. 281–310). Jossey-Bass.

Zimmerman, B. (2021). *Make Belief Comix.* www.MakeBeliefComix.com

3 Ethical Issues in Art Therapy and Career Counseling

In this chapter, ethical frameworks for the practice of career counseling and career development utilizing art therapy strategies will be examined. The authors will identify, reference, and explain key components of the National Career Development Association Code of Ethics (2015); the Art Therapy Credentials Board Code of Ethics, Conduct, and Disciplinary Procedures; the American Counseling Association Code of Ethics; and the National Career Development Association (2009) statement of Minimal Competencies for Career Counseling and Development. The authors will describe art therapist/counselor responsibilities of competence and integrity in the delivery of services which address, assess, document, and consider multicultural factors that influence clients' career development contexts, needs, and concerns. Additionally, the authors will outline competencies required for incorporating art-based strategies into treatment, and the role of supervision in supporting learning and ethical practices of applying art therapy approaches to career development intervention.

For the purposes of this book, the exploration of ethical guidelines will primarily focus on the ethics of career counseling and its interface with art therapy and the means to navigate the challenging and ambiguous situations that arise while working as a helping professional. Questions that should be answered for readers as they read and review this chapter include: Is it ethical for me to combine art therapy and career counseling methods when I have been primarily trained in one of the disciplines? What are my ethical obligations to clients who are seeking career development and decision-making guidance? How do my skillsets and competencies regarding career counseling and art therapy interventions inform what I ethically state about the strengths and limitations of the services I am able to provide? What ethical guidelines related to multicultural competency inform art therapy and career counseling practices? What are some models of ethical thinking that I can consider when approaching ethical dilemmas involving career counseling and art therapy?

Overview: Introduction to Ethical Practice

To guide and ensure that helping professionals practice their professions in a manner that continually considers client welfare and does no harm to those who entrust themselves to their care, professional associations and credentialing bodies articulate the ethical guidelines and behaviors necessary for such practice. Habbal and Habbal (2016) note that ethical guidelines are also written to "improve ourselves and the society around us as a whole" (p. 116). In reference to career counseling, Katsarov et al. (2020) assert that mental health professionals must address these ethical guidelines on several levels, a microlevel, which includes counselor interaction with clients that respects and supports client privacy, dignity, and autonomy; the organizational level which addresses issues of

DOI: 10.4324/9781003035756-3

need and justice in terms of dedicated provision of support, and a societal level, where broader political issues of social inclusion, opportunity for self-direction, dignity, and stability of the economy are taken into account. Mental health professionals have layers or responsibility to consider as they approach each interaction or intervention implemented relevant to career and life goals.

Art therapists, counselors, and other mental health professionals enter into their professions with the intention of supporting individuals, families, and community groups in attaining their optimal functioning and quality of life with awareness of social contexts. Achievement of this aspiration is reliant on therapist striving towards being their best self and serving others well. To support practitioners and those they serve, professional organizations articulate ethical principles and values to guide mental health professionals' behaviors. These principles outline art therapists' and career counselors' obligations to foster client autonomy, avoid causing harm, and to promote client mental health and well-being (AATA, 2015; ACA, 2014; NCDA, 2015). Art therapists are also called to cultivate imagination and "support creative processes for decision-making and problem solving, as well as meaning making and healing" (AATA, 2015, p. 1). Across disciplines, ethical foundations of professional practice include providing equitable and fair treatment, honoring commitments, fulfilling responsibilities, and dealing truthfully in their work with others (AATA, 2015; ACA, 2014; NCDA, 2015).

To illuminate ethical principles and values, ethical codes of conduct provide therapists with descriptions of specific behaviors and practices that are required (ACA, 2014; ATCB, 2019; NCDA, 2015). Core categories of behaviors include responsibility to clients, informed consent, professional competence and integrity, standards of conduct related to confidentiality and privacy, multicultural competency and nondiscrimination, the nature and boundaries of the professional relationship, accurate communication of one's scope of practice and associated services and their limitations, documentation, as well as clarity about financial arrangements for services provided (ACA, 2014; ATCB 2019; NCDA, 2015).

All of these general categories, as well as their sub-topics, are relevant to clinicians regardless of training specialty and all client groups and treatment concerns. Ethical codes provide a building block for ethical decision-making but do not answer every question related to complicated real-life occurrences. Principles of practice can often be vague and abstract as well (Castro-Atwater & Hohnbaum, 2015). Additionally, ethical codes and state laws may at times conflict with each other, prohibiting the construction of a singularly correct response. Furthermore, many situations that clinicians face are not straightforward and require further contemplation, consultation, and consideration to ensure that the best practice pathway is being taken for the benefit of clients.

Combining Art Therapy and Career Counseling

Readers of this book are likely well aware of their professional association's and credentialing organization's ethical principles, guidelines, and disciplinary codes, but may be less familiar with related professionals' ethics codes even though significant overlaps in acceptable standards exist. Consequently, those practicing or preparing to practice creative career counseling within their mental health practices will need to be familiar with more than one set of guidelines to enhance their navigation of required competencies which support the integration of art-based methods into career development and decision-making. Additionally, helping professionals must take into consideration state laws and mandates that inform their particular professional practice.

The professions of art therapy and career counseling are both multifaceted in nature and require extensive knowledge and skills to practice them in an ethical manner. Moon (2006) described the ethical practice of art therapy as an artful balancing of competence and aware-ness. He emphasized the importance of art therapists' knowledge and ability to understand and facilitate the therapeutic relationship, art processes, and an art space that can pro-mote healing opportunities for clients. Furman (2013) asserted that art therapy prac-tices consist of a complex weaving together of art, symbolism, physical interaction with art processes, and engagement with subjective content that must be approached with thoughtful consideration of ethics and necessary competency. She contended that ther-apists who practice outside of their competency will very likely cause harm and empha-sized the interdependence between competence and beneficial practices. For example, lack of counselor understanding of media properties and their influence on the acti-vation of client emotions may result in opening concerning feelings too quickly and exceeding the therapist's skills at helping a client manage those feelings and associations. Springham (2008) highlighted evidence that significant harm to a client can the result when well-meaning but untrained practitioners utilize art-based practices that they do not fully understand how to use in the context of clients' vulnerabilities and concerns. In Springham's presented example, a counselor's prompt for a client to paint and confront their addiction led to emotional and physical harm to the client, as the client engaged in a physical confrontation with the artwork. Di Maria (2019) further explained that, while it is essential for art therapists to understand ethical codes, informed consent procedures, and work policies, it is equally necessary to be aware of personal biases and blind spots that may interfere with ethical behavior and facilitation of best practices.

The responsibilities of career counselors are also multidimensional. Career coun-selors combine relational counseling skills and techniques in concert with specialized knowledge and skills that support career exploration and choices that may impact their clients' emotional, physical, and economic well-being throughout their lifespan (ncda. org). Consequently, lack of awareness of personal biases, cultural contexts of clients, or limitations of assessment tools that provide guiding information can translate into lim-iting opportunities and subsequent harm. For both art therapists and career counselors, committing to lifelong learning regarding core art therapy and counseling skills and multicultural competency is a necessity (Brown, 2002; Flores & Heppner, 2002; Talwar, 2010; ter Maat, 2011).

Ethical Models

Fortunately, numerous decision-making models have been created to support mental health professionals' efforts to facilitate consideration and action regarding ethical dilemmas that arise in practice (Pryzwansky & Wendt, 1999). Ethical models outline strategies for clinicians to explore internal reflections and values as well as external guidelines to ethical decision-making and its consequences. Each model offers a dif-ferent structure for approaching an ethical question. For example, some models utilize acronyms to assist therapists in recalling the steps they must take to address the compo-nents of decision-making (Hartel & Hartel, 1997; Hauck & Ling, 2016).

Hartel and Hartel (1997) offered the acronym SHAPE which stands for Scrutinize, Hypothesize, Analyze, Perform, and Evaluate. Scrutinizing calls therapists to engage their senses in detecting the signs of the problem at hand. Hypothesizing entails utiliz-ing knowledge of the situation and ethical guidelines to develop a solution to the prob-lem. Next, in the analyzing step, the mental health practitioner critically considers the developed solution, and finally, in the Perform and Evaluate stages, the therapist imple-ments the plan then checks and double checks the results of their actions. Hartel and Hartel found that applying the SHAPE acronym in circumstances that were perceived as moderately busy or stressful improved speed and accuracy of team-oriented decision-making. Having a systematic way of approaching a clinical concern and communicating about the possible decisions related to the concern was shown to be more effective than using intuition alone.

Similarly, art therapists Hauck and Ling (2016) created an ethical decision-making model that may be memorable for art therapists and creative counselors due to its acronym "DO ART." DO ART represents, Dilemma, Options and Outcomes, Assistance, Responsibility, and Take Action. In this model, the first step towards decision-making begins with defining the ethical **dilemma**. In general, Hauck and Ling, define an ethical dilemma as a situation when more than one ethical code or principle must be considered, and the determination of the ethical path to follow regarding the situation is complex or unclear. Next, **options** for prevention or remediation of a dilemma are considered. Once these options are identified, each possibility's potential positive and negative **outcomes** must be thought out. Yet, these deliberations do not need to be conducted alone: seeking **assistance** from peer and supervisors, or being aided by an exploration of literature on relevant themes and ethical principles enriches the decision-maker's knowledge and widens perspectives to be considered. Still, the art therapist or counselor facing the ethical dilemma must take **responsibility** for the choice of actions in terms of potential benefit or harm to involved parties. With all of this in mind, the therapist finally **takes action** on the soundest route to resolving the ethical concerns.

Using Ethical Models to Explore Issues of Competency

To explore how these models can be used to consider career counseling and art therapy ethics, two case scenarios are presented regarding the important ethical issues of therapist competency and accurate representation of expertise.

The Case of Annie

Utilizing Hartel and Hartel's SHAPE model for approaching decision-making, consider the case of Annie. Annie is a Board-Certified Art Therapist (ATR-BC) and has been in private practice for several years. She works with adults who are often going through life transitions including career transitions. She has found that using the Bridge Drawing (Hays & Lyons, 1981) or the Road Drawing (Hanes, 1995) has been helpful to her clients as they are exploring career paths. To build her private practice referrals she decides to add "Career Specialist" to her list of specialty areas listed on her practice webpage. Scrutinizing the situation, a question may arise, is Annie sufficiently qualified to list career specialist on her webpage? Would a listing of a career specialty accurately reflect her training and competency to potential consumers? Assuming that she had no specific training in career development and decision-making, what would be appropriate for Annie and for a practitioner to do as a bystander of this situation?

Step two, hypothesizing, could begin with an exploration the ethical codes related to advertisement. Given that Annie is an art therapist, one may start by looking at the ATCB Code of Ethics, Conduct and Disciplinary Procedures for guidance. For example, the ATCB Code 2.51 notes that "art therapists must ensure that all advertisements shall provide sufficient and appropriate information about their professional services to help the layperson make an informed decision about contracting for those services" (ATCB, 2019, p. 8). Additionally, art therapists are responsible for ensuring their advertisements, in any media, are accurate. Furthermore, art therapists "must not use names or designations for their practices that are likely to confuse or mislead the public" (ATCB, 2019, p. 8).

Specialty areas may only be listed if the art therapist has the education, training, and experience that meet recognized professional standards of practice.

Finally, exploring national and state laws and guidelines regarding career professionals' title protection, credentials, and/or licensure, would help a practitioner understand salient regulations. In the case that a practitioner did not find title protection or licensure laws have been broken, a practitioner's primary concern may be regarding the clarity and appropriateness of Annie's specialty designation.

In the performing stage, a practitioner may ask Annie about her advertisement, as well as the experience and qualifications which merit the career specialty designation. If she affirmed that she had minimal training or successful experience in facilitating career exploration, a practitioner could communicate their discomfort with the specialty designation and note that the listing may be misleading to the public. Based on Annie's subsequent actions, for example, taking down the designation or declining to take down the designation, a practitioner would evaluate if any further action would be needed to promote protection of the public and what the consequence of those actions may be.

The Case of Cindy

Cindy is a credentialed career counselor who has always enjoyed arts and crafts as a hobby. She is also familiar with art therapy as a profession as their practice group has an art therapist who rents out one of the office suites one night a week. Cindy has been working with a young woman who has experienced work issues related to sexual harassment at work. Cindy plans to bring in clay to her next session to help her client experience and release anger regarding the work events, as she's heard the art therapist say that clay is a good art medium to explore feelings. It is important to note that Cindy has taken a ceramics class, and feels comfortable working with clay.

On the evening before the session with the young woman, Cindy sees the art therapist in the office suite kitchen and excitedly tells the art therapist of her plan to work with clay to explore the work environment sexual harassment issue, then quickly leaves to attend her next session. As an art therapist, considering what Cindy just shared, it is clear that Cindy is well trained as a career counselor; however, there are concerns that Cindy may not be fully cognizant of the therapeutic properties of clay and how it may open up expression and emotions related to the harassment or other life experiences. Client welfare and the art therapist's role are the primary concerns in this situation.

Using the DO ART Model (Hauck & Ling, 2016) the art therapist must first define the ethical dilemma. Is Cindy at risk for doing harm to her client? Is she practicing within the scope of her professional training and competence? What is the responsibility of the art therapist to intervene, educate, or report Cindy, if necessary, to her credentialing body for the unethical practicing outside her scope of training and competency? What additional information is needed to determine if Cindy may be at risk for causing harm, and if so, what is the art therapist's responsibilities to Cindy's client, if any? What are the art therapist's options for action? A few possible options will be explored next.

Option 1: Since Cindy is a credentialed career counselor, Cindy is responsible for adhering to the NCDA Code of Ethics as well as "all applicable federal, state, local and or institutional statutes, laws, regulations, and procedures" (NCDA, 2015, p. 9). The NCDA Code Section C, Professional Responsibility, C.2.a states, "Career professionals practice only within the boundaries of their competence, based on their education, training, supervised experience and national professional credentials" (p. 9). Additionally, the code C.2.b refers to the adoption of new specialty areas (which may include incorporation of creative modalities such as art within career development) and notes, "While developing skills in new specialty areas, career professionals take steps to ensure the competence of their work and to protect others from possible harm" (NCDA, 2015, p. 9). The American Counseling Association Code of Ethics (2014) mirrors this language and requirements for all counseling professionals.

The NCDA (2015) Code (I.2.a) requires career counselors to act when they have knowledge or concern that a colleague may be violating ethical standards including those addressing competency. However, NCDA Code I.2.b directs career professionals, if feasible, to informally address and possibly resolve concerns with the career professional prior to taking the concern to the ethics committee. This option may be utilized provided that the client's confidentiality rights are not violated. If a career counselor is uncertain about the occurrence of a violation and the necessity of reporting, they can consult with a supervisor or others knowledgeable about the NCDA code to seek further direction. NCDA Code I.2.f warns against initiating unwarranted complaints.

Option 1 Outcomes: If after gathering more information from Cindy and attempting to resolve the concern directly with her, the conclusion is that Cindy should be reported for her conduct to the NCDA because she is practicing outside of her scope of training and competency and is harming clients, the art therapist would provide truthful evidence of the violations to the NCDA ethics committee, certification bodies, licensing boards, or other appropriate institutional authorities. Importantly, art therapists are bound by their professional ATCB (2019) Code (1.5.9) "to cooperate with any ethics investigation by any professional organization or government agency … when requested or when necessary to preserve the integrity of the art therapy profession" (p. 5).

Based on the determination of the applicable review board, Cindy may or may not be sanctioned for practicing outside of her scope of competent practice. If sanctioned, the board or panel would follow its disciplinary policies and procedures to determine the appropriate consequence that could range, for example, from a formal reprimand, mandatory remediation, additional educational requirements, to more severe consequences such as suspension of certification and notification of other agencies (ATCB, 2019).

Option 2: Credentialed art therapists are bound to conduct themselves in alignment with the Art Therapy Credentials Board Code of Ethics, Conduct, and Disciplinary Procedures (ATCB, 2019) Code 1.21, directs art therapists to file a complaint with the ATCB if there is reason to believe that another credentialed art therapist is violating the law or standards of the ATCB code such as practicing outside of their scope of training or competency. In this example, the art therapist considers reporting Cindy for practicing art therapy without training to the ATCB.

Option 2 Outcome: Since Cindy is not a credentialed art therapist, the ATCB does not have jurisdiction over her credential or review of her professional practices. Cindy is not specifically obligated to follow the ATCB code of conduct and disciplinary procedures. Therefore, this option would not be a viable means to protecting Cindy's client or further preventing harm of clients in the future.

Option 3: According to ATCB Code 1.5.8, art therapists are encouraged to promote public understanding of the principles and profession of art therapy, including presenting information to other mental health professionals while accurately conveying the necessary competency and qualifications for practices of methods taught. Considering this ethical code, the art therapist may decide to reach out to Cindy to express concern and offer some information about the qualities of clay and the possible ramifications of working with clay to address a traumatic situation. They may offer consultation and note the training required to skillfully navigate art media within a therapeutic context.

Option 3 Outcomes: Cindy may or may not welcome the information offered. She may reconsider using clay as an option within the career counseling session or may consider getting further training to be sure she could use art-based strategies in a competent manner. Additionally, Cindy may discuss potential collaboration or supervision regarding her case provided the client has granted permission for such sharing of case information. Alternatively, Cindy may be offended by the inquiry, and the professional relationship with Cindy may be strained.

According to the DO ART framework for ethical decision-making seeking assistance to support consideration of options is recommended. Hauck and Ling (2016) suggest pursuing several forms of assistance including consultation with a supervisor or colleague or exploration of literature that addresses relevant concerns. A search of literature relevant to this case may lead to the writings of Rosen and Atkins (2014) who explore the boundaries of practice that inform use of creativity and expressive arts media or play therapist Stauffer's (2019) examination of ethical concerns related to her competency to use of drawing processes in her play therapy practice. After reviewing source assistance and carefully weighing the risks and benefits of each option and their outcomes, it is the art therapist's task to move forward with responsible action.

Adding Art to Ethical Decision-Making Processes

For both art therapists and non-art therapists, art exploration can be utilized as an excellent tool for reflection and enrichment of ethical decision-making processes. In this regard, Hauck and Ling (2020) have expanded on their DO ART model (Hauck & Ling, 2016) by making recommendations for complementary art processes. Hauck and Ling (2020) assert that structured art activities "can simplify the decision-making process by organizing the components in a clear and concise way" (p. 35). They proposed utilizing a tri-fold art surface with three sections on each side of the page for artistic exploration of each of the DO ART model elements, Dilemma, Options and Outcomes, Assistance, Responsibility, and Take Action. For example, Hauck and Ling (2020) adapted drawings such as the Bridge Drawing (Hays & Lyons, 1981) and Draw a Person in the Rain (Verinis, Lichtenberg, & Henrich, 1974) that have been traditionally used to explore goal orientation and response to stressors respectively, and have offered them as drawing structures to imagine the pathway towards taking action and to appraise the rewards and risks of accepting responsibility for determined actions. After each section of the model is explored via art processes and products, the artist can holistically reflect on the ethical decision-making courses of action via the visual representations. An example of an art therapy student's artistic exploration of ethical decision-making stages and selected outcomes of art related to Cindy's case is provided in Figures 3.1 and 3.2.

These figures provide artwork as related to a student narrative demonstrating responses to these questions and a student's perception of the art-informed DO ART process:

> The DO ART process helped me compare the different outcomes side by side and assess my own role. I appreciated the use of the person standing in the rain directive as it allowed me to address the more emotional side of my role. The stop light illustration with the different ethical codes helped me to visualize how the ethical codes applied to the described situation. The internal and external assistance portions were less impactful than they could have been since I was not actually getting the assistance from other professionals or resources. Visualizing the different paths that would lead to the options helped me visualize what the impact of the various options might look like. Overall, I think this would be a great companion to active exploration of an ethical dilemma.

Figure 3.1 Student artwork 1: DO ART Process

Open-Ended Art Processes

Additional art-based strategies may be used for exploring and understanding ethical considerations that may be faced while addressing career issues in counseling and art therapy. Fish (2012) asserts that therapist response art, art created by the clinician as a means to explore and contain difficult material or countertransference in response to a client, can be used as a tool in supervision to identify and address potential ethical issues that may arise. This art process does not have a particular structure that needs to be followed. Any art medium can be utilized to grapple with a dilemma that needs further exploration and understanding before actions are considered and taken.

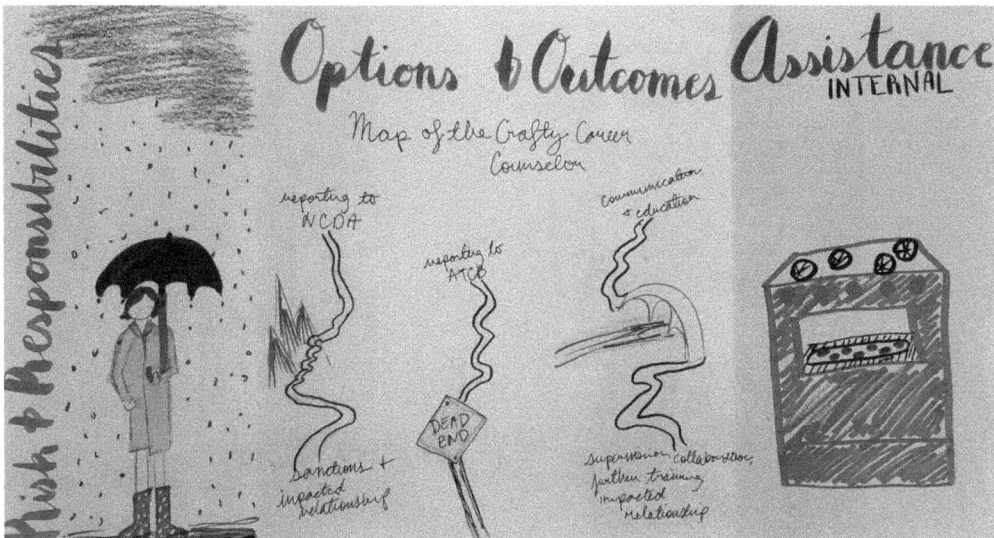

Figure 3.2 Student artwork 2: DO ART Process

For example, an art therapist or career counselor may utilize artwork and processes to begin the scrutinizing process identified in the Hartel and Hartel (1997) SHAPE model. Considering the case of Annie once again, it is possible that Annie herself may experience some discomfort or ambivalence about listing herself as a career specialist. To investigate this uncertainty, art engagement could be utilized to explore what has not yet been articulated or clarified regarding Annie's ambivalence. An open-ended question or intentional theme for artmaking, such as, "What are the boundaries of my expertise?" or, "What do clients need to know about my expertise and limitations to make an informed decision about selecting me as a care provider?" could stimulate the art therapist's kinesthetic, sensory, and affective engagement with felt experience and provide a symbolic visual product for reflection and consideration. A supervisor could guide Annie in such a process. The following artwork and discussion demonstrate what this art exploration may look like.

To begin the reflection, Annie, decided to create two different "bubble figures" to explore the roles and responsibilities of art therapists and career counselors and to examine where those roles may overlap (Figure 3.3). She reviewed career counselor definitions and ethical codes of conduct articulated her perceptions of art therapists' scope of practice and selected colors to represent facets of professional roles and practice settings that she attributed to each profession.

Next, she explored her own training and levels experience and created the "bubble self-portrait" shown in Figure 3.4. As she looked at her self-portrait, she identified that she did have some general experience with supporting people through career transitions,

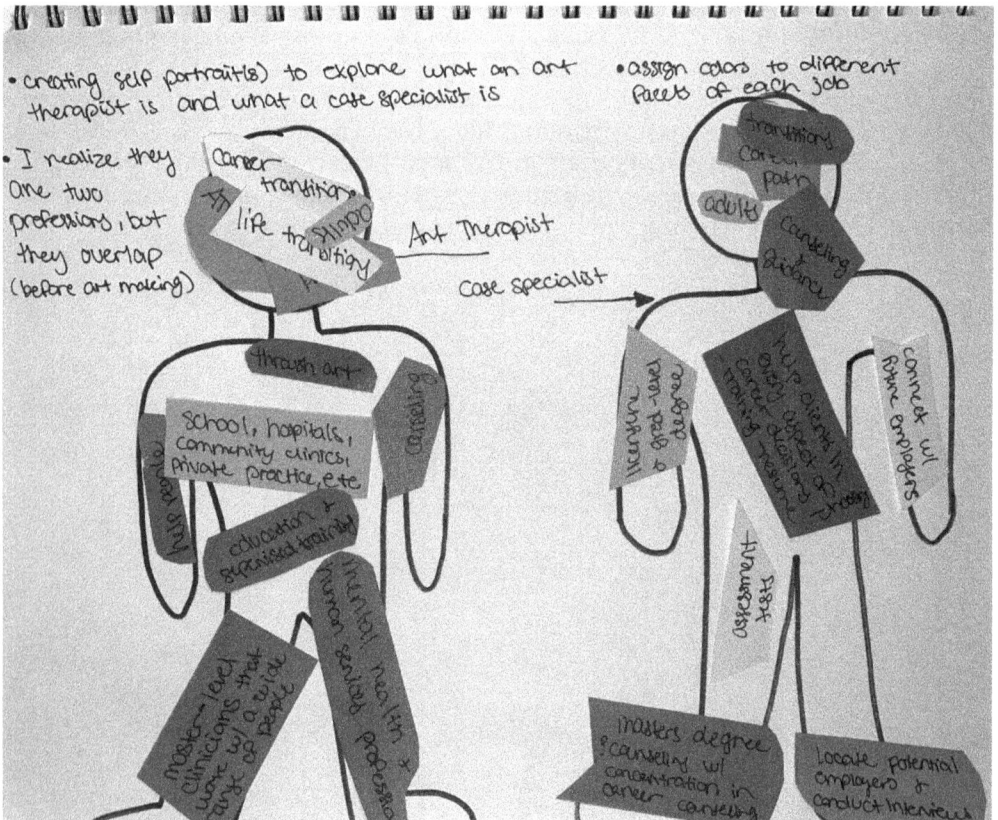

Figure 3.3 Art Therapist and Career Counselor Comparison

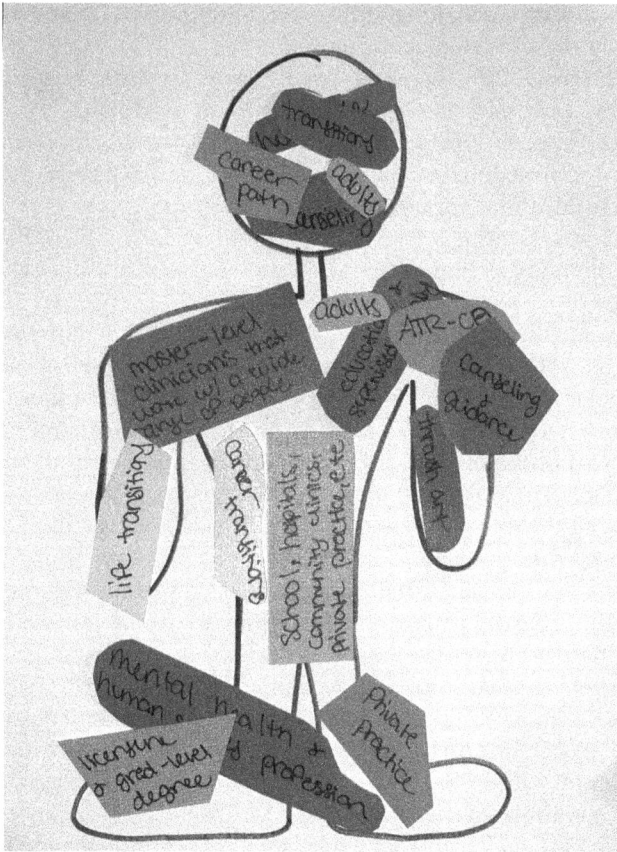

Figure 3.4 Bubble Self-Portrait: Annie Explores Her Training

but that she really didn't have the same level of training and expertise in "all things career." In the end, Annie decided that stating that she was a career specialist may be misleading to potential clients and took down the language from her website. As she enjoyed addressing career life issues and felt that was in her scope of practice, she considered new ways to articulate this interest to clients while also establishing a "when to refer to a career counselor" list for herself, so she would make appropriate referrals to career counselors when clients' needs surpassed her competency level.

Can I Ethically Combine Art Therapy and Career Counseling Approaches?

It is not taboo for career counselors to use creative arts methods, and it is not forbidden that art therapists address clients' work and life goals and decision-making process. Rosen and Atkins (2014) asserted that counselors can use creativity in counseling and defined creativity in counseling as "a broad term for practices that typically include a variety of therapeutic approaches used in a creative way" (p. 298). They reported that the counseling profession has long been familiar with the power of the arts to support expression, development, and well-being and that this history is evidenced in counseling literature. Yet, they also identified necessary familiarity with art media and counselor recognition of the power of the arts to quickly lower defenses and evoke emotional responses as prerequisites for art-based work. To utilize art processes, qualified practitioners must generate safe and secure spaces for artmaking experiences and must be able to hold and handle what may arise from the provided art processes.

Career counselors have also incorporated creative methods into their career counseling strategies. For example, career counselors have used collage to help college students explore career interests (Jahn, 2018), utilized various arts media to support clients in creating career-focused genograms to understand family career influences (Chope, 2005), or provided additional genogram-related drawing tasks to extend clients' awareness of career narratives, values, and goals (Di Fabio, 2010). Swank and Jahn (2018) offered sand tray methods to illuminate and enhance college students' career decision-making processes.

Barba (2000), an art therapist and Licensed Mental Health Counselor, represents one of a very small group of art therapy professionals who have incorporated and formally written about strategies for an art therapy approach to career life-planning. Based on her private practice work, Barba developed a guide for those seeking career change and satisfaction and offered art prompts to stimulate readers' imagination and creativity to support examination of personal qualities and interests as well as work/life visions and values. Even though few have written about their career-focused art therapy facilitation experiences, it is likely that many art therapists have used both art and verbal counseling techniques to address clients' work/life concerns that have occurred at various stages of their lives.

Strategies of career counselors and art therapists do overlap and can be competently performed by trained professionals based on sufficient understanding of both career counseling and art therapy strategies and their ramifications for client well-being and empowerment. Professionals who combine art and career practices must consider the boundaries of their expertise and limit the scope of their practice to what they can adeptly manage. Consequently, taking an honest inventory of one's knowledge, skills, and proficiency is essential. A tool, such as the Career Counseling Self-Efficacy Scale (O'Brien et al. 1997), can provide a means for evaluating areas of self-efficacy and challenge related to a broad range of career counseling knowledge, skills, and interventions. When completing the scale, professionals rate their ability to select instruments to use for assessing career interests; communicate knowledge of local and national information regarding job markets; help a client identify internal and external barriers to career decision-making and more. Yet, as previously stated, self-assessments can be subject to bias and blind spots, and more objective or external resources for evaluation may be needed (Di Maria, 2019). Examining self-rating results with a supervisor is highly recommended.

Utilizing Supervision and Outcome Monitoring to Answer Competency Questions

Supervision is an excellent forum to explore uncertainties about one's professional scope and competency levels. The ACA (2014) Code and NCDA (2015) Ethics Code, C.2.d, admonish both counselors and career counselors to continually monitor their effectiveness and to seek supervision to evaluate their efficacy as needed. The ATCB (2019) Code, 1.2, states that "art therapists "shall seek regular consultation and or/supervision with fellow qualified professionals" to ensure professional competence and integrity (p. 3).

For example, Rosen, a counselor, sought supervision from Atkins, a psychologist, counseling educator, and expressive therapist, to help Rosen determine if her use of expressive therapies within counseling was competent and ethical (Rosen & Atkins, 2014). Within the assistance of supervisory discussions and support, Rosen was able to define similarities and differences between counseling and expressive therapies' professional practices, recognized necessary knowledge and skills required for art-based work, and clarified the need to identify herself as a counselor who utilized creative methods, not a creative arts therapist.

Pinner and Kivlighan (2018) expressed concern that self-assessment and consultation with supervisors may be insufficient processes for verifying professional competency and effectiveness due to the subjective nature and communication of experiences. Furthermore, Pinner and Kivlighan stated that the accrual of additional clinical experiences did not necessarily equate to greater clinical expertise. To boost accuracy of competency evaluation, the authors recommended clinicians engage in routine outcome monitoring (ROM) to determine the boundaries of proficiency and to prevent harm. ROM processes consist of assessing clients' outcomes on a regular basis to ensure client benefit is being achieved. Outcome monitoring can be completed through regular use of an evidence-based measure specific to clients' career goals. Pinner and Kivlighan also noted that clients who participated in regularly completing and reviewing ROM measures with their therapist also demonstrated better therapy outcomes than those who did not.

Cardoso and Sales (2019) found particular value in the use of the Personal Questionnaire (PQ; Elliott et al., 2016) as a ROM structure to assess career development and decision-making progress. Unlike a pre-formed questionnaire, the PQ is an individualized questionnaire co-constructed with the client. The questionnaire evolves from an interview process and an exchange of ideas that help the counselor and client clearly define the career problem list. After the list is agreed upon, the client rates the amount which the problem bothers them on a 7-point scale, 1 being the smallest extent and 7 largest. This client and counselor use the tool to assess the extent to which the problems have resolved at different stages of treatment. Reviewing such measures with the client promotes dialogue, supports clients' goal attainment, and assists counselors in identifying potential limitations of their own skills necessary for advancing clients' aims. Art therapists, counselors, and career counselors should be prepared to utilize multiple methods to check for competency and to address ethical dilemmas that may arise.

Examining the Ethics of Multicultural Competency

Adequate preparation and skill in providing culturally sensitive services to people of a variety of backgrounds and abilities is another essential area of therapist competency and ethical practice. The professions of art therapy, counseling, and career counseling acknowledge and advocate for culturally responsive work with all clients. The American Art Therapy Association (AATA, 2015) defines multicultural and diversity competency as:

> the capacity of art therapists to continually acquire cultural and diversity awareness of and knowledge about cultural diversity with regard to self and others, and to successfully apply these skills in practice with clients. Art therapists maintain multicultural and diversity competence to provide treatment interventions and strategies that include awareness of and responsiveness to cultural issues.
>
> (p. 8)

The ACA (2014) Code of Ethics, the NCDA (2015) Code of Ethics, and the ATCB (2019) Code of Ethics, Conduct and Disciplinary Procedures feature several specific regulations that outline professionals' ethical obligations to culturally sensitive practice. The NCDA (2015) requires that:

> career professionals recognize historical and social prejudices and misdiagnoses and pathologizing of certain individuals and groups and the role career professionals can play in avoiding the perpetuation of these prejudices through proper diagnosis, recommendations and provision of services.
>
> (p. 14)

Finally, the Art Therapy Credentials Board (2019) dictates that credentialed art therapists engage in ongoing training to develop and improve cultural competence throughout their careers.

Multicultural Competency Guidelines

While several ethical codes apply to multicultural competency, even more detail is provided regarding ethical behaviors in professional organizations' multicultural competency documents. The NCDA (2009) Multicultural Career Counseling Minimum Competencies and American Art Therapy Association's (2015) Art Therapy Multicultural/Diversity Competencies were created to articulate and amplify components of culturally informed care in terms of the knowledge, skills, attitudes, and behaviors that are building blocks of culturally sensitive work. Accordingly, the NCDA addresses the key areas of career professionals' multicultural proficiency; understanding the strengths and limits of theory and their application to clients being served; awareness of one's own cultural beliefs and assumptions that may impact professional behavior and decision-making; understanding of the role of assessment and knowledge assessments options and limits regarding their applicability to people of various backgrounds; engagement in evaluation and use of technology to ensure technologies sensitively match with client needs, abilities, and access, and that necessary support for technology use is provided. Career counselors are admonished to incorporate guidelines and research into the development of appropriate programs, seek feedback from the group members to improve program design quality, and undergo continuing training and supervision to enhance the cultural sensitivity of their services.

The AATA (2015) Multicultural/Diversity Competencies describe three main categories: art therapist awareness of their personal values, beliefs, and assumptions; art therapist knowledge of clients' worldviews; and art therapist skills in developing and implementing appropriate interventions and strategies that are sensitive to religion and biculturalism. These aspirational guidelines share much of the spirit of the NCDA (2009) Multicultural Competencies yet add items related to the specialized aspects of the art therapy profession. For example, art therapists must be aware of symbolic traditions, bias that may exist within art-based assessment and their interpretation, and the manner in which cultural art traditions may influence participation, art materials selection, and creation of imagery.

Given the great importance of multicultural and diversity competency, Chapter 6 in this book will be devoted to further explorations of these important concepts and will address career counseling and art therapy in a manner which:

> honors multicultural perspectives, takes into consideration the specific values, beliefs, and actions influenced by a client's race, ethnicity, culture, national origin, color, gender, gender identity, sexual orientation, class, age, marital status, political belief, religion, geographic region, mental or physical disability, and historical or current experiences with the dominant culture.
>
> (AATA, 2015, p. 1)

Viewpoints that consider microlevel, organizational levels, and societal levels of fair and equitable practices of career counseling and art therapy service provision will also be investigated.

Summary

Art therapy, counseling, and career counseling have unique components as helping professions but also share valued principles of ethical behavior and empowering clients on their paths towards well-being and career and life role satisfaction within their larger familial and social environments. In this chapter, we explored the ethical requirement of doing no harm and understanding one's areas of competencies. Methods to assess competencies and to consider ethical dilemmas were outlined as informed by professional ethical principles and codes, multicultural competencies, ethical models, art-based reflection processes, and routine outcome monitoring. This chapter was not constructed as a comprehensive view of all ethical codes and principles that affect art therapists and career counselors, but was designed to provide examples and stimulus for further examination of the ethical bases of art therapy and career counseling practices.

Discussion Questions and Activities

1 List as many personal ethical issues that you face on a weekly basis (e.g., lying about why you were late for a meeting, letting someone use your store card for a discount). What made these ethical dilemmas? How did you go about deciding what to do? What feelings did you have in the process and afterwards? Do you still think it was the right decision? Would you make the same decision again, or process how you made the decision differently?

2 **Cases to Consider for Further Learning**
   Ethical concerns may arise in various career counseling and art therapy circumstances. Below are some additional cases to explore for discussion, art exploration, and decision-making. For each dilemma below, consider the following: What is the ethical dilemma? What are the applicable sections in the ACA and NCDA Code of Ethics and the ATCB Code of Ethics, Conduct and Disciplinary procedures? Which specific codes come into play? Which ethical model would you use to explore this dilemma further and why? How would a different model possibly look? What art processes would you use to clarify your considerations? What would likely lead to the best outcome? How would you proceed and what might that look like?

   a A client brings in some career test results from a free test on the Internet. She is very excited about the suggestion that she would be "matched" to being an electrical engineer. When you ask about the test, you realize it is a color test where the person is given a list of careers that best match the color preferences of the individual.
   b Consider a career center that is also a training institution. Thus, all the sessions are video-recorded and saved on the center's secure server.
   c A practitioner decides that as part of their business, they want to provide career services over the Internet, using primarily video conferencing through services such as Skype, Facetime, or Zoom.
   d What advice would you give to a practitioner who enjoys using social media (Facebook, blogging, Twitter, Pinterest, Instagram, etc.)?
   e A specialist sees clients in their office, but has most of their resources (career assessments, e-books, how-to-videos, etc.) online.
   f A specialist is working with a client who says that they do not have regular access to a computer or the Internet to research potential occupations. The client asks if they can borrow the specialist's tablet to access the information during the week.
   g A practitioner decides that they will provide career counseling in a virtual world such as Second Life. What are some ethical considerations they should explore prior to making this decision?
   h A practitioner really enjoys using a career app, finding it to be very relevant to their clients. However, the tool isn't grounded in theory, nor is there empirical evidence that the tool works. This tool linked on her website.
   i A career practitioner likes to hang out in various chat rooms and uses them as a marketing opportunity for their practice.

3 Joy is working on her master's degree in counseling and this is her first semester. She has accepted a graduate assistantship working in the campus library doing critiques for the university career center after completing a week-long training seminar. Just a few weeks into her new position, Joy sits down with Amy, for what starts out as a typical critique. Amy tells Joy that she has been unemployed for several months and she feels a lot of pressure because her bills are piling up. Amy then says: "I feel lost and alone; I sometimes just want to end it all." Joy has not discussed the limits of confidentiality with Amy.

4 Alex is a counselor at a high school, helping Raina decide what to do after she graduates. Raina has had a tough year; she has shared with Alex that her parents had just finalized a messy divorce about 6 months ago. Alex suggested Raina get support from the school counselor, but doesn't know what the outcome was. Raina recently set up a meeting with Alex to discuss her options, and wanted to have her mother there because Raina has been living with her and they have grown close in the past 6 months or so. Alex meets with Raina and her mother 3 times, and come up with a plan for which major Raina should choose and which universities she should visit. A few days later, Alex receives a phone call from Raina's father, who is very angry, demanding to know why he wasn't included on these meetings since he is the father and is going to be paying for all of this. He demands to know everything that went on in the meetings Alex had with Raina, and if Alex doesn't comply, he threatens to sue.

References

American Art Therapy Association. (2015). Art therapy multicultural and diversity competencies. www.arttherapy.org/upload/Multicultural/Multicultural.Diversity%20Competencies.%20 Revisions%202015.pdf

American Counseling Association. (2014). ACA code of ethics. www.counseling.org/resources/ aca-code-of-ethics.pdf

Art Therapy Credentials Board (2019). ATCB code of ethics, conduct, and disciplinary procedures. www.atcb.org/Ethics/ATCBCode

Barba, H. N. (2000). *Follow your bliss! A practical, soul-centered guide to job-hunting and career life planning.* Universal Publishers.

Brown, D. (2002). The role of work and cultural values in occupational choice, satisfaction, and success: A theoretical statement. *Journal of Counseling & Development, 80,* 48–56.

Cardoso, P. & Sales, C. (2019). Individualized career counseling outcome assessment: A case study using the personal questionnaire. *The Career Development Quarterly, 67,* 21–31, https://doi. org/10.1002/cdq.12160

Castro-Atwater, S. & Hohnbaum, A. (2015). A conceptual framework of "top 5" ethical lessons for the helping professions. *Education, 135*(3), 271–278.

Chope, R. (2005). Qualitatively assessing family influence on career decision making. *Journal of Career Assessment, 13*(4), 395–414.

Di Fabio, A. B. (2010). Life designing in 21st century: Using a new strengthened career genogram. *Journal of Psychology in Africa, 20*(3), 381–384.

Di Maria, A. (2019). Factors that can influence the ethical decision-making process. In A. Di Maria (Ed.), *Exploring ethical dilemmas in art therapy: 50 clinicians from 20 countries share their stories* (pp. 3–11). Routledge.

Elliott, R., Wagner, J., Sales, C. M. D., et al. (2016). Psychometrics of the Personal Questionnaire: A client-generated outcome measure. *Psychological Assessment, 28,* 263–278. doi:10.1037/pas0000174

Fish, B. (2012). Response art: The art of the art therapist. *Art Therapy: Journal of the American Art Therapy Association, 29*(3), pp. 138–143.

Flores, L., & Heppner, M. (2002). Multicultural career counseling: Ten essentials for training. *Journal of Career Development, 28*(3), 181–201.

Furman, L. (2013.) *Ethics in art therapy: Challenging topics for a complex modality.* Jessica Kingsley.

Habbal, Y., & Habbal, H. B. (2016). Identifying aspects concerning ethics in career counseling: Review on the ACA code of ethics. *International Journal of Business and Public Administration, 13*(2), 115–124.

Hanes, M. J. (1995). Utilizing road drawings as a therapeutic metaphor in art therapy. *American Journal of Art Therapy, 34*(1), 19–23.

Hartel, C., & Hartel, G. (1997). Assisted intuitive decision making and problem solving: Information-processing-based training for conditions of cognitive busyness. *Group Dynamics: Theory, Research, and Practice, 1*(3), 187–199.

Hauck, J., & Ling, T. (2016). The DO ART model: An ethical decision-making model applicable to art therapy. *Art Therapy: Journal of the American Art Therapy Association, 33*(4), 203–208. https://doi.org./10.1080/07421656.2016.1231544

Hauck, J., & Ling, T. (2020). Applying art therapy directives to ethical decision making. *Art Therapy: Journal of the American Art Therapy Association, 37*(1), 34–41. https://doi.org/10.1080/07421656.2019.1667669

Hays, R. E., & Lyons, S. J. (1981). The Bridge Drawing: A projective technique for assessment in art therapy. *The Arts in Psychotherapy, 8*(3–4), 207–217. https://doi.org/10.1016/0197-4556(81)90033-2

Jahn, S. A. B. (2018). Professional issues and innovative practice: Using collage to examine values in college career counseling. *Journal of College Counseling, 21*, 180–192.

Katsarov, J., Albien, A. J., & Ferrari, L. (2020). Developing a moral sensitivity measure for career guidance and counselling. *Journal for Perspectives of Economic Political and Social Integration, 25*(1), 45–65.

Moon, B. L. (2006). *Ethical issues in art therapy.* Charles C. Thomas.

National Career Development Association. (2009). NCDA Minimum Competencies for Multicultural Career Counseling and Development. www.ncda.org

National Career Development Association. (2015). NCDA code of ethics. www.ncda.org/aws/NCDA/asset_manager/get_file/3395

O'Brien, K. M., Heppner, M. J., Flores, L. Y., & Bikos, L. H. (1997). The Career Counseling Self-Efficiency Scale: Instrument development and training applications. *Journal of Counseling Psychology, 44*(1), 20–31. doi:10.1037/0022-0167.44.1.20

Pinner, D. H., & Kivlighan, D. M., III. (2018). Ethical implications and utility of routine outcome monitoring in determining boundaries of competence in practice. *Professional Psychology: Research and Practice, 49*(4), 247–254. http://dx.doi.org/10.1037/pro0000203

Pryzwanksy, W. B., & Wendt, R. N. (1999). *Professional and ethical issues in psychology.* Norton Professional Books.

Rosen, C. M., & Atkins, S. S. (2014). Am I doing expressive arts therapy or creativity in counseling? *Creativity in Mental Health, 9*, 292–303. https://doi.org/10.1080/15401383.2014.906874

Springham, N. (2008). Through the eyes of the law: What is it about art that can harm people? *International Journal of Art Therapy, 13*(2), 65–73. https://doi.org/10.1080/17454830802489141

Stauffer, S. (2019). Ethical use of drawings in play therapy: Considerations for assessment, practice, and supervision. *International Journal of Play Therapy, 28*(4), 183–184. http://dx.doi.org/10.1037/pla0000106

Swank, J. M., & Jahn, S. (2018). Using sand tray to facilitate college students' career decision making: A qualitative inquiry. *The Career Development Quarterly, 66*, 269–278. https://doi.org/10.1002/cdq.12148

Talwar, S. (2010). An intersectional framework for race, class, gender, and sexuality in art therapy. *Art Therapy: Journal of the American Art Therapy Association, 27*(1), 11–17.

ter Maat, M. (2011). Developing and assessing multicultural competence with a focus on culture and ethnicity. *Art Therapy: Journal of the American Art Therapy Association, 28*(1), 1–7.

Verinis, J. S., Lichtenberg, E. F., & Henrich, L. (1974). The draw-a-person-in-the-rain technique: Its relationship to diagnostic category and other personality indicators. *Journal of Clinical Psychology, 30*(3), 407–414.

4 The Role of Assessment in Art Therapy and Career Counseling

This chapter will introduce the reader to history of assessment in career development and several philosophies regarding the place of assessment in supporting client understanding of career development aptitudes, strengths, goals, values, and more, to enhance case conceptualization and treatment planning. Criteria for choosing assessments, descriptions of assessment categories, assessment tools, validity and reliability of assessments, multicultural issues related to selection and administration of assessments, and interpretation of assessment outcomes will be outlined. Scholarly works related to roles and types of assessments available to art therapist/counselors will be utilized as referenced resources. Importantly, this chapter will also examine the strengths and limitations of standardized assessments, informal assessment tools, interview strategies, and art-based approaches to gathering important information regarding clients' career development concerns and goals. Non-standardized and informal art-based strategies such as the creative career genogram and an art-based career values assessment will be described and illustrated.

Exploring and Utilizing Standardized or Informal Assessments

History of Career Assessment

"Assessment" has a long history in the counseling field. From the beginning of time, individual differences have been noticed in intelligence, skills, aptitudes, personality types, preferences, and so on, and as psychology emerged as a field, we began trying to identify, classify and predict outcomes from these differences. As examples, early Chinese psychologists identified five emotions, as well as yin and yang; Hippocrates identified four humors; Aristotle proposed that while thinking is rooted in perception, sometimes this is flawed; and the Renaissance period saw a rising interest in understanding the individual. Early career assessments were used to help identify which individuals would be best suited for which jobs in the military, in response to wars. Thus, the early career assessments focused on matching "conditions of success" for specific occupations (Parsons, 1909) with traits, skills, and aptitudes for learning specific skills. As psychology shifted its focus across the years, career assessments mirrored those changes. Interest and values inventories began to emerge. Non-standardized approaches to career assessment began to appear. With a current national push on career readiness, more inventories addressing readiness have been emerging. Career assessments today are varied in the constructs they measure, as well as how they are administered and interpreted.

DOI: 10.4324/9781003035756-4

Types and Purposes of Career Assessments

Each individual career assessment has a stated purpose. Similar to reviewing the treatment purpose for a medicine, it is important to review the purpose for each specific assessment, to increase the likelihood that the chosen assessment will positively address the treatment goal. A person wouldn't apply a steroid cream to treat a fever, and a counselor shouldn't administer an interest inventory to help a client clarify their values. Thus, having an understanding for the general types of career assessments that exist as well as their general purpose, will help a counselor in determining which type is recommended for their client. Table 4.1 identifies some of the most common types and purposes of career assessments.

Choosing a Career Assessment

The decision to use a career assessment should be based on the client's needs and the degree to which a particular assessment can best address those needs. Thus, the first step in choosing a career assessment is to thoroughly understand what the client's needs and goals for career counseling are and matching those to the career assessments available. Also important is understanding the client's personality, as well as their cultural context in

Table 4.1 Common types, purposes, and examples of career assessments

Type of career assessment	General purpose	Examples
Classifications (interests, values, skills, personality, aptitudes)	Identify specific characteristics; for some, linking these to a list of matching options	ASVAB NEO-PIR Self-Directed Search Strong Interest Inventory Work Values Inventory
Career Indecision	Identify how decided a person is, or aspects that may be contributing to career indecision	Career Decision Scale Career State Inventory
Career readiness	Determine readiness to make a career decision; identify potential barriers to being ready	Career Attitudes and Strategies Inventory Career Salience Inventory My Vocational Situation
Career beliefs	Identify beliefs that may help/ hinder the career decision-making process	Career Decision Making Self-Efficacy Scale Career Thoughts Inventory Career Outcome Metacognition Survey
Career Stress	Identify stressors specific to work	Career Tension Scale Job Stress Survey Occupational Stress Inventory Vocational Meaning & Fulfillment Surveys
Career Transitions	Identify areas that may hinder/ support them as they engage in or consider a career transition	Barriers to Employment Success Inventory Career Transition Survey Re-employment Success Inventory
Computer-assisted career guidance systems	Provide an interactive experience where one can use multiple combinations of assessments to see matching results	SIGI FOCUS Kuder Career Planning System
Card sorts and other qualitative tools	Client-driven approaches that often result in a unique product, with the goal of creating a springboard for deeper conversation about the specific topic.	Career Genogram Career Style Interview Career System Interview Card Sorts My Career Chapter My System of Career Influences Virtual Card Sort

making career decisions, and what type of career assessment experience they might benefit most from. Some clients might prefer a lengthier, more comprehensive, structured assessment that results in a report or a list of options for further exploration, whereas others might prefer a more creative expression of their identities and a less structured approach that provides confirmation and affirmation of who they are and opens a door for conversations about future possibilities. Still others might prefer a combination of these two approaches.

In addition to knowing our clients, a knowledge of specific career assessments is required to ensure that ethical options are provided. The National Career Development Association provides a resource called "A Comprehensive Guide to Career Assessments" that included in-depth reviews of standardized and non-standardized career assessments, including psychometric properties of the objective inventories, administration and interpretation steps, research that has used the assessment, and an overall evaluation of the resource. Ethically speaking, knowing whom the assessment was normed on, as well as reliability and validity information, reading level, and limitations (including cultural) should be key considerations when determining if an assessment is the appropriate tool for your client.

Just as clients have goals for career counseling, career assessments are created with specific purposes in mind. The assessment purpose might include identifying and clarifying specific aspects of a person's self-knowledge, such as interests, values, skills, aptitudes, strengths, or personality. Some assessments, such as computer-assisted career guidance programs, might look at various aspects of an individual and combine them in an overall report. They might also be used to unearth career beliefs or negative career thoughts, or to determine career readiness. The outcome purpose could be to provide a comprehensive picture of the attributes being measured, create a list of careers and/or training options that best match the individual's responses, highlight areas that might need further discussion with a practitioner, and recommend next steps.

A final consideration for choosing an assessment is the counselor's familiarity with the assessment. Ethical standards from art therapy and career development associations as well as counseling accreditation bodies require counselors to limit their use of assessments to those for which they have received training and supervision. This includes reading the assessment's professional and technical manuals if they exist, taking the assessment themselves, and working with a supervisor to understand the results. In addition, a counselor might practice administrating and interpreting the assessment through roleplays or in conjunction with an experienced counselor or supervisor so they can gain experience and know how to approach challenging profiles.

Integrating Career Assessments into the Career Conversation

A major misperception of career counseling and conversations involving careers is that it can be summed up in giving clients a test that points them to matching career options. Best practices would suggest that this "test and tell" approach is not optimal for helping individuals make informed career decisions. Osborn and Zunker (2016) suggest a process for integrating career assessments into the overall counseling process – a process that might result in the decision not to use a career assessment. The recommended steps include:

1 **Analyze the client's needs**. Ask enough questions to understand what the gap is for the client. What information do they need to help them move forward in their career decision-making and problem-solving process?
2 **Establish the purpose for an assessment**. Once the need(s) are determined, the counselor should identify what outcomes are being sought for taking an assessment. Is it to clarify one's interests or to see what options match certain individual characteristics?

Or is the goal to determine what barriers or negative thoughts may be limiting a person's career decision, or perhaps to measure career readiness? Specifying a desired outcome for an assessment is a prerequisite for the third step.

3 **Determine instruments**. Assessment possibilities should be clearly related to the client's goal(s). More than one option should be presented to the client to invite and hear their voice for treatment options. The options might include standardized or non-standardized assessments.

4 **Utilize results**. Once the decision for an instrument is made and the individual completes the assessment, the counselor then discusses with the client how the results address the client's need(s) and the reasons why they took the assessment. What was learned from the assessment? What still needs to be learned?

5 **Make a decision**. As part of the discussion of the assessment results, a decision must be made by the client and counselor. The decision could be to take another assessment, or to begin exploring options using career information, or to commit to a major or career change.

One step appears to be missing in this recommended sequence. Between choosing an instrument and utilizing the results, NCDA specifies that prior to providing a career assessment, the career professional must orient clients to the assessment. This orientation should begin with a reiteration of the purpose of the assessment, what will be the output of the assessment, and how the results will address the client's needs and goals. An overview of the assessment should include instructions on how to complete the instrument, and if it is an online assessment or computer-assisted career guidance program, how to navigate the system. Also important is to let client's know what to do if they get stuck while taking the assessment, and what to do once they have completed the assessment. If possible, the counselor should "check in" with the client at least once during the assessment and ask how the process is going, and to answer any questions.

Interpretation of Assessment Results

Clients vary in the amount of assessment interpretation they desire from a counselor. Some inventories generate reports that are several pages long, and some clients will prefer to read those results independently, and may or may not want to discuss next steps with a counselor. Some clients will prefer an in-depth explanation of scales and subscales, while others will want to jump straight to "the list." Understanding and respecting a client's preferences for interpretation will serve to enhance the working alliance that has been established.

Recommendations for interpreting objective assessment results include:

- **Begin by reiterating the purpose for the assessment**. Most assessments that link to options do not have as their purpose the identification of THE ONE career a person should pursue. Instead, often the purpose is to expand a person's options based on the information the person inputs. Re-stating the purpose for the assessment will keep the conversation focused on the overall goal for career counseling.

- **Ask the client for their preference in discussing the inventory results**. Would they prefer to read over the results themselves (if a report is given)? If so, would they like a list of questions to guide them as they read the results? Would they like a brief or more in-depth interpretation? Do they want to do it right after they've completed the assessment or would they prefer some space between taking the assessment and discussing the results?

- **Ask the client for their general reactions to taking the assessment**. What was the experience like for them? Were they able to take their time? Were the questions easy or difficult to answer? What did they think of the questions? How did they approach taking the assessment?
- **Ask the client for what they think (or hope) the results will show**. Most objective career assessments are not designed to produce results that will surprise the test-taker. If a person indicates they like working with people, the results will likely show occupations that involve working with people. If the results differ from what the client was thinking or hoping they would show, the conversation might focus on why that potentially happened.
- **Examine the overall results first**. Before diving into subscales and their potential meaning, take a look at what the overall results are suggesting. Do they have a high or low undifferentiated profile, or are there clear peaks and valleys? Do their interests seem to be consistent or all over the place? Is there a very short or long list of options? Do the results seem to mirror what the client has shared verbally or do they differ?
- **Explore subscales and individual items**. For instruments that have subscales, looking at these results can provide nuance. For example, the Self-Directed Search compares interests and competencies across the RIASEC types. Examining if a person's interests are high but competence is low in an area may lead to a suggestion for gaining more training in that area. If the reverse is true, the client might be encouraged to see if there are other occupations that might use their skills and also tap their interests. The overall results of the Career Thoughts Inventory might indicate lower levels of negative career thoughts, but in examining the individual items, a couple of specific problematic thoughts might be elevated and worth discussing.
- **Present the results tentatively and in small doses**. Even the most reliable instruments have a margin of error, so results should be stated in a tentative manner, such as "the results are suggesting that you might want to consider ..." or "some options you might want to explore ...." When launching into the interpretation, it is very easy to move out of discussion mode and into lecture mode. Watching client non-verbal responses, inviting client comments, and monitoring the balance of who is speaking most can steer a counselor away from monologuing.
- **Invite reactions to the results and interpretation**. Throughout the interpretation, ask the client for their responses to the interpretation. Do the results resonate with the client? Were there any surprises or concerns about the results? Do they want to provide some context around the results? For example, a client's results might indicate occupations in a specific area where they've had a great deal of experience, but are no longer interested in being in that field. In that case, the results are skewed to reflect the person's experiences. A different assessment might suggest that others' opinions are complicating their ability to commit to a career, but the client may provide a cultural context that these opinions, while complicating the decision, are not negative, but valued.
- **Determine next steps**. It is desirable that the results of the assessment will push the client forward in making their career decision. However, it may also be that the client enjoyed taking the career assessment and would like to take additional ones to gain a more comprehensive view of themselves and options. Or, it could be that the results were unsatisfactory and taking another assessment is desirable to provide a different perspective. It could be that the next step is to focus counseling conversations on examining and challenging negative career thoughts, or perhaps engaging with career information to learn more about career options or to narrow career options.

Recommendations for interpreting qualitative/subjective assessment results include:

- **Begin by reiterating the purpose for the assessment**. As with the first recommendation for interpreting objective assessments, it can be helpful to reiterate the goal for engaging in the particular assessment activity. The outcome goals may be similar to the goals for using objective measures (e.g., identifying interests, listing out barriers or impacts on career decision making), but the process is different. Unlike many of the standardized assessments that provide a list of options that match a person's specific characteristics, these qualitative approaches do not result in a matched list, but lend themselves more to discussion and clarification of the issues involved with career decision-making.
- **Ask the client for their general reactions to engaging with the assessment or activity**. What was the experience like for them? How did they approach the task? What thoughts and feelings were they experiencing when they started, during the process, and at the end?
- **Ask the client to offer their interpretations of the product they produced**. The product that is produced is generated from the client. While they might be responding to a prompt, the result is very different than reading a report that is generated from responses to items on an inventory. Reports are predictable in their format and results. A counselor knows what to expect. With client-created products, each outcome will be very different, and as the client is the one who created the product, asking the client to share the meaning they are seeing is a recommended first step.
- **Offer observations and ask questions**. Some non-standardized approaches like card sorts (Osborn et al., 2016) or My Career Story (Savickas & Hartung, 2012) have recommended "process" questions for counselors to ask or instructions to follow, while others might not. Observations might include repeated themes that are emerging in the product or in the client's description of the product, or elements that were present in discussions prior to the assessment but are missing in the final product. A counselor might ask clients if there were any surprises that emerged, or to identify the most salient considerations such as in the case of interests or options. Other questions should tie into the overall goal for engaging with the assessment, such as "One of our goals for doing this was to get a better understanding of what's important to you in making this career decision. How do you think this process has addressed that?"
- **Determine next steps**. As with standardized career assessments, the ultimate goal is to help a client gain more clarity about their situation and make progress in their career decision. After completing a non-standardized assessment, a client may want to take a standardized inventory that links with options, and might be in a better place to do that as they may have more clarity on their interests, values or skills. Or, they may need to discuss barriers that were identified, and create strategies on how to best address them. It could be that through the experience, they prioritized what was most important to them in making a career decision, and are now ready to examine career information using that knowledge as a rubric for evaluating options.

Use of Other Assessments

Mental Health Assessments

As mental health issues such as anxiety and depression have been increasing among adults, colleges and universities are also seeing a rise in these cases. Adults and students don't leave their mental illness outside the door when seeking counseling to address their career needs. Many researchers (Hayden & Osborn, 2020; Finklea & Osborn, 2019; Walker & Peterson, 2012; Rottinghaus et al., 2009; Saunders et al., 2000) have found relationships among career and mental health constructs. Low, flat scores on interest inventories might be indicative of depression. Dysfunctional career thoughts have been correlated with depression, anxiety, and other mental health outcomes such as worry. Practitioners should refer to the technical manuals and when possible, review recent research associated with any career assessment they are using, to see if scores on the instrument are associated with other constructs, including mental health. Alternatively, a practitioner might want to utilize standardized mental health instruments such as the anxiety and depression inventories to accompany the career instruments. If higher levels of depression are found, a counselor may want to hold off on administering an interest or skill inventory to assure that the client is not in a depressed state when completing the inventory, which will negatively bias the results.

Counselor-Created Assessments

Characteristics common to a specific clientele group may emerge over time. For example, if a counselor's primary clientele are military members or veterans, they may hear issues related to transitions, or knowing how to translate military experiences into civilian job skills. As a counselor works with repeated individuals from a specific group, they may learn that certain issues are especially relevant to that group, and routinely ask about these issues. Over time, the counselor may decide that they want to add items to an intake sheet or create their own career assessment. Or, an art therapist may find that an art directive that was designed for mental health counseling adapts well for their clients' career issues. Another possibility is that a counselor creates their own intervention that seems to resonate with clients. All of these examples represent a response to client needs, and thus have great potential merit and utility. Counselors developing assessments, whether objective or subjective in nature, must consider ethical principles when creating, administering and interpreting these tools. In most of these cases, the interpretation should be offered tentatively, such as "It seems as if ____ is a very important consideration for you when thinking about your options." In the absence of evidence of strong psychometric properties, a counselor should steer away from statements that suggest options based on results from an inventory they create and focus instead on how discussions about the client's responses help with understanding and addressing the client's career concern.

Multicultural Issues Related to Selection and Administration of Assessments

Given the weight of career decisions that are made, often in large part on the basis of career assessment results, counselors must assure that the inventories being used are appropriate, reliable, and valid for the client who is using them. Culturally sensitive career counseling goes beyond assuring that norming processes and psychometric properties are appropriate, and chooses, administers, and interprets assessments within a cultural context. Many career assessments now report equivalence of results for different genders, races, and ethnicities, but not every identity is represented or reported on. When intersecting identities are considered, it is clear that no assessment will be able to have adequate representation of samples from each unique combination of identities to provide consistent results. Thus, the onus is on the counselor to ask about a client's identities, experiences, cultural background, and other impacts such as cultural belief system (Flores et al., 2003; Ridley et al., 1998) that might be affecting their career choice, and then integrate the assessment into this knowledge. This might include a discussion of bias, discrimination and societal barriers that the client may have faced. Other possible topics of inclusion might be how cultural and societal values, or family expectations, might interact with the individual's career decision.

A counselor also needs to be aware of any perceived power dynamics that can come across especially during an interpretation of a career assessment, and instead work to create an atmosphere in which the client feels comfortable to contradict a finding, suggested options, or even interpretations. Another way to promote a shared balance of power is to present all results and interpretations tentatively. A counselor might start by asking the client to share what they expect or hope the results to show, or what people who are close to them might expect the results to show (Flores et al., 2003).

Using Art-Based Methods for Exploration and Case Conceptualization

A Brief History of Art Therapy Assessments

The scope of art therapists' work with clients often includes arts-based assessments used formally or informally to aid case conceptualization. Yet, many early art-based assessments were originated by psychologists and psychiatrists who used drawing prompts and activities as projective methods to explore client concerns, relational dynamics, or developmental considerations. These paper and pencil art-based assessments included the House-Tree-Person drawing series (HTP: Buck, 1948) designed to explore clients' personality components and relationships with others, the Kinetic Family Drawing, a drawing of one's family doing something, created to explore perceptions of family relationships (Burns & Kaufman, 1970), and Draw-a-Person (Machover, 1952) used to examine clients' self-concept. In concert with drawings, clients were asked to note associations or describe stories related to their artwork to provide further material for interpretation. While these assessments were frequently used by psychologists and other mental health professionals in the past to support the understanding of client diagnoses and concerns, training in and use of these processes have diminished in favor of training in evidence-based brief scales that are devised to measure clients' experiences of diagnostic symptoms (Piotrowski, 2015). Questions about the reliability and validity of interpretations derived from projective methods have remained a concern as there is no universally accepted standards for interpretation of drawings or symbols. Additionally, meanings of drawings and symbols are influenced by a client's personal and cultural contexts, adding to variability in projective assessment responses and accuracy of interpretations. Variations in application of projective assessments and lack of therapist awareness of how their cultural lens or biases may influence interpretation are also problematic.

Consequently, art therapists have grappled with the need for more rigorous evaluation of reliability and validity of art-based assessments and their applications (Betts, 2006, 2016). Deaver (2016) also noted the need for collecting normative samples of drawings for comparison to drawings of clinical populations. Appropriately, professional ethics require that art therapists "carefully evaluate the specific theoretical bases and characteristics, validity, reliability and appropriateness of each instrument" (Art Therapy Credentials Board, 2021, p. 9).

The aforementioned concerns and standards have fostered assessment refinement and creation of formal art-based assessments developed through research processes. One assessment that has undergone extensive research is the Diagnostic Drawing Series (DDS; Cohen, 1985; Cohen, Mills, & Kijak, 1994; Cohen & Mills; 2016), conceived of as an art-based means for clarifying diagnosis and treatment planning for individuals aged 13 or over. This assessment protocol includes a free drawing, a drawing of a tree, and a picture related to how they are feeling using lines, shapes, and colors using pastels. The DDS and its scoring systems have been established and refined over the years. Standardized materials and administration procedures as well as rating manuals that provide evaluative guidance regarding the graphic qualities of artworks; metaphors and symbols revealed; and client physical behavior, verbalizations, associations, and articulated art titles in order to distinguish between "mental health and illness in adults using DSM Diagnoses, contributing to a diagnostic process; or supporting or confirming a diagnosis" (Cohen & Mills, 2016, p. 562). Normative studies of the DDS have also been completed to provide a basis for comparison and clinical findings.

Diverging from projective frameworks for understanding clients, Gantt and Tabone (1998) created an assessment rating scale, the Formal Elements of Art Therapy Scale (FEATS), that is most typically utilized with the administration of the Person Picking an Apple from a Tree Drawing. Instead of interpretation, evaluators utilize the rating scale to evaluate 14 visual aspects of the work, including prominence of color, implied energy, space, details of objects and environment, realism, and more, that may be considered graphic equivalencies of symptoms associated with four diagnostic categories of major depression, schizophrenia, organic mental disorder, and bipolar disorder. Ongoing research is providing additional impetus for assessment measure refinement and validation (Bucciarelli, 2011).

Another art therapy assessment example, Silver's (2005) Draw-a-Story, is a well-researched screening for depressive symptoms and risk for aggression for teens and adults, prompts examinees to select from a group of stimulus drawings and combine elements of the selected in a drawing of their own. Examinees are then asked to tell a story about their drawings. In the case of Silver's Draw-a-Story, evaluative rating scales address the themes of the story related to humor, emotional functioning, and self-image as opposed to the image interpretation or graphic qualities.

Art therapists frequently differ in their views on the nature and role of assessment in art therapy, some preferring a more informal approach to considering art processes and processes within the therapy context. In this regard, assessment within art therapy incorporates observational processes of clients' interactions with the art materials, interactions with the examiner/therapist, and attention to verbal and non-verbal communications that occur during assessment engagement (Gilroy, Tipple, & Brown, 2012). This is particularly evident in the case of family art evaluations. Art therapists have devised specific sequences of individual and interactive art experiences that reveal family themes and structures as they actively navigate decision-making, art processes, and discussions. Kwiatkowska's (1978) Family Art Evaluation that engages family members in a free drawing, a family portrait, and an abstract family portrait and Landgarten's (1981) Family Art Assessment where families are asked to engage in a non-verbal team art task, a non-verbal family art task, followed by a verbal family art task are among the most well-known art therapy evaluations for assessing family structures and patterns. When utilizing these art assessment processes, art therapists combine their objective observations and subjective analyses of family actions, creations, and verbalizations to summarize family dynamics and formulate treatment plans (Asawa & Haber, 2016).

McNiff (2009) advocated for a client-centered approach to art evaluation methods emphasizing reliance on collaboration with the client in the exploration of their artworks over the span of the therapeutic relationship. Within this frame, imagery is collected over time, and therapist and client join together to witness the unfolding of the client's unique visual and symbolic language used to reflect experiences, feelings, perceptions, and ideas. In this context, the client is validated as the expert on their visual language and meaning of their works.

Expanding on this consideration for clients' expertise on their personal symbols, a client's cultural context must also be respectfully taken into account when working towards an understanding of a person, their art, and their art process and art imagery. Cultural experiences and contexts influence people's responses to materials, themes, generation of symbols, and associations with symbols revealed in assessment processes. Art therapists work with clients from a variety of cultural contexts and experiences and must be sensitive to the need for relevant adaptations and test equivalence to ensure cross-cultural applications of art-based assessments are appropriate (Betts, 2013). Additionally, art therapy assessment processes should be reviewed for bias, and art therapists must also reflect on their own potential for biases in administration and interpretation. In this regard, the Art Therapy Credentials Board (2021) has illuminated art therapists' responsibilities regarding awareness of art therapy assessments limitations and applicability in the ATCB Code of Ethics, Conduct, and Disciplinary Procedures. They require art therapists to "carefully evaluate the specific theoretical bases and characteristics, validity, reliability and appropriateness of each instrument" (Art Therapy Credentials Board, 2021, p. 9) and to "proceed with caution when attempting to evaluate and interpret performance of any person who cannot be appropriately compared to the norms for the instrument" (Art Therapy Credentials Board, 2021, p. 9).

Using Visual Information and Artistic Processes as Career Assessment

As of this date, art therapists have not designed formal art therapy assessments for use in examining clients' perspectives or skills related to career considerations. While art therapists may use informal assessments during therapeutic situations where career and life design arises as a presented component, few have published these practices. Barba (2000), an expressive art therapist, offered creative means for exploring career related self-knowledge and career interests. She asserted that imaginal processes enhanced career exploration and decision-making. Barba encouraged her clients to utilize creative exercises to re-imagine themselves, employers, and relationships with employers. To promote reconsideration of one's personality for example, Barba asked clients to name a personal trait they perceived as a weakness. Next, clients were invited to externalize this trait and give it form. Clients were encouraged to use clay, drawing materials, or creative writing processes to do so. Following externalization and reflection, clients were invited to describe the creation and reflect upon inquiries such as: What is it? How does it serve you? What does it have to teach? Barba posited that awareness of personality traits, including perceived weaknesses, could help clients understand their best fit with career options and environments. In another described intervention, Barba encouraged clients to imagine their "bliss moments" and create images or stories that reflected them. Following the creative process, clients were asked to identify implied interests and talents implied by the art or stories. Such creative methods for investigating personality traits and interests can be combined with formalized career interest and skill surveys to broaden data available for exploration.

In a related manner, occupational therapists have utilized expressive arts assessment processes in exploring occupational client profiles (Eschenfelder & Gavalas, 2018). Specifically, expressive therapy approaches were designed to stimulate communication of meaningful experiences and interests that enable client-centered treatment planning. One such art-based occupational assessment process is the Gunnarsson's Tree Theme Method (TTM; Gunnarsson & Eklund, 2009). In this multi-staged art process, clients are asked to paint a tree with roots, a trunk, and a crown symbolizing their personality, interests, and relationships. These themes are explored through five different tree paintings which represent different stages of life including the present, childhood, adolescence, adulthood, and the future. Painting and reviewing works are followed by storytelling, occupational story-making, goal-setting, and treatment planning.

Some career counselors have also incorporated imaginal or arts-based processes in their assessment repertoires. For example, career counselors have utilized guided imagery (Jahn, 2018; Stoltz, Apodaca, & Mazahreh, 2018), sand tray (Killam, Degges-White, & Michel, 2016; Swank & Jahn, 2018) and collage processes (Burton & Lent, 2016; Jahn, 2018; Killam et al., 2016), to collect qualitative information regarding clients' career interests, influences, and values. Jahn (2018) noted that creative formats in career counseling supported increased client engagement, promoted deeper access to emotions, and allowed for "processing that is not limited by verbal expression" (p. 184). Jahn emphasized that creative processes often revealed hidden values, which left unexplored, might cause distress during the career decision and life planning process.

Taylor and Savickas (2016) demonstrated that art-based processes could be incorporated into a narrative life-design approach to career counseling by inviting clients to explore career problems through drawing. Following My Career Story Workbook (Savickas & Hartung, 2012) exercises that elicit valued life themes and stories, Taylor and Savickas utilized the Pictorial Narrative intervention to invite clients to depict their career problem and their preferred outcome using color pencils and paper. After placing these images together, counselor and client view and dialogue about what they see. "Baby steps" pictures, which involve the client being asked to depict small movements that can be taken towards the preferred outcome, can also be included as a part of the described career intervention. Themes that appear in the My Career Story and Pictorial Narrative drawings are then interwoven into discussions of career life design efforts, values, and aims between client and counselor.

Decision Space Worksheet

The Decision Space Worksheet designed by Peterson, Lenz, and Osborn (2016) is a cognitive information processing theory (CIP) informed projective career assessment with a visual component. This assessment is utilized to understand clients' concerns related to a career problem and how these concerns may affect the client's readiness for career decision-making. Peterson, Lenz, and Osborn note that assessment is "a quick effective way for clients to grasp the comprehensiveness of what is happening in their life in the moment" (p. 4). Clients are instructed to state a career problem or decision they are working on, and then identify any thoughts, feelings, people, finances, or other items that may have an influence on this career concern and then are asked to rate each item as positive, negative, or neutral. The visual component of the assessment consists of a circle that represents the career decision space. Clients are asked to draw a circle within the circle to represent each influence on their list, utilizing the size of each circle to represent the relative importance of that item within the career decision space and to label each circle with the number that matches the list. Having multiple tools available for the client, such as colored pencils, pens, markers, watercolors, and so on, can help engage the creative process when they move to representing the issues on paper. As demonstrated in Figure 4.1, the task of creating circles to represent the career influences may be interpreted widely and creatively providing rich information for client and career counselor discussions.

Processing the DSW

Once the client has completed the DSW, the practitioner might begin the processing by asking about their general experiences completing the DSW, with a question such as "What was this experience like for you? What thoughts and feelings came up as you were working

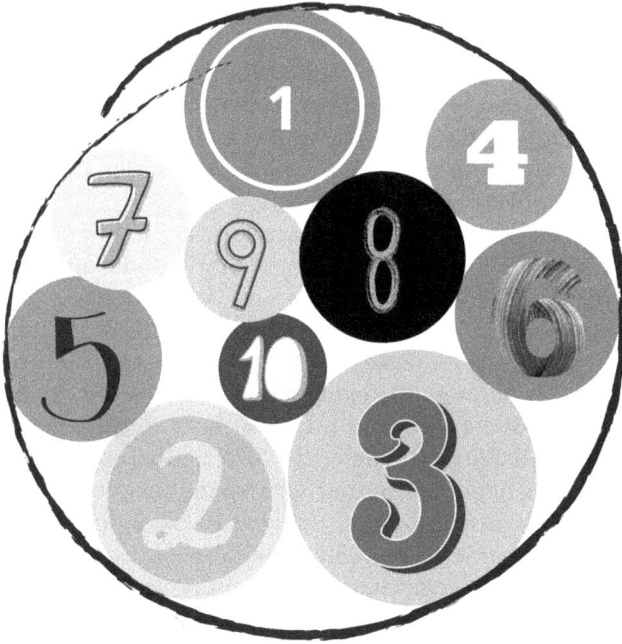

Figure 4.1 Decision Space Worksheet Example

on this?" Other questions might focus on the original decision the client wrote down – "Tell me more about that" or "Now that you've gone through this activity, would you like to add anything else to what you wrote here?" Practitioners can then review the written list of elements and valences, asking such questions as "What is your impression of this list?" or "How does each item affect your career decision?" or "Are some of the valences slightly stronger than others?" or "Do some of these go hand-in-hand or influence each other?"

For the visual representation, after asking the client to share their general impression, the practitioner might guide the client to look for themes or patterns or relationships, or to identify the elements that seem to be of the most concern. The practitioner might consider, as the client speaks, whether there is a clear tendency towards more cognitive or affective elements, the presence of an underlying negative self-concept, or external pressures impacting the career decision. At this point, the practitioner may decide to move to a more formal assessment of readiness or negative career thinking, or may work with the client to identify next steps. For example, if "fear of the unknown" is an element, helping the client make the unknown known might be a next step.

Career-Focused Genograms

Another assessment utilizing a visual format is the Career Genogram. Chope (2005) described the Career Genogram as a diagram that depicts a person's "occupational family-tree" and "the most commonly recognized and frequently administered qualitative instrument for gathering information about the influence of the family in career decision making" (p. 406). As such, career-focused genograms may be utilized for different age groups including teenagers, college students, and adults. For example, in the case of a homeless youth, Setlhare-Meltor and Wood (2016) offered the career genogram to explore existing career narratives as a first step toward building new narratives. Storlie et al. (2019) utilized the Career Genogram assessment with college students and found that undeclared college freshmen experienced the Career Genogram as an effective method to identify family gender and generational patterns related to career types, career satisfaction, and career/work attitudes. Students also stated they experienced increased awareness of family narratives and how they influenced their career options and decision-making considerations. Kakiuchi and Weeks (2009) utilized a related occupational transmission genogram with adult couples to effectively explore generational career values and the effects on couple and family roles and dynamics.

Chope (2005) outlines the following processes for the career genogram: First a client must research the career choices of their family of origin and extended family; next, the client is asked to depict these family members and their careers symbolically on paper via drawing materials; finally, the client is encouraged to reflect on family career themes, beliefs, and values that have been passed on to them directly or indirectly. However, in an effort to connect with clients and to expand expression, some career counselors have added creative processes of collage, sand tray, and more to their genogram assessment protocols (Buxbaum & Hill, 2013; Killam et al., 2016; Setlhare-Meltor & Wood, 2015).

Di Fabio (2020), for example, advocated for expanding genogram interventions by adding supplementary creative prompts. Using this expanded approach, clients are encouraged to create a career jewel box which contains career life dreams; a set of "mirror" reflection artworks that engage clients in representing their personal qualities and traits as they perceive them, and another image that reflects their qualities and traits as others may perceive them; a letter or scroll that features career messages passed on by family members; and finally, a list of mottos that family members expressed regarding career and life constructs. Client and counselor review artworks together, looking and listening to stories that help reveal recurrent themes related to career influences, interests, and conflicts. With knowledge of these themes, counselor and client thoughtfully design career life goals and intervention plans.

Thus far, art therapists have not written about work with career-focused genograms. However, art therapists (Hoshino & Cameron, 2008; Schroeder, 2015) have embraced the genogram structure as an art therapy tool that may be employed to illuminate family patterns and influences. They demonstrate that genograms' structures do not have to be limited to paper and pencil, circle and squares. Genograms can be freely interpreted and depicted with creative symbols and materials including but not limited to drawing, painting, collage, sculptural media, and natural objects. Creative symbols and media extend expressive options and may amplify clients' perceptions and experiences.

To demonstrate the potential of creative career-focused genograms within art therapy and career counseling relationships examples are provided below. In the career development and art therapy course at Florida State University, students explored their own career genograms and family career influences. Regarding Figure 4.2, one student followed a traditional career genogram three-generation structure while utilizing drawn representations and collage to depict her sibling's career, her parents and their siblings' careers, and her grandparents' careers. This student noted that some of her family career history, including dedicated military service, was not familiar to her prior to the assignment, and that investigating family career history deepened her understanding of family career influences. As she reflected, she noted that providing service to others was a value that she had inherited. She also noted that hard work and economic security were valued by as many family members, and many had professional roles in science- and finance-related fields. She reported family stories of dedication to work that at times limited time with family, and alternative stories from other members of the family where the centrality of family and work/life balance was emphasized. She noted that she experienced some conflict related to family pressures to choose a career that would guarantee economic

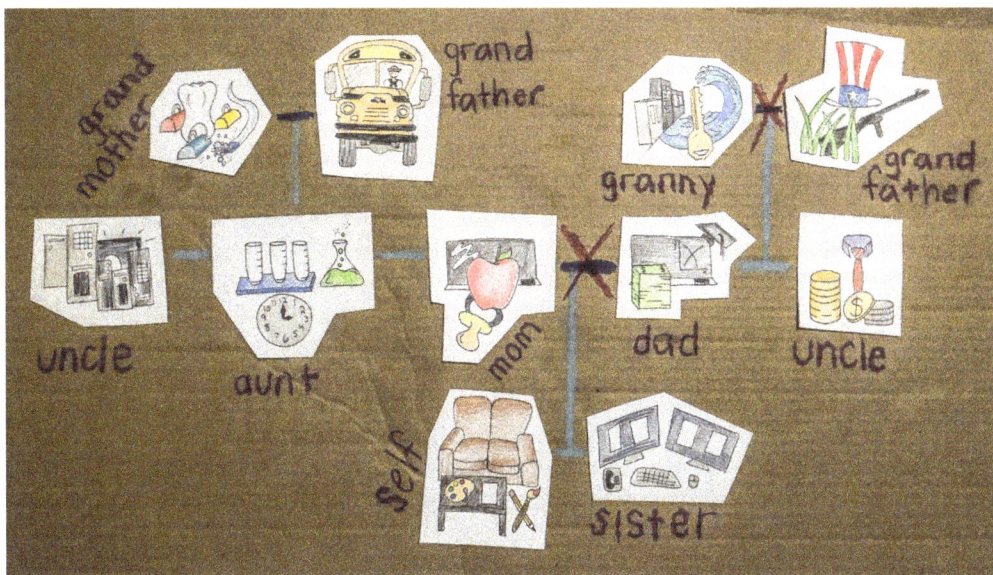

Figure 4.2 Career-Focused Genogram Example

security in opposition to her own choice to pursue a career of art and service. In a career counseling setting, a professional would further explore emerging themes to address the career influences and any challenges they presented for the student. Figure 4.2 shows a career-focused genogram.

Career genogram extensions described by Di Fabio are explored in the two art examples in Figure 4.3. On the left, a second art therapy student utilized collage items to represent family messages that had been passed down to her about career pathways. She noted that many of these messages were very encouraging, emphasizing personal agency and choice related to career aspirations. However, a second group of messages accentuated the importance of staying geographically close to family so that family ties could be readily maintained. Responding to Di Fabio's (2020) jewel box prompt,

Figure 4.3 Examples: Extended Career Genogram Components a. Family Values Letter and b. Jewel Box

the student was able to explore her own interest and values that influenced her career preferences (figure on right). Jewel box items included representations of family, home, leisure, travel, animals, art, learning, and school. The student found that by reviewing these images side by side she furthered her understanding of what career values she shared with family and those that were distinctly her own. In a career counseling context, the professional may offer this series of career genogram art reflections to expand the client's awareness of family influences. With this awareness, a client can accept or change family-provided narratives and move forward with creating their own guiding career story.

Summary

Assessments in career counseling take a variety of forms, from objective normed measures, card sorts, and qualitative interviews, to arts-informed inquiries. These career development assessments and processes target a variety of career-oriented concerns such as identifying career interests, values, barriers to decision-making, and more. Practitioners need to be thoughtful regarding assessment selection to ensure that assessment measures address client career counseling goals. Additionally, competency in administration and interpretation of measures and critically evaluating the validity of the measure and its applicability to the person being served are essential for ethical practice. Thus far, art-based assessments have predominantly been utilized to elicit qualitative information that may contribute to client and therapist understanding of career influences and barriers. Finally, it is important to recognize that assessment is only one component of a comprehensive career counseling relationship. Professionals must be sensitive to clients' broader life experiences and report, explore, and communicate assessment results in ways that are accurate, manageable, and supportive of client goals.

Discussion Questions and Activities

1   How would you respond to the following situations?

    a   A minority adolescent female client brings in a copy of results from a career assessment that was normed on older white males. She is asking for an interpretation of the results.

    b   A client brings in results from a reliable, valid inventory for which you have not been trained or received supervision on, and wants you to interpret the results.

    c   A client brings in results from an inventory with known reliability and validity issues, excited about the results, and wants you to interpret and integrate the results into the session.

    d   A colleague has an idea for creating a non-standardized career assessment to use with clients who are having career decision-making problems.

    e   A client has completed an interest inventory and has a completely flat profile (low, high, or in the middle, across the board).

    f   A client brings in results from two different inventories that are contradictory in the occupations recommended the client pursue and avoid.

2   What would a comprehensive career assessment set contain? Can you locate any assessments that are comprehensive?

3   If a client takes an inventory that identifies career thoughts/beliefs, or career decision-making self-efficacy, and the results suggest that the client is struggling in one of these areas, how would you proceed?

4 Compare how you might assess the common career elements (e.g., interests, skills, values, aptitudes, career beliefs) with standardized, structured assessments as well as non-standardized approaches.

5 Choose a standardized and non-standardized career assessment that you think would likely be of value for your clientele. (Note: many sample reports of standardized career assessments are available online.) How would you introduce the career

The Decision Space

Directions:

- The large circle below represents the total decision space.
- Within the large circle, draw smaller circles that represent the magnitude or the relative importance of each item listed on the Decision Space Worksheet (DSW).

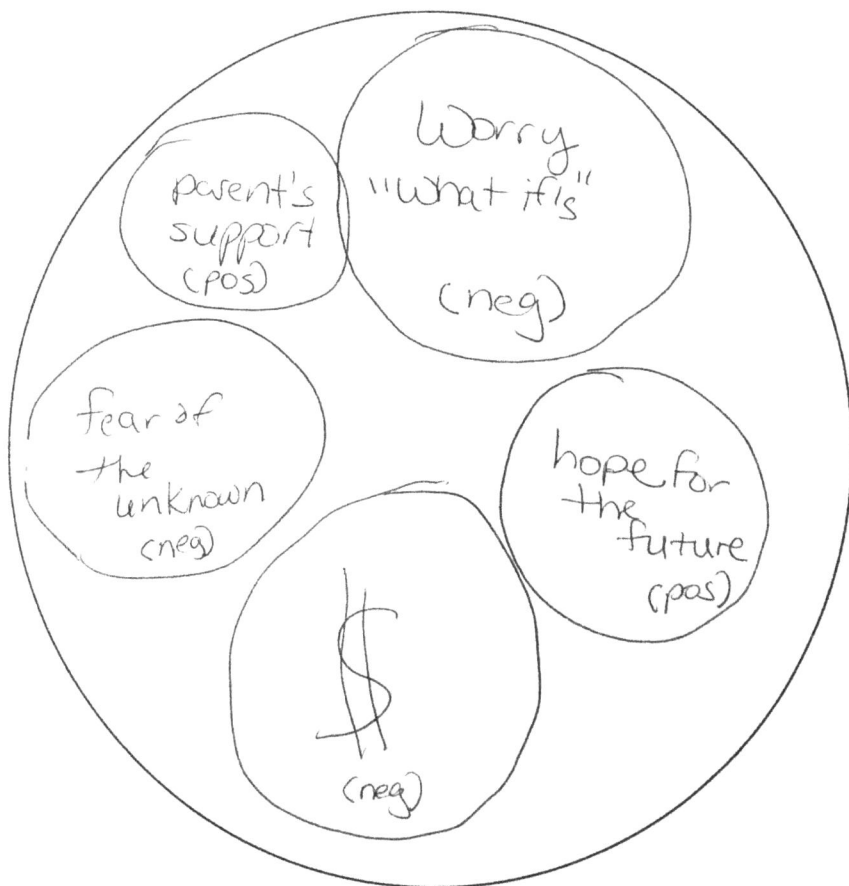

Figure 4.4 Decision Space Worksheet for Discussion Question

Source: Center for the Study of Technology in Counseling & Career Development, Florida State University, Tallahassee, FL.

assessment? What key aspects would you want to discuss? How would you go about interpreting the results? How would you integrate into the process of career counseling? How would you incorporate cultural awareness and sensitivity into these discussions?

6   What advantages and disadvantages do you see in using visual arts-based formats to collect career assessment data?

7   How might you prepare yourself to competently combine visual arts-based methods and standardized structured career assessments to address clients' career problems? What training, supervision, or resources would you seek? How would you evaluate your assessment skills?

8   Find an online "fun" career assessment such as one that uses Star Wars characters to describe personality types, or one that prescribes which careers are best suited for a person based on a preferred color. Take the assessment and reflect on the results. How accurate were they? Now imagine a client comes in having printed out the results of such an "assessment." What might be the pros and cons associated with this type of tool? What ethical considerations are in play? How might you handle the situation? What would you do next?

9   Consider that you have a client who is trying to choose a major. You have them complete a Decision Space Worksheet to show what concerns are impacting their decision. Their DSW results are presented in Figure 4.4. What would your next steps be with this client? How would you help to process these results? If you wished to add another creative element to the process, what might you do, and for what reason?

References

Art Therapy Credentials Board. (2021). ATCB Code of ethics, conduct, and disciplinary procedures. www.atcb.org/wp-content/uploads/2020/07/ATCB-Code-of-Ethics-Conduct-Disciplinary Procedures.pdf

Asawa, P. & Haber, M. (2016). Family art assessment. In D. Gussak & M. Rosal, *The Wiley handbook of art therapy* (pp. 524–533). John Wiley & Sons.

Barba, H. N. (2000). *Follow your bliss! A practical, soul-centered guide to job-hunting and career life planning*. Universal Publishers.

Betts, D. (2006), Art therapy assessments and rating instruments: Do they measure up? *The Arts in Psychotherapy, 33*(5), 422–434.

Betts, D. (2013). A review of the principles for culturally appropriate art therapy assessment tools. *Art Therapy: Journal of the American Art Therapy Association, 30*(3), 98–106.

Betts, D. (2016). Art therapy assessments: An overview. In D. Gussak & M. Rosal (Eds.), *The Wiley handbook of art therapy* (pp. 501–513). John Wiley & Sons.

Bucciarelli, A. (2011). A normative study of the Person Picking an Apple from a Tree assessment. *Art Therapy: Journal of the American Art Therapy Association, 28*(1), 31–36

Buck, J. N. (1948). The H-T-P test. *Journal of Clinical Psychology, 4*, 151–159.

Burns, R. C., & Kaufman, S. H. (1970). *Kinetic Family Drawings (K-F-D): An introduction to understanding children through kinetic drawings*. Brunner-Mazel.

Burton, L. & Lent, J. (2016). The use of vision boards as a therapeutic intervention. *Journal of Creativity in Mental Health, 11*(1), 52–56.

Buxbaum, E. H., & Hill, J. C. (2013). Inclusive career genogram activity: Working with clients faced with forced career transitions to broaden the mind and encourage possibilities. *Career Planning and Adult Development Journal, 29*(4), 45–59.

Chope, (2005). Qualitatively assessing family influence on career decision making. *Journal of Career Assessment, 13*(4), 395–414.

Cohen, B. M. (Ed.). (1985). *The Diagnostic Drawing Series handbook*. Author.

Cohen, B. M., Mills, A., & Kijak, A. K. (1994). An introduction to the Diagnostic Drawing Series: A standardized tool for diagnostic and clinical use. *Art Therapy: Journal of the American Art Therapy Association, 11*(2), 105–110.

Cohen, B. M., & Mills, A. (2016). The Diagnostic Drawing Series (DDS) at thirty: Art therapy assessment and research. In D. E. Gussak, & M. L. Rosal (Eds.), *The Wiley handbook of art therapy* (pp. 558–568). John Wiley & Sons.

Deaver, S. P. (2016). The need for norms in formal art therapy assessment. In D. E. Gussak & M. L. Rosal (Eds.), *The Wiley handbook of art therapy* (pp. 600–606). John Wiley & Sons.

Di Fabio, A. B. (2010). Life designing in 21st century: Using a new strengthened career genogram. *Journal of Psychology in Africa, 20*(3), 381–384.

Eschenfelder, V. G., & Gavalas, C. M. (2018). Expressive art to facilitate the development of the occupational profile: A scoping review. *The Open Journal of Occupational Therapy, 6*(1), 1–15. https://scholarworks.wmich.edu/ojot/vol6/iss1/8

Finklea, J. T., & Osborn, D. (2019). Understanding relationships between commitment anxiety and career tension. *Journal of Employment Counseling, 56*, 117–126. doi:10.1002/joec.12126

Flores, L. Y., Spanierman, L. B., & Obasi, E. M. (2003). Ethical and professional issues in career assessment with diverse racial and ethnic groups. *Journal of Career Assessment, 11*(1), 76–95. https://doi.org/10.1177/106907202237461

Gantt, L., & Tabone, C. (1998). *Formal Elements Art Therapy Scale: The rating manual.* Gargoyle Press.

Gilroy, A., Tipple, R., & Brown, C. (2012). *Assessment in art therapy.* Routledge.

Gunnarsson, A. B., & Eklund, M. (2009). The Tree Theme Method as an intervention in psychosocial occupational therapy: Client acceptability and outcomes. *Australian Occupational Therapy Journal, 56*(3), 167–176. http://dx.doi.org/10.1111/j.1440-1630.2008.00738.x

Hayden, S. C., & Osborn, D. S. (2020). Impact of worry on career thoughts, career decision state, and cognitive information processing-identified skills. *Journal of Employment Counseling, 57*(4), 163–177. doi:https://doi.org/10.1002/joec.12152

Hoshino, J., & Cameron, D. (2008). Narrative art therapy within a multicultural framework. In C. Kerr, J. Hoshino, J. Sutherland, et al. (Eds.), *Family art therapy: Foundations of theory and practice* (pp. 193–220). Routledge.

Jahn, S.A.B. (2018). Professional issues and innovative practice: Using collage to examine values in college career counseling. *Journal of College Counseling, 21*, 180–192.

Kakiuchi, K. S. & Weeks, G. R. (2009). The Occupational Transmission Genogram: Exploring family scripts affecting roles of work and career in couple and family dynamics, *Journal of Family Psychotherapy, 20*(1), 1–12. https://doi.org/10.1080/089752502716467

Killam, W. K., Degges-White, S., & Michel, R. E., (Eds.), (2016). *Career counseling interventions: Practice with diverse clients.* Springer.

Kwiatkowska, H. (1978). *Family art therapy and evaluation through art.* Thomas.

Landgarten, H. B. (1981). *Clinical art therapy.* Brunner-Mazel.

Machover, K. (1952). *Personality projection in the drawing of the human figure.* Charles C. Thomas.

McNiff, S. (2009). *Arts based research.* Jessica Kingsley.

Osborn, D. S., Kronholz, J. F., & Finklea, J. T. (2016). Card sorts. In M. McMahon & M. Watson (Eds.), *Career assessment: Qualitative approaches* (pp. 81–88). Sense Publishing. Retrieved from www.sensepublishers.com/catalogs/bookseries/career-development-series/career-assessment/

Osborn, D. S., & Zunker, V. G. (2016). *Using assessment results for career development* (9th ed.). Cengage Learning.

Oster, G. D., & Gould Crone, P. (2004). *Using drawings in assessment and therapy* (2nd ed.). Brunner-Routledge.

Parsons, F. (1909). *Choosing a vocation.* Garrett Park Press.

Peterson, G., Lenz, J. & Osborn, D. (2016). *Decision Space Worksheet (DSW) activity manual.* Florida State University Center for the Study of Technology in Counseling and Career Development.

Piotrowski, C. (2015). Clinical instruction on projective techniques in the USA: A review of academic training settings 1995–2014. *SIS Journal of Projective Psychology & Mental Health, 22*, 83–92.

Ridley, C. R., Li, L. C., & Hill, C. L. (1998). Multicultural assessment: Reexamination, reconceptualization, and practical application. *The Counseling Psychologist, 26*(6), 827–910.

Rottinghaus, P. J., Jenkins, N., & Jantzer, A. M. (2009). Relation of depression and affectivity to career decision status and self-efficacy in college students. *Journal of Career Assessment, 17,* 271–285. https://doi.org/10.1177/1069072708330463

Saunders, D. E., Peterson, G. W., Sampson, J. P., Jr., & Reardon, R. C. (2000). Relation of depression and dysfunctional career thinking to career indecision. *Journal of Vocational Behavior, 56,* 228–298. https://doi.org/10.1006/jvbe.1999.1715

Savickas, M., & Hartung, P. (2012). My career story: An autobiographical workbook for life-career success. Vocopher. www.vocopher.com/CSI/CCI_workbook.pdf

Schroeder, D. (2015). *Exploring and developing the use of art-based genograms in family of origin therapy.* Charles C. Thomas.

Setlhare-Meltor, R., & Wood, L. (2016). Using life-design with vulnerable youth. *The Career Development Quarterly, 64,* 64–74.

Silver, R. (Ed.). (2005). *Aggression and depression assessed through art.* Routledge.

Stoltz, K. B., Apodaca, M., & Mazahreh, L. G. (2018). Extending the narrative process: Guided imagery in career construction counseling. *The Career Development Quarterly, 66,* 259–268.

Storlie, C. A., Lara Hilton, T. M., McKinney, R., & Unger, D. (2019). Family career genograms: Beginning life-design with exploratory students. *The Family Journal: Counseling and Therapy for Couples and Families, 27*(1), 84–91.

Swank, J. M., & Jahn, S. A. B. (2018). Using sand-tray to facilitate students' career decision-making: A qualitative inquiry. *The Career Development Quarterly, 66,* 269–278.

Taylor, J. M., & Savickas, S. (2016). Narrative career counseling: My career story and pictorial narratives. *Journal of Vocational Behavior, 97,* 68–77.

Walker, J. V., & Peterson, G. W. (2012). Career thoughts, indecision, and depression: Implications for mental health assessment in career counseling. *Journal of Career Assessment, 20,* 497–506.

5 Relational Development and Processes in Art Therapy and Career Counseling

This chapter will outline and describe the central importance of the therapeutic relationship in fostering successful alliances and outcomes with and for clients. Readers will be provided with descriptions of therapist and client considerations that may impact the development or maintenance of a working alliance at the beginning, working, and closing phases of art therapy and career counseling. Recommendations for building and sustaining alliances through art-based and verbal strategies suitable to each stage will be provided. A significant part of the chapter will be devoted to explaining how the presence of artmaking materials, art interventions, and art products may shift and enhance the therapeutic relationship. Rationale for and use and methods for therapist engagement in reflective artwork to explore and identify countertransference issues and supervisory concerns will be offered. Finally, ethical issues related to confidentiality and the boundaries of the therapeutic relationship will be reiterated.

The Importance of the Therapeutic Relationship

In any application of art therapy, counseling, and career development, the effectiveness of an intervention is dependent on the quality of the relationship that is developed between practitioner and client. Therefore, to prepare for successful navigation of career themes with the client, attention needs to be paid to the components that contribute to a positive therapeutic relationship.

What constitutes a helpful therapeutic relationship that supports constructive treatment outcomes? Gullo et al. (2012) asserted that, within psychotherapy, a "real relationship" is characterized by genuineness, and realism supports positive outcome. When a therapist and client are genuine, they engage with each other in an authentic way. Words and actions come from a true and caring place that is in alignment with personal characteristics, resources, and energies. When a client and therapist's experiences are framed by realism, perceptions and experiences that one holds for the other are accurate and suited to the context. In this realistic relationship, the client and the counselor/art therapist understand the aims and abilities of the other within their working arrangement. In this context, achievable outcomes well-matched to client concerns, problems, and goals are mutually agreed upon.

Patterson et al. (2014) noted that clients' beliefs and expectations for therapy (positive, negative, or in between) also have a strong effect on therapeutic processes and client outcomes. Accordingly, when clients approach their therapeutic counseling work with personal commitment and when they hold beliefs that their therapist will present positive traits such as warmth, nurturance, knowledge, and problem-solving skills, they achieve stronger collaborative relationships and treatment outcomes. Client motivation and beliefs in the helpful nature of counseling and art therapy, may exist prior to the beginning of the therapeutic relationship, but are always important to nurture and support.

DOI: 10.4324/9781003035756-5

The Working Alliance

The working alliance is a term that has been utilized to describe the relational core of therapeutic interaction and effectiveness across therapy disciplines and approaches. Bordin (1979) defined the working alliance as an achievement of consensus regarding the goals of therapy, the tasks or methods of therapy, and the bond or personal connection between client and therapist. Numerous research studies have been conducted to explore the dynamics and components of the working alliance with the aim of supporting mental health clinicians fine-tuning their approaches to effective client care (Falkenstrom et al., 2014; Horvath, 2018; Patterson, Anderson, & Wei, 2014). Practitioners from the disciplines of psychotherapy, medicine, psychiatry, social work, and more concur that a good alliance is an essential factor which predicts client progress.

In the past, many assumed that career counselors were less reliant on the therapeutic relationships than other counseling-related modalities (Masdonati et al., 2014). Only in more recent years has research been conducted to address the influences of the working alliance on career counseling outcomes. Masdonati et al. (2009) reported study results which confirmed that a strong working alliance in career counseling positively aligned with clients' satisfaction with career interventions as well as life satisfaction. Additionally, Masdonati et al. (2014) found that the greater the working alliance was considered, the more clients reported a decrease in a lack of career information. When career counseling clients evaluated their working relationship with the counselor as positive, they also reported a greater decrease in problems with career decision-making.

Adding Art to the Working Alliance Equation

Art therapists have also conceptualized and addressed the working alliance and its role in therapy but have factored in the presence of art materials, artmaking processes, and the resulting artworks that have been produced. Art processes and products become the focus of shared attention and a central place to meet and establish connection (Isserow, 2013). Springham and Huet (2018) identified artwork as "an arena of exchange between artist and viewers" (p. 7). Yet, communication between art therapist and client is not restricted to artmaking and viewing; communication also includes visual, verbal, and non-verbal exchanges and joint activity. Such art exchanges expand information resources and communication potential within the career counseling relationship.

Within therapy sessions, art therapists utilize the art materials as an intermediary presence within the client and art therapist relationship, and the art product within art therapy has often been identified as being the third presence in the room (Schaverien, 1992). Schaverien noted that triangular relationship between the maker, therapist, and images leads to a dynamic conversation that is characteristically different from those that occur in verbal psychotherapies. These triangular conversations rely upon the therapist's skilled perceptions of clients' art-based drives, needs, and expressions. Kramer (2000) described the perceptual skill of art therapists as "the third eye" and the skillful use of art-based intervention strategies to support client expressive intentions as the development and use of "the third hand." First and foremost, these terms and strategies reflect an art therapist's ability to observe and empathize with client visual communications, experiences, artmaking processes, and needs. Art therapists use their understanding of the quality of the materials, tools, and methods for working with materials, and knowledge of what qualities of materials may evoke as someone is using them to unobtrusively scaffold client efforts.

The Expressive Therapies Continuum is a framework for understanding art material properties and their functions within the art therapy process (Hinz, 2020; Lusebrink,1990). Hinz asserted that visual arts materials provide variable opportunities for information processing and expression and evoke engagement on multiple levels that range from sensory and kinesthetic experiences, perceptual and affective experiences, cognitive engagement and creative applications of imagination. Those who choose to incorporate creative art processes in career counseling need to be aware of the influence of media properties and processes on clients' art explorations and responses. For example, offering a client a more controlled medium such as colored pencils and directing them to focus on a particular career theme may foster a client's cognitive consideration of career topic in contrast to a sensory or kinesthetic approach which may evoke or channel emotional responses to career themes addressed via looser or more physically challenging materials such as paint and clay.

Additionally, art therapists learn about the processes of mentalization, symbolic representation, and how clients may or may not wish to explore the visual expression via verbal language (Morrell, 2011). Holmqvist et al. (2019) noted that imagery may contain past and present feelings as well as wishes for the future and that the process of creating art can support management of overwhelming feelings. Whether or not a client chooses to discuss these feelings, or the symbolic meaning of their imagery, it is important for the therapist to demonstrate a positive and empathetic reception to the art. The art therapist's accepting and validating response to art can be compared to verbal therapists' bestowal of unconditional positive regard to clients' verbal and non-verbal presentations. Therapists may impart these positive outlooks through verbal, non-verbal, or artistic communication. Artistic responses offered by therapists to reflect compassionate understanding may include art that is sensitively designed to mirror the client's presenting expression and concerns (Lachman-Chapin, 2001).

When an art therapist creates an artistic response and explores it with a client, the therapist is reflecting, "Here is what I am taking away from your expressions, is this accurate?" versus "This is what you are saying with your artwork," as clients are the experts on their artistic expressions.

When examining symbolic meaning of artwork with a client, it is important to appreciate that symbolic meanings of art imagery can exist on many levels that are influenced by personal, familial, and cultural contexts (Swan-Foster, 2018). Consequently, art therapists and counselors working with clients through creative arts and imagery must take care to avoid mislabeling or misinterpreting artwork based on their personal biases or cultural lens. Inaccurate interpretation of artwork by the therapist can lead to client detachment from the image and a rupture of the therapeutic relationship.

Harnessing Art Processes to Build a Working Alliance

Bat Or and Zilcha-Mano (2019) worked to explore how the working alliance could be conceptualized and measured in art therapy; the result was the Art Therapy Working Alliance Inventory (ATWAI), based on Horvath and Greenberg's (1989) Working Alliance Inventory which measures alliance in verbally orientated helping relationships. Based on their research, Bat Or and Zilcha-Mano found that positive working alliance in art therapy relied on the client's trust and perception that art media exploration and engagement were effective as a therapeutic process, that art tasks assisted them in communicating thoughts and feelings to the therapist, and that the art therapist's presence, support and technical artistic assistance during sessions were positive.

Basic Skills in Building a Therapeutic Relationship

While art therapists rely heavily on art and art processes for therapeutic communication and connection, both beginning counselors and art therapists need training and practice the with building block skills of helping relationships. These building blocks include active listening, accurate reflection of clients' experiences, empathy, or a compassionate understanding of clients' particular experiences and contexts, and a non-judgmental warmth known as unconditional positive regard based on the work of Carl Rogers (as cited in Cochran and Cochran, 2015). These skills are valued across theoretical frameworks and are necessary for therapeutic work.

Unfortunately, perfect understanding and reflection do not always occur within the therapeutic relationship in spite of our best efforts. An art therapist may suggest a particular material only to find that the client has an aversion to that material, or invite a creative reflection on a theme that a person is not ready to address. A career counselor may miss cues about familial influences that a client is facing in regard to career decision-making and will need to step back, listen closely, and gather more information regarding the family influences and conflicts. Consequently, helping professionals need to cultivate personal humility and non-defensiveness when their reflections, interpretations, or interventions are deemed inaccurate or a poor fit for the clients' experiences. These "bumps in the relationship" provide an opportunity for further exchanges and attunement to client meanings and needs. A collaborative working through of therapeutic ruptures can move a therapeutic relationship back to health and result in positive outcomes for clients. Building, repairing, and strengthening relationships are cornerstone practices of effective art therapy and career counseling (Paul & Charura, 2015).

Communicating the Nature and Boundaries of Art Therapy and Career Counseling

Consent Forms

Credentialing bodies and professional associations provide art therapists and counselors with guidelines on informing clients about professional qualifications, the scope of provided services, fee structures, and more in their ethics documents (ATCB, 2021; AATA, 2020; ACA, 2014; NCDA, 2015). State and local laws also provide guidance on consent requirements pertaining to their regions. To ensure informed consent, a client must be apprised of the rights and responsibilities of engaging in and disengaging from treatment, the roles of both therapist and client, the nature of confidentiality and its limits including a duty to report, and the processes and procedures that may be utilized as part of treatment. As art therapy includes the creation of imagery, a description of how artwork will be retained or documented should be provided. Art therapists and counselors must also provide clients with information about situations in which processes and outcomes of therapy may be shared with a supervisor, treatment team, family member, or insurance company, and the type of client agreement necessary to release treatment information. This information is provided to clients in written form for review and formal consent.

Given the significant development of telehealth options for providing career and mental health care, it is also important to become familiar with the secure telehealth platforms that comply with the Health Insurance Portability and Accountability Act's

(HIPAA) standards for protecting client information. Using technological means to engage in counseling from distant locations creates a unique set of circumstances that require further definition and explanation within consent processes. The American Psychological Association (2020) has designed an excellent checklist of telehealth consent considerations for mental health professionals. Topics that should be reviewed with your client prior to engaging in telehealth services include: understanding of digital platforms and equipment that may be used for telehealth; the use of secure internet versus public Wi-Fi to ensure privacy; and the selection of spaces for necessary to protect confidentiality and reduce distractibility in a home or alternate setting. Communication strategies and responsibilities related to emergencies, technological glitches, and other considerations related to session protocols should be clearly established.

As these guidelines outline the boundaries of care, it is important that art therapists and counselors review these policies with clients at the beginning of treatment to provide an opportunity for questions and to confirm comprehension. When a person is unable to consent for themselves, and a guardian has provided consent on a client's behalf, review of processes, roles, and confidentiality should be discussed with the person receiving treatment, and their assent to treatment gained.

Gathering Information to Achieve Holistic Understanding

After consent is obtained, the important task of gathering client information to support a holistic understanding of the client begins. In some settings, a client is asked to report biopsychosocial information via an agency form prior to starting treatment or in tandem with an agency representative. In these cases, completed forms are provided to the clinician for review with the client. Sensitive review of intake information along with respectful inquiry and support for clients to share the contexts of their life stories set a tone for the therapeutic relationship that will unfold.

Various forms of intake processes and interviews are conducted to collect and consider this type of information. For example, Gehart (2016) designed forms for clinicians to utilize in the initial interview process to gather necessary information. Utilizing these intake forms or outlines, clinicians collect demographic information about the person and their significant others related to their age, ethnicity, relational status, and their scholastic level and/or occupation. Presenting problems are explored as clinicians elicit and record the client's perspectives. When appropriate, similar information is ascertained from significant others (caregivers, guardians, partners, parents, spouses) to obtain a multifaceted view of the presenting concerns.

Gently exploring background information such as trauma history; substance abuse history; precipitating events such as recent school, life, or work stressors; related family history; and prior counseling and art therapy experiences results in a fuller picture of the client. Similarly, discovering clients' strengths, resources, and dimensions of diversity remains an essential process for understanding the whole person. In that regard, personal, social/relational, and spiritual resources are discussed and acknowledged. Dimensions of diversity include, but are not limited to, information regarding potential resources and challenges the client may experience related to age, gender identification, sexual orientation, cultural backgrounds, socioeconomic status, religion, regional community, language(s), family background, family configuration, and abilities. It is essential to recognize a person's life history and cultural contexts as interwoven components of their presenting career story or concerns. See Chapter 6 for a more thorough exploration of multicultural considerations in career counseling and art therapy.

When formulating a treatment plan with their clients, clinicians use gathered information to support conceptualization of the operational dynamics involved with the career problem. Additionally, a career counseling theoretical framework may also guide the understanding and articulating of the career considerations and goals. Therapist theoretical orientation with a client may be shaped by training in a particular theoretical model, a client's characteristics and presenting case concerns, and optimally, a mix of these factors. Theory perspectives and how they are applied to career counseling and art therapy are further addressed in Chapter 2.

Intakes and Interviews

Career-Focused Approaches

What information does a career counselor/art therapist need to obtain to establish rapport and guide the collaborative work ahead? It is important for practitioners to ascertain the main purpose the client is seeking assistance during the first session. In many career counseling settings, it is expected that help seeking will focus on career issues. Yet, in other settings, career counselors are trained and expected to also provide mental health counseling and support conversations about blended career and mental health concerns. Counselors, art therapists, and related helping professionals who do not specifically specialize in career counseling may find that career concerns arise as a small or central component of life challenges presented by their clients. In any of these situations, once the career-related problem is identified, it is important to invite discussion on the types of conflicts, distress, interests, and goals that have motivated their help-seeking behavior.

Career Intake Forms

Career counseling agencies, career centers at colleges and universities, as well as independent service providers have designed intake forms to collect client information and interests in advance of the initial interview. These forms can streamline the interview process by providing the clinician with preliminary themes for career conversations. Career intake forms may share common factors such as collection of clients' demographic information and gathering of information related to career history, career interests, and current motivations for attending career-focused counseling. However, forms may also differ in content related to the service provider's or institution's primary theoretical orientation. For example, Box 5.1 demonstrates a portion of a career intake form used in the Florida State University Career Center that shows alignment with cognitive information processing theory (Sampson et al., 2004). Consequently, their intake form questions are designed to illuminate career decision-making patterns and thoughts in addition to information about current career interests and desired pursuits. Importantly, information regarding client's previous or current participation in mental health counseling is also collected to ensure a broad snapshot of the client's experiences and support a more comprehensive conceptualization of career considerations. Counselor review of a client's completed form acquaints the counselor with the client's primary concerns and experiences that will be further considered within the initial interview.

Portion of Intake Form

For the statements below, please rate using the scale below:

	Strongly disagree	Disagree	Neither agree nor disagree	Agree	Strongly agree
I feel anxious about my career concerns.	1	2	3	4	5
I feel I know the next steps needed to attain my career goals.	1	2	3	4	5
I feel confident that I can make the next steps to attain my career goals.	1	2	3	4	5

Please read the question carefully and respond with the most appropriate answer for you by circling one of the following responses: poor, fair, good, very good, or excellent.

	Poor	Fair	Good	Very good	Excellent
Knowledge of your values, interests, and skills.	1	2	3	4	5
Knowledge of the career options you are considering.	1	2	3	4	5
Career decision-making skills.	1	2	3	4	5
Awareness of an ability to control your self-talk/the way you talk to yourself	1	2	3	4	5

In terms of your current career decision, which of these bests describes where you are in the process? Place a check next to the appropriate statement below (CHECK 1):

____ Knowing that I need to make a choice

____ Understanding myself, options, decision-making, and thoughts

____ Expanding and narrowing my options

____ Prioritizing my options

____ Implementing my first choice

____ Knowing I made a good choice

Art-Based Intakes

While traditional intake forms are important in the practice of a broad range of clinicians, art therapist and career counselors may also want to look at creative ways to gather initial information about clients' career concerns and goals to stimulate opening dialogues. In some cases, art therapists and/or career counselors may use structured worksheets with creative components to provide a format for clients to consider their goals and possible paths towards their goals. An example of a visual option is the Career Concept Form created by Parker-Bell (2021; Figure 5.1). During an intake process, the individual would be asked to fill in as much as they currently know about their career goals, career qualities, rewards of pursuing such a career, supports and resources that would enable them to pursue their goal, and skills, talents, or interests that will help them be successful and/or satisfied with the career. Additionally, individuals would be invited to list or fill in steps they believe they would need to take to move towards their

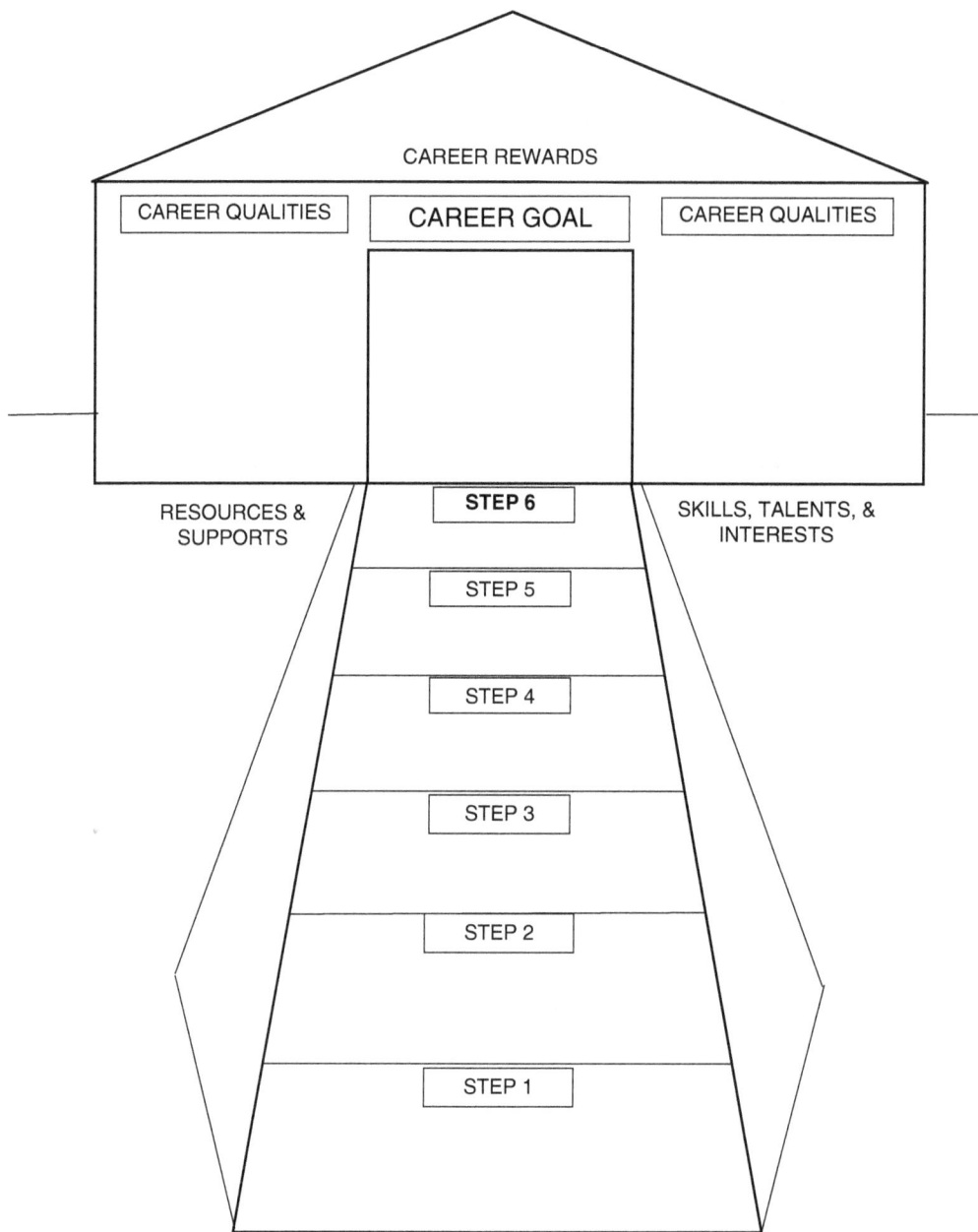

CAREER REWARDS

CAREER QUALITIES

CAREER GOAL

CAREER QUALITIES

RESOURCES & SUPPORTS

SKILLS, TALENTS, & INTERESTS

STEP 6

STEP 5

STEP 4

STEP 3

STEP 2

STEP 1

© BPB 2021

Figure 5.1 Career Concept Form

career goal. The practitioner would emphasize that it is perfectly acceptable to leave any parts of the form blank if they do not have ideas about how to fill those sections of the form. Once completed, the Career Concept Form would be viewed and discussed together to gauge the client's current career development conceptualization status.

In the example of the Career Concept Form (Figure 5.2), much of the form is completed, and it would appear that the person has some familiarity with the field of accounting, support of family for pursuing the career option, and interests that may align with the career focus. Given this visually presented information, the practitioner may ask the

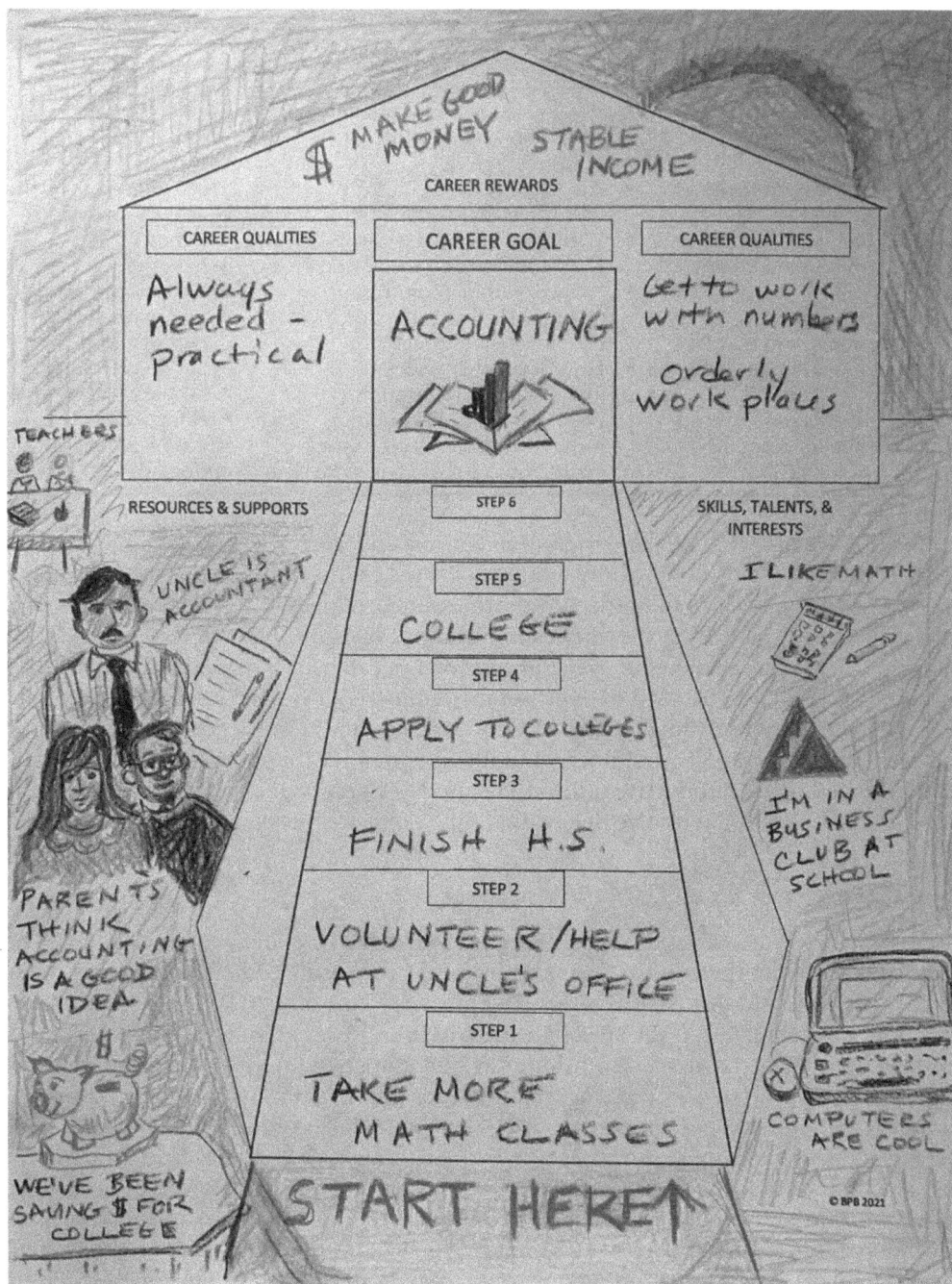

Figure 5.2 Completed Career Concept Form

individuals specific questions they may have about the steps towards their goal or other factors or barriers they may be concerned about.

Moving from Intake Forms to Interview Processes

The initial meeting with a client is a tremendously important. It is the first opportunity to welcome your client, make them feel comfortable, explain the concepts and limits of

Table 5.1 Sample opening questions

Career history and hopes	Career influences and resources	Career decision-making
• Tell me about your occupational and educational history • What career options are you considering? • If you had to choose one career today, what would you choose? • Finish this sentence: At this point in my career development, I would like to … • Finish this sentence: By our last session together, I would like to accomplish …	• What role has your family played in how you see your career options? • Are there certain rules your family has about careers? • What role has your culture played in how you see options? • What are some other resources or supports that influence your career considerations? • How have other issues such as mental health, economic resources, or discrimination influenced your career experiences, interests, or concerns?	• How do you typically go about making decisions? • How would you like this decision to be different? • What other factors are important to you as you making this career decision? • What do you think is keeping you from making a career decision or reaching your goal?

confidentiality and to support the development of a connection that will enable productive therapeutic work. Utilizing information collected via the intake form, a therapist will use open-ended questions to spark conversation aimed at identifying client concerns and career themes. Establishing the client's motivation for beginning the therapeutic relationship is a good place to begin. What brings you by? Table 5.1 is a sampling of questions and inquiries that may be used to open conversations about career development factors.

Each client response (both verbal and non-verbal) should influence the direction of the therapist's subsequent questions within the interview. Throughout the session, a therapist's non-judgmental reflective skills will be used to summarize primary concerns identified and cultivate collaborative determination of career counseling goals.

Formalized Interviews and the Life Career Assessment

More structured means to gaining information related to a client's career history, concerns and work/life themes are also used in career counseling. Life Career Assessment (LCA; Gysbers & Moore, 1987; Gysbers, Heppner, & Johnston, 2014) is one such framework which is facilitated in the style of a structured interview. Using this narrative postmodern approach, the career counselor/art therapist asks questions related to work experiences, education and training, relationships and friends, a typical day, as well as strengths and obstacles (Gysbers et al., 2014). For example, in terms of work experiences, a client is invited to discuss their last two work experiences which may be a paid or volunteer positions. For each position, they are asked to discuss what they liked best what they liked least about it. Next, the career counselor/art therapist seeks clients' views on education and training experiences. Similarly, the client's likes and dislikes about their various levels of education and types of training are ascertained. Clients are also asked to describe stories of their leisure activities, social engagement, and experiences with friends. These latter questions help illuminate client approaches and preferences regarding acquisition of job knowledge skills, how they tend to engage with others, and potential interest areas that may be applied to the career context. Narratives related to their typical day also provide clues to how they navigate their time within a spectrum from systematic or spontaneous as well as preferences for independent or dependent engagement related to work and decision-making. Finally, a client is asked about strengths and obstacles. What does the client see as their resources and in what way do these resources support their life journey? How do obstacles they identify relate to their current juncture in career concerns and decision-making? A counselor/art therapist will ask follow-up questions and use reflective statements to mirror themes that occur in the descriptions.

During the initial interview, both life and work themes are revealed and are integral to the career counseling/art therapy experiences. Together, the counselor and client collaborate and come to consensus on themes that appear significant. These themes will inform problem formulation, goal setting, and treatment plan development.

Starting with Art

Art-based methods are also valuable for stimulating exploration of career concerns and aspirations within an initial session. The Bridge Drawing originated by Hays and Lyons (1981) is one art-based method that may be utilized. Hays and Lyons created the Bridge Drawing as a means to explore clients' internal and external journeys from one state of being or space to another using the visual metaphor of the bridge. Since that time, art therapists have utilized this drawing and metaphor as a way to examine clients' goals, future orientation, and perceptions regarding presented obstacles and overall well-being (Darewych & Campbell, 2016). Materials provided for the tasks include 12″ × 18″ white paper and eight classic color markers, yellow, orange, red, blue, green, purple, black, and brown. Hays and Lyons' (1981) directions for the Bridge Drawing were "Draw a bridge from someplace to someplace. … Indicate with an arrow the direction of travel … place a dot to indicate where {you} are in the picture" (p. 208). Following the bridge creation, clients were invited to describe their drawing in words. Later researchers provided more specific directions for clients, asking participants to "Draw a bridge connecting where you are now to where you would like to be. Place yourself somewhere in the picture" (Teneycke et al., 2009, p. 299). While some evaluative methods have been created to consider elements of mood or mental health symptoms indicated by the drawings, most typically, the Bridge Drawing task is used more informally as a means to explore motivation and life transition themes. An artist may approach the work spontaneously to allow less conscious themes to reveal themselves during post-creation reflective processes.

To address career goals specifically, Casado-Kehoe (2016) developed a structured Career Bridge drawing process and referred to the bridge as a "Life Bridge." Clients or activity participants were warmed up to imaginal and creative process through counselor-led guided imagery. Clients were asked to visualize this bridge, where they were at that moment, and where they were headed career-wise. Clients were provided a variety of art materials including crayons, markers, paint, and a choice of paper. In contrast to the art therapist-designed versions, clients were directly asked to attend and create various parts of the bridge with specific concepts in mind. For example, the pillars of the bridge were to be created and filled in with words that described their current and previous work experiences. Additionally, on the bridge surface, clients were instructed to write the steps that they would need to take to get to their career destination. Casado-Kehoe also outlined questions that therapists could pose to enhance client exploration. These questions included:

- Tell me about your drawing.
- What is your dream career?
- What steps will you need to take to pursue this career?
- What skills or work experiences have helped you so far to prepare you for this career?
- As you travel through your Bridge of Life, what reminders may help you when things become challenging?
- What could you tell yourself that would help you cross the bridge and achieve your career goals? (Casado-Kehoe, 2016, p. 166)

Figure 5.3 Student Career Bridge 1

It is important to consider the positives and negatives of providing very structured directions for creation and reflection upon the Life Career Bridge. On a positive note, the structured approach to art and questions provides a framework for facilitating clients' thinking about career aspirations and experiences. On the other hand, a very structured approach centered on cognitive processing may reduce occurrences of the "happy accidents' of artistic processes that sometimes illuminate deeper, less conscious associations and meanings that can be considered when one is completed with the artwork. Some FSU graduate art therapy students exploring the structured approach suggested by Casado-Kehoe felt restricted by the outlined parameters. Notably, art therapy students are comfortable with art processes and familiar with less structured creative investigations into personal perspectives and experiences. Clients with less artistic experience and comfort may prefer a structured approach to reduce anxiety about artmaking processes and skill. Two career bridge images are included here as examples.

Related to Figure 5.3, the first student reflected on her career bridge as follows:

> On the left side of my Career Bridge are symbols for the past jobs, internships, education, and volunteer experiences that helped shape the path I am on. I drew myself about halfway across the bridge almost on the other side of the FSU logo symbolizing that I have almost completed my graduate experience. On the right side are my future career goal of becoming an LMHC and ATR. I recognize that the right side is less specific and contains less images. I believe this is because I am still uncertain of where I will be employed and what population I would like to work with.

In the second image (Figure 5.4), another student reflected on work-related experiences that formed her interest in art therapy. Note that in both cases, several directions suggested by Casado-Kehoe (2016) were not followed, but imagery provided avenues for rich discussions about current perceptions of career pathways.

Career Collage and Headline Story

Another art-based means to eliciting career themes is the Career Collage Story. Collage is the creative combination of magazine images, words, and other two-dimensional

Figure 5.4 Student Career Bridge 2

materials which together form a composition that may be created to reflect a particular theme or may be constructed spontaneously in response to the available materials. Collected images and materials are generally glued to a base paper or posterboard type surface to form the final montage. Stallings (2016) described collage as a less threatening art medium for those who may not be comfortable with other art processes that can be used to address a variety of therapeutic considerations. Collage processes may also support enhanced verbal expression for populations that are less inclined to speak or those who may benefit from a visual stimulus to prompt memories or associations. Jahn (2018) advocated for the use of collage in career-focused exploration to facilitate engagement in career counseling and to elicit motivational and affective reflection.

When providing collage as a medium for creative and reflective work, it is beneficial to present variety of precut images from magazines reflective of culture and age group, a variety of color paper, tissue papers, scissors, and glue; and drawing materials such as markers, color pencils are provided so that clients may add to the collage as they wish. Career concerns and interests may be represented by magazine images, or may be suggested via colors and shapes torn or cut from paper and additional drawn lines, shapes, or symbols.

Clients are asked to create a collage that reflects their current career development interests and concerns. Upon completion of the collage, the client is asked to provide a headline for their collage as if it was the illustration for a featured newspaper story about their career interests, concerns, or status. Next, clients are invited to explore the who, what, when, where, and how of the story as it may be described to readers. This part can be completed in written form or informally discussed with the art therapist counselor. Based on this reflection and discussion, themes related to career concerns, interests, and contexts are illuminated and considered for goal setting and treatment planning.

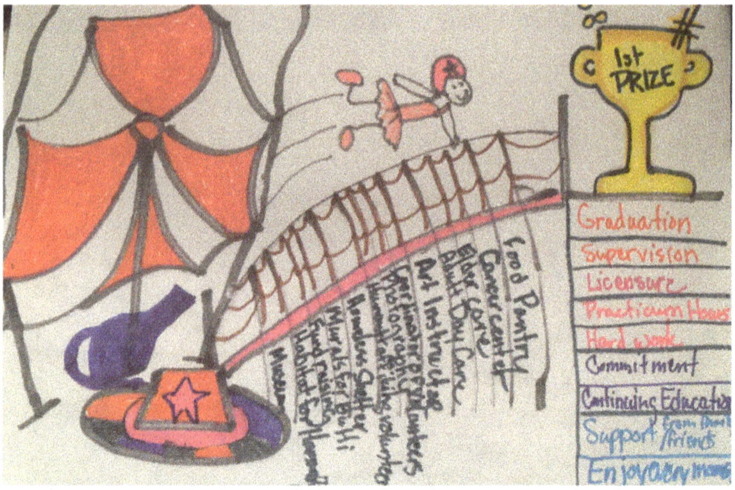

Figure 5.5 Student Example: Jane Rockets onto Art Therapy Scene

Supporting written storytelling following the art process can also add to the information shared and considered between therapist and client.

Upon reviewing her Bridge Drawing (Figure 5.5), one therapy student reflected that her career story headline would be "Jane Rockets onto Art Therapy Scene" and that she would achieve "death defying feats in the field of art therapy to help others upon her graduation." She wrote:

> I feel like I'm being shot out of a cannon sometimes. It took a long time to get here but it's going so fast now. I need to remind myself to enjoy every moment to get to the end of the bridge where my art therapy career awaits. Few people will teach you how to get shot out of a cannon, and even fewer people will design the actual cannon. But I will do both.
>
> Bella Nock, Sarasota, FL

Another student struggled with creating a career headline and artwork (Figure 5.6). She noted that while she was aware of communities she wished to serve as an art therapist, she was unclear about many details at this juncture due to societal events related to racial strife and inequities. In her case, she found it more valuable to create a career genogram, which helped her explore her career influences, as opposed to examining her desired future. These process and discussions provided an opportunity for the student to explore her interest in revisiting and possibly recalibrating her career goals (see Figure 5.7).

Career Problems

As noted above, intake forms, interviews, and art processes provide means for identifying and expanding upon the career concerns that motivated the client to reach out for assistance. As an art therapist or counselor, it is important to be familiar with various problems that may arise and to understand factors which contribute to these problems as well as strategies to address them. Career problems identified within the art therapy and counseling setting may include educational major or career choice or change, expanding

Figure 5.6 New Art Therapist in Town

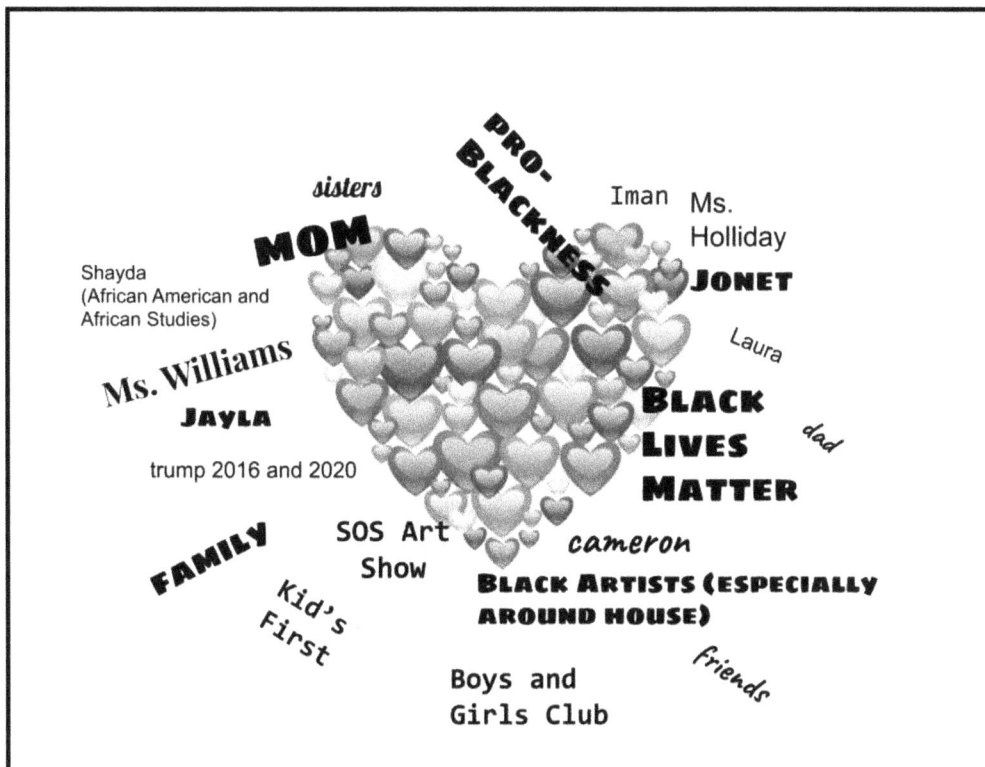

Figure 5.7 Sample Alternative Career Genogram

or narrowing career or educational options, negative career thinking, job search concerns related to tasks such as résumé writing, interviewing, and networking to name just a few. Career problems may also be associated with pre-foreclosure on career options, which means that a client had only considered or engaged in a few job paths instead of exploring a full spectrum of jobs or careers that may have interested or suited them. Some clients may seek assistance following an experience of unemployment or underemployment. A person is underemployed when their education, training, or skills are not being utilized within the work setting and they may be overqualified for their current position, for example a person with a master's in business administration working as a stockperson in a big box store. Clients may seek assistance when they are transitioning between careers spurred by a shift in work/life roles or interests, changes in the employment setting or marketplace, and moves related to a partner's job relocation, to name a few possible scenarios.

Additionally, counselors and art therapists can extend their knowledge of the scope of career problems as identified and described within the frame of career development theories. For example, a proponent of Holland's theories would evaluate and identify problems related incongruence between the person's personality and their career choice. A career counselor trained in cognitive information processing theory would be attuned to problems of dysfunctional career thinking. A clinician whose work may be influenced by the person–environment correspondence theory (Eggerth, 2008) may explore and identify work problems related to the fit between the client's values and the work setting's values. For example, a nurse who highly values the relationship with patients may experience a lack of fit and dissatisfaction with their job when the work setting demands and priorities diminish their ability to cultivate those relationships.

Knowing Your Client Holistically: Addressing Mental Health

Mental health concerns may also be intertwined with identified career problems. For example, a client's experience of depressive symptoms or negative thinking may interfere with full engagement or enjoyment of their work and result in occupational dissatisfaction and/or reduced performance in their work setting. Additionally, unreasonable work setting demands or discriminatory practices experienced by a client may precede a client's experience of distress, mental health symptoms, and subsequently influence their orientation to work and job seeking processes. Consequently, exploring wellness and mental health concerns at the beginning of the art therapy/counseling relationship warrants art therapist and counselor time and attention. This integration may take various forms depending on the clients' needs and wishes, service provider settings, and theoretical orientations. Two examples of how mental health and career concerns may be integrated are included below.

Integrating Mental Health in Career Service Centers

Lenz et al. (2010) advocated for combined mental health career counseling approach within organizations while acknowledging administrative, logistical, and perceptual challenges. Career service centers also have the option to utilize career theories and strategies that integrate mental health and career concerns such as the CIP theory. The FSU Career Center applies the CIP theory and Holland's theory and service providers are trained to assess and address both concerns.

Specifically, a differentiated service delivery model (Sampson, 2008; see Figure 5.8) is used, with the goal of providing clients with the level of service their career concern

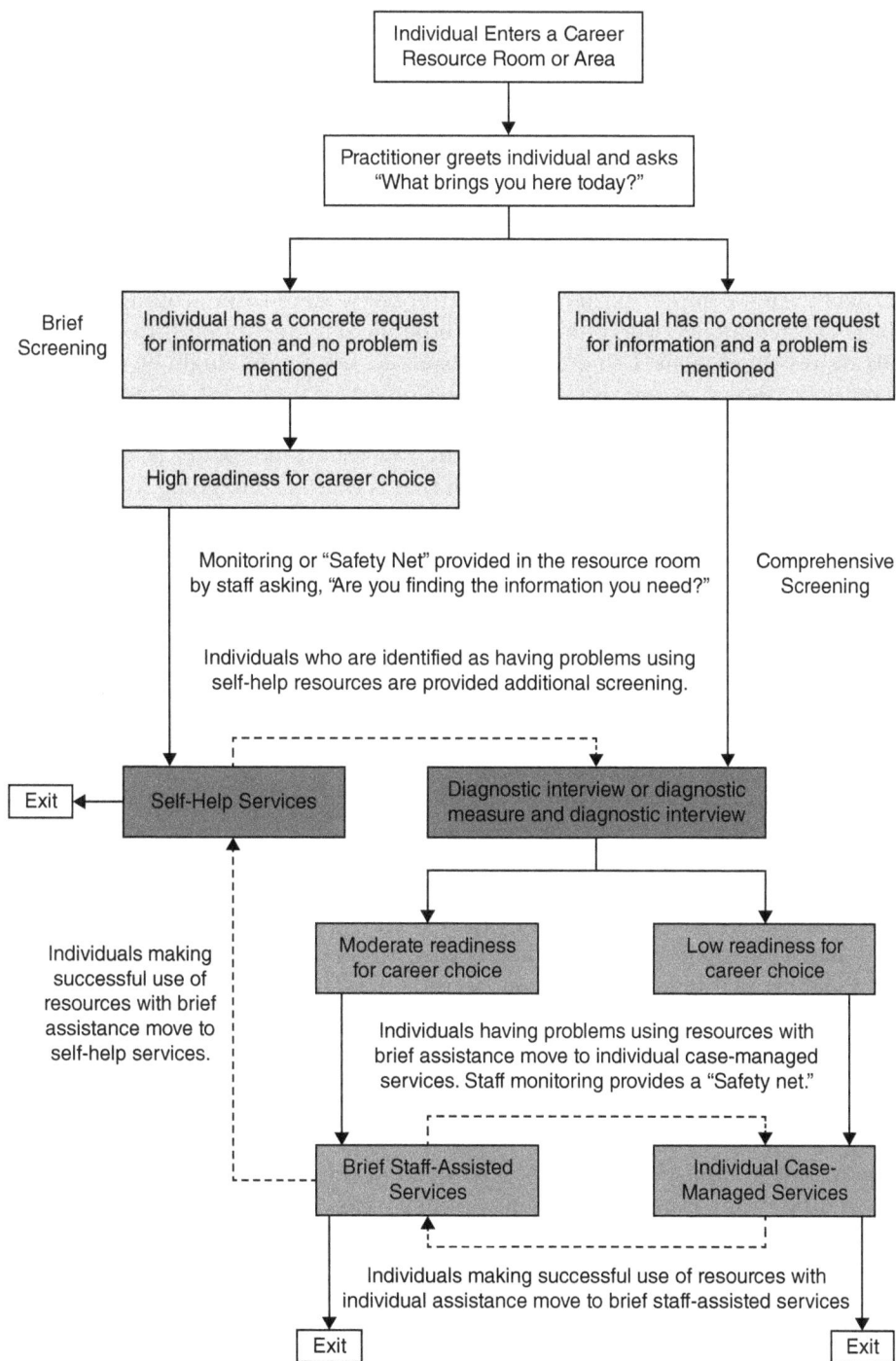

Figure 5.8 Service Delivery Sequence for Drop-In Career Services.

Source: Adapted from "Using readiness assessment to improve career services: A cognitive information process-ing approach," by J. P. Sampson, G. W. Peterson, R. C. Reardon, and J. G. Lenz, 2000, The Career Development Quarterly, 49(2), p. 162. https://doi.org/10.1002/j.2161-0045.2000.tb00556.x. Copyright 2000 by the National Career Development Association. Adapted with permission.

requires. As an individual enters the center, they meet with a career advisor who talks with them for about 15–30 minutes to gain an understanding of their career concern as well as their readiness to engage in the career decision-making and problem-solving process. Readiness is determined by their capability to engage at that time in light of the complexities that are impacting their decision. If it seems the person has a straightforward need, and is ready to engage (i.e., high capability/low complexity), interventions would center on a self-directed mode. For example, someone wanting to learn about job searching would be shown a variety of resources on that topic. If that person has multiple concerns, or has a moderate level or readiness (e.g., high capability/high complexity or low capability/low complexity), a career practitioner would likely encourage them to use the brief-assisted model, where they work a little bit at a time, often with different advisors to address their goals. Using the same example, the person might be encouraged to work on their résumé at one visit, explore developing their network at another visit, and build interview skills at another. Finally, if a person, in that initial visit, demonstrates low readiness (i.e., low capability/high complexity), a career practitioner is likely to recommend an individual case-managed approach that is similar to ongoing individual counseling. This allows the individual to address the complexities in a deeper manner, focus on mental health concerns that might be impacting or be exacerbated by the career concern, and to break the goals into even more manageable steps.

While the model may appear to suggest three distinct tracks, in reality, clients may move across the three different platforms. For example, a person may start as self-directed and realize they need more support; or as part of the individualized case-managed approach, they work outside of session time with a career advisor on tasks such as résumé writing. Research has supported each of these three approaches as being effective (Kronholz, 2015; Osborn et al., 2016; Whiston et al., 2017).

In addition to the service delivery model, the FSU Career Center uses handouts based on CIP theory (Sampson et al., 2020; Sampson et al., 2004) to help frame the client's career concern and to identify areas for focus, such as "What's Involved in a Career Choice," and a handout on decision-making. These were described in detail in Chapter 2. Holland's theory is often utilized to help clients as they identify career and major options based on their characteristics. Finally, to identify and address dysfunctional career thoughts that impede the career decision-making process, the Career Thoughts Inventory (Sampson et al., 1996a) and Career Thoughts Inventory Workbook (Sampson et al., 1996b), both based in CIP theory, are utilized.

Integrating Career Services into Mental Health Treatment

Art therapists and counselors in predominantly clinical settings may frequently find themselves working in situations where clients' primary reason for seeking services is related to mental health concerns, but career concerns are also present. One model for providing integrative services was described by Ellison et al. (2015) who created a program for emerging adults with significant mental health conditions and employment preparation or career exploration needs. Residential care center residents, aged 16–21, received placement and support for supported employment, education, peer mentorship, career development efforts centered on personal choice, exploration, agency, and more. Ellison et al. noted that positive work and school experiences for those experiencing serious mental health conditions led to self-sufficiency, engagement in typical activities of emerging adulthood, self-esteem, agency, and decreased stigma. For this group, career development and mental health services were disseminated from one location with collaboration and communication among career specialists and mental health professionals central to the approach. Individualized care and peer mentorship were designed to address developmental stages of a young adulthood and mental health considerations throughout each step of career exploration, job search, job skill development, placement support, and support for work engagement on a continuous basis. Ultimately, this combination of adapted career and mental health service provision was found to be more effective in supporting successful employment and sustained work engagement than the provision of vocational services alone.

Goal Setting and Action Plans

The working phase of career counseling and art therapy constitutes the core action segment of treatment. Identification and exploration of problems takes place and interventions are implemented. To ensure action plans are meaningful to the client, teamwork is necessary. Elliott et al. (2016) recommended clinicians use the Personal Questionnaire (PQ) early in the relationship, to engage the client to identifying, ranking, and rating the identified problems they have been experiencing. Cardoso and Sales (2019) asserted that the PQ was suited to career counseling as it provides a means to incorporate subjectivity and cultural meanings into goal development. Using a 3 × 5 card for each problem, the client writes out the problem and rates it on a scale from 1 to 7 to indicate the level it bothered them, 1 representing not at all and 7 the maximum possible. After client and therapist review the cards, the client ranks the problems in order of importance to them. With information regarding career development and mental health concerns identified, the art therapist/counselor and client collaborate to form working goals and plans for treatment that are suited to the individual's circumstances and needs. As treatment plans are executed, rankings and ratings of the problems are revisited to assess the efficacy of the action plans. This regular review process has been shown to strengthen the client's perception of the working alliance throughout the treatment relationship.

Career development action plans target many goals. These goals include expanding self-knowledge, increasing occupational knowledge, exploring training resources, developing job search skills, and more. After overarching treatment aims have been determined and a theoretical approach is matched to client considerations and needs, specific goals and plans for treatment should be developed that are observable, time specific, achievable, and clearly articulated (Gysbers, Hepner & Johnston, 2014). For example, a client may have a broad goal of selecting a career direction, but this goal should be broken down into smaller measurable and obtainable action steps. For example, Step 1: Client will complete career interest assessment process by X date. Step 2: Client will complete and reflect upon art-based inclusive genogram by X date to explore influences on career interests and decision-making. Step 3: Client will identify their personal career values by completing a career values card sort and art process by X date. Step 4: Client will identify three careers that they would like to learn more about by X date. Step 5: Client will identify skills, interests compatible to each job by X date through review of career information, and so on.

Another way of managing multiple client goals is through an individual career learning plan (see Table 5.2). A client can list multiple goals, such as choosing a major, creating a résumé, and learning about training options, and then create steps to accomplishing those various goals, and to keep track of them on one document. This also can be used as a way to track progress.

Table 5.2 Sample of a Blank Individual Career Learning Plan

Individual Learning Plan

[Insert address of career center or school]

Goal(s): #1 _____

#2 _____

#3 _____

Activity	Purpose	Estimated time required	Goal #	Priority

The purpose of this plan is to select resources and services that may be useful in making a career choice. Activities or resources included on the plan can be added or subtracted as needed.

Name	**Date**	**Staff Member**	**Date**

Exploring Self-Knowledge in the Working Phase of Treatment

Values Card Sort and Portrait

To address the general goal of self-knowledge and the more specific goal understanding one's career values, a career card sort may be offered. Card sorts provide a visible and active way to explore ideas and concepts that may not be as easily identified or articulated via an open-ended question-and-response processes. Instead of asking, "What are your career values?" a card sort provides the opportunity to ask, "Which of these career values resonate with you?" The Virginia Commonwealth University (VCU, n.d.) Career resources values card sort provides 24 different values. Values include: ability to work independently; believing in the work that I do; working with many people in a social atmosphere; and more. A client will be invited to look through the cards, and in this case are asked to note which values they must have, would like to have, or don't need. Reflective questions or artwork may follow such an activity.

One art-based extension to the card sort is the Career Values Portrait. Clients are provided a choice of two-dimensional art materials, and are asked to create an artwork that incorporates and reflects three to five of their most important career values. Symbols, shapes, colors, lines, and textures may be used to express associations with the values. Creative exploration, visual reflection, and discussion may expand or confirm initial responses to the card-sort process.

Graduate art therapy students in an FSU Career Counseling and Art Therapy class, were asked to complete a values card sort. Following the ranking of their career values, they engaged in the Career Values Portrait process. Upon completed the artmaking process one particular art therapy student chose to include the cards from the card sort in her artwork (Figure 5.9) and commented on the role the Values Portrait played in helping her consider career values and priorities.

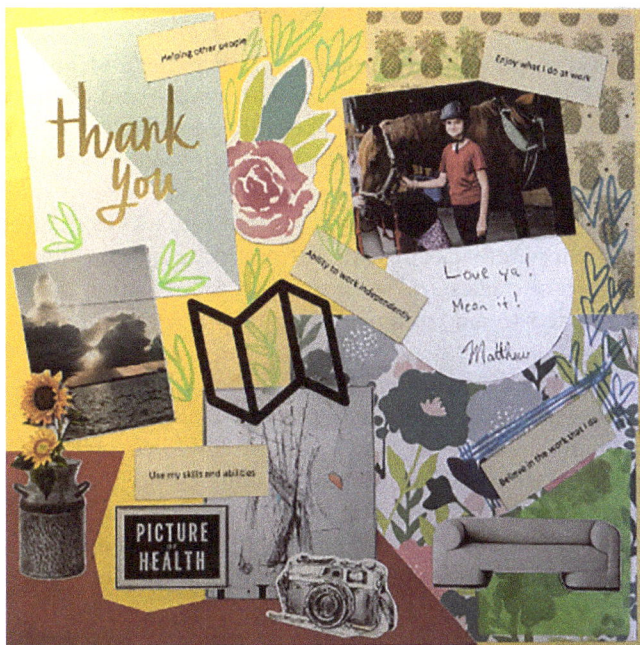

Figure 5.9 Student Example Career Values Portrait

This student reflected:

> Matching imagery with my career values was gratifying and reassuring. Creating this image also made abstract values both concrete and personal for me. I placed the cards into the collage in close proximity to images or sections that represent them.

Exploring Dominant Qualities

Another example of an art-based intervention for the working phase of treatment is Barba's (2000) Exploration of Dominant Qualities. If a client's treatment goals relate to exploring personal traits they perceive may interfere with their career satisfaction, career effectiveness, or desired work/life roles, this active method can assist with externalizing the trait and examining it dimensionally. Her instructions are as follows:

1 Think about a personal trait that you have defined as a weakness
2 Externalize the thing and give it substance. That is, draw it, shape it in a lump of clay, write a poem that captures its different aspects. Take some time to reflect upon your creation.
3 Ask yourself the following questions.
4 What is it?
5 How did it originate?
6 How does it serve you?
7 What challenges, opportunities, or dangers does it present?
8 How do you, or can you, compensate for its other side, its shadow?
9 If it could speak, what might it say?
10 What does it have to teach?
11 What does it have that you need? (Barba, 2000, p. 40)

Considering Treatment Progress and Closure

Throughout the working phase of treatment, action plans and interventions are carried out. Clients work towards their goals and art therapist and client explore progress together. During the review, efforts are acknowledged and celebrated. As goals are achieved, anticipating and planning for termination is also important. Such planning will include discussions about how many sessions will be needed or remain prior to the ending of art therapy/career counseling. Still, stalls or setbacks in treatment progress are also to be expected. These setbacks provide the clinician and the client the opportunity to explore experienced obstacles and to revisit and refine action plans. Further assessment may also be needed to aid understanding of problems, interests, and influences more fully.

Ideally, the working phase of treatment will transition into a closing phase when action plans have been completed and goals accomplished. However, other situations may also prompt consideration of closure with a client. These situations include extended periods of client inaction, lack of depth of meaning of sessions, or premature closure when a client leaves counseling during the beginning or working phases of treatment prior to goal attainment. As in any phase of treatment, it is important for the art therapist/counselor to reflectively examine clients' status and readiness for closure and to initiate closing processes as indicated.

Tasks of the closing phase of treatment include review of content of art therapy and career counseling sessions, review processes and outcomes that have been explore and completed, acknowledgment and celebration of clients' gains and strengths, and evaluation of what went well and what went poorly during sessions. Additionally, it will be important to address feelings regarding the end of the counseling and art therapy relationship and provide clear and direct structure for the next steps for the client, and to articulate the role of the art therapist counselor as an available resource in the future. For the purposes of this chapter, relational closure and review of client strengths and gains in the closure process will be emphasized.

Headley et al. (2015) noted that facilitating the ending of the therapeutic relationship in counseling may be viewed in different ways. On one hand, it can be viewed as a guided mourning process related to the loss of the supportive therapeutic relationship. On another hand, it can be seen as a welcomed celebration of the evolutionary process where the client no longer needs the support of the therapist for their continued development. Landgarten (1991) asserted that termination of the therapeutic relationship can be an ambivalent experience of gratification and mourning for both client and therapist related to the caring that is afforded to joint efforts at goal attainment. Appropriate management of the closure of therapy experiences deepens the therapeutic relationship through the exploration of the transformative processes and roles that have occurred and provides opportunities for mutual appreciation to be expressed.

Headley et al. (2015) asserted that creative approaches to addressing closure experiences in counseling can be advantageous noting that sensory aspects of the creative process can assist with the exploration of experiences and aid communication of closure sentiments. In the creative termination process described by Headley et al., drawing and painting materials as well as a collection of varied sized and shaped rocks (Figure 5.10) are introduced as tangible means for client and therapist to co-create and explore therapeutic gains and relational experiences. Working side-by-side, client and therapist create and then take turns sharing their reflective representations. Clients are invited to choose a small container such as small pouches, boxes, or baskets to take the meaningful symbols of their experiences with them in the session's final moments. As selected rocks are exchanged or offered to the therapist as a gift or remembrance, the therapist may designate a special basket or jar as place to visibly honor these emblems of achievement and relational connection.

Figure 5.10 Creating and Exchanging Rocks for Closure

A Portfolio Review of Career Counseling Art Therapy Experiences

The physical and visual nature of art production within career counseling and art therapy provides a different type of opportunity to review therapeutic/counseling experiences that can enhance closure. Landgarten (1991) advocated for art therapists to thoughtfully review collected art with their clients and suggested attending to artworks that highlight experiences without reopening issues that have been addressed and closed. Art therapists see artworks "not merely as symbols of past experiences but also as stimuli that can evoke, revive and preserve past experiences" (Salomon & Levinger, 2020, p. 7). Consequently, it is advisable to review artworks and the meanings prior to the final session so that the last session may be reserved for relational closure and celebrations. An art portfolio review supports client witnessing of their journey from a different vantage point and encourages reflection on therapeutic experiences and gains.

As the relationship closes, clinicians and clients must revisit the guidelines that were established regarding the retention or release of clients' artworks. Dependent on determined agreements, therapists may retain photographed client artwork for client records and/or clients. Ethical guidelines regarding the management of art products created in sessions may be found in national art therapy organization or credentials board ethics documents such as the Art Therapy Credentials Board (2021) Code of Ethics, Conduct, and Disciplinary Procedures, and the American Art Therapy Association (2020) Ethical Principles for Art Therapists.

Additional Art Processes for the Closing Phase of Treatment

Reviewing client accomplishments at the close of treatment may include revisiting the career bridge drawing created at the beginning of the relationship. To provide a visual example for comparison, the professional may invite a client to create a second bridge drawing to note their current place on their career journey and to represent any new experiences or resources that they may use to support their ongoing career efforts. Next, similarities and differences between the two drawings would be explored and progress that has been made in achieving career direction and goals would be acknowledged and celebrated.

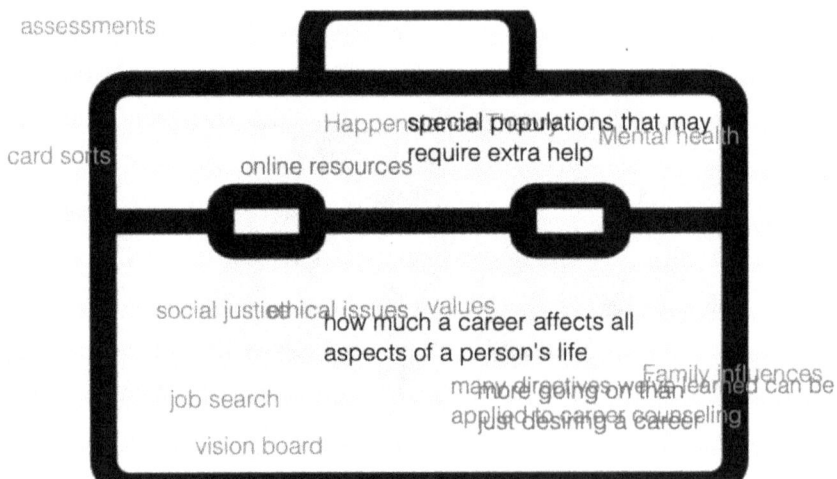

Figure 5.11 Collective Tool box

Another art-based means of summarizing achieved career learning may include the creation of a career skills toolbox. Using a preformed toolbox outline, the client can be asked to symbolically represent the skills and learning that they are carrying with them into their future life and experiences. Alternatively, a client may be encouraged to embellish the inside and outside of a small box, to represent and reflect their current career beliefs, skills, and accomplishments. In each form, the box can be used as a reminder of gains made in and outside of sessions.

The toolbox image in Figure 5.11 represents a graduate level Career Counseling and Art Therapy class Zoom meeting whiteboard-created toolbox in which students posted words that related to learning they achieved during the career-focused class. In this case, students also identified concepts they would continue to consider as they applied course concepts to clinical practice.

Summary

Basic counseling and art therapy skills are foundational in establishing and sustaining working alliances throughout the phases of career counseling and art therapy. These phases of treatment include gaining consent, establishing relationships through sensitive inquiry to identify career problems, setting career- and life-related goals, addressing problems through theory-informed treatment planning and intervention strategies, progress evaluations, and closure of therapy. From beginning to the closing phase of the relationship, art therapy interventions can be used to illuminate career concerns, aid exploration, and expand communication options for clients and professionals.

Discussion Questions and Activities

1 Review your practicum, internship, practice, or work setting consent forms: Are all practice guidelines included, clearly written, and accessible? What processes do you employ to ensure client understanding?
2 What type of environment and art therapy/counselor behavior do you believe would support your telling of your career concerns and goals?
3 Create an artwork that reflects your career story or concerns. How would you wish to explore these with art therapist or career counselor? How can you use this experience to inform your work with clients?
4 What means do you use to foster collaboration with clients on goal setting and evaluation? In what ways might you expand those practices?
5 What are other creative ways that you have provided closure to therapy? How might these methods be applied to career counseling concerns?

References

American Art Therapy Association (2020) Ethical principles for art therapists. https://arttherapy. org/ethics/

American Counseling Association. (2014). ACA code of ethics. www.counseling.org/resources/ aca-code-of-ethics.pdf

American Psychological Association (2020). Informed consent checklist for telepsychological services: www.apa.org/practice/programs/dmhi/research-information/informed-consent-checklist

Art Therapy Credentials Board (2021). Code of ethics, conduct, and disciplinary procedures. www.atcb.org/wp-content/uploads/2020/07/ATCB-Code-of-Ethics-Conduct-Disciplinary Procedures.pdf

Barba, H. N. (2000). *Follow your bliss! A practical, soul-centered guide to job-hunting and career-life planning.* Universal Publishers.

Bat Or, M., & Zilcha-Mano, S. (2019). The Art Therapy Working Alliance Inventory: The development of a measure. *International Journal of Art Therapy, 24*(2), 76–87.

Bordin, E. S. (1979). The generalizability of the psychoanalytic concept of the working alliance. *Psychotherapy: Theory, Research & Practice, 16*, 252–260. https://doi.org/10.1037/h0085885

Cardoso, P. & Sales, C. M. D. (2019). Individualized career counseling outcome assessment: A case study using the Personal Questionnaire. *The Career Development Quarterly, 67*, 21–31. https://doi.org/10.1002/cdq.12160

Casado-Kehoe, M. (2016). Bridge of life: Creating a career path. In W. K. Killam, S. Degges-White, & R. E. Michel (Eds.), *Career counseling interventions: Practice with diverse clients* (p. 166). Springer.

Cochran, J. L., & Cochran, N. H. (2015). *The heart of counseling: Counseling skills through therapeutic relationships* (2nd ed.). Routledge.

Darewych, O. H., & Campbell, K. B. (2016). Measuring future orientations and goals with the Bridge Drawing: A review of the research. *Canadian Art Therapy Association Journal, 29*(1), 30–37.

Eggerth, D. E. (2008). From theory of work adjustment to person–environment correspondence counseling: Vocational psychology as positive psychology. *Journal of Career Assessment, 16*(1), 60–64. https://doi.org/10.1177/1069072707305771

Elliot, R., Wagner, J., Sales, C. M. D, et al. (2016). Psychometrics of the Personal Questionnaire: A client-generated outcome measure. *Psychological Assessment, 28*, 263–278. https://doi.org/10.1037/pas0000174

Ellison, M. L., Klodnick, V. V., Bond, G. R., et al. (2015). Adapting supported employment for emerging adults with serious mental health conditions. *The Journal of Behavioral Health Services & Research, 42*(2), 206–222.

Falkenstrom, F., Granstrom, F., & Holmqvist, R. (2014). Working alliance predicts psychotherapy outcome even while controlling for prior symptom improvement. *Psychotherapy Research, 24*(2), 146–159, http://dx.doi.org/10.1080/1080/10503307.2013.847985

Gehart, D. (2016). *Case documentation in counseling and psychotherapy: A theory-informed competency-based approach.* Cengage Learning.

Gullo, S., Lo Coco, G. & Gelso, C. (2012). Early and later predictors of outcome in brief therapy: The role of real relationship. *Journal of Clinical Psychology, 66*(6), 614–619, https://doi.org/10.1003/jclp.21860

Gysbers, N. C., Heppner, M. J., Johnston, J.A. (2014). *Career counseling: Holism, diversity, and strengths* (4th ed). American Counseling Association.

Gysbers. N. C., & Moore. E. J. (1987). *Career counseling: Skills and techniques for practitioners.* Prentice-Hall.

Hays, R. E., & Lyons, S. J. (1981). The Bridge Drawing: A projective technique for assessment in art therapy. *The Arts in Psychotherapy, 8*(3), 207–217. https://doi.org/10.1016/0197-4556(81)90033-2

Headley, J. A., Kautzman-East, M., Pusateri, C. G., & Kress, V. E. (2015). Making the intangible tangible: Using expressive art during termination to co-construct meaning. *Journal of Creativity in Mental Health, 10*, 89–99. https://doi.org/10.1080/15401383.2014.93815

Hinz, L. D. (2020). *Expressive therapies continuum: A framework for using art in therapy* (2nd ed.). Routledge.

Holmqvist, G., Roxberg, A., Larsson, I., & Lundqvist-Persson, C. (2019). Expressions of vitality affects during therapy and the meaning for inner change. *International Journal of Art Therapy, 24*(1), 30–39, https://doi.org/10.1080/17454832.2018.148069

Horvath, A. O. (2018). Research on the alliance: Knowledge in search of a theory. *Psychotherapy Research, 28*(4), 499–516.

Horvath, A. O., & Greenberg, L. S. (1989). Development and validation of the working alliance inventory. *Journal of Counseling Psychology, 36*(2), 223–233.

Isserow, J. (2013). Between water and words: Reflective self-awareness and symbol formation in art therapy, *International Journal of Art Therapy*, *18*(3), 122–131. http://dx.doi.org/10.1080/17454832.2013.786107

Jahn, S. A. B. (2018). Professional issues and innovative practice: Using collage to examine values in college career counseling. *Journal of College Counseling*, *21*, 180–192.

Kramer, E. (2000). *Art as therapy: Collected papers of Edith Kramer*. Jessica Kingsley.

Kronholz, J. F. (2015). Self-help career services: A case report. *Career Development Quarterly*, *63*, 282–288.

Lachman-Chapin, M. (2001). Self psychology and art therapy. In J. Rubin (Ed.), *Approaches to art therapy* (2nd ed., pp. 66–78). Brunner/Routledge.

Landgarten, H. B. (1991), Termination: Theory and practice. In H.B. Landgarten & D. Lubbers (Eds.). *Adult art psychotherapy: Issues and Applications* (pp. 174–198). Brunner-Routledge.

Lenz, J. G., Peterson, G. W., Reardon, R. C., & Saunders, D. E. (2010). Connecting career and mental health counseling: Integrating theory and practice. Retrieved from http://counselingoutfitters.com/vistas/vistas10/Article_01.pdf

Lusebrink, V. B. (1990). *Levels of imagery and visual expression in therapy*. Plenum Press.

Masdonati, J., Massoudi, K., & Rossier, J. (2009). Effectiveness of career counseling and the impact of the working alliance. *Journal of Career Development*, *36*, 183–203. https://doi.org/10.1177/0894845309340798

Masdonati, J., Perdix, S., Massoudi, K., & Rossier, J. (2014). Working alliance as a moderator and a mediator of career counseling effectiveness. *Journal of Career Assessment*, *22*(1), 3–17. https://doi.org/10.1177/1069072713487489

Morrell, M. (2011). Signs and symbols: Art and language in art therapy. *Journal of Clinical Art Therapy*, *1*(1), 25–32. http: digitalcommons.lmu.edu/jcat/vol1/iss1/8

National Career Development Association. (2015). NCDA code of ethics. www.ncda.org/aws/NCDA/asset_manager/get_file/3395

Osborn, D., Hayden, S. C. W., Peterson, G. W., & Sampson, J. P., Jr. (2016). Effect of brief staff-assisted career service delivery on drop-in clients. *Career Development Quarterly*, *64*, 181–187. Retrieved from http://fsu.digital.flvc.org/islandora/object/fsu%3A543803 doi:10.1002/cdq.12050

Parker-Bell, B. (2021). [Student handout for career development class]. Art Therapy Program, Florida State University.

Patterson, C. L., Anderson, T., & Wei, C. (2014). Clients' pretreatment role expectations, the therapeutic alliance, and clinical outcomes in outpatient therapy. *Journal of Clinical Psychology*, *70*(7), 673–680.

Paul, S., & Charura, D. (2015). *An introduction to the therapeutic relationship in counselling and psychotherapy*. Sage.

Salomon, M. & Levinger, S. (2020). The experience of art therapists who work in private practice when retaining clients' artworks after therapy termination. *The Arts in Psychotherapy*, *70*, 2–9. https://doi.org/10.1016/j.aip.2020.101684

Sampson, J. P., Jr. (2008). *Designing and implementing career programs: A handbook for effective practice*. National Career Development Association.

Sampson, J. P., Osborn, D. S., Bullock-Yowell, E., et al. (2020). *An introduction to CIP theory, research, and practice* (Technical Report No. 62). Florida State University, Center for the Study of Technology in Counseling and Career Development. Retrieved from http://fsu.digital.flvc.org/islandora/object/fsu%3A749259

Sampson, J. P., Peterson, G. W., Lenz, J. G., et al. (1996a). *Career Thoughts Inventory*. Psychological Assessment Resources.

Sampson, J. P., Peterson, G. W., Lenz, J. G., et al. (1996b). *Career Thoughts Inventory workbook*. Psychological Assessment Resources.

Sampson, J. P., Jr., Reardon, R. C., Peterson, G. W., & Lenz, J. G. (2004). *Career counseling and services: A cognitive information processing approach*. Brooks/Cole.

Schaverien, J. (1992). *The revealing image: Analytical art psychotherapy and practice*. Routledge.

Springham, N., & Huet, V. (2018). Art as a relational encounter: An ostensive communication theory of art therapy. *Art Therapy: Journal of the American Art Therapy Association*, *35*(1), 4–10

Stallings, J.W. (2016). Collage as an expressive medium in art therapy. In D. Gussak & M. Rosal (Eds.), *The Wiley handbook of art therapy* (pp.163–167). John Wiley & Sons.

Swan-Foster, N. (2018). *Jungian art therapy: Images, dreams, and analytical psychology*. Routledge.

Teneycke, T., Hoshino, J., & Sharpe, D. (2009). The Bridge Drawing: An exploration of psychosis. *The Arts in Psychotherapy, 36*, 297–303.

Virginia Commonwealth University. (n.d). Values card sort. https://careers.vcu.edu/media/vcu-careers/docs/ValuesCardSort.pdf

Whiston, S. C., Li, Y., Mitts, N. C., & Wright, L. (2017). Effectiveness of career choice interventions: A meta-analytic replication and extension. *Journal of Vocational Behavior, 100*, 175–184. http://dx.doi.org/10.1016/j.jvb2017.03.010

6 Diversity and Social Justice in Career Counseling and Art Therapy

In this chapter, frameworks for considering and addressing cultural influences, resources, and barriers to career development will be offered. For the purposes of this chapter, cultural groups may pertain to racial or ethnic identity, socioeconomic class, gender identification, sexual orientation, physical or mental disability, religious affiliation, and other marginalized intersectional identities. The chapter includes a review of related ethics, professional multicultural competencies, cultural humility, and social justice frameworks designed to prepare clinicians for ongoing reflection and sensitive cross-cultural career guidance. Application of career counseling theories and approaches that emphasize interrelationships between social systems and individuals' career development will be emphasized.

It is important to recognize the inherent power dynamics that exist in the career counseling relationship. Art therapists, counselors, and career counselors fill supportive and influential roles in the lives of clients who are navigating career exploration and decision-making efforts. Such efforts impact clients emotionally, physically, socially, and economically throughout their lifespans. Consequently, career counseling professionals must strive to understand their clients and the contexts in which they live in order to provide adequate service. The journey to understand others' experiences begins with self-awareness of cultural experiences, biases, and privilege and continues with expanding one's knowledge and understanding of the individual, their salient cultural values, and the broader systemic structures that may support or limit access to equitable career development and economic opportunities. Art therapists and career counselors also have the opportunity to advocate for organizational and systemic changes that may support equitable access to rewarding career experiences.

Defining Diverse

For the purposes of this chapter, diverse populations will be broadly defined as those that are considered non-dominant, minority, or oppressed groups within the broader population being considered. Due to the brevity of this chapter, the authors will provide an overarching view of considerations related to some but not all minority, non-dominant, or marginalized groups of people. In preparation for professional practice, it is important for career counseling professionals to explore and address experiences specific to the individual who is engaging in career exploration and their experiences of salient intersectional identities. For example, a client may identify as Hispanic, lesbian, middle-aged, cisgender female, and Catholic and the influence of these cultural affiliations on their daily experiences and the presenting career issue may vary. Art therapists also have multifaceted identities that may align with the dominant cultural groups that

DOI: 10.4324/9781003035756-6

are privileged or those that are marginalized. The therapeutic relationship is influenced by the interactions of client and therapist identities, experiences, and perceptions.

Career Counseling in a Multicultural Society

Sultana (2017) described culture as a complex matrix of sets of experiences, orientations, strategies and rituals that are developed over time by a group and its institutions to navigate life experiences. He further asserts that members of a group are socialized into a community's patterns of behavior, and their responses to experiences become automatically enacted with little consciousness or awareness. He notes that meaning-making contexts can serve to inform social relationship structures but can be dysfunctional when they limit development of new responses to challenges, or when different responses to action or meaning-making are perceived as threats. When career counselor and client have been acculturated to different sets of community wisdom, experiences, and supported actions, clashes in systems may occur within the therapeutic relationship.

Sultana (2017) further posited that career counseling practitioners may intend to help those who have not shared their group affiliations or experiences but can be vulnerable to falling into habits or practices that that prevent sensitive cross-cultural work from occurring. He identified five specific pitfalls that career counselors may fall into. These include: incipient racism/monoculturalism; romanticization of culture; restricted notions of equality; exoticization of culture; cultural essentialism and reductionism. The pitfall of incipient racism or monoculturalism refers to the hesitance of helping professionals to acknowledge their own discomfort with differences and subsequent failure to face instinctive fears and explore their responses. Romanticization of culture pertains to a failure to recognize and challenge oppressive or unjust practices in other cultures, which may originate from a fear of being perceived as racist. In this regard, career counseling spaces test art therapists' and counselors' skills to explore cultural frameworks and to accommodate for them, but to also take a stand when necessary. Sultana described a restricted notion of equality as one that equates equality with the absence of discrimination. He asserts that concepts of equality need to include anti-discriminatory practices that go beyond tolerating diversity but respecting diverse practices and advocating for inclusion. Exoticization relates to the practice of emphasizing the strangeness or otherness of a group. Finally, cultural essentialism and reductionism pertains to ascribing to stereotypical and generalizing thinking of a culture which reduces the career counselor's ability to acknowledge variations of values and experiences among people who share one particular aspect of identity such as country of original or religious group.

Given all of the potential pitfalls that one can experience on self-awareness journeys, career counseling art therapists must prepare themselves for uncomfortable moments of self-reflection and learning as they strive to provide thoughtful service. Still, Sultana (2017) notes:

> While all inhabitants of multicultural societies are called upon to make serious and sincere efforts to meet others on their own terms, and thus to cross cultural borders, it is critical that we do not assume that such 'crossings' are the same for those from subordinate groups as they are for those in power, or that we all pay the same toll at the border.

(p. 454)

Art therapy and career counseling professionals must humbly commit themselves to ongoing reflection and education regarding cross-cultural art therapy and counseling practices and recognize the power dynamics inherent in helping relationships.

Ethics and Multicultural Skills

Related Professional Ethics

Embarking on a journey towards multicultural competency is more than aspirational, it is an ethical obligation. The National Career Development Association (NCDA, 2015) requires credential holders to adhere to codes of ethics that include expectations for behaviors regarding diversity and cultural sensitivity. Practitioners are called to honor diversity and promote social justice through fulfillment of fundamental principles of fostering client autonomy; non-maleficence, or avoiding actions that may cause harm; beneficence, supporting mental health and well-being; objectivity, or providing service in an equitable manner; accountability, fulfilling one's responsibility and trust inherent in counseling relationships; and veracity, working truthfully with professional contacts.

The ethical principles for art therapists created by the American Art Therapy Association (AATA, 2013) share many of the fundamental values identified by the NCDA, but use slightly different language in some areas. In addition to principles of autonomy, non-maleficence, and beneficence, AATA chose the terms fidelity, justice, and creativity to describe art therapists' responsibilities. Fidelity requires art therapists to act with integrity towards others, to be honest and accurate in their professional relationships, and to be truthful in their work. Justice is defined as committing to treating all persons with fairness and ensuring that they have equal access to services. Creativity pertains to fostering imagination for self-understanding, and supporting creative processes for "decision-making and problem-solving, as well as meaning-making and healing" (AATA, 2013, p. 1).

The Art Therapy Credentials Board (ATCB, 2021) also sets specific guidelines for behavior that credentialed art therapists are bound to follow, in the form of the ATCB Code of Ethics, Conduct, and Disciplinary Procedures. Two codes pertinent to fair and just treatment of people from diverse backgrounds include Code 1.24, which compels art therapists to develop and continually expand their multicultural competence and training, and to use practices that are in accordance with a client's or group's diverse identity dimensions, and 1.25, which details the necessity of art therapists to communicate in ways that are developmentally and culturally sensitive. The code requires art therapists to seek assistance such as appropriate translation support when language or communication barriers occur.

Unfortunately, these ethical guidelines provide general descriptions of values and conduct but lack detailed direction on how to approach the process of becoming more culturally sensitive and applying such sensitivity to career counseling art therapy work. Consequently, professional organizations have developed more detailed documents that further outline expectations for practitioner attitudes and behaviors.

Multicultural Competencies

The National Career Development Association (NDCA, 2020) has established a list of competencies that serve as a baseline for self-reflection and preparation to "promote the career development and functioning of individuals of all backgrounds" (p. 1). Career counselors are expected to:

- understand the strengths and limitations of career theories and utilize theories that are appropriate for the population being served
- be aware of their own cultural beliefs and assumptions and incorporate this awareness into decision-making with clients
- continue to develop individual and group counseling skills so that they may respond appropriately to client needs
- understand psychometric properties of career assessments to ensure appropriate selections and interpretations
- assess information and technology resource options to ensure these are sensitively matched to the needs of diverse populations
- provide focused support on use of information, resources, and technologies
- utilize professional research and guidelines in developing and implementing career development programs for diverse populations
- incorporate research, guidelines, experience, and stakeholder evaluation of services and apply this knowledge in creating a culturally sensitive career development program.

Art Therapy Multicultural and Diversity Competencies

Similarly, the American Art Therapy Association (2015) created a competencies document to describe developmental approaches to enabling effective work with diverse populations. These approaches incorporate a sequence of efforts that cultivate art therapist awareness, knowledge, and skills. For each of the core identified areas – Art Therapist Awareness of Personal Values, Biases, Assumptions; Art Therapist Knowledge of Client Worldviews; Art Therapist Skills in Developing and or Implementing Appropriate Interventions, Strategies, and Techniques with Sensitivity to Language, Religion, and Biculturalism – attitudes and beliefs, knowledge and skills benchmarks are outlined. Examples of these competencies are provided below:

I.A.4 Attitudes and Beliefs: Culturally competent art therapists recognize how their own cultural background, cultural identity, assumptions, and experiences including aesthetic experiences, and experiences in the arts have influenced attitudes, values, and biases about psychological, creative, and art making processes, including developmental changes.

(AATA, 2015, p. 2)

II.B.2 Knowledge: Culturally competent art therapists understand how race, culture, and other aspects of diversity may affect personality formation, vocational choices, manifestation of psychological disorders, help-seeking behavior, creative process, image making, experiences with the arts, and the appropriateness or inappropriateness of art therapy approaches.

(AATA, 2015, p. 4)

III.C.2 Skills: Culturally competent art therapists are able to design and offer art therapy interventions and experiences that take into consideration their clients' diverse art traditions, preferences for art materials, and their beliefs and practices related to the creation of imagery.

(AATA, 2015, p. 6)

Competencies and Cultural Humility

Given the scope of necessary learning, one may question if competency is attainable. Others have asked if competency models are desirable. Art therapists Bodlovic and Jackson (2019) advocated for moving away from competency models that may bolster expectations that specific approaches can be learned as frameworks for working with specific cultural groups. Instead, they incorporated an art-based cultural humility training model inspired by the work of Tervalon and Murray-García (1998). This paradigm emphasized the necessity for practitioners to commit to a lifelong journey of self-exploration and critique. Helping professionals are guided to explore barriers they may be experiencing in regard to felt and expressed compassion towards clients and are obliged to correct power imbalances inherent in therapist–client relationships. Accordingly, clients are to be upheld as experts on their own lived experiences, and the adoption of non-paternalistic engagement with individuals and formation of advocacy partnerships within communities is emphasized.

Competencies and Social Justice Practice

Gipson (2015) also questioned the sufficiency of knowledge, skill, and awareness-based competencies in preparing art therapists for equitable professional practice with diverse populations and argued that deeper commitments to social justice issues and actions are needed. She asserted that critical consciousness needs to be raised and stressed that art therapists need to examine their own relationships with power, privilege, and structures that maintain systemic oppression. Viewpoints of those who have experienced marginalization and race-related transgressions need to be heard, respected, and their concerns addressed.

Crucil and Amundson (2017) noted that individually focused career counseling interventions may not solve presenting career issues when clients experience systemic oppression. They reflected:

> you become aware that the traditional employment counseling approach might not be enough of an intervention; the presenting problem may not lie with the client, but perhaps it lies with the greater social system that the client (and you) live within. This realization is one that comes from an understanding that individual functioning – and career development – is rooted in the social systems (i.e., family, community, and society) within which clients live.
>
> (Crucil & Amundson, 2017, p. 2)

In this regard, Crucil and Amundson (2017) outlined important ways for professionals to provide social justice-informed career counseling practice. These suggested processes included cultivating self-awareness, but moved further into actions. They asserted that career counselors should be prepared to facilitate social justice interventions that incorporate advocacy and empowerment on an individual and family level, noting that such interventions are as important as policy level actions. These actions consist of, but are not limited to, culturally attuned interventions that build self-esteem and support self-efficacy. In school or community settings, career counselors should act as an ally for individuals, identify systemic barriers, and utilize communication skills to dismantle organizational structures that interfere with career development. On a public and social political level, Crucil and Amundson claimed it behooved career counselors to utilize their expertise in career development and employment discrimination to advance advocacy measures on a larger systemic scale.

Acknowledging Career Barriers

In order to disrupt career development barriers, one must first recognize the broad range of barriers that clients may experience. Barriers can take many forms such as "stereotyping, discrimination, lack of role models, bias in education or employment, and harassment" (Sampson et al., 2013, p. 101). These barriers influence internal experiences of career development self-efficacy and limit career pathways.

Discrimination in the Workplace

In 2019, Glassdoor conducted a diversity and inclusion study which polled adults 18 and over about their workplace experiences. In the United States, 61% of those surveyed endorsed that they had witnessed or experienced workplace discrimination based on age, gender, race, or LGBTQ status. Of all respondents from United States, United Kingdom, France, and Germany, 30% had experienced or witnessed racism in the workplace and 24% had experienced or witnessed LGBTQ discrimination. Adults in the United States reported highest percentages of witnessing or experiencing racism and ageism, with 42% and 45% of participants noting these occurrences.

Discrimination Influences Unemployment

People who identify as transgender have experienced greater unemployment rates than the national average (James et al., 2016). According to the 2015 transgender survey (James et al., 2016), 30% of survey respondents lost a job, or did not receive advancement, or experienced mistreatment related to their gender identify or expression within the work setting. Additionally, 77% of those surveyed stated they experienced conditions that led to hiding or delaying their gender transition, or that they left their jobs in order to evade workplace mistreatment.

Racial Disparities in Occupational Access

In their study of US employment trends, Byars-Winston et al. (2015) examined US census and labor force data collected from 1970–2010 and found that gendered and racial disparities continued to be perpetuated in occupational realms. Specifically, Byars-Winston et al. analyzed 35 occupations and found that White women and Asian men and women were more likely to fill professional status work roles while Black, Hispanic, and Native American men and women were more likely to be employed in occupations that have been characterized as low skill, low status, and low-income earning.

Undocumented Immigrant College Students

Kantamneni et al. (2016) studied the experiences of undocumented immigrant college students and found that they had inner resources of resiliency, supports, and coping skills and that they also experienced barriers to academic and work-related decisions and outcomes. As they matriculated through the early school experiences, they often experienced stress related to discrimination, potential discovery, and fears of deportation. Additionally, their pursuits of college may be shaped by limited access to scholarships and financial aid. In the college setting, undocumented college students may experience lack of support from staff or faculty and insufficient options for cultural or social connection.

Lower-Income Students

Lower-income students have not been provided equivalent educational resources such as quality teaching, supplies, and academic supports that are available to more affluent peers in their school systems (Ibrahimovic & Potter, 2013). Low-income students are less likely to be exposed to information regarding ongoing educational opportunities, college application processes, or available financial aid resources. Additionally, lower-income students may need to contribute to family earnings instead of seeking education that may lead to higher earning potential. Unfortunately, low-income students who have not been provided equal resources compete for jobs in the workforce with those with who have had significantly more school resources and career-focused preparation (Ibrahimovic & Potter, 2013).

Socioeconomic Status, Meaningful Work, and Appropriate Intervention

Autin and Allan (2019) explored the impact of socioeconomic privilege on pursuit and attainment of work that is meaningful to an individual. While they found that meaningful work was equally desired across groups of varying socioeconomic status, socioeconomic privilege appeared to significantly increase access to meaningful work. Those with limited socioeconomic privilege frequently experienced barriers to access, in part due to the necessity of attending to their basic needs.

In this regard, counselors need to understand client contexts and shape interventions accordingly. Autin and Allan (2019) noted that exploring clients' career passions can be appropriate for both privileged and less privileged groups. However, the correct sequencing of interventions can be crucial. When barriers are not experienced due to a privileged status, interventions may quickly focus on plans for picking majors or careers. When barriers are experienced due to less privileged socioeconomic status, opening up conversations about systems of privilege and oppression and designing interventions that present options for overcoming barriers may be more immediately relevant and necessary.

A Sampling of Theory-Informed Practices

As noted above, career interventions need to be responsive to clients and their contexts. Additionally, it is important to identify theoretical models and approaches that inform these career interventions. Much has been written about theoretical frameworks and how well suited or less suited they are to diverse populations. A limited sampling of theories and approaches that have been matched to the needs of diverse groups will be described. This sampling begins with the more broadly applied psychology of working theory; and further includes LGBTQ affirmative career counseling with a client with multiple marginalized identities; narrative career theory with young African females who have experienced migration and resettlement; social cognitive career theory and social political development theory applications with Latinx youth; expressive arts approaches combined with positive youth development concepts for low-income urban youth; and expressive arts offerings for female schoolchildren from Haiti. Additionally, four principles for supporting positive occupational identity and economic equity for Latinx and African American youth will be outlined.

Psychology of Working Theory (PWT)

PWT (Blustein et al., 2019) provides a theoretical framework specifically aimed at increasing inclusiveness and equity in career development, and it is especially helpful for those of working age. One assumption of PWT is that an individual's context or identities (e.g., social class, race, gender) cannot be separated from their work experiences. They state that work provides three functions, including survivability (e.g., meeting basic needs), social connection and contribution to society, and self-determination (e.g., the ability to plan for one's work future). They suggested that a practitioner first explore whether a client is able to meet their basic needs, and any expectations of meeting the survival needs of others. Questions about social connectivity should include the work environment, but also extend to other environments. Are the main meaningful relationships the client has at work, or do they have no close work relationships? What impact is the career concern having on feelings of connectedness? For example, if a person is considering quitting or relocating, how would their social connectedness change? To what degree does the client feel the work allows them to make a contribution to society, and how do they feel about that? Finally, how self-determined is the individual about shaping their future career steps? How much agency/volition does the client believe that they have or actually have in their career choices?

Practitioners should listen for and inquire about clients' experiences with work such as harassment and discrimination, and explore these in greater detail. They might also discuss different identities the client ascribes to, possible intersections of those identities, and how these might have impacted their work experiences. When a client shares negative experiences, in addition to re-affirming their worth, a practitioner might also explore how they might advocate for themselves, or identify ways to address (or avoid) the situation in the future.

LGBTQ Affirmative Career Counseling Model

Speciale and Scholl (2019) articulated an affirmative approach to working people identifying as LGBTQ along with other marginalized identities. Their approach to career counseling combined the work of Zunker (2016), feminist vocational models, narrative therapy constructs, and multicultural career counseling models that acknowledge systemic oppression, require relational empathy, and facilitate empowerment. Speciale and Scholl noted six stages of model they utilized: pre-counseling preparation; establishing an affirmative client counseling relationship; identifying and exploring identity issues and barriers; understanding how biases and discrimination limit career opportunity; collaborative selection of assessment approaches and plan development; and selecting and enacting the client's future story.

The beginning stages of the models will be addressed here. In the first stage, the counselor is expected to explore their own identities and examine any pre-existing biases about the client's cultural identities and career pathways. Through these explorations, the career counselor is compelled to address any barriers they may have to empathizing with the client's experiences. Additionally, the counselor is obligated to complete out of session research work prior to the first session to obtain information on histories of oppression and privilege that may be relevant to the particular client's identities, affiliated groups, and presenting problems. Following this preparation, the counselor works to establish their role as ally and build a working alliance with the client. As the alliance is being built, the counselor should anticipate some hesitance or trust given historical experiences of oppression and/or past negative experiences with counseling or helping relationships, and consider this a normal part of the relationship development process. Clients should be provided time to reveal their stories and be supported with client-centered reflections that empathetically acknowledge their experiences.

Narrative Approach with Refugees

Based on their qualitative research with young African females with refugee backgrounds, Abkhezer et al. (2018) asserted a narrative inquiry approach was effective in creating a space for the young women to tell their career stories and the impact of their migration and settlement experiences on their current and future career plans. The researchers employed narrative career counseling processes that included a focus on reflection, attention to meaning-making, as well as fostering connectedness, learning, and agency of the participants. They maintained that narrative approaches to career counseling provided refugees with an opportunity "to re-contextualize their skills, strengths, knowledge, and career plans" (Abkhezer et al., 2018, p. 17). Researchers maintained that a career counseling environment designed to support individuals' vocalization of new or silenced narratives provided participants with avenues for deconstruction of past stories and reconstruction of new ones that could aid in future life and career plans.

Social Cognitive Career Theory (SCCT) and Social Political Development Theory (SPDT) with Latina/o Immigrant High School Students

McWhirter et al. (2019) identified two theories as the philosophical base of their program Advocating for Latina/o Achievement in School Program (ALAS), designed to support career development of Latina/o immigrant youth. They noted that SCCT (Lent, Brown, & Hackett, 1994, 2000) was well-suited to this purpose because of its focus on contextual supports and barriers and its promotion of agency and self-efficacy beliefs related to positive career outcomes and goals. In alignment with SCCT theory, the ALAS program supported exploration of prior experiences of school achievements and provided opportunities for new ways of navigating and experiencing academic performance. Group-based methods included encouragement and reinforcement of effort; support of persistence towards desired academic outcomes; facilitating learning of stress management strategies; provision of Latina/o role models to expand ideas about potential success; and provision of college and career resource materials to reduce informational barriers to career planning. McWhirter et al., also incorporated social political development theory (SPDT; Watts et al., 2003) premises into the ALAS program. This framework supports individuals' knowledge, emotional preparation, and cultivation of capacities needed for action and resistance to political and social systems that are oppressive and fosters movement towards liberation from these constraints. In this regard, McWhirter et al. provided programs to build community; enhance cultural pride; promote critical reflection; and create opportunities for the development and use of advocacy skills.

Four Principles of Practice for Strong Occupational Identity for Black and Latinx Youth

The JFF organization, whose mission is to support equitable career outcomes for Black and Latinx youth, provided broader but complementary goals for intermediary career intervention programs. Specifically, Hoffman et al. (2020) outlined four principles that may serve to expand economic advancement opportunities for Black and Latinx youth. These four principles include 1) applying best practices that support the most marginalized; 2) focusing on youth assets; 3) building cultural competence; and 4) enabling youth to exercise self-advocacy.

Hoffman et al. (2020) provided examples of each of these four principles. For example, a best career counseling practice includes review of labor market information to help youth evaluate trends regarding workforce demands and potential earnings of particular jobs in their communities. Additionally, supporting youth in understanding the difference between "lifeboat" jobs that fill urgent economic needs and "lifetime" jobs that may provide economic security, and how they may capitalize on skills learned in lifeboat jobs to build pathways to lifetime jobs was also cited. Because of anticipated barriers and internalized false stereotypes that youth of color may experience, youth of color may question the worthiness of devoting efforts to overcoming obstacles related to college attendance or training for higher paying careers. By focusing on community and youth assets and the rejection of stereotypes, students can be supported in exploring and pursuing interests and overcoming anticipated obstacles. The third principle, building cultural competence refers to providing opportunities for youth to explore and understand different cultural practices that are expected in varied settings. Additionally, practitioner work with employers to reduce exclusionary cultural practices was also emphasized. Finally, given the unfortunate frequency of discrimination in the workplace, practitioners must be ready to "listen, learn, and lead regarding racial inequity" (Hoffman et al., 2020, p. 9) to help youth identify and address such challenges.

Expressive Arts Approaches with Diverse Populations

Forrest-Bank et al. (2016) combined an expressive arts approach with a positive youth development (PYD: Lerner, 2005) framework to support youth from low-income urban areas. Forrest-Bank et al. identified Lerner's core premises of PYD as the 6 Cs, Competence, Connection, Character, Confidence, Caring and Compassion, and Contributions, which are linked to adolescent thriving. PYD programs aim to help youth build these characteristics so they may successfully navigate life challenges. PYD programs introduced youth to protective resources such as academic support, recreational activities, arts engagement, social-emotional skills training, mentoring, and more. While there remains a need for more research on the effectiveness of PYD afterschool programs, preliminary findings suggested a positive impact on rates of behavior challenges, school retention, and motivation for academic achievement that expand student career readiness and their contributions to society. Forrest et al. emphasized that the expressive arts are particularly associated with prosocial communication and values. In partnership with the Art from Ashes (AfA) organization, Forrest-Bank et al. provided and studied the effectiveness of an expressive arts afterschool PYD program with high-risk urban youth. The program consisted of a series of workshops that focused on "expression, connection, and transformation" (Forrest-Bank et al., 2016, p. 433). In this case, a four-week therapeutic poetry protocol was tested. Those that attended the poetry group showed increases in academic performance and social competence measures compared to a control group.

Rice et al. (2018) utilized expressive arts processes within a social work program that aimed at providing hope and opportunities for self-reliance to children and adults experiencing poverty in Haiti. In their specific research project, Rice et al. incorporated expressive arts as a means to explore cultural contexts related to perceived gender roles and career goals of Haitian school-aged girls. Girls were asked what it means to be a girl in Haiti, viewed a related film and story book about Haitian girls' educational dreams, and were asked to draw, using paper and color pencils, what they wanted to do after they completed school. In group settings, facilitators encouraged participants to show their drawings and fostered discussions on the type of work they desired and steps needed to achieve their educational or career aspirations. Through this process, Rice et al. learned about traditional gendered roles and expectations for women in Haitian culture and the girls' perceptions about opportunities for education, jobs (that did not require education) and careers (work that required further education or professional training), as well as barriers to education and career pursuits. While this protocol was not designed as a career intervention, it demonstrated that expressive arts programs can provide a forum to reveal important information about cultural career contexts that can be used to build career development programs in partnership with the community.

Adapting Creative Career Interventions in Accordance with Diversity Dimensions

The Art Therapy Credentials Board (2021) in the Code of Ethics, Conduct and Disciplinary Procedures, outlined therapists' obligation to utilize practices that are in accordance with a client's or group's diverse identity dimensions. To illustrate an adaptation of a creative process to identity dimension and community contexts, the genogram and inclusive genograms will be explored.

As described in the assessment chapter, the career-focused genogram is a frequently employed qualitative assessment that explores family career themes and patterns and their influence on career decision-making. The standard genogram structure is a series of circles and squares representing females and males and their careers in three generations of one family. Art therapists can use a variety of art media to creative symbol-focused approaches to the genogram to enhance the expressive qualities; however, the underlying structure of the genogram is biased towards traditional family structures and assumes that clients may have access to information about generations of family members (Buxbaum & Hill, 2013). People who were adopted, raised in foster families, blended families, same-sex parent families, or configurations of family where extended family members play important influential roles may not feel the typical genogram structure is a fit for their experiences. Additionally, traditional career genograms do not have structural components to represent or consider significant career influences that exist outside the family, such as friends, mentors, and teachers.

Buxbaum and Hill (2013) offered the inclusive career genogram as an expanded creative structure aimed to be more responsive to clients' constructs of family and career influencers. They defined the inclusive career genogram as inclusive career genogram as a "means to visually map, illustrate, document, and construct a diagram that is an expanded, inclusive, and comprehensive sphere of influence that includes multiple life characters drawn from family, culture, and the person's own individual life context and themes" (Buxbaum & Hill, 2013, p. 50). Influences represented may encompass employers, teachers, coworkers, community role models, societal role models, fictional characters, songs, hobbies, memorable moments, or places that hold significance for the client.

When introducing the task, Buxbaum and Hill (2013) provided clients with a list of potential influences as described above to stir client consideration of the wider scope of career influences that they may have experienced. Using markers on a large posterboard or whiteboard, clients were asked to create a symbol of self in the center of the surface using any shape, form, or symbol that represented them. Following this step, clients represented selected career influences using written words, shapes, or symbols and placed them on the page. The clients were then asked to create lines between their self-symbol and the influence symbols using the type of line to characterize the significance of the influencing relationship. For example, short lines or thicker lines could indicate greater importance to the client and longer, thinner lines could connote less connection or influence. During the subsequent discussion of the artwork, client and clinician reflected on patterns that emerged and made connections to stories and themes that were revealed in

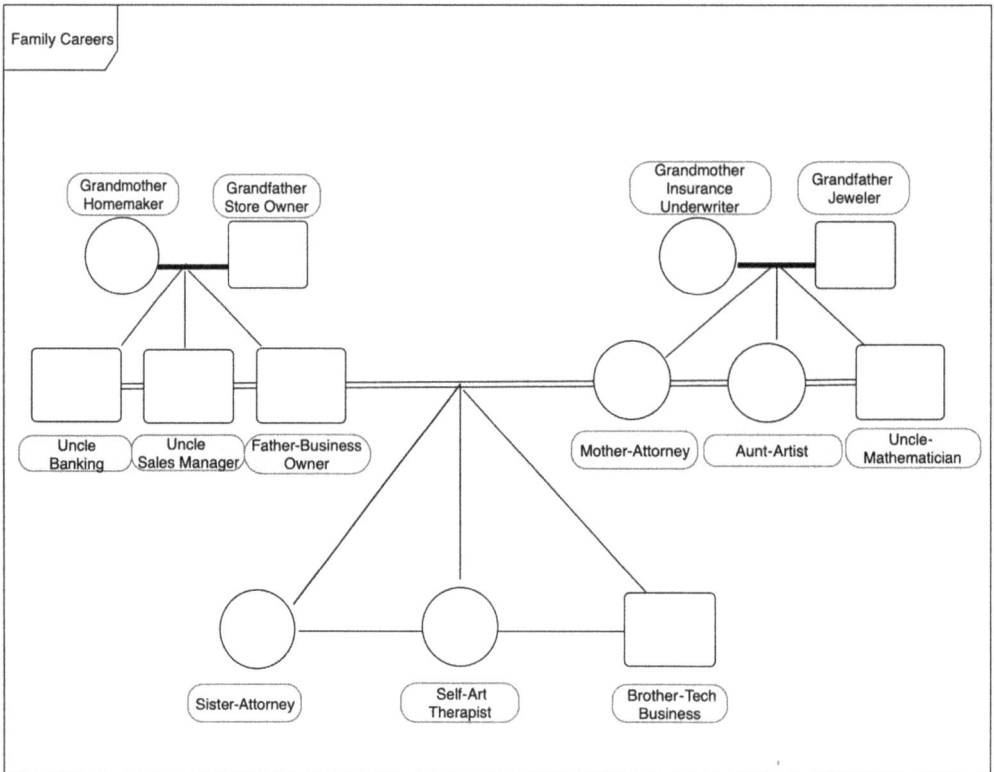

Figure 6.1 Traditional Career Focused Genogram Structure

the interview process. Buxbaum and Hill asserted that this type of intervention helped adults with unexpected work transitions integrate lifespan influences into their career revisioning processes.

In a separate forum, graduate art therapy students enrolled in a Career Development and Art Therapy Course at FSU were asked to create two personal career-focused genograms, one traditionally structured (Figure 6.1) and a genogram based on Buxbaum and Hill's (2013) inclusive model (Figures 6.2 and 6.3). When completed, they were asked to identify the advantages and disadvantages of each process. Following the completion of both processes, several students noted that they felt more comfort with the inclusive genogram format as it allowed them to represent and consider important influences and figures like art teachers or mentors that were outside their family frameworks. Other students explicitly expressed some discomfort with the traditional career-focused genogram. In these instances, they noted that they had gaps in knowledge of family members due to family divorces, multi-generational traumas, or family histories of oppression that limited options for their families to pursue desired occupational identities. Other students noted that they had relied on people and influences outside their families due to negative messaging received from family members. Accordingly, students appreciated having broader options of identifying and considering other role models or fictional characters as carriers of career life messages as part of their career genogram creation. While the class experience did not constitute research, it provides some indication that the inclusive career genogram may be a more welcoming structure for examining career influences.

Figure 6.2 Student M. Inclusive Genogram

Figure 6.3 Student S. Inclusive Genogram

Other Art Therapy Applications

While art therapists typically explore and adapt art media and art processes to learn about their clients and to help support them in the attainment of their life goals, art therapists also use their art skills to expand self-awareness and to explore their responses to therapeutic relationships and clients (Fish, 2016). The following processes are offered for the purposes of promoting self-exploration and thoughtful cross-cultural work with clients. As with any art processes, adaptations may be made to best suit the needs of the artists involved.

Learning about Yourself: Cultural Humility and the Cultural Vessel

The cultural vessel art process was created and offered as a part of Bodlovic and Jackson's (2019) cultural humility education work with art therapy students, which may also have application for career counseling students. To address cultural humility creatively, students were asked to "create a bag, toolkit or vessel out of paper a metaphorical holding" of biases assumptions, beliefs, skills as they examined prejudicial systems and oppression and concepts of "colonialism, racism, classism, sexism, heteronormativism, and ableism" (Bodlovic & Jackson, 2019, p. 3). "Isms" were described as mental constructs derived from social influences which could lead to operational biases. As these beliefs and biases were confronted, students were called to add to their creation and review and replace components with new perceptions, thoughts, and understanding. Using a creative process and product to express, hold, examine, and discard beliefs and assumptions is an important undertaking for art therapists who are engaging in professional work including career development guidance with diverse populations. As practitioners, when approaching one's own ongoing humility work, encouragement is given to create and revisit a personal cultural vessel, bag, or toolkit and replace or discard assumptions and beliefs that have been transformed as in Figure 6.4.

Figure 6.4 Origami and Collage Cultural Vessel

Relational Dynamics: Exploring Cross-Cultural Differences with Clients

Art therapist Dye (2017) developed a Universal Theory Approach to facilitate her inter-cultural art therapy work in South Africa. Her approach addressed important components of her model: Acknowledge, Identity, Culture, Individual, Race, Language. She explained that clients and therapists need to acknowledge culture-specific influences on the client's life. Secondly, Dye asserted that therapeutic aims should center upon building and acknowledging clients' personal, cultural, and racial identities. Dye noted that navigating between cultural influences and individual concerns should be handled delicately, with one needing more attention than the other at different times in therapy. In regard to race and language, Dye emphasized these factors cannot be ignored and must be addressed. Prior to new work with a client Dye would complete research related to cultural constructs and create her similarities and differences that were reflected in the client and therapist cultures to increase awareness and acknowledgment of such considerations. Dye (2017) also valued addressing cultural and racial differences between art therapist and client and the emotions that may arise related to those differences gently but directly with clients. She noted that such acknowledgment reduces unspoken tensions that may otherwise occur and communicates interest in learning about a client's racial and cultural experiences.

To address similarities and differences between therapist and client in a non-aggressive way, Dye (2017) offered an art-based structure to foster communication. For her described process, Dye utilized a large sheet of paper and paint or other materials such as collage. The large sheet of paper is divided into three columns marked similarities and differences between therapist and client, as applicable. In the space below therapist and client list, or represent, similarities and differences as they are learning about each other's cultural experiences. Dye introduced lighter topics such as celebratory traditions prior to moving to more emotion-laden topics relevant to treatment issues. Free flowing conversations were encouraged and positive connections were built.

Dye (2017) noted these exercises provided opportunities for expression of interest, discussion, reinforcement of cultural values, and pride. She recommended that therapists create a positive atmosphere, verbalize their interest and appreciation regarding learning about culture, be sensitive to client responses that may indicate they are unsure and are concerned about being judged, and in those cases, provide clarification that they are not being rejected or judged. Dye acknowledged that these discussions can be sensitive for both client and therapist. Accordingly. therapists should be prepared to acknowledge aspects of their own culture that may be viewed negatively without defensiveness.

Focusing on career counseling, a dialogue could be conducted regarding concepts of work and career. This process provides opportunities for acknowledgment of similarities and differences about career concepts, values, and access and barriers experienced. Figure 6.5 is a sample created through digital art means.

Art Processes for Exploring Clients' Salient Identities

Art can be used to creatively transform existing diversity frameworks into visual springboards for storytelling, acknowledgment, and understanding. For example, Hays (2016) utilized the ADDRESSING acronym to identify aspects of identity that may be salient for clients. ADDRESSING stands for Age (or generational experiences), Developmental disabilities, Disabilities acquired, Religion (or spirituality), Ethnicity (or race), Socioeconomic status, Sexual orientation, Indigenous status, National origin, and Gender. Taking time

SIMILARITIES	DIFFERENCES	DIFFERENCES
Therapist Name: AT Client Name: CL	**Therapist Name:** AT **Cultural Groups**(s): White Cisgender Female, Middle Socioeconomic Class, Jewish, Midwest origins, 2nd generation born in US on one side of family, 3rd generation on other side from Eastern Europe, middle-aged	**Client Name:** CL Cultural Groups (s): Latina, Cisgender, Catholic, 3rd generation born in USA, Mexican American, college-aged

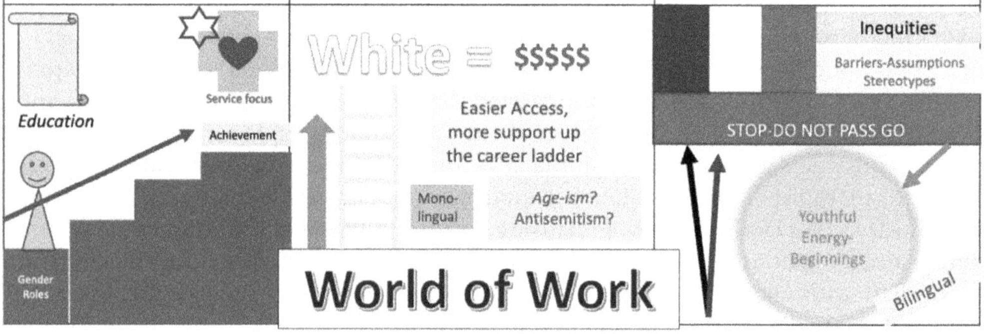

Figure 6.5 Similarities and Differences Exploration

to explore a client's salient identity components through interview or art can provide the therapist with a broader understanding of client context, values, and experiences. Art works that explore the ADDRESSING identity components can take many forms, including a hand created book (Figure 6.6) with a creative page devoted to each of the factors and their relevant experiences with them.

Alternatively, Loden's (2010) dimensions of diversity model provides two spheres of primary and secondary dimensions of diversity, the primary fitting into the center of the secondary dimensions. The primary dimensions of diversity include physical abilities and characteristics, age, race, ethnicity, sexuality, gender, spiritual beliefs, income, and class. Secondary dimensions, or the outer sphere, include work experience, communications

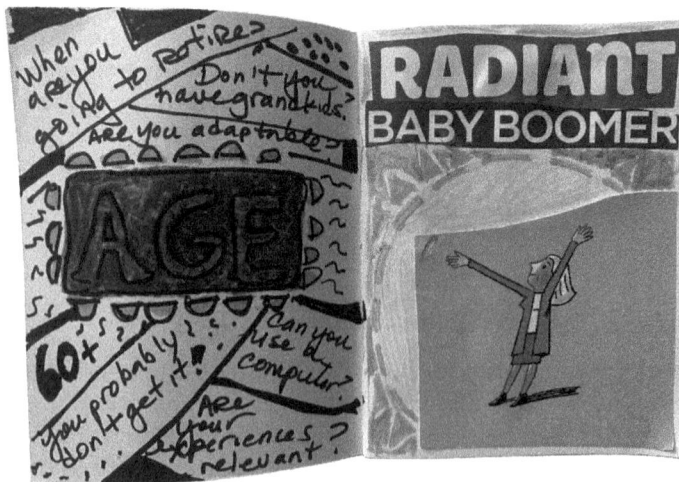

Figure 6.6 Age and Generational Identity Page from ADDRESSING book

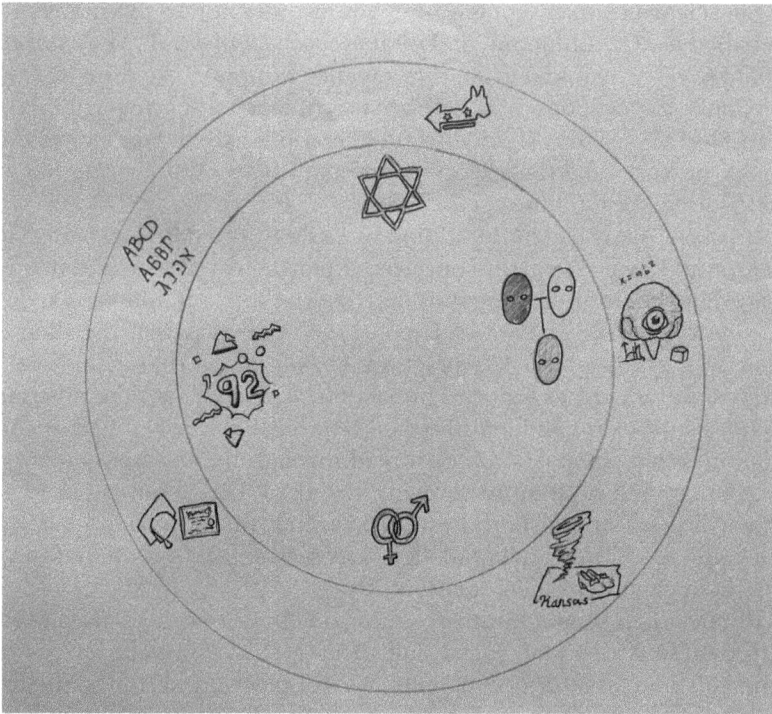

Figure 6.7 Dimensions of Diversity Example: Primary and Secondary Considerations

style, cognitive style, family status, political beliefs, education, geographic location, organization role and level, military experience, work style, and first language. Clients may use the circles to represent factors that are currently present in their lived experiences. Having a visual example of these dimensions can foster discussions on what dimensions are currently meaningful to the client. Along a list of these factors, forms with pre-drawn circles can be offered as a base for created or written representations. Figure 6.7 provides an example of a person's artistic response to the diversity model stimulus. In this case, primary factors included Judaism as a spiritual and cultural identification, bi-racial identity, heterosexuality, and millennial generation affiliation. Visual learning style, proficiency with several languages, educational accomplishment, Midwestern roots, and Democratic political leanings were described as salient secondary dimensions of identity.

Case Study Example

To demonstrate how dimensions of diversity may be addressed within a professional career counseling and art therapy framework, the following case is presented. Carolyn is a second semester Latina first year university student who presents at the Career Center uncertain about her next steps. For as long as she can remember, she's wanted to be a doctor, just like her grandmother. When asked why, she says she wants to help people. She was consistently on the Dean's list in high school, and she received a scholarship to study pre-med. She wants to be known as a medical leader within the Hispanic community and serve as a mentor to other Latina high school students to go into medicine. However, during her first semester, she struggled to make Cs in her science courses, despite hours of studying and working with a tutor. During this current semester, she's finding herself bored with her science courses, but enjoying her introduction to psychology course. She says she's terrified about failing out, and what everyone will think. She's talked with her parents about the dilemma, and while they say they'll support anything she wants to do they are also quick to point out that there are lots of psychology majors flipping burgers at a local fast-food restaurant. Carolyn is seeking guidance on whether to change to a different major or to re-take the science courses in hopes of improving her chances of being admitted to medical school.

The career practitioner started the session by expressing a desire to better understand the context around Carolyn's career concerns, exploring the factors and the people who have influenced her decision-making thus far. To start, the practitioner asked Carolyn to share more about her family and close friends, their career paths, and their influences on her career path to this point. The practitioner then noted that in addition to family, we often carry other identities that can impact our career plans. The practitioner then gave Carolyn a list of example identities as a reference and asked her to consider the different identities that she holds. Carolyn read through the list and nodded with some recognition, but seemed hesitant to verbalize details. When asked about her response, Carolyn noted, "I don't know where to start. I can tell you what is most salient, but it's complicated." The practitioner acknowledged her discomfort and offered that it may be easier for her to explore her salient identities visually.

The practitioner then suggested that creating a collage may be a good place to start. After bringing out scissors, glue sticks, and three boxes of pre-cut images specifically curated to include images of diverse people, types of places, and things, the practitioner instructed Carolyn to select one to three images that related to each identify factor that she has experienced as relevant to her current career concerns and place them on an 18″ × 24″ page, wherever she felt they belonged. The practitioner noted that she could cut or trim images any way that she would like. The practitioner's rationale was to gain an understanding of Carolyn's cultural background and how her intersectional identities informed her career concerns (Evans & Sejuit, 2021). In this case, artwork was utilized to reduce the discomfort regarding disclosure and to build relationship. Collage was specifically selected due to the ease of the process and the stimulating nature of preexisting imagery. Figure 6.8 shows the collage.

Figure 6.8 Carolyn's Identity Collage

After Carolyn completed the collage, the practitioner invited her to note one or two images that seemed to be the most important to her at this moment. Quietly, the practitioner and Carolyn reviewed the artwork together. After a minute or two, Carolyn, pointed out the mannequin figure in the top center. She noted that the figure was on a tightrope, and that represented her trying to navigate different career influences related to her identities. She noted her identities as cisgender heterosexual female as represented by images on the left which included the female figure, the jogging male, and the heart. She said she felt some pressure to make her romantic relationship a greater priority than schoolwork at times, which further challenged her attempts to get good science grades. The images on the right represented her physician grandmother, her connections to her family's roots in Mexico, their immigration journey, and her spirituality and Catholic faith. She described her faith as an influence that draws her into a life of service, caring for those in her community. Under the mannequin figure, she noted, was a brain and comic conversation balloon, which represented her interest in psychology. The images of the females below the brain, represented her in conversation with a college roommate as well as age/generational factors. Carolyn stated that she was from the second generation of family members to be born in the US, and that she felt some pull towards being more independent of family obligations like some of her non-Latinx peers. She wished at times that she could make career decisions without worrying so much about family reactions. She sighed, "My community needs mental health care too!"

The practitioner then asked Carolyn to give some examples of important decisions she had made in the past, and how these values impacted her decision-making. Some of the themes that emerged from analyzing past decisions in this way were prayer and seeking spiritual guidance, the importance of hearing and honoring her family's voices while also maintaining her own, and ultimately seeking diligently to find a solution that pleased herself, her family, and God. The practitioner then asked Carolyn to talk about how each had impacted her current career concern so far, and how she would like them to play a role going forward as she worked on the career decision. This step demonstrated the practitioner's cultural sensitivity and a purposeful integrating of Carolyn's cultural values into the career decision-making process. They would re-visit these three values in upcoming sessions when talking about self and options knowledge.

The practitioner used culturally sensitive strategies to address Carolyn's career concerns. Evans and Sejuit (2021) recommended in addition to asking the client about how they view themselves, to ask how their family describes them. They also suggested using an "Occtalk and Psychtalk" exercise in which Carolyn listed options she was considering in one column (i.e., occtalk), and adjectives (i.e., psychtalk) that came to mind in the second column. The practitioner adjusted this activity by adding columns suggested by Carolyn to include important family members' perceived attitudes towards those options. After this step, the practitioner asked Carolyn if she wanted to expand the options she was considering or go with the ones on her list. She said she wanted to start with the ones she had listed, learn more about those, and then if she didn't feel like she had a good option, would return to it. Together, they brainstormed ways that Carolyn could learn about the options on her list. This included using her network, such as her grandmother, to learn about options, but also looking at labor market information (Hoffman et al., 2020) in O*NET, and culturally specific sources such as diversity.com, IMdiversity, and employdiversity.com. In subsequent sessions, Carolyn shared about the information she was gaining, as well as reflections on her family's thoughts as well as her own. She described how prayer about the decision had helped calm her stress about the different pressures, and how she felt that all of the options she was considering would contribute to society, something she felt was in alignment with God's purpose for her life. As she reviewed options, she decided to take some time to commit to a decision, and made a plan to spend the rest of the semester engaging in more shadowing and researching of her options. Together, the practitioner and Carolyn created a plan to help her explore each, and agreed to meet back the following semester to determine next steps.

Summary

Art therapists and career counselors have an ethical responsibility to continually expand their self-awareness and awareness, knowledge, and skills regarding the values, beliefs, customs, and experiences of diverse populations. In addition to multicultural competencies, it is important for art therapists and counselors to practice cultural humility and multi-level social justice approaches to support clients in overcoming barriers to career development opportunities, achievements, and positive and equitable work environments, and developing self-efficacy and self-advocacy skills. When designing career interventions, care must be taken to investigate appropriate theories and best practices that respectfully address clients' cultural contexts, values, and goals. Additionally, adapting art therapy methods and materials in alignment with cultural art traditions and clients' contextual experiences is essential.

Discussion Questions and Activities

1 What has your career development journey involved? What levels of access or barriers to education and career pursuits did you experience? Art Prompt: Fold a paper in half. On one side write Access. On the other side write Barriers. On each side create symbols that represent encounters with support or aspects of identity that affected your access to education, career preparation resources, job opportunities, and work environment satisfaction? How might awareness of your experiences of privilege or barriers help or interfere with acknowledging, considering, and respecting clients' experiences?

2 What kinds of processes can you utilize to support your development of cultural humility and commitment to ongoing learning?

3 What are some ways that you can advocate for career access and equity on an individual, organizational, or systemic level?

4 What are some ways that you can learn about salient cultural art traditions and their material preferences? How might artmaking experiences in career counseling help you form a partnership with clients regarding their career development experiences and goals?

References

Abkhezer, P., McMahon, M., Glasheen, K., & Campbell, M. (2018). Finding voice through narrative storytelling: An exploration of career development of young African females with refugee backgrounds. *Journal of Vocational Behavior, 105*, 17–30.

American Art Therapy Association. (2013). Ethical principles for art therapists. https://arttherapy. org/wp-content/uploads/2017/06/Ethical-Principles-for-Art-Therapists.pdf

American Art Therapy Association. (2015). Art therapy multicultural and diversity competencies. www.arttherapy.org/upload/Multicultural/Multicultural.Diversity%20Competencies.%20 Revisions%202015.pdf

Art Therapy Credentials Board. (2021). Art Therapy Credentials Board code of ethics, conduct, and disciplinary procedures. www.atcb.org/wp-content/uploads/2020/07/ATCB-Code-of-Ethics-Conduct-DisciplinaryProcedures.pdf

Autin, K. L. & Allan, B. A. (2019). Socioeconomic privilege and meaningful work: A psychology of working perspective. *Journal of Career Assessment, 33*(2), 60–68. https://doi.org.10.1177/1069072719856307

Blustein, D. L., Kenny, M. E., Autin, K., & Duffy, R. (2019). The psychology of working in practice: A theory of change for a new era. *The Career Development Quarterly, 67*(3), 236–254. https://doi.org/10.1002/cdq.12193

Bodlovic, A., & Jackson, L. (2019). A cultural humility approach to art therapy multicultural pedagogy: Barriers to compassion. *The International Journal of Diversity in Education, 19*(1). https://doi.org/10.18848/2327-0020/CGP/v19i01/1-9

Buxbaum, E. H., & Hill, J. C. (2013). Inclusive career genogram activity: Working with clients facing forced career transitions to broaden the mind and encourage possibilities. *Career Planning and Adult Development Journal, 29*(4), 45–59.

Byars-Winston, A., Fouad, N., & Wen, Y. (2015). Race/ethnicity and sex in US occupations, 1970–2010: Implication for research, practice, and policy. *Journal of Vocational Behavior, 87*, 54–70.

Crucil, C. & Amundson, N. (2017). Throwing a wrench in the work(s): Using multicultural and social justice competency to develop a social justice-oriented employment counseling toolbox. *Journal of Employment Counseling, 54*, 2–11.

Dye, L. (2017). *Using art techniques across cultural and race boundaries: Working with identity.* Jessica Kingsley.

Evans, K. M. & Sejuit, A. L. (2021). *Gaining cultural competence in career counseling.* National Career Development Association.

Fish, B. (2016). *Art based supervision: Cultivating therapeutic insight through imagery.* Routledge.

Forrest-Bank, S. S., Nicotera, N., Bassett, D. M., & Ferrarone, P. (2016). Effects of an expressive art intervention with urban youth in low-income neighborhoods. *Child Adolescent Social Work Journal, 33*, 429–441. https://doi.org/10.1007/s10560-016-0439

Gipson, L. R. (2015). Is cultural competence enough? Deepening social justice pedagogy in art therapy. *Art Therapy: Journal of the American Art Therapy Association, 32*(3), 142–145. doi:10.1080/07421656.2015.1060835

Glassdoor Inc. (2019). Diversity & inclusion study 2019. https://about-content.glassdoor.com/app/uploads/sites/2/2019/10/Glassdoor-Diversity-Survey-Supplement-1.pdf

Hays, P. A. (2016). *Addressing cultural complexities in practice: Assessment, diagnosis, and therapy* (3rd ed.). American Psychology Association.

Hoffman, N., Murphy, L., & Seaton, G. (2020). How intermediaries can help Black and Latinx youth develop a strong occupational identity: Four principles of practice. Building Equitable Pathways Series. Jobs for the Future (JFF). Eric Number: ED11198: www.jff.org

Ibrahimovic, A., & Potter, S. (2013). Career counseling with low-income students: Utilizing social cognitive career theory and the theory of circumscription and compromise. *Career Planning and Adult Development Journal, 29*, 60–71.

James, S.E, Herman, J. L, Rankin, S., et al. (2016). *National Center for Transgender Equality.* https://transequality.org/sites/default/files/docs/usts/USTS-Full-Report-Dec17.pdf

Kantamneni, N., Shada, N., Conley, M. R., et al. (2016). Academic and career development of undocumented college students: The American dream? *The Career Development Quarterly, 64*, 318–332. https://doi.org/10.1002/cdq.12068

Lent, R. W., Brown, S. D., & Hackett, G. (1994). Toward a unified social cognitive theory of career/academic interest, choice, and performance. *Journal of Vocational Behavior, 45*, 79–122.

Lent, R. W., Brown, S. D., & Hackett, G. (2000). Contextual supports and barriers to career choice: A social cognitive analysis. *Journal of Counseling Psychology, 47*, 36–49.

Lerner, R. M. (2005). Promoting positive youth development: Theoretical and empirical bases. In R.M. Lerner (Ed.), White paper prepared for the Workshop on the Science of Adolescent Health and Development, National Research Council/Institute of Medicine. National Academies of Science. Loden Associates (2010). Primary and secondary sources of diversity. www.loden.com/Web_Stuff/Dimensions.html

McWhirter, E. H., Rojas-Aruauz, B., Ortega, R., et al. (2019). ALAS: An intervention to promote career development among Latina/o immigrant high school students. *Journal of Career Development, 46*(6), 608–622. https://doi.org/10.1177/0894845319828543

National Career Development Association. (2015). NCDA code of ethics. www.ncda.org/aws/NCDA/asset_manager/get_file/3395

National Career Development Association. (2020). Minimum competencies for multicultural career counseling and development. www.ncda.org/aws/NCDA/asset_manager/get_file/26627

Rice, K., Girvin, H., Frank, J. M., Corso, L. S. (2018). Utilizing expressive arts to explore educational goals among girls in Haiti. *Social Work with Groups*, *41*, 1–2, 111–124. https://doi.org/10.1080/01609513.2016.1258620

Sampson, J. P., McClain, M. C., Musch, E., & Reardon, R. C. (2013). Variables affecting readiness to benefit from career interventions. *The Career Development Quarterly*, *61*, 98–109.

Speciale, M. & Scholl, M. B. (2019). LGBTQ affirmative career counseling. *Career Planning and Adult Development Journal*, *35*(1), 22–35.

Sultana, R.G. (2017). Career guidance in multicultural societies: identity, alterity, epiphanies and pitfalls. *British Journal of Guidance & Counseling*, *45*(5), 451–462. https://doi.org/10.1080/03069885.2017.1348486

Tervalon, M. & Murray-García, J. (1998). Cultural humility versus cultural competence: A critical distinction in defining physician training outcomes in multicultural education. *Journal of Health Care for the Poor and Underserved*, *9*(2), 117–125.

Watts, R. J., Williams, N. C., & Jagers, R. J. (2003). Sociopolitical development. *American Journal of Community Psychology*, *31*(1–2), 185–194.

Zunker, V. (2016). *Career counseling: A holistic approach*. Cengage.

7 School-Based Career Counseling and Art Therapy

Conceptualizations of one's career begin in childhood, and are shaped through experiences one has via interactions with parents, teachers, school counselors, classes, clubs, and peers, all of which come together in a school-based setting. In this chapter, we discuss career development standards (including the career component of the ASCA model) in schools, and how these can be achieved in creative ways in K-12 schools.

Stage Theories

Developmental career theories were reviewed in Chapter 2 and are summarized in Table 7.1. While most developmental theorists would agree that the actual ages bookending each stage may have somewhat fuzzy boundaries, it is the unique characteristics and tasks associated with each stage that merit a counselor's focus. By understanding the general stage a person is in, the counselor can determine if they are on track, behind, or ahead of where they should be, and can provide interventions that are appropriate.

Two non-career theorists that provide a useful context for understanding and intervening in younger populations are Erikson and Piaget. Erikson (1950) identified eight stages

Table 7.1 Comparison of developmental career theories and their stages

	Child	Early–mid adolescence	Mid–late adolescence and young adulthood
Ginzberg	**Fantasy** (before age 11) – play oriented where one tries out different "jobs" and makes initial value judgments about work	**Tentative** (11–17) – a time of transition where youth learn of work requirements and begin to recognize their interests, skills, etc.	**Realistic** (17 and older) – interests integrate with skills and other personal characteristics, leading to exploration, crystallization to a career field, and specification where one commits to a job or training
Super	**Growth** (14 and younger) – the self-concept is developing, as are attitudes towards the world of work		**Exploration** (14–25) – learn about career options through trying them out in classes and jobs, resulting in development of skills and making a tentative choice
Gottfredson	**Ages 4–5** – oriented to size and power; concrete thought process **Ages 6–8** – oriented to sex roles with self-concept being influenced by gender stereotypes	**Ages 9–13** – oriented to social valuation, with greater self-awareness, more introspective thinking, and identification of aspirations	**Age 14 and older** – oriented to unique, internal self, self-in-situation, and awareness of prestige level, development of preferences

DOI: 10.4324/9781003035756-7

of psychosocial development, with five of them occurring during childhood and adolescence. Career elements can be seen in the desired virtue to be developed. The stages, ages, and desired outcome virtues include:

- trust versus mistrust (age 0 to 18 months) with a desired outcome virtue of hope
- autonomy versus shame and doubt (18 months–3 years), with a desired outcome virtue of will
- initiative versus guilt (3–5 years), with a desired outcome virtue of purpose
- industry versus inferiority (5–13 years), with a desired outcome virtue of competency
- identity versus confusion (13–21 years), with a desired outcome virtue of fidelity.

Piaget (1971) identified four stages of cognitive development, all of which occur during the K-12 ages. The stage, age range, and descriptions of tasks to be accomplished during each stage include:

- Sensorimotor (age 0 to 2 years), involves curiosity about the world, and coordination of motor responses with senses, with an outcome goal of object permanence.
- Preoperational (2–7 years), involves symbolic thinking, learning to speak and understand language, development of imagination, with an outcome goal of conservation (e.g., water volume will stay the same regardless of whether it is poured into a different-sized container).
- Concrete operational (7–11 years), involves attachment of concepts to concrete situations; logical thought can be used, but only applied to physical objects.
- Formal operations (11 and older), involves theoretical, applied thinking, abstract logic and reasoning, with a capability for strategic thinking and planning.

Seeing a K-12 person through the overlapping lenses of these theories will allow a counselor to understand how a career concern might fit with where the person is psychosocially, and also to make sure that the words and intervention a counselor uses are appropriate for the client's cognitive level. For example, asking a client to use metaphors to describe their career concern is appropriate for someone who has reached formal operations, but is not appropriate, and would likely be, at best, unfruitful and, at worst, frustrating and discouraging, for someone at an earlier cognitive level.

Career Development Goals in K-12 Settings

Our individual identities begin prior to birth, with each person's DNA being unique to themselves, and these identities are further shaped as we engage with the world around us. This "world" for most young children through adolescence is comprised mainly from interactions in a school environment. As such, professional associations such as the National Career Development Association (NCDA) and the American School Counselor Association (ASCA) have identified guidelines for helping children and adolescents progress in their career and vocational identity. While these guidelines and indicators are many, and very specific, reviewing them can provide an art therapist or career counselor with ideas on how to support school counselors in their charge to help students in their career development.

Career development is one of three domains that ASCA identifies as mindset and behavioral foci for school counselors to enhance in K-12 students. The career

Table 7.2 ASCA career development standards, guidelines, and sample indicators

Standard	Guideline 1	Sample indicators	Guideline 2	Sample indicators
Develop career decision-making skills based on integrated knowledge of the world of work and self	Develop career awareness	Become aware of personal characteristics like interests and skills	Develop employment readiness	Write a résumé
Identify career-related goals and strategies for achieving those goals	Acquire career Information	Use the Internet for career information	Identify career goals	Create and maintain a career-planning portfolio
Understand relationships among personal characteristics, education/training, and the world of work	Acquire knowledge to achieve career goals	Describe how work can affect lifestyle	Apply skills to achieve career goals	Work well in a team

development domain includes two standards: to help students a) with their understanding of how school and work are connected, and b) plan and eventually transition successfully from school to their next destination. Further, ASCA provides three national standards, each further defined by two specific guidelines, which are in turn defined by multiple objectives. The ASCA career development standards, guidelines, and indicators are provided in Table 7.2. Note that ASCA does not identify grades in which these standards and guidelines should be addressed. The full ASCA model can be purchased at schoolcounselor.org.

NCDA has also specified a developmental framework of domains, goals, and sample indicators (see Table 7.3). NCDA also divides indicators by learning stages into knowledge acquisition, application, and reflection (evaluation).

For example, one indicator addresses communication skills, and is divided into identifying effective communication skills (knowledge acquisition), demonstrating those skills (application), and evaluation their use of communication skills (reflection). The complete list of guidelines is available at www.ncda.org/aws/NCDA/asset_manager/get_file/3384?ver=16587.

Some common themes exist across these two frameworks, such as increasing building self- knowledge, increasing career awareness and career exploration, accessing and using career information, engaging in career decision-making, and creating, implementing, and evaluating a personal career plan. In the sections that follow, we'll explore career development programs and strategies for elementary, middle, and high school levels.

School Programming

In a school setting, a counselor might provide services through individual counseling, group counseling, classroom guidance or workshops, through clubs or organizations, or before-/after-school activities. In addition to these time-limited interventions, a counselor might want to create an overall career program that is implemented in a systematic way throughout the school year and across different grade levels. Developing career-related programs within a school setting requires the buy-in and support of administrators, teachers, parents, and students, in order for the program to be successful (Zunker, 2016). Issues discussed in the program design chapter (Chapter 14) are appropriate considerations for establishing a program in school settings.

Table 7.3 NCDA career development framework with sample indicators

Domain	Goal	Sample indicator
Personal social development	Develop understanding of yourself to build and maintain a positive self-concept.	Identify your interests, likes, and dislikes.
	Develop positive interpersonal skills including respect for diversity.	Identify effective communication skills.
	Integrate personal growth and change into your career development.	Demonstrate adaptability and flexibility when initiating or responding to change.
	Balance personal, leisure, community, learner, family, and work roles.	Show how you are balancing your life roles.
Educational achievement and lifelong learning	Attain educational achievement and performance levels needed to reach your personal and career goals.	Assess how well your attitudes and behaviors promote educational achievement and performance.
	Participate in ongoing, lifelong learning experiences to enhance your ability to function effectively in a diverse and changing economy.	Describe the requirements for transition from one learning level to the next (e.g., middle school to high school, high school to post-secondary).
Career management	Create and manage a career plan that meets your career goals.	Develop a career plan to meet your career goals.
	Use a process of decision-making as one component of career development.	Evaluate the effect of personal priorities, culture, beliefs, and work values in your decision-making.
	Use accurate, current, and unbiased career information during career planning and management.	Judge the quality of the career information resources you plan to use in terms of accuracy, bias, and how up-to-date and complete they are.
	Master academic, occupational, and general employability skills in order to obtain, create, maintain, and/or advance your employment.	Demonstrate the ability to use your academic, occupational, and general employability skills to obtain or create, maintain, and advance your employment.
	Integrate changing employment trends, societal needs, and economic conditions into your career plans.	Identify employment trends that affect your career plans.

Many career-focused activities can be adjusted for developmental level. Some examples include:

- career day/week/month with career-related activities, contests, special speakers
- career fairs where a number of local employers come to share with students
- education and training fairs
- career-related games such as career bingo, alphabet games (how many occupations can you list that begin with the letter "a"), or online games such as Kahoot!
- career fantasy days where everyone dresses up in career-related costumes
- guest speakers
- National Career Development Month and poster conference (ncda.org)
- career of the week (highlight diverse people in different careers)
- career-related field trips
- posting career guides and information online, in parent newsletters, etc.
- "windows" of career uniforms
- practice fairs, where students can practice interviewing, etiquette, résumé writing, communication skills
- highlight training opportunities

- challenge school clubs and organizations to link activities to building self- and options knowledge
- ask school media centers to organize displays of career-related information
- provide teachers with careers and career information related to their subject/topics.

In their book, *Expressive Arts Interventions for School Counselors*, Degges-White and Colon (2015) include additional activities such as vision boards, collages, and guided imagery activities that can be adjusted for the appropriate level. Career cards engage students in designing 3″ × 5″ cards that represent career options based on their preferred activities. Another activity involves asking students to identify heroes they admire or are inspired by from movies and collect information on that character, including a picture and general description of the character, how they identify with the character, how the character inspires them, and how the character influences their future career ideas. From that information, they create and present a poster.

Many states provide curriculum to enhance career knowledge and skills in students. These might be located online on department of education websites, or in career education links. For example, Florida's department of education includes a PDF guide for self-assessment as related to career, as well as a teacher's guide, and a link to the state's career information delivery system, which describes several lesson plans. In the next sections, we'll describe several examples of career programs specific to elementary, middle, and high school students.

Elementary Career Programs

Enterprise Village

This elementary program is a hands-on event hosted by the Stavros Institute (www. stavrosinstitute.org/enterprise-village) and features integration between economic education in the schools and hands-on roleplaying of jobs in an environment staged with local business names and stalls. Elementary students apply for and work in one of 20 different jobs in this staged employment area, such as mayor, journalist, and banker. They work on teams, set and work toward goals, receive a paycheck, and can spend that paycheck at one of the storefronts.

Journey in the World of Professions and Work

This 10-unit program (Ginevra & Nota, 2018) was created for children centered on Life Design principles (Savickas et al., 2009) and specifically targets two aspects of career adaptability, i.e., curiosity and career concern. For two hours weekly, a career counselor provides a combination of didactic and experiential activities. The module titles for career concern include: "Let's get to know each other to work together"; "Hurrah for school … for our future"; "Work changes … let's look for change and think about the future"; "Let's project ourselves into the future"; and "Nuggets of optimism and hope." The modules focused on curiosity are titled: "Let's think about work"; "Exploring professions beyond their labels"; "Let's continue to explore … probing jobs and workers"; "Diversity makes work more meaningful"; and "Work, family, community … hurrah for different relationships." Following the lesson, students completed a multiple-choice quiz on the content; students scoring less than an 8 were involved in additional meetings on that topic until they achieved the score. Compared to a control group, students (with a mean age of 10.65 years) who participated in the training scored higher on multiple outcomes, including hope, optimism, curiosity, career exploration, occupational knowledge, information, planning, and time perspective (Ginevra & Nota, 2018).

REACH Career and College Readiness Curriculum

Designed specifically for fourth graders, the goal for this program was to identify and relate knowledge about self with jobs and career paths, with an added goal of building positive self-efficacy beliefs about their readiness for work and or additional training (Allen et al., 2019). These goals were addressed in six 50-minute lessons delivered over eight weeks that included a check in question, brief presentation of information, an activity applying the information, and time for reflection. The names of the six lessons included: value sort, vision board, goal setting, reality check, career exploration, and college exploration. The program was delivered during regular class time as a course, as the state allotted school counselors time to schedule students for counseling-related lessons.

Other Elementary Activities

One creative approach for elementary students would be to create an online game, such as Kahoot! where students have to guess answers to career-related questions. Some of these might be "What is the number one employer in our city?" or show a picture of a job-related task and ask students to guess the occupational title, among other questions. Career charades is a fun way to expand career awareness. Students could be given common titles such as "firefighter" or "doctor," or more challenging ones such as "engineer" or "counselor." This could also be turned into a partnering or smaller group activity. Sometimes, elementary schools will hold career fairs, which could be an opportunity for a practitioner to stand at a table and share about career information. Figure 7.1 shows a picture of one author (Osborn) doing just that. To increase awareness of RIASEC-related

Figure 7.1 Osborn at Elementary Career Fair

occupations, she created a simple posterboard that described the six RIASEC types, and had students guess what occupation might be under the one most like them. This was accompanied with a very important reinforcer (candy on the table).

Elementary students also enjoy helping others, and if given a "case," will have many ideas. For example, they can be given descriptions of an individual's traits, such as "she likes helping people, and if someone is sad around her, she'll try to find ways to comfort them. What kind of job do you think she'd be good at?" A more physical activity might involve asking students to reach their arms up to the sky as high as they can, and to pretend they can touch their dreams. They can be suggested to hold their dreams in their hands, and then tap their chests as an indicator to put their dreams in their hearts. They can then be directed to create a "dream drawing," where they can illustrate what their dream is. Co-creating career cheers is yet another activity, where they can create individually or in partnerships or teams chants that encourage them to pursue their dreams. One example of an echo chant is, "I can be" (I can be), "anything I want to be", "there's nooooooo stopping me" (there's no stopping me).

Middle School Career Programs

CareerStart Program

Defined as a whole school engagement program, CareerStart (Orthner et al., 2010) aims to help middle school students (especially those at high risk for dropping out) develop a plan for their career future that will simultaneously impact school engagement, academic success and career exploration. To achieve this goal, career lessons are integrated into the standard core courses to address the age-old question of "When will I ever use this information?" by highlighting careers that do use that information as well as local labor market information on those specific careers. CareerStart seeks to integrate parent/guardian engagement through activities such as an interview with their student. Resources and suggestions are provided for other school staff, such as the school librarian, social workers, and counselors. The program also encourages engagement with local employers for career fairs and guest speaking.

#CHICAS Club

The #CHICAS club (Edirmanasinghe & Blanigan, 2019) was a middle school club for Latina students focused on building research skills, self-efficacy, as well as community building, sponsored by one of the school counselors. The students created the name of the club, which was an acronym of the following words: *Científicas* (scientists), *Héroes*, *Inteligentes* (intelligent), *Confidente* (confident), *Activistas* (activists), and *Soñadores* (dreamers). Together, they brainstormed how to increase school engagement by other Latina students, created a research project, and from their results, implemented school changes such as distributing school information in Spanish and English, and accommodating Hispanic Heritage Month celebrations. This program is an example of how a club can organize activities to purposely build skills, networks, and confidence.

RIASEC & CIP-Based After-School Career Group

Osborn and Reardon (2006) delivered a six-week after-school career program shaped on cognitive information processing theory (Sampson et al., 2020; Sampson et al., 2004) and utilizing Holland's (1997) RIASEC theory. The first and last sessions were saved for opening and closing respectively. The remaining 30-minute sessions focused on the four components identified by CIP as essential ingredients for career decision-making, that is, self-knowledge, options knowledge, decision-making, and metacognitions, with activities, such as the Self-Directed Search: Career Explorer (middle school version), to accompany each. Other activities included researching options and games to address decision-making and self-talk. Comments from students in the final session indicated gains in the four areas, and a preference for more time and an increased number of sessions.

Florida's Career and Education Planning Course

Florida currently requires all middle school students to complete a career and education course prior to being promoted to high school. In their educational toolkit, available at www.fldoe.org/academics/college-career-planning/educators-toolkit/, modules with lesson plans that outline the lesson objective, materials required, length of time needed, a detailed description of the activity, online resources, discussion questions, and evaluation criterion, are provided. Lessons are cross-walked with current standards. Current modules include: understanding the workplace, self-awareness, exploring careers, goal-setting/decision-making, workplace skills, career and education planning, and job search.

Mapping Vocational Challenges Career Development Program (MVC)

Turner and Lapan (2005) described the use of the MVC, a computer-assisted career program within the context of a group. The MVC (Lapan & Turner, 1997, 2000) consists of three main components: career exploration, career mapping, and career interpretation. The career mapping module requires students to rate 90 occupations for interest, perceived gender type, efficacy, parent support, and value (degree to which an occupation would be personally rewarding). In group, the counselor provides the maps, and focuses discussion on the intersection of their interests in relation to their perceived gender type of occupations to raise awareness of the influence of these perceptions. Students are encouraged to identify occupations of high interest but of different gender type, that is, non-traditional career options. Discussion of tasks and other specific information associated with occupations of interest is then facilitated. An evaluation (Turner & Lapan, 2005) of this group intervention found that males increased in Artistic, Social, and Conventional interests, while females increased in Realistic, Enterprising, and Conventional interests as a result of participation. Other gains were seen in efficacy for career exploration, career planning, and vocational development.

Project Hope for Health Science

Ali et al. (2017) modified an existing career intervention program to increase math/science achievement and career exploration in the health sciences for rural Latino middle school students. Based in social cognitive career theory (Lent, 2020), the sessions included: Session 1: introduction to health science career information via a Jeopardy-like game; Session 2: interest identification with RIASEC codes and linking to health science careers; Session 3: exploring the impact of culture and family, as well as barriers and supports for career success through career narratives and drawings; Session 4: exploring culture and community resources related to health science careers and information through a bingo game; Session 5: conducting mock interviews using health science students as the interviewer, focusing on connecting students' interests with health science positions; and Session 6: a field trip to a university that include hands-on and career exploration activities within health services programs. The program evaluation found that participation in the program resulted in math/science self-efficacy beliefs for both Latino and European American students, increases in health science career interests for Latino students, and increases in health science career self-efficacy for European American students.

High School Career Programs

¡Adelante!

Designed for 9th and 10th grade Latinx students, this program (Arriero & Griffin, 2019) utilized community asset mapping (i.e., pooling together formal and informal resources from those in the surrounding community) to increase students' knowledge and skills, promote their ethnic identity, increase their attendance at and graduation from school, and to increase their awareness of post-secondary options. To be included, students were required to meet weekly, and parents were required to attend two meetings each month, which were led in Spanish, and in which childcare, dinner, and raffle prizes were provided. Parents were also invited to attend English as a second language classes on the nights of the student sessions. Student sessions focused on identifying character traits, sharing about a Latinx role model who demonstrated a character trait, hearing from and talking with a guest speaker, and collaboratively working on a district-wide cultural event. The guest speakers were from Latinx backgrounds, and also shared at the parent meetings, about topics such as immigration and politics. Latinx college students from geographically close colleges and universities shared about their experiences and resources such as financial aid.

My Career Story Homeroom Activity

Cadaret and Hartung (2021) developed a three-week classroom intervention focused on career decision-making using the *My Career Story* workbook (Savickas & Hartung, 2012). This took place in five homeroom classes an urban high school comprised of mostly African American, Puerto Rican, and Dominican 11th grade students. In the first session, establishing a working alliance was the key goal, and once that occurred, the students went through four questions of the MCS which had them identify their role models, favorite magazines/television shows/websites, a current favorite book or movie, and their favorite saying or motto. Each question was presented to the large group first along with the discussion of an example along with clarifying questions from the group leader. Small groups were then formed, where the same format followed but with the goal of more individual participation.

During the second session, the focus was on the plot and theme of the favorite book or movie, and students were encouraged to explore these in greater detail, describing the self that was represented, identifying RIASEC interests, and exploring what scripts might be revealed by the favorite story. They then examined their favorite motto and explored how that might be advice to themselves in their current career decision. Following this discussion, the group leader helped them examine occupations via O*NET, concluding with a unified statement about their career narrative that they shared with their group members. The final session revolved around the theme "Enact My Story," where goal setting, identifying strategies and brainstorming possible ways to meet goals occurred and barriers/potential solutions were discussed. Supports for decision-making were identified, and the sessions concluded with reminders of goals and self-advice that came

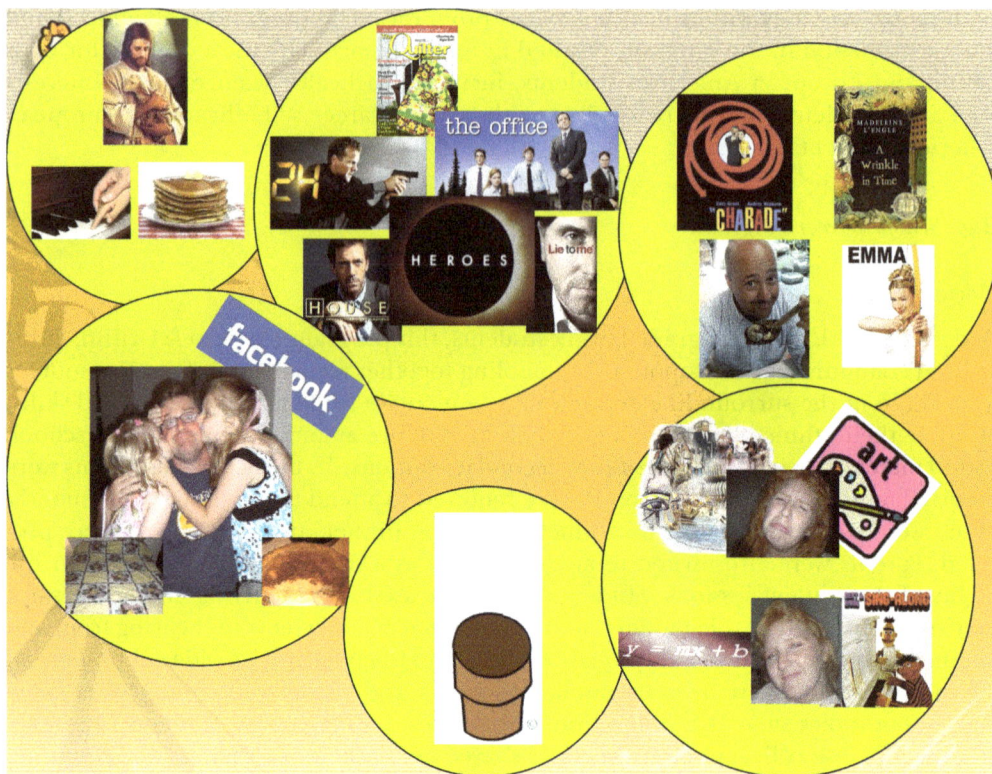

Figure 7.2 Visual representation of MCS responses

from the favorite motto. Pre–post tests revealed increases in vocational identity, as well as increases in control and confidence aspects of career adaptability.

A potential adaptation of this approach is to encourage students to use technology to demonstrate their answers to the MCS. Figure 7.2 shows an example of one student's visual representations to each of the questions.

My Future Is Mine

When a high school in China saw a need for career programming, they partnered with a research group who created a five-unit/five classes, lecture and activity balanced course. Unit 1, called "Development of My Career," used self-portraits and the idea of "running through the tunnel of time" to emphasize a positive attitude towards the present and the future, and the idea of career planning. Units 2–4 focused on exploring interests, personality, and abilities and relating these to major options. Unit 5 was entitled "My Choices of Humanities/Social Sciences or Sciences/Technology," and emphasized having a positive attitude and initiative, as well as the logistics of choosing a major. To study the impact of this course, Gu et al. (2020) implemented it three ways: an actual five-week course, infusing course content into whatever course the students were taking at that same period; or core teachers presenting the content through homeroom instruction. They also included a control group. Unfortunately, they didn't compare the efficacy of the different approaches, but combined them and found that the course significantly reduced students' reported career decision-making difficulties, and improved their self-appraisal and problem-solving as compared to the control groups.

Nontraditional Career Fair

This one-day fair presents a twist on the traditional career fair, in that 15 individuals employed in occupations that are under-represented by their gender presented and shared their experiences with the local high schools and the community, with a goal of expanding attendees' perceptions of career options. The fair was created from a collaborative partnership between the local Private Industry Council and the local community college and state university. Examples of females in non-traditional careers were border patrol officer, firefighter, and computer repair technician. The males in non-traditional careers included hair stylist, nurse, respiratory therapist, and receptionist. During lunch, an active-duty female pilot from the local United States Marine base spoke about pursuing a career regardless of perceived gender rules. In their evaluation, the researchers (Kolodinsky et al., 2006) found that attendees' confidence in performing duties of various occupations increased.

STEM-Focused Career Programs

Given the national interest and need for workers in STEM-related (science, technology, engineering, and mathematics) occupations, many colleges offer scholarships and other incentives for students pursuing majors in one of these areas. In turn, middle and high schools often create programs that focus on identifying and encouraging students to consider these paths. Having mentors and role models available at events such as career fairs for students is a powerful and important intervention, especially for females and under-represented students (Carlone & Johnson, 2007). Another recommendation is to connect STEM careers to values such as helping, to combat occupational stereotypes (Wang et al., 2013). Fouad (1995) created a six-week unit for eighth grade students that aimed to increase awareness of math and science careers, as well as self-esteem and greater numbers enrolling in math and science courses. She found moderate increases for each of those goals. Another study examined the effect of nine 50-minute group counseling sessions, comprised of didactic and experiential activities, focused on building STEM self-efficacy and general career decision-making self-efficacy. The first four sessions focused on career information specific to STEM careers, and the last four focused on self-efficacy sources, followed by a ninth wrap-up session. These researchers found that students in the STEM group had significant gains immediately following the group and three months after, compared to those who were in the control group.

Classroom-Based Career Activities

One opportunity practitioners might take advantage of in the schools is classroom guidance in actual classes, homerooms, or during lunch or after school.

Supporting Teachers in Providing Career Development

Practitioners might find opportunities to address career development via teacher contacts. Some possibilities include providing:

- a list of occupations associated with a specific subject (e.g., careers associated with criminology)
- opportunities such as the National Career Development Association's Poetry and Artwork contest

- weekly career development tips (how to learn more about career options, building skills, etc.)
- online game links the practitioner finds or prepares, such as Kahoot!, where students can compete on issues related to career development and job search
- in-person games and activities such as career bingo, career charades, crossword puzzles, or word find games.

In addition to these activities, a practitioner can talk with interested teachers about how what other resources or activities might be helpful or welcomed, such as co-developing and delivering a career lesson plan.

Example of an Impromptu In-Class Career Activity

At the end of class one day, a teacher found that there was about ten minutes remaining before the end of class, and decided to spend that time focusing on students' career development. The teacher looked through a list of "suggested career activities" that the art therapist had shared and landed on an alphabet challenge. There were two options: the first was where students listed as many occupations per letter as they could think of, and the second where students were limited to one letter. The teacher decided to go with the latter, focusing on the letter "A." To minimize chaos at the whiteboard, she decided to divide the students into small teams and have one person from each team write out their answers. She gave them the instructions that they had one minute to generate as many career titles as they could, without online help, that started with the letter A, and that there would be rewards (candy) for the group that came up with the most unique career, the most careers, and so on. She passed out sticky notes for them to write their responses on. At the end of one minute, the representatives came to the board and posted the results. Duplicates of the same title had to be stacked on top of each other. They then looked at the remaining list. She passed out candy as promised and then asked a few questions, such as, "What do you think of this list?" and "Do you think we got most of the 'A' job titles that are out there?" She then taped up a list of occupations from the online Occupational Outlook Handbook (www.bls.gov/ooh/a-z-index.htm#A) next to the sticky notes (see Figure 7.3), and said, "This is page 1 of about 15 pages' worth of job titles starting with the letter A. What do you think?" Students were surprised by how many they were. She asked, "Is it possible that you are limiting your options because you don't know what exists?" She finished the class by showing the link to the online Occupational Outlook Handbook and providing a QR code that she generated that went right to the page, and encouraged them to take some time to see what other options existed past what they currently were aware of.

At the beginning of the next class, she started by saying she wanted to follow up on the previous day's activity. She had all the students stand up, and said she would be describing one of the occupations from the "A-list." Students were to sit down when they heard something that did not fit with their interests, values, skills, or preferences. She did this until there she reached the end of her list or until there was only one person left standing. The descriptors included:

- makes over $100,000 a year
- works with computers
- must have analytical skills
- must have strong communication skills
- creates charts and tables

Student Ideas

Online OOH "A" Occupations - 1st page

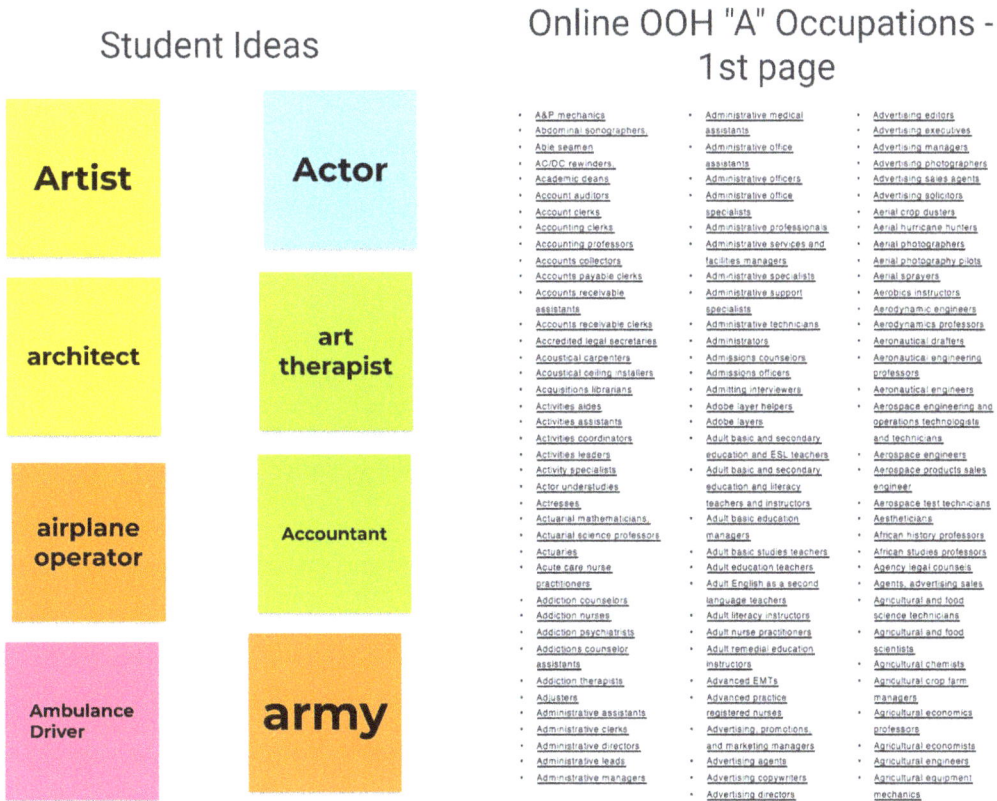

Artist	Actor
architect	art therapist
airplane operator	Accountant
Ambulance Driver	army

- A&P mechanics
- Abdominal sonographers,
- Able seamen
- AC/DC rewinders,
- Academic deans
- Account auditors
- Account clerks
- Accounting clerks
- Accounting professors
- Accounts collectors
- Accounts payable clerks
- Accounts receivable assistants
- Accounts receivable clerks
- Accredited legal secretaries
- Acoustical carpenters
- Acoustical ceiling installers
- Acquisitions librarians
- Activities aides
- Activities assistants
- Activities coordinators
- Activities leaders
- Activity specialists
- Actor understudies
- Actresses
- Actuarial mathematicians,
- Actuarial science professors
- Actuaries
- Acute care nurse practitioners
- Addiction counselors
- Addiction nurses
- Addiction psychiatrists
- Addictions counselor assistants
- Addiction therapists
- Adjusters
- Administrative assistants
- Administrative clerks
- Administrative directors
- Administrative leads
- Administrative managers

- Administrative medical assistants
- Administrative office assistants
- Administrative officers
- Administrative office specialists
- Administrative professionals
- Administrative services and facilities managers
- Administrative specialists
- Administrative support specialists
- Administrative technicians
- Administrators
- Admissions counselors
- Admissions officers
- Admitting interviewers
- Adobe layer helpers
- Adobe layers
- Adult basic and secondary education and ESL teachers
- Adult basic and secondary education and literacy teachers and instructors
- Adult basic education managers
- Adult basic studies teachers
- Adult education teachers
- Adult English as a second language teachers
- Adult literacy instructors
- Adult nurse practitioners
- Adult remedial education instructors
- Advanced EMTs
- Advanced practice registered nurses
- Advertising, promotions, and marketing managers
- Advertising agents
- Advertising copywriters
- Advertising directors

- Advertising editors
- Advertising executives
- Advertising managers
- Advertising photographers
- Advertising sales agents
- Advertising solicitors
- Aerial crop dusters
- Aerial hurricane hunters
- Aerial photographers
- Aerial photography pilots
- Aerial sprayers
- Aerobics instructors
- Aerodynamic engineers
- Aerodynamics professors
- Aeronautical drafters
- Aeronautical engineering professors
- Aeronautical engineers
- Aerospace engineering and operations technologists and technicians
- Aerospace engineers
- Aerospace products sales engineer
- Aerospace test technicians
- Aestheticians
- African history professors
- African studies professors
- Agency legal counsels
- Agents, advertising sales
- Agricultural and food science technicians
- Agricultural and food scientists
- Agricultural chemists
- Agricultural crop farm managers
- Agricultural economics professors
- Agricultural economists
- Agricultural engineers
- Agricultural equipment mechanics

Figure 7.3 Sample In-Class Whiteboard Activity

- must have a bachelor's degree
- typically work in teams
- typically work 40 hours a week
- uses math and statistics
- most work for insurance companies.

At the end of the activity, she asked students to guess what the position was. She then projected the information on the screen and asked students to share why they sat down when they did. She ended the activity by reinforcing the main idea that in order to narrow down that 15-page list of "A" occupations, they needed to know enough about themselves and the options they were considering. She showed the students the O*NET (www.onetonline.org) and Occupational Outlook Handbook (www.bls.gov/ooh/) sites, along with QR codes to get to them quickly, and how they could search the databases quickly to see options that matched different criteria. She ended by flashing a picture of the school counselors and art therapist who could work with students on an individual basis to help with their career plans.

Art Therapy and School-Based Services

The practice of art therapy has been incorporated into school services for over 50 years in many locations around the world (Moula et al., 2020). For example, in 2013, 12.5% of surveyed American Art Therapy Association members noted they worked in school settings (Elkins & Deaver, 2015). More dramatically, Karkou (2010) noted that 60% of United Kingdom's registered art therapists reported working with children in schools, and Israeli art therapists have reported that art therapy services are considered vital to their school-based mental health teams (Regev et al., 2015). While art therapy services are not available in all schools, art therapists do provide individual and group art therapy services in elementary, middle school, and high school, and alternative educational settings. Deboys et al. (2017) found that children and their parents valued receiving art therapy services in school, as they considered school a safe environment to address concerns.

School-Based Art Therapy Purposes and Processes

Art therapy services are differentiated from art education services in that art therapy promotes non-verbal communication to address students' social and emotional needs as opposed to the instructive aims of art education (Gonzalez-Dolginko, 2018). Hannigan, Grima-Farrell, and Wardman (2019) asserted that the inclusion of creative art therapy approaches in school settings provide opportunities to maximize students' capabilities as individuals and community members and allowed for the appreciation of students' unique ways of learning. Thus far, humanistic child-centered theoretical approaches to school-based art therapy services have proved most effective (Moula et al., 2020). Children have reported liking the active nature of artmaking within art therapy and have found it easier to express and explore their feelings or concerns through imagery (Deboys et al., 2017).

According to Moula et al. (2020), the main purposes of art therapists' efforts in school systems have centered on supporting children's self-esteem, self-confidence, self-expression, improved mood, communication skills, resilience, and reduction of behaviors that may interfere with learning. Additionally, art therapists have facilitated interventions that reduce mental health symptoms related to depression, anxiety, and attention concerns. Isis et al. (2010) noted art therapists creatively addressed students' test anxiety and supported the retention of students who may have otherwise discontinued their schooling. In Deboys et al.'s (2017) small qualitative study, interviewed children, parents, and teachers agreed that the children made gains in targeted treatment areas in response to art therapy interventions, particularly when aims for treatment were clearly communicated to all involved.

To establish further confidence in school-based art therapy services and to support opportunities for students, Ramirez, Haen, and Cruz (2020) conducted a study of school-based art therapy groups for high school students of color from a low-income neighborhood that performed at various levels of academic achievement. Participants were provided a 12-week structured group program where they addressed themes supporting self-exploration and mastery via a variety of art media and tasks such as collage, clay work, self-portraits, and landscapes. Compared to a control group of equivalent high school students, participating students demonstrated significantly reduced inattention and hyperactivity and improved personal adjustment, self-esteem, and self-expression. Findings were established through analysis of Behavior Assessment System for Children, Second Edition (BASC-2) scores which were collected before and after the 12-week program. Based on these findings, Ramirez, Haen, and Cruz (2020) posited:

> Considering the overlaps between mental health and academic success, art therapy has the potential to enhance the learning environment by increasing emotional language and expression, as well as fostering students' capacity for academic inquiry and evaluation.

(p. 6)

These promising findings suggest that art-based methods may also be effective in supporting exploration and achievement of foundational career development goals and objectives. An art therapy-informed approach may be particularly effective at fostering self-knowledge and interpersonal skills important for career decision-making.

Links between expressive arts, group work with children and adolescents, support of socio-emotional development and career counseling have been formed. Citing the particular developmental considerations of children and teens preferences for non-verbal communications and preadolescents' vacillation between abstract and concrete thinking, Lindo and Ceballos (2020) advocated for the use of creative approaches to foster middle students' essential cognitive and socio-emotional career readiness. To that end, they created and implemented a career intervention protocol called the Child Adolescent Career Construction Interview (CACCI). This guide was adapted from the Career Construction Interview (CCI: Savickas, 2015) which elicits career and life design narratives and adds arts-based components to support students in exploring self-concept and meaningful life themes that may influence career readiness and career exploration. Lindo and Ceballos suggested that the program could be implemented in school counseling or mental health settings.

Lindo and Ceballos' eight-week protocol consisted of seven group sessions and one final individual session with each student. These sessions included an introductory group where clients used sand tray miniature toys to represent and describe themselves to others; sessions focused on drawn or created responses to questions about favorite TV characters, social media site, or magazines utilized to explore interests, a favorite story to explore themes of problem-solving; advice to themselves to promote trust in their power to problem-solve, identification and creative depiction of heroes to explore self-concept, and depiction of early recollections to explore client contexts and behaviors. Counselors and students returned to sand tray processes for the final group session where participants were asked to represent their group experience and address termination with other group members. During the final individual session with the counselor, student and counselor reviewed a summary of students' statements and created expressions. This final review session was designed to consolidate the learning and to foster dialogues that helped students apply gained self-awareness to academic and career development goals.

Lindo and Ceballos reported positive outcomes for group participants. However, more research will be needed to further demonstrate the protocol's effectiveness in supporting youth and career aims. Additionally, Lindo and Ceballos suggested that additional career interventions such as the administration of career interest assessments could stimulate further dialogues and maximize gains received from the expressive arts group.

Art-Based Interventions for School-Based Career Development

As noted in the first half of this chapter, K-12 career development programs often employ active means to support career exploration and learning. To demonstrate how art therapy processes may be utilized as an active means to supporting students of various ages and stages in their career development, some art-based options will be explored in more detail. As in all art therapy contexts, practices must be bracketed by the therapist's skill at cultivating relational engagement and attunement to cultural, contextual, and developmental needs of the specific group.

Elementary School

In concert with the aims of *Journey in the World of Professions and Work* program created by Ginevra and Nota (2018), the following activity is described. This activity includes a book

Figure 7.4 Fantastical Career Example: Silly Hat Stacker. Copyright Wilson Bell, 2022.

reading, artmaking, and group discussion and focuses on the goal of promoting career curiosity and concern. While a variety of children's books provide kid-friendly explorations of career options, one of my favorite books on this topic is *When I Grow Up*, written by Al Yankovic and illustrated by Wes Hargis (2011). This book is particularly well suited to fostering career curiosity and imagination about career options. The main character in the book creates fantastical not-yet-existing career options and enthusiastically describes his grandfather's varied career interests and engagement, normalizing career changes over a lifespan. This book was designed for children 4–8 and is also available in an audiobook format. Following a book reading or listening time, children would be asked to create at least one fantastical career option using drawing and painting materials suitable for the age group. Figure 7.4 shows one created example. Artworks would then be reviewed and students' creative career options and stories would be welcomed and celebrated. The facilitator could then encourage students to reflect on the many work roles they have seen in day-to-day life, expanding student exposure through group discussions.

Middle and High School

The following process is appropriate for middle and high school students and addresses the ASCA Career Development Standard regarding promoting understanding of relationships among personal characteristics, education/training and the world of work. Hermann and Hasha's (2015) Career Haiku activity is designed to increase students' exploration of talents and interests and to support development of long-term career goals. In the sequence described by Hermann and Hasha, students are invited to reflect on their interests, strengths, skills, and career ideas and then discuss these ideas within small groups. Students are then introduced to the history and practice of haiku poetry, a Japanese form of poetry that consists of a total of 17 syllables, 5 syllables in the first line, 7 syllables in the second line, and 5 syllables in the final line. This poem structure allows for meaning to be captured in powerful short statements. After review of haiku examples, students are asked

Figure 7.5 Studio 2020.

> Clay work is for me
> Hands and heart need to feel mud
> Dirt into function. (S. W.)

to create haiku poems about a career interest which was generated by their reflections. Poems' foci can be further defined to focus on identifying the career, describing why they are interested in that career, and their overall goal or what skills they need to reach the career goals. Finally, completed haikus are read and discussed in the small groups.

Hermann and Hasha noted that artmaking could be substituted for the haiku poetry in cases where such structures may be too cumbersome or not well-suited to the client population's learning strengths and challenges. Still another way to support creative exploration of career concerns is to combine art and poetry processes. In this combined process option, students are encouraged to begin the career exploration by capturing digital photographs of hobbies, interests, places, or things that represent their skills or strengths. After reviewing these images in small groups and learning about the haiku poetry process, the students use the stimulus of a selected photograph to write their poem about the career interest. Figures 7.5 and 7.6 provide sample photographs and poems regarding two of many possible career interests.

These photographs and haiku examples demonstrate how creative explorations stimulate processes of investigation and further thinking about career interests. The photograph of the clay wheel and the accompanying haiku reflect the valuing of physical engagement with materials and harnessing creativity to make functional items for others. The photograph of the pipes and the related haiku reflect an interest in mechanical process and service to others. Snapshots capture ideas and record interests for consideration and can be used to prompt next stages of investigation regarding occupational characteristics and training requirements. The creation of haikus supports reflection and the encapsulation of feelings and associations with career options. Haikus may also reveal important themes to be further explored as students work to solidify career interests and values.

Figure 7.6 Pipe: A Career in Plumbing.

> Splash, a pipe has burst
> In a panic, they call me
> I fix it quickly.

Summary

Career development goals have been proposed by various theorists and professional associations. Most high schools have as a goal for their graduates to transition to being productive, satisfied citizens. The experiences leading up to that point serve as the springboard for that to happen. Many avenues exist to achieve the general career goals of helping students learn more about themselves, the world of work, decision-making skills, and self-efficacy. Program design, implementation and evaluation within the context of a school system will be most effective if it is integrated into existing programs and engages the entire system (i.e., teachers, parents, students, school staff, community members, local businesses). More recently, art therapists and creative career counselors have joined the teams of professionals working to support students' self-awareness and career development. Creative methods, well-suited to youth, are providing new avenues for students to reflect on these important developmental tasks.

Discussion Questions and Activities

1 Considering developmental level and career goals, design a career curriculum for either elementary, middle, or high school students.
2 Contact the guidance department at local elementary, middle, and high schools and/ or visit their websites to see the type of career programs they offer their students. What's there? What's missing? What could be enhanced? Are elements of integrating expressive arts evident?
3 Interview someone you know that falls within the pre-K-12th grade. Ask about their career goals, interests, and perceived skills.

```
A B I H U W M K G T A H P J K
I S P N I J R N B E R C Y O N
Z G Q E Z O I S T C T R H S O
R Z D Y W K A H X H I A A J I
F M O M A D I D J N S E Z G T
S B A E E N W U E O T S T G A
O E P T K F W X S L I E W Q Z
T S Y I H M E U X O C R K K I
C X N W R I T I N G K B Q Z N
Z G B Z U T K M I Y T D V Z A
G N I V L O S M E L B O R P G
P I H S R E D A E L P B D O R
X M X V R U F S N X E C P P O
L I S T E N I N G T W R J B P
H H R W R C K I Q U F M Q P H
```

Figure 7.7 Word Search Puzzle, Created with Discovery Education Puzzlemaker https://puzzle-maker.discoveryeducation.com/word-search/result

4   Complete the word-search puzzle for career-related skills in Figure 7.7. Words include artistic, math, research, technology, leadership, organization, speaking, thinking, listening, problem-solving, teamwork, writing. Do you think this is a helpful way to teach students about career skills? How might you vary this activity for developmental level or topic?

5   Consider the different career options you explored throughout your childhood and adolescence. What helped you gravitate towards certain fields and away from others? What implications might you apply to developing a career-related curriculum for different milestones?

6   If you are an art therapist working in a school setting, explore opportunities to collaborate with school counselors or teachers responsible for career development curriculum. What does the current career development program at your school look like? How might you creatively engage with the program or individual students to help build the socio-emotional and cognitive skills that promote career readiness?

References

Ali, S. R., Brown, S. D., & Loh, Y. (2017). Project HOPE: Evaluation of health science career education programming for rural Latino and European American youth. *Career Development Quarterly*, *65*(1), 57–71. https://doi.org/10.1002/cdq.12080

Allen, A. H., Jones, G. D., Baker, S. B., & Martinez, R. R. (2019). Effect of a curriculum unit to enhance career and college readiness self-efficacy of fourth grade students. *Professional School Counseling*, *23*(1), 1–9. https: 10.1177/2156759X19886815

Arriero, E., & Griffin, D. (2019). ¡Adelante! A community asset mapping approach to increase college and career readiness for rural Latinx high school students. *Professional School Counseling, 22*(1), 1–9. https://doi.org/10.1177/2156759X18800279

Cadaret, M. C., & Hartung, P. J. (2021). Efficacy of a group career construction intervention with urban youth of colour. *British Journal of Guidance & Counselling, 49*(2), 187–199. https://doi.org/10.1080/03069885.2020.1782347

Carlone, H. B., & Johnson, A. (2007). Understanding the science experiences of successful women of color: Science identity as an analytic lens. *Journal of Research in Science Teaching, 44*, 1187–1218.

Deboys, R., Holttum, S., and Wright, K. (2017). Processes of change in school-based art therapy with children: A systematic qualitative study. *International Journal of Art Therapy, 22*(3), 118–131. https://doi.org/10.1080/17454832.2016.1262882

Degges-White, S., & Colon, B. R. (Eds.) (2015). *Expressive arts interventions for school counselors.* Springer.

Edirmanasinghe, N., & Blanigan, K. (2019). Demystifying the research process: A career intervention with Latinas. *Professional School Counseling, 22*(1b), 1–6. https://doi.org/10.1177/2156759X19834433

Elkins, D. E., & Deaver, S. P. (2015). American Art Therapy Association, Inc.: 2013 membership survey report. *Art Therapy: Journal of the American Art Therapy Association, 32*(2), 60–69. https://doi.org/10.1080/07421656.2015.1028313

Erikson, E. H. (1950). *Childhood and society.* Norton.

Fouad, N. A. (1995). Career linking: An intervention to promote math/science career awareness. *Journal of Counseling and Development, 73*(5), 527–534.

Ginevra, M. C., & Nota, L. (2018). 'Journey in the world of professions and work': A career intervention for children. *The Journal of Positive Psychology, 13*(5), 460–470. https://doi.org/10.1080/17439760.2017.1303532

Gonzalez-Dolginko, B. (2018). Status report on art therapists in public schools: Employment and legislative realities. *Art therapy: Journal of the American Art Therapy Association, 35*(1), 19–24. https://doi.org/10.1080/07421656.2018.1459116

Gu, X., Tang, M., Chen, S., & Montgomery, M. L. T. (2020). Effects of a career course on Chinese high school students' career decision-making readiness. *Career Development Quarterly, 68*(3), 222–237. https://doi.org/10.1002/cdq.12233

Hannigan, S., Grima-Farrell, C., Wardman, N. (2019). Drawing on creative arts therapy approaches to enhance inclusive school cultures and student wellbeing. *Issues in Educational Research, 29*(3), 756–773.

Hermann, K. M., & Hasha, L.R. (2015). Career story haiku. In S. Degges-White & B. Colon (Eds.), *Expressive arts interventions for school counselors* (pp. 227–229). Springer.

Holland, J. L. (1997). *Making vocational choices: A theory of vocational personalities and work environments.* PAR.

Isis, P. D, Bush, J., Siegel, C. A., & Ventura, Y. (2010). Empowering students through creativity: Art therapy in Miami-Dade County public schools. *Art Therapy: Journal of the American Art Therapy Association, 27*(2), 56–61.

Karkou, V. (2010). *Arts therapies in schools: Research and practice.* Jessica Kingsley.

Kolodinsky, P., Schroder, V., Montopoli, G., et al. (2006). The career fair as a vehicle for enhancing occupational self-efficacy. *Professional School Counseling, 10*(2), 161–167. https://doi.org/10.5330/prsc.10.2.cp27m53023041k64

Lapan, R.T., & Turner, S. (1997, 2000). *Mapping Vocational Challenges Career Development Program.* All Rights Reserved.

Lent, R. W. (2020). Career development and counseling: A social cognitive framework. In S. D. Brown, & R. W. Lent (Eds.), *Career development and counseling: Putting theories and research to work* (pp. 129–164). Wiley & Sons.

Lindo, N. A., & Ceballos, P. (2020). Child and adolescent career construction: An expressive arts group intervention. *Journal of Creativity in Mental Health, 15*(3), 364–377. https://doi.org/10.1080/15401383.2019.1685923

Moula, Z., Aithal, S., Karkou, V., & Powell, J. (2020). A systematic review of child-focused outcomes and assessments of arts therapies delivered in primary mainstream schools. *Children and Youth Services Review, 112*, 104928. https://doi.org/10.1016/j.childyouth.2020.104928

Orthner, D. K., Akos, P., Rose, R., et al. (2010). CareerStart: A middle school student engagement and academic achievement program. *Children & Schools, 32*(4), 223–234. https://doi.org/10.1093/cs/32.4.223

Osborn, D. S., & Reardon, R. C. (2006). Using the Self-Directed Search: Career Explorer with high-risk middle school students. *The Career Development Quarterly, 54*, 269–274.

Piaget, J. (1971). The theory of stages in cognitive development. In D. R. Green, M. P. Ford, & G. B. Flamer (Eds.), *Measurement and Piaget* (pp. 1–11). McGraw-Hill.

Ramirez, K., Haen, C., & Cruz, R. F. (2020). Investigating impact: The effects of school-based art therapy on adolescent boys living in poverty. *The Arts in Psychotherapy, 71*, 1–6. https://doi.org/10.1016/j.aip.2020.101710

Regev, D., Green-Orlovich, A., Snir, S. (2015). Art therapy in schools: The therapist's perspective. *The Arts in Psychotherapy, 45*, 47–55. https://doi.org/10.1016/j.aip.2015.07.004

Sampson, J. P., Osborn, D. S., Bullock-Yowell, E., et al. (2020). *An introduction to CIP theory, research, and practice* (Technical Report No. 62). Florida State University, Center for the Study of Technology in Counseling and Career Development. Retrieved from http://fsu.digital.flvc.org/islandora/object/fsu%3A749259

Sampson, J. P., Jr., Reardon, R. C., Peterson, G. W., & Lenz, J. G. (2004). *Career counseling and services: A cognitive information processing approach*. Brooks/Cole.

Savickas, M. L. (2015). *Life design counseling manual*. Retrieved from www.Vocopher.com

Savickas, M. L., & Hartung, P. J. (2012). My Career Story: An autobiographical workbook for life-career success. www.vocopher.com.

Savickas, M. L., Nota, L., Rossier, J., et al. (2009). Life designing: A paradigm for career construction in the 21st century. *Journal of Vocational Behavior, 75*, 239–250. doi:10.1016/j.jvb.2009.04.004

Turner, S. L., & Lapan, R. T. (2005). Evaluation of an intervention to increase non-traditional career interests and career self-efficacy among middle-school adolescents. *Journal of Vocational Behavior, 66*(3), 516–531. https://doi.org/10.1016/j.jvb.2004.02.005

Wang, M. T., Eccles, J. S., & Kenny, S. (2013). Not lack of ability but more choice individual and gender differences in choice of careers in science, technology, engineering, and mathematics. *Psychological Science, 24*, 770–775.

Yankovic, A., & Hargis, W. (2011). *When I grow up*. Harper.

Zunker, V. (2016). *Career counseling: A holistic approach*. Cengage.

8   Positive Psychology in Career Development and Art Therapy
Emphasizing Strengths

In this chapter, career concerns will be addressed through positive psychology and positive art therapy lenses. Highlighted concepts will include benefits of generating hope, identifying strengths and resources, and cultivating meaning and purpose in the occupational realm. Additionally, examples of career development strategies and art-based interventions will be described. Positive psychology, art therapy, and career counseling concepts and tactics will be applied to various career stages such as early career preparation; transition from school to the world of work; transforming mid-career workplace challenges; and late career challenges and transitions including retirement. Examining and applying identified strengths will be a primary emphasis.

Positive Psychology

In recent years, positive psychology concepts originated by Seligman and Csikszentmihalyi (2000) have grown in popularity and inform many helping professions' orientation to improving client well-being and functioning in various life realms including career domains (Panc, 2015). Seligman and Csikszentmihalyi described positive psychology as the study and cultivation of human flourishing and personal fulfillment in contrast to disease-oriented models of psychology which have focused on pathology, repair, and amelioration of distress. Efforts in positive psychology practice aim to stimulate change through fostering positive subjective experiences and attending to positive traits, strengths, and virtues. Positive traits enumerated by Seligman and Csikszentmihalyi include personal courage, perseverance, originality, aesthetic sensibility, and wisdom, among others, notably "capacity for love and vocation" (Seligman & Csikszentmihalyi, 2000, p. 5). Additionally, identified virtues such as responsibility, altruism, civility, and work ethic are relevant to success in many educational, work, and community contexts.

Positive Psychology and Career Development

Panc (2015) summarized the underpinnings of positive psychology as relating to hedonism and eudaimonic philosophical traditions which emphasize boosting pleasure and reducing pain or expanding happiness through actualization of one's true and best self, respectively. More specifically, Panc noted that hedonism-oriented interventions centered on cultivating good feelings while eudaimonic interventions emphasized taking action and functioning well. To test and implement positive psychology tenets, researchers and practitioners have implemented a variety of positive psychology interventions (Panc, 2015). Themes of these interventions have included conceptualizing one's best self, expressing optimism and gratitude, cultivating positive thoughts, identifying strengths, and projecting positive outcomes for oneself in the future.

DOI: 10.4324/9781003035756-8

Panc outlined study results that suggested individuals with greater experiences of good feelings, or positive affect, took more action to achieve goals. Those who endorsed experiencing more positive feelings were more likely to engage in new experiences and interacted more with others. Additionally, people who experienced higher levels of happiness expressed greater satisfaction with their work, reported more positive relationships with supervisors and colleagues, had better success at finding new work after a period of unemployment, and generated more income throughout their careers. Based on these research conclusions, Panc advocated for incorporating positive psychology interventions into career development programs to maximize individuals' potential for achieving optimal career outcomes.

Dik et al. (2015) also posited that career counseling strategies align well with positive psychology concepts and interventions, due to their mutual appreciation of the importance of cultivating meaning and purpose in work. Dik et al. maintained that all career development theories explored the topic of meaning in some manner and that a numerous range of career development applications are designed to generate purposeful and meaningful work engagement. According to Dik et al., positive psychology-informed career applications addressed perceiving and living a calling; cultivating positive emotions; gratitude; work hope, the experience of positive work goals and the agency to achieve them; as well as flow, where people are positively focused and engaged in goal-directed effort. Additionally, positive psychology-compatible career interventions may entail highlighting strengths that can be applied in work settings and job crafting, which encourages individuals to purposefully adjust their thoughts or actions regarding work engagement to improve work satisfaction.

Peterson et al. (2017) described a model of vocational meaning in work, with four levels. Each builds upon each other, starting with survival (consisting of basic needs such as food and shelter), egocentrism (which consists of self-enhancement needs such as promotion and privileges), group welfare (which consists of team enhancement needs such as contributing to a group, or helping the group reach its goals), and universalism (such as transcendence needs such as seeing work as a calling from God or reaching fulfillment in life). They suggest that, after assessing which of these sources for meaning are most important to a client, a practitioner would then assess the degree to which the person's current employment is meeting those needs. When there is a discrepancy, practitioners should discuss how to close the discrepancy. For example, if team enhancement is identified as a key way in which a person achieves meaning at work, and they assess their current work as not providing many opportunities for team enhancement, the conversation might center on whether the person can meet that need through other avenues, such as leisure or volunteer activities, or if they could negotiate to work on projects or redesign their work responsibilities to allow them to fulfill that need. Another alternative would be to consider leaving the position for a job that would fulfill that need.

In addition to meaning and purpose in work, several other career counseling concepts and interventions can be approached from a positive psychology perspective. Strengths are one aspect of self-knowledge that will be addressed later in this chapter. Another important area includes the role of psychology constructs in enhancing career adaptability. Buyukgoze-Kavas (2016) found that hope, resilience, and optimism significantly predicted career adaptability for 415 undergraduate students in Turkey. Buyukgoze-Kavas stated that all of these constructs are important psychological resources for individuals in their career decision-making. Hirschi (2014) found positive relationships between hope and career planning, career decidedness, and career self-efficacy.

Other overlaps between career and positive psychology include self-talk and career thoughts. In addition, career counseling has become more affirming of the connection between career and mental health (Marks et al., 2021). For example, research has found that negative career thoughts and depression predicted poorer meaning in life (Buzzetta et al., 2020), and negative career thoughts were also associated with poorer coping strategies (Bullock-Yowell et al., 2015). Higher levels of personal well-being, a component of positive psychology, predict lower levels of negative thoughts surrounding career commitment anxiety, and moderately predict vocational identity (Strauser et al., 2008). Helping individuals to honestly see themselves and their options and to have confidence in their future are interventions career practitioners should be employing on a regular basis with their clients.

Positive Art Therapy

Art therapists Wilkinson and Chilton (2013) asserted that art therapy principles and strategies can be well-aligned with positive psychology frameworks, as creative processes utilized in art therapy cultivate exploration of meaning through metaphoric content; shift energy and achievement of flow through the balancing of skill and challenge in art engagement; and foster positive experience and mood. They noted that offering art prompts that include a positive focus increased positive moods to a greater extent than art prompts that invite clients to express experiences of stressful situations. Still, they explained that positive art therapy approaches are not aimed at glossing over negative experiences but are designed to provide opportunities for people to access strengths and resources or states of being that can support navigation through concerns and promote flourishing. Wilkinson and Chilton highlighted several creative interventions utilized to cultivate meaning, sense of purpose, or positive affect in various conditions. For example, with a group of cancer survivors, Wilkinson and Chilton invited survivors to honor their resilience, an ability to thrive following challenge, through recalling what brought them hope during difficult times and asked them to assemble found object sculptures that reflected their experiences. During and following the completion of artworks, cancer survivors were able to uncover meaningful and positive aspects of their experiences and evidence of their strengths.

Darewych and Bowers (2017) advocated for positive psychology-informed art therapy interventions and highlighted the role that art processes can play in cultivating imagination. They discussed the relationship between mental imaging, drawing, and the ability of humans to conceptualize things that are not currently present. They noted that this capacity can be utilized to revisit experiences or memories in symbolic visual forms and provide opportunities for people to attribute new meanings to these events. In this regard, Darewych and Bowers outlined simple art processes that encouraged imagination such as the scribble drawing originated by early American art educator and art therapist, Florence Cane. Using Cane's (1983) approach, a person is invited to spontaneously scribble on paper, review the result, and identify a symbol or object they had perceived or could be created from the scribble. Next, the artist amplifies their associations through embellishing the scribble drawing and marks. When meanings are ascertained, these can be explored within the therapeutic and further transformation and positive action may be stimulated.

Some preliminary research demonstrates support for these assertions. Pictet et al. (2011) demonstrated that generating mental imagery can influence emotional responses. In their study, the researchers sought to confirm or refute that imagination could be engaged to promote positive mood. Using picture and word cues, the researchers exposed adults experiencing dysphoric moods at a mildly depressed level to digital pictures of common objects and regional locations paired with words that suggested positive/negative emotional outcomes or neutral conditions. After seeing the image and words, the researchers prompted participants to utilize mental imagery to "imagine the combination of the next picture and word as if you were actively involved" and were then asked to rate the vividness of the image they experienced (Pictet et al., 2011, p. 888). Following image and word exposure and mental imagery practice, participants were invited to engage in a behavioral fishing game task. Researchers found that participants who were exposed to and generated positive mental imagery performed significantly better on the task compared to those in neutral or negative image and word conditions. Based on their findings, they suggested that generating positive imagery from picture and word cues can stimulate increased positive affect and performance for those experiencing dysphoria.

Counselors have also used art-based methods to support clients' positive visualization and goal attainment. Burton and Lent (2016) asserted that creative arts processes and non-verbal explorations helped increase client awareness of personal resources and supported visualization of goals. Burton and Lent aligned their theoretical orientation to solution-focused behavior therapy, but this approach shares common factors with positive psychology, as it focuses on generating desired future experiences instead of focusing on problems or distress. To assist clients with identifying goals and visualizing their future, Burton and Lent engaged their client in creating vision boards. Vision boards may be created with a variety of digital arts frameworks and traditional art surfaces such as canvas, paper, bulletin boards to be embellished by digital images, magazine images and words, drawing materials, and other accessible materials. To start, clients were invited to consider their values and how these values informed their life and work aims. Next, Burton and Lent encouraged clients to write down a few goals to focus on before engaging in the creative process. Following the client's completion of the vision board, time was dedicated to exploring clients' visually expressed aims. Burton and Lent asserted that vision board engagement effectively fostered client and counselor communications and inspired clients to work towards creating the lives that they had imagined.

Identifying and Using Strengths

Once goals are set, how do people set out to achieve them? What traits or resources help people enact their action plans? Positive psychologists have often emphasized the use of personal strengths to generate positive outcomes and subjective experiences of well-being (Owens et al., 2019; Peterson & Seligman, 2004). However, people may have difficulty identifying their strengths or have limited vocabulary to articulate strengths they experience. Consequently, introducing formalized assessments which provide clients an avenue for learning about their strengths can be advantageous. Owens et al. (2019) and Robertson (2018) reported that career practitioners frequently utilized positive psychology assessments to assist clients in determining their strengths. Two assessments designed to increase strengths awareness are the Clifton StrengthsFinder (Rath, 2007) and the Values in Action Institute Inventory of Strengths (VIA-IS: Peterson & Seligman, 2004). The Clifton Strengths Finder helps clients identify their clusters of talent that can be transformed into strengths. The VIA-IS exposes clients to 24 different character strengths, inviting examinees to assess the degree these strengths relate to them. Upon completion of the assessment, examinees learn their five top character strengths based on their endorsements. Robertson described the VIA-IS as a well-researched and positively focused system for individuals to identify and learn about their dominant strengths. Dik et al. (2015) asserted that using one's signature strengths at work may lead to perceptions of work as more meaningful and that use of signature strengths increased well-being.

Art therapists have also utilized the VIA-IS. For example, Darewych and Bowers (2017) used VIA-IS as a preliminary stimulus for strength identification and application. Pairing the VIA-IS with art therapy processes, Darewych and Bowers invited clients to complete the VIA-IS followed by a "my strengths collage" using paper, magazines, markers, paint, and other drawing materials. Through viewing and discussing completed artworks including selected symbols and imagery, clients gained awareness of their strengths and how they may be applied to their everyday life.

Louis and Lopez (2014) described the range of aims that strengths-based intervention may target once strengths have been illuminated. For example, strengths-based interventions may emphasize increasing the frequency of strength utilization, modifying strengths use related to situational demands, or cultivating further growth of a particular strength. Overall, Louis and Lopez asserted that strengths-based interventions should help clients describe identified strengths and articulate how these strengths can be developed and used in varying degrees. Additionally, Louis and Lopez explained that strength-based interventions need to be refined to support clients' desired outcomes, rely on evidence-based practice, and be used over a period of time to extend and reinforce learning. Interventions may be initiated in a variety of settings including but not limited to mental health practices, career counseling centers, schools, and workplace settings.

Strengths and Job Decision-Making: The Case of J.

In the following case, the VIA-IS and art therapy approaches are utilized to support a graduate art therapy student in her efforts to refine her career direction and job search strategies following graduation. J. noted that she was confident about her chosen field of art therapy but was unsure of the type of work setting that would be the best match for her personality and skills. To help the student narrow her focus, the practitioner recommended J. begin her exploration by completing the VIA-IS. Upon completion of the assessment, J. revealed that her most significant strengths were creativity, curiosity, and humility. J. read the provided descriptions of the traits and agreed that these findings suited her. Still, J. was unclear about how knowledge of these traits may help refine her job selection process. Consequently, the practitioner invited J. to create symbols that reflected her strengths and then create images of work environments that would be conducive, complementary, or supportive to each strength.

First, J. created an image (Figure 8.1) that represented her creativity. She reported that, "My creativity symbol is my hands, synthesizing strings of information or materials, to create something new." When thinking of an ideal work environment where she could use this strength, she was inspired to create an environment full of colorful strings that she could weave together with her creative hands.

J. noted that she struggled in creating a symbol that reflected her curiosity. After reflecting on some of the curiosity descriptions, she resonated with being open to new experiences and enjoying the process of discovery. J. decided to depict her curiosity as a brain that contained different roads, paths, and locations (see Figure 8.2). She explained that the symbol represented her past journeys and love for exploring new places on an intimate level. Then, J. more confidently created a work environment image. To support her curiosity, J. asserted that an ideal work environment would offer many different pathways and stimulus for new discovery.

In terms of humility, J. found this to be an easier symbol to create. She likened humility to wildflowers that thrive in different climates and environments in a complementary fashion as opposed to a dominating manner. For the humility symbol, she created a flower form in the shape of a human silhouette (see Figure 8.3). For their environment, she produced a pattern that represented a lush grass for the flowers to flourish in.

Figure 8.1 J's Creativity Representation

Figure 8.2 J's Curiosity Representation

Figure 8.3 J.'s Humility Representation

After creating the three symbols and their environments, J. reflected that her ideal employment setting would embrace her traits and provide opportunities for creativity, avenues for discovery, and a culture that promoted the flourishing of both staff and clients. At the end of this process, J. decided to cut each trait-related work environment into strips and weaved them together to an open basket-like structure to integrate her environmental preferences and desires (See Figure 8.4).

At the close of the art series, J. remarked that the process of exploring her strengths in a creative and meaningful way "made it easier for me to answer and assimilate some of the questions I had about what my future work environment might look like, and that it's important for those future sites to give space to these three strengths." J.'s increased self-knowledge of traits and values provided self-awareness that would be important to employ during her job search and decision-making steps.

Capitalizing on Strengths to Address Barriers

It is important to acknowledge that pursuit of meaningful work suited to one's strengths may be experienced as a luxury when economic disparities, systemic oppression, or other barriers interfere with career preparation resources and job access. However, examining and bolstering strengths may help individuals identify inner or outer resources that they can use to navigate obstacles and move towards career goals. Smit et al. (2015) worked with a group of adolescents from an under-resourced rural township in South Africa

Figure 8.4 J's Integration of Creativity, Curiosity, Humility, and Their Environments

and designed participatory visual strategies to engage learners in processes to support strength identification and cultivate hope and agency regarding post-secondary school options. Their program included student engagement in mind-mapping and photovoice activities as well as discussions that centered on their influential personal and systemic challenges, constructive choices available, and assets that may boost or sustain them during next life stages. Smit et al. conceded that fostering awareness of assets and risk factors does not singularly ensure resilience, but asserted that cultivating awareness of personal and societal resources increases critical thinking, problem-solving, and optimism.

To start their work with students, Smit et al. (2015) invited students to engage in mind-mapping. Mind-mapping is a type of concept mapping that utilizes visual formats to express ideas that are currently formulating (Butler-Kisber & Poldma, 2010). Frequently, such maps are completed by writing along with drawing or sketching of ideas and diagrams of relationships between concepts providing a visual way to examine them. In Smit et al.'s (2015) study, students were asked to organize their thoughts about career and life goals in visual form by creating a symbol of these concepts in the center of a page. Next, they were encouraged to depict their thoughts about associated assets and barriers radiating out from the central form.

Following the mind-mapping activity, students were engaged in photovoice activities. Photovoice methods use photography processes to encourage people to reflect and identify community strengths and concerns and to stimulate examination of important issues through the review of photographs (Wang & Burris, 1997). Smit et al. provided disposable cameras and invited participants to take a minimum of photographs of items in their environments that represented related barriers or assets. Photographs were printed, and students selected two images to reflect on in written form and discuss within a group forum. Smit et al. adapted Wang's (1999) SHOWED method to structure student narratives. These structures entailed responding to questions "What do you **S**ee?"; "What is really **H**appening?" "How does this relate to **O**ur life?" **W**hy does this problem/issue or

Figure 8.5 SHOWED Method Example

strength exist? "How can we be **E**mpowered by our understanding?" and "What can we **D**o to address this problem issue?" (Smit et al., 2015, p. 126). The included example from the author (Parker-Bell; see Figure 8.5) demonstrates how the SHOWED method may be used to explore a selected photograph.

S I **See** a flawed but beautiful multicolored class that can hold and reflect light.
H **Happening**: The glass is holding the light and is inviting further investigation and engagement.
O **Our life**: I enjoy multifaceted, multicolored dimensional experiences. I can appreciate overarching beauty which includes things that other people may see as flaws.
W **Why**: Family influences and appreciation for varied interests and ways of being.
E **Empowered**: The message empowers my personal acceptance and self-appreciation and invites me to expand this view to others.
D **Do**: At times when the flaws capture my attention and thoughts, don't lose sight of the beauty and fullness of the whole experience.

According to Smit et al. (2015) mind-maps and photovoice activities not only helped students in identifying strengths and concerns they experienced; they helped reveal relevant considerations to teachers. Consequently, teachers were able to attune their career support strategies to students' personal and community contexts. Using the image of the glass and accompanied SHOWED reflection as a basis for career exploration, a practitioner may explore how the author's varied interests and pleasure experienced in investigating multifaceted phenomena may help with overcoming career exploration obstacles and match with a range of career options.

Building on Strengths to Increase Job Satisfaction

Following career selection and job attainment, positive psychology tenets and strategies can support clients' optimum functioning and flourishing within work environments (Owens, Allan, & Flores, 2019; Owens, Flores, Kopperson, & Blake, 2019). For example, positive psychology frameworks can help clients consider and apply their positive characteristics and strengths as they negotiate work environments. Additionally, fostering hope and empowerment may increase clients' perceptions of agency and lead to greater work fulfillment.

Owens et al. (2019) defined work fulfillment as job-related experiences that provided satisfaction, meaning, positive engagement as well as positive workplace emotions. Individuals' perceptions of work fulfillment are based on interaction among personal characteristics, cultural contexts, and environmental and societal considerations. For example, two people may have the same personal strengths and skills, but their access to resources or job opportunities may differ. One person may live in a region that has bountiful job openings in their area of competency while the other resides in an area where employment options are sparse. Work climates can also differ. For instance, a workplace may be supportive or discriminatory to workers in similar roles in response to their identities, triggering markedly dissimilar experiences of worker satisfaction or distress. Unfortunately, work fulfillment is more likely to occur when fewer barriers are experienced and where work efforts are valued and supported. When systemic oppression or policy inequities occur, practitioner support and advocacy are necessary. However, where clients do have some control, practitioners can support clients in applying their strengths and resources to address work factors and build positive experiences.

In this regard, practitioners who operate from a positive psychology framework build a therapeutic alliance with clients and work collaboratively to cultivate hope, adaptability, strengths, and empowerment (Owens et al., 2019). According to Owens et al., hope-based practices start with the client determining their broader work and life goals. If obstacles are experienced, hope is sustained through the generation of multiple routes to achieve goals. When clients experience unexpected or new career challenges, the practitioner may emphasize interventions that foster development of adaptability and flexibility. When work environments present challenges, practitioners may assist clients in identifying and developing positive character traits and skills. Practitioners also support clients in identifying how they may use their strengths and skills to promote positive work environments.

Putting Strengths and Positive Strategies to Work at Mid-career: Job Crafting

Wrzesniewski and Dutton (2001) described job crafting as processes that promote worker agency and empowerment through modification of thoughts, tasks, and shifting of work-setting relationships. When individuals engage in job crafting, they activate opportunities to shape work-setting design and social frameworks which, in turn, may support positive work meaning and worker identities. It is important to note, however, that individuals may not have the opportunity to job craft or may not choose to job craft due to the additional effort required. Wrzesniewski and Dutton also emphasized that job crafting may activate workplace changes but does not replace organizations' responsibility to evaluate and improve work environments.

Yet, when work settings offer some freedom to approaching responsibilities, individuals may elect to craft their work tasks, relationships, or work-related thoughts to enhance satisfaction with work engagement. For example, a person may engage in task crafting when they ask their employer to increase the proportion of tasks which matches their interests and skill sets within their daily work assignments, or to modify tasks which they are required to accomplish to make them more achievable. When workers adapt, reframe, or build work-setting social connections to strengthen their sense of teamwork, this constitutes relational job crafting. Cognitive job crafting may include a client's efforts to restructure their thoughts about work experiences or the value of their work to others. Individuals may also engage in cognitive job crafting when they focus on rewarding aspects of their work as opposed to concentrating on perceived organizational flaws.

Combining Job Crafting with Art Therapy: The Case of Ms. G.

Ms. G., a 52-year-old single Caucasian female, sought career-related assistance when she found herself overwhelmed and frustrated with a job she used to enjoy. Ms. G. described her work setting as demanding due to high level expectations for performance and ever-expanding workloads. Ms. G. had worked for a large banking company in their corporate human resources department. Ms. G. noted that she had been promoted two times during her eight years at the company and that she was responsible for developing new worker training and ongoing staff development regarding client interactions. She worked with regional trainers and would test new training strategies and content at area branches. Of late, she had been tasked with more administrative duties related to trainer evaluations. She felt that the task assignment reflected the company's trust in her but also resulted in longer workdays for her. Ms. G. also admitted to holding some resentment when she perceived younger administrative supervisors were exploiting her unmarried and childless status. She reflected on a time when a supervisor commented that he appreciated her taking late tasks on, not only because she performed well, but because it helped married and parenting colleagues go home to their families in a timely manner. Although she was offended, it was hard for her to say no to last minute assignments. At this juncture, she wasn't sure if she should stay with the company and try to make the job work or seek new alternatives. As she reflected on job seeking, she expressed concern about potential agism in the job marketplace and was ambivalent about having to prove herself again at a new company, should she find an opportunity.

After further conversation, the practitioner and Ms. G. determined that the initial treatment goal would be to explore her experiences and potential for improving job satisfaction at her current work setting. The career practitioner chose a positive psychology and art therapy approach to creatively help Ms. G. capitalize on her strengths to build hope and agency regarding her current position. To find out more information about Ms. G.'s work preferences, the practitioner invited Ms. G. to create an image of her ideal workday. Selecting colored pencils from a range of materials, Ms. G. took great care and time with her image (see Figure 8.6). Ms. G. started the image along the borders adding drawings and words to describe work characteristics and tasks. Next, she created a central circle which she labeled "quiet time for productive synthesis and creativity." She spent considerable time and energy on embellishing the circle.

Ms. G. reflected on her image and noted that she was somewhat surprised that quiet time was central in her ideal workday image as she really did enjoy working with others and managing a variety of tasks related to staff training. She observed that the additional administrative tasks had slowly eroded her quiet time which she had used to synthesize new information and approaches to training development. She agreed that her ideal day would involve fewer administrative tasks, more interaction with colleagues and trainees, and more acknowledgment and appreciation of her talents and work efforts. Her ideal workday would also involve a to-do list that could be completed by 6 pm. Ms. G. stated that she liked the core aspects of her training work and would like to explore ways to devote

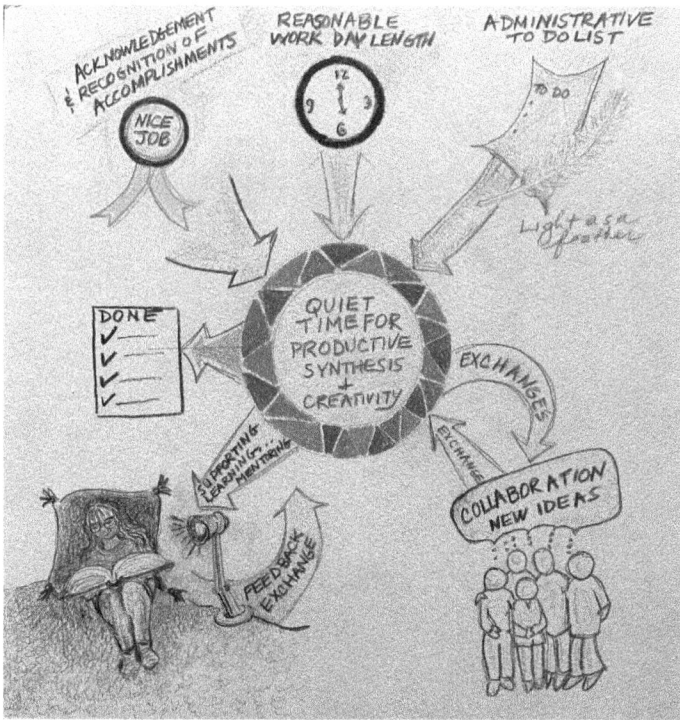

Figure 8.6 Ms. G's Ideal Workday Image

more time to those responsibilities. At the close of the session, Ms. G. and the practitioner agreed to explore perceived barriers to achieving that goal.

Session 3 began with Ms. G. eagerly starting on the depiction of her work obstacles. Using watercolor crayons, she created an image dominated by a clock and lists (Figure 8.7). Beneath the clock and between two lists, Ms. G., described that she had created a self-symbol and that she was holding up very heavy weights, time pressures, and to-do lists. She noted that the red, orange, and yellow circle represented her quiet, creative, productive time as well as her head. She compared the size of this circle to the central circle in her first image and posited that the current circle was much smaller than ideal. She remarked that just looking at the work evoked distress and caused her to lose sight of positive aspects of her work.

After exploring some of these feelings, the practitioner reflected the client's strength in being able to sustain engagement and successfully complete many important tasks, yet also noted a theme of lack of control and burden. The practitioner inquired about Ms. G.'s level of freedom to shape her workdays. Ms. G. stated that she generally had a good deal of freedom in structuring her days when she did not have training commitments. Additionally, Ms. G. noted that she felt burdened by heavy workloads and short deadlines which caused her to be more reactive versus proactive about planning her days. At this juncture in the session, the practitioner introduced the concept of job crafting and asked Ms. G. if she was interested in learning more and experimenting with job crafting processes to increase positive experiences and greater work fulfillment. Ms. G. agreed that job crafting could be a good place to start and that she would look forward to learning more.

In session 4, Ms. G. and the practitioner reviewed the previous artwork and then discussed the three types of job crafting: task crafting, relational crafting, and cognitive

Figure 8.7 Ms. G's Depiction of Work Obstacles

crafting. Examples of these strategies were provided. Next, the practitioner invited Ms. G. to create an image that reflected job crafting tasks that she could potentially try within her work setting. In response, Ms. G. returned to color pencils. She traced a large circle on a page and repeated the circle design that represented her quiet productive time in the center of the larger circle. She divided the outer portions of the large circle and labeled them cognitive, task, and relational, and followed by adding symbols and words to represent possible job crafting tasks. When she was finished with her drawings, she cut out the circular composition and laid it on top of the ideal workday obstacle image (Figure 8.8 and 8.9). Ms. G. stated that putting the circle on top of the distressing image already increased her sense of personal power.

Ms. G. and the practitioner reviewed Ms. G.'s job crafting circle. Ms. G. explained that potential task crafting could involve reducing some of her work tasks by delegating appropriate administrative tasks to others. She said it was reasonable for her to assign analysis of training evaluation data to a colleague within her department, so that she could mainly focus on writing the quarterly summary reports based on the analysis. She also explained that she could reduce work interruptions by closing her door and turning off her email alerts for a one- to two-hour time span during some days to make room for report writing and "creative synthesis time." Regarding cognitive job crafting tasks, Ms. G. identified that she could take time at the end of each day to list and reflect on her accomplishments and provide herself with "attagirl" recognitions instead of waiting to hear that from her supervisors. She noted that she could also choose to look at her work as a glass half-full versus glass half-empty phenomenon by reminding herself of an aspect of her work she enjoyed each day. When reflecting on relational job crafting, Ms. G. acknowledged that she could improve her communication with administrative supervisors who may not be aware of some of the discomfort she had been experiencing.

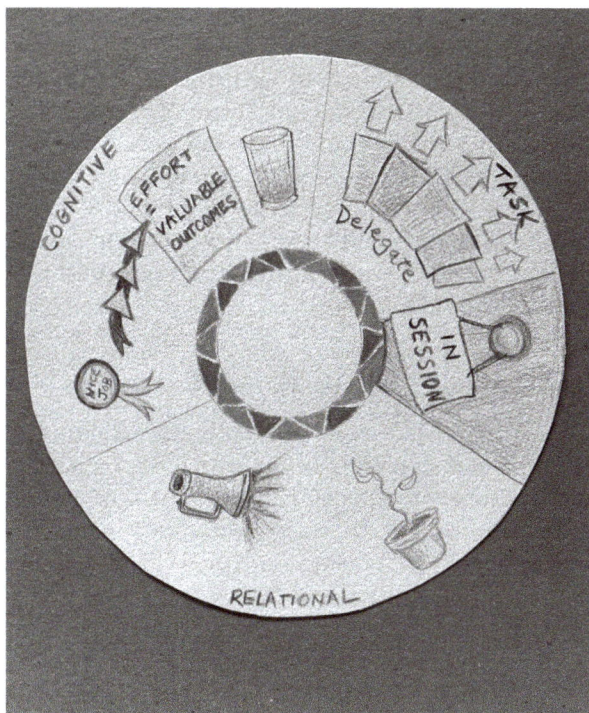

Figure 8.8 Ms. G's Job Crafting Tasks

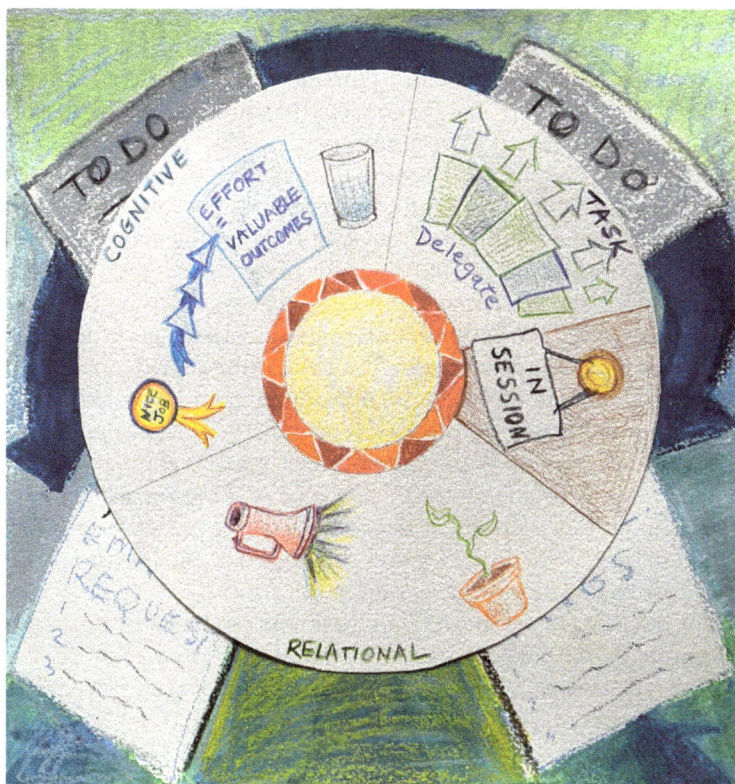

Figure 8.9 Ms. G's Overlay of Job Crafting Tasks and Ideal Workday Obstacle Image

She said it was reasonable to request the establishment of regular workload planning meetings with administration. Finally, Ms. G. stated that she could nurture stronger social relationships with coworkers to help foster teamwork and reduce isolation regarding the administrative tasks she had taken on. At the end of the session, Ms. G. reiterated that it was helpful to identify ways she could shape her work experiences.

Additional sessions with Ms. G. focused on creating and reflecting upon strengths and skills that she could utilize to operationalize her identified job crafting tasks. Ms. G. began to implement these strategies and benefited from a return to more fulfilling work experiences that included "creative synthesis time" and relationships that were essential to her job satisfaction and fulfillment.

Positive Career Interventions for Later Career Concerns

In later phases of career, adults may experience vulnerability to career changes related to job marketplaces, economic downturns, or shifting work qualification expectations that require attainment of new competencies. These situations may result in unexpected work transitions, underemployment, or earlier than anticipated retirement. Brandan et al. (2013) asserted that positive psychology-informed career counseling can be utilized to support coping resiliency, self-efficacy, and community efficacy for adults in this career stage. Peila-Shuster (2012) posited that it may be advantageous for adults to articulate strengths, and then identify how these strengths may be utilized in life's next chapter, whether it be a new work situation or retirement.

Once strengths are recognized, clients can apply their strengths in new positions or settings, cultivating meaningful engagement in work, volunteer opportunities, and/or leisure pursuits.

Brandan et al. (2013) identified strengths-based assessments that may be offered to initiate this work with later career individuals. For example, a practitioner may use the Strengths, Weaknesses, Opportunities, and Threats (SWOT) analysis format to open conversations about a client's resources and concerns. Inquiries regarding work and interpersonal skills, available personal or community networks, and history of achievements may unfold conversations regarding strengths. Questions about obstacles experienced, or areas of life they experienced difficulties meeting their goals, could reveal potential weaknesses to be addressed. Additional questions regarding life dreams and support systems may uncover opportunities that had not been considered. Finally, discussions regarding threats such as health concerns or experiences of agism provide openings for support and problem-solving. Brandan et al. recommended that practitioners evaluate clients' readiness for such conversations before embarking on this approach.

Alternatively, Brandan et al. (2013) endorsed matching and converting components of the SWOT analysis to cultivate new perspectives and strategies. Client and practitioner work together to connect strengths to opportunities, such as connecting language abilities to the demand for interpreters in healthcare settings or to reconsider weaknesses and threats as opportunities. For example, the threat of being passed over for advancement due to lack of familiarity with cutting edge technologies in the industry, could be reclassified as an incentive to seek out training opportunities.

A visual way of helping clients move from weakness or threat to strength or opportunity may incorporate a four-part collage series that practitioners may offer in individual or group settings. Clients begin with a four-fold horizontal page and are instructed to write what they are moving from (weakness or threat) on the first panel to what they are moving towards (strength or opportunity) on the final panel. The two center panels will be used to reflect and represent positive aspects of these characteristics that may help

Figure 8.10 Example 1: Four Part Collage Series Illustrating Movement

them move towards the final panel. Clients are provided magazines or precut images and text, in addition to glue and scissors and asked to use representative words or images on each of the panels. Two examples of this process are provided in Figures 8.10 and 8.11.

In Figure 8.10, Client A identified his weakness as being too bold and emotional on the job. Client A said his supervisor had recently written him up for having a "loud and aggressive tone" when voicing his frustration with his work team and their performance."

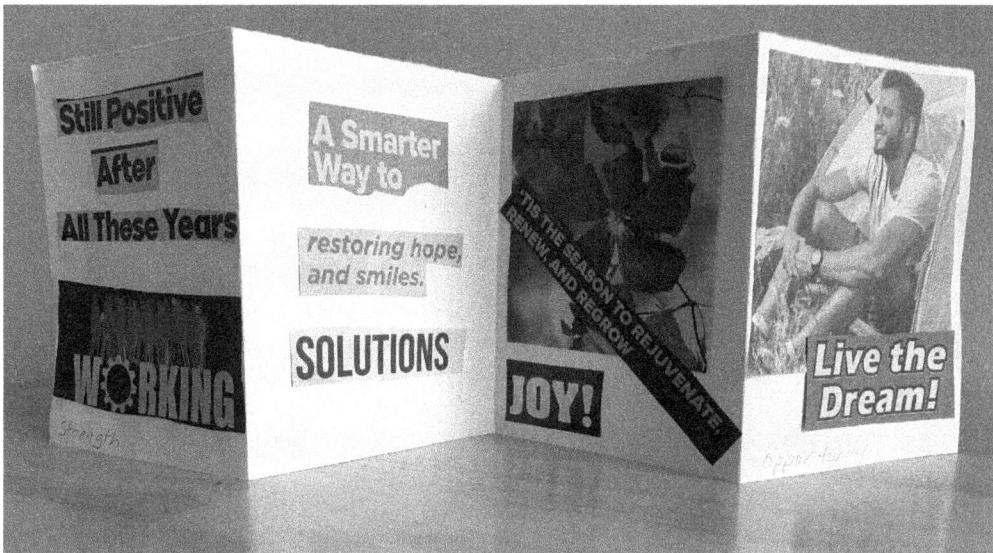

Figure 8.11 Example 2: Four Part Collage Series Illustrating Movement

He admitted he was frustrated but felt that he shouldn't have been "punished" for bringing up legitimate concerns to his team. Now he felt like quitting. However, he was hesitant to leave his job given his age and concerns about competing with younger managers for new positions. In exploring the positive aspects of his boldness, he reflected that he brought power and spark to his work, and that he was interested, alert, and effective at completing the tasks he took on. In the final frame, he was able to identify aspects of his boldness as a strength, as he considered himself decisive and able to get jobs done in short order. He felt these traits, coupled with experience, could be valuable and appreciated in many work settings and became more optimistic about finding a new position that might be a better fit.

In Figure 8.11, Client B reflected on a personal strength of maintaining positivity after 30 years of hard work as a teacher. As pension rules were shifting, she made the hard decision to retire and take advantage of best payouts, though psychologically she was not sure she was ready to leave the classroom. When discussing her collage, she explained that her experience in the classroom helped her see solutions that could be achieved instead of dwelling on challenges. The third panel represented her budding ability to see her new circumstances as a something that could be joyful or rejuvenating. Finally, Client B said that her positivity could help her see her retirement as an opportunity to "live the dream," as she enjoyed spending time with her son and his family and now had the time and financial means to do so.

Attention to strengths, weaknesses, opportunities, and threats can lead to solution-focused conversations and efforts. Practitioners may use solution-focused questioning strategies identified by Brandan et al. (2013) to illuminate the client's previous experiences of overcoming career challenges, adjusting to new work settings, and thriving following personal challenges. Identifying and acknowledging the client's repertoire of resilience skills stimulate the clients use of these skills in new situations.

Summary

Positive psychology and positive art therapy tenets may be utilized at all stages of career development to activate hope, identify strengths, support self-efficacy, and foster resilience in the face of work barriers and the pursuit of meaningful work. Strengths-based career assessments and approaches can be enhanced by using art-based interventions to activate positive imagery and creative approaches to problem-solving. Practitioners play an important role in supporting clients' experiences of empowerment as they work to use their skills and strengths and opportunities to meet career objectives.

Discussion Questions and Activities

1 **Self-reflection 1**: During your childhood, adolescence, or early adulthood, how did others' feedback or attention to your perceived strengths shape your career interests or pursuits? What personal or communal resources have you considered most influential in your career development? How did you utilize these strengths and resources to navigate challenging times during your career development pathways? Using any art media, create an artwork that reflects a strength that continues to support you in your achievement of work/life goals.
2 **Self-reflection 2**: Consider a current work or volunteer experience. How might job crafting tasks be applied to improve your satisfaction with roles and responsibilities?
3 **Self-reflection 3**: Create a "Favorite Workday" image. What does that image reveal about work experiences that are meaningful to you?

4 **Self-reflection and Application**: Identify a time in your life when you experienced a barrier to achieving a desired educational or career goal. At that time, how might you have experienced a career practitioner's guidance or intervention that emphasized a positive or strengths-based focus? Whether your reaction was positive, negative, or somewhere in between, how might this response shape your use of positive psychology and art therapy career interventions with clients? What techniques would you use to sensitively encourage hope without minimizing barriers?

5 **Application**: What career or art therapy assessments might you use to gain further understanding of a client's strengths, resources, or values regarding meaningful work? How could the chosen assessment help you formulate a career development treatment plan?

6 Consider what brings you meaning in your work and life? What needs do you have that you look to work to fulfill? How is your work fulfilling those needs? When there is a mismatch between what gives you meaning in work and what your current work provides, what would recommended next steps be? Are there other ways to meet those needs? Can something be negotiated with your employer to increase the likelihood that your needs will be met? Would receiving more training or seeking out different projects help meet your needs?

References

Brandan, M. M., Goddard, N. A., Kabir, B., et al. (2013). Resilience and retirement, coping self-efficacy: Implementing positive psychology during times of economic hardship for late-career individuals. *Career Planning and Adult Development Journal, 29*(4), 25–36.

Bullock-Yowell, E., Reed, C. A., Mohn, R., et al. (2015). Neuroticism, negative thinking, and coping with respect to career decision state. *The Career Development Quarterly, 63*(4), 333–347.

Burton, L., & Lent, J. (2016). The use of vision boards as a therapeutic intervention. *Journal Creativity and Mental Health, 11*(1), 52–65. http://dx.doi.org/10.1080/15401383.2015.1092901

Butler-Kisber, L., & Poldma, T. 2010. The power of visual approaches in qualitative inquiry: The use of collage making and concept mapping in experiential research. *Journal of Research Practice, 6*(2): 1–16.

Buyukgoze-Kavas, A. (2016). Predicting career adaptability from positive psychological traits. *The Career Development Quarterly, 64*(2), 114–125. https://doi.org/10.1002/cdq.12045

Buzzetta, M. E., Lenz, J. G., Hayden, S. C. W., & Osborn, D. S. (2020). Student veterans: Meaning in life, negative career thoughts, and depression. *Career Development Quarterly, 68*(4), 361–373. https://doi.org/10.1002/cdq.12242

Cane, F. (1983). *The artist in each of us* (rev. ed.). Art Therapy Publications.

Darewych, O. H., & Bowers, N. R. (2017). Positive arts interventions: Creative clinical tools promoting psychological well-being. *International Journal of Art Therapy, 23*(2), 62–69.

Dik, B. J., Duffy, R. D., Allan, B. A., et al. (2015). Purpose and meaning in career development applications. *The Counseling Psychologist, 43*(4), 558–585. https://doi.org/10.1177/0011000014546872

Hirschi, A. (2014). Hope as a resource for self-directed career management: Investigating mediating effects on proactive career behaviors, life and job satisfaction. *Journal of Happiness Studies, 15*(6), 1495–1512. doi:10.1007/s10902-013-9488-x

Louis, M. C., & Lopez, S. J. (2014). Strengths interventions: Current progress and future directions. In A. C. Parks, & S. M. Schueller (Eds.), *The Wiley handbook of positive psychological interventions* (pp. 66–89). Wiley.

Marks, L. R., Hyatt, T., Saunders, D., et al. (2021). The intersection of career and mental health from the lens of cognitive information processing theory. *Journal of the National Institute for Career Education and Counselling, 47*(1), 38–43. doi:https://doi.org/10.20856/jnicec.4706

Owens, R. L., Allan, B. A., Flores, L. Y. (2019). The strength-based inclusive theory of work. *Counseling Psychology, 47*(2), 222–265. https://doi.org/10.1177/0011000019859538

Owens, R. L., Flores, L. Y., Kopperson, C., & Allan, B. A. (2019). Infusing positive psychological interventions into career counseling for diverse populations. *Counseling Psychology, 47*(2), 291–314. https://doi.org/10.1177/0011000019861608

Panc, I. R. (2015). Positive psychology interventions: Evidence-based resources for students' career development. *Journal of Educational Science, 5*(2), 51–61.

Peila-Shuster, J. J. (2012). Using strengths to construct the new life chapter. *Career Planning and Adult Development Journal, 28*, 21–32.

Peterson, C., & Seligman, M. E. P. (2004). *Character strengths and virtues: A handbook and classification.* Oxford University Press/American Psychological Association.

Peterson, G. W., MacFarlane, J., & Osborn, D. (2017). The Vocational Meaning Survey (VMS): An exploration of importance in current work. *Career Planning and Adult Development Journal, 33*(2), 49–59. Retrieved from http://fsu.digital.flvc.org/islandora/object/fsu%3A543789

Pictet, A., Coughtrey, A. E., Matthews, A., & Holmes, E. A. (2011). Fishing for happiness: The effects of generating positive imagery on mood and behavior. *Behavior Research and Therapy, 49*(12), 885–891.

Rath, T. (2007). *StrengthsFinder 2.0.* Gallup Press.

Robertson, P. J. (2018). Positive psychology and career development. *British Journal of Guidance & Counseling, 46*(2), 241–254. https://doi.org/10.1080/03069885.2017.1318433

Seligman, M. E. P., & Csikszentmihalyi, M. (2000). Positive psychology: An introduction. *American Psychologist, 55*, 5–14. https://doi.org/10.1037/0003066X.55.1.5

Smit, S., Wood, L., & Neethling, M. (2015). Helping learners think more hopefully about life school: The usefulness of participatory visual strategies to make career education more contextually relevant. *Perspectives in Education, 33*(3), 121–140.

Strauser, D. R., Lustig, D. C., & Çiftçi, A. (2008) Psychological well-being: Its relation to work personality, vocational identity, and career thoughts. *The Journal of Psychology, 142*(1), 21–35. https://doi.org/10.3200/JRLP.142.1.21-36

Wang, C. C. (1999). Photovoice: A participatory action research strategy applied to women's health. *Journal of Women's Health, 8*(2), 185–192.

Wang, C. C., & Burris, M. A. (1997). Photovoice: Concept, methodology, and use for participatory needs assessment. *Health, Education, & Behavior, 24*(3), 369–387. https://doi.org.proxy.lib.fsu.edu/10.1177/109019819702400309

Wilkinson, R. A., & Chilton, G. (2013). Positive art therapy: Linking positive psychology to art therapy theory, practice, and research. *Art Therapy, 30*(1), 4–11.

Wrzesniewski, A., & Dutton, J. E. (2001). Crafting a job: Revisioning employees as active crafters of their work. *Academy of Management Review, 26*(2), 179–201.

9 Career Decision-Making

This chapter will address the complexity of career decision-making and possible factors that may impede or support career decision-making readiness. Career decision-making assessments, models, and interventions will be identified and explored. Finally, examples of interventions that align with career development theories such as cognitive information processing theory and chaos theory will be highlighted, with a special emphasis on how creative and artistic interventions may be intertwined with established career counseling structures and practices.

Navigating Career Decision-Making

The experience of career indecision is one of the most common reasons individuals pursue career counseling experiences (Gati & Levin, 2014). Career choice is a complex process, and many factors may contribute to individuals experiencing obstacles to career decision-making. Gati and Levin described several associated factors that can make this process complex and challenging. These factors included large amounts of career alternatives to choose from; broad range of variations in terms of type and length of training required to prepare for career options; uncertainty that exists regarding self and the world of work; necessity of compromise during the decision-making process; social barriers to career access or options; and worries regarding making a wrong decision.

Additionally, Gati and Kulcsar (2021) asserted that contemporary decision-making processes have been shaped by shifting economies, resulting in more unknowns in terms of long-term career predictability. Recent pandemic experiences have also cultivated atmospheres of unpredictability. Consequently, current career explorers are called to embrace ambiguity and uncertainty, incorporate flexibility, and conceptualize change as a normal part of movement towards optimal career positions. Taking time to explore career influences and bringing them into clearer awareness is also an essential part of the decision-making process.

Exploring and Addressing Clients' Concepts of Self and Career Efforts

Readiness to Engage in Career Problem-Solving and Decision-Making

When career decision-making junctures occur, individuals may or may not be ready to address them. Sampson et al. (2013b) described career decision-making readiness as a capability to manage complex internal and external variables related to career choice. Notably, the state of readiness is not stagnant. Readiness can shift as internal experiences change. For example, an individual may be motivated to reevaluate the type of career that may satisfy them and would be less ready to make a career decision until the evaluation is complete. Or a person who was confident about career choice may experience self-doubt

DOI: 10.4324/9781003035756-9

after experiencing a negative career event. Readiness for career decision-making may also occur when external demands related to family or career unexpectedly expand or retract. Many factors may influence low readiness for decision-making. Additional factors include personality characteristics, negative thinking about self or career decision-making processes, gaps in understanding of career information, challenges with decision-making strategies, personal circumstances that may include external barriers to education or work access, lack of exposure or success with previous career resources and interventions, and more. As noted in previous chapters, practitioners may engage in formal or informal assessment methods to clarify a client's readiness for career decision-making processes to fine-tune career counseling interventions.

Creative Self-Efficacy

During contemporary career choice processes, individuals must process numerous amounts and types of information related to career pathways options which can understandably be experienced as daunting. Given this complexity, Storme and Celik (2018) asserted that creativity and confidence in one's creativity are central to career decision-making processes. Storme and Celik posited that individuals who lack confidence in their capacity to solve original and complex problems, a demonstration of low creative self-efficacy, are prone to experiencing challenges with career decision-making. Based on study findings, Storme and Celik found that college students who reported low creative self-efficacy scores demonstrated lower levels of self and career exploration, increased dysfunctional beliefs or lack of realistic assessments about their career paths, and greater levels of career indecisiveness. Additionally, Storme and Celik discovered that those with lower levels of ambiguity tolerance had more difficulty with career decision-making and may experience career confusion. Based on these findings, Storme and Celik recommended that career counselors' approaches focus on building confidence in creative problem-solving, addressing dysfunctional beliefs or fears related to career decision-making, and supporting clients' organization and integration of information gathered in the career exploration and decision-making phases.

Emotional Intelligence and Self-Efficacy

Santos et al. (2018) added to the dialogues about self-efficacy and career decision-making through their studies of the relationship between emotional intelligence and self-efficacy. In their research framework, they described emotional intelligence as a person's ability to appraise their emotion, appraise others' emotions, and an ability to regulate and use emotion to inform actions, in accordance with the theories of Wong and Law (2002). Santos et al. found that, most significantly, people who had challenges with comprehending their own emotions and difficulty applying emotions to personal actions experienced greater challenges with career decision-making. Additionally, those who had challenges with appraising and applying emotions frequently experienced challenge with self-efficacy that in turn impacted self-efficacy beliefs regarding career decision-making. In response to these findings, Santos et al. recommended interventions be focused on developing emotional intelligence and career decision-making self-efficacy. They asserted that interventions that focus on self-reflection and expression of emotions may increase emotional intelligence which may then be used to motivate action regarding career goal formulation. Recommended interventions for improving career self-efficacy related to supporting self-knowledge, occupational knowledge, goal identification, and advancing clients' knowledge and comfort with career planning and problem-solving.

Creative Methods Used to Support Career Self-Efficacy and Decision-Making

Art Therapy and Self-Efficacy

Providing opportunities for personal art expression may support self-efficacy. Kaimal and Ray (2017) found that healthy adults that engaged in one-hour sessions of free artmaking within a studio setting facilitated by an art therapist, reported increased positive affect and perceived self-efficacy, based on participant-completed Positive and Negative Affect Schedule (Watson et al., 1988) and the General Self-Efficacy Scale (GSES; Schwarzer & Jerusalem, 1995) questionnaires before and after artmaking sessions. Facilitating art therapists provided participants with a choice of three materials and their non-judgmental support. Participants selected their material, determined the processes they wished to engage in, and identified imagery and themes to develop. These open-ended opportunities supported individual engagement in creative problem-solving and decision-making skills.

Forgeard et al. (2021) also sought to understand how supported unstructured art sessions may promote self-efficacy in adults. In their study, adults with clinical diagnoses, such as mood and anxiety disorders, engaged in supported free-choice art group art sessions. Results of self-report assessments administered before and after art engagements demonstrated that adults experienced an improvement in mood, general self-efficacy, and creative self-efficacy at the end of sessions. In this study, self-efficacy pertained to perceptions of control or material of tasks and creative self-efficacy referred to confidence in their ability to create new and useful ideas or outcomes. Additionally, group participants found the stimulation of art processes to be activating allowing for more energized engagement in activities.

Researchers need to implement more specific studies to determine if open studio processes can influence career self-efficacy. Supported art session engagement may be used to supplement focused career interventions if increased evidence demonstrates that confidence in creative and expressive realms may be transferred to career decision-making domains.

Sand Tray

Sangganjanavanich and Magnuson (2011) and Swank and Jahn (2018) advocated for the use of sand tray in career counseling to support career decision-making processes. Swank and Jahn asserted that semi-structured sand tray interventions can effectively assist with supporting college student career self-efficacy through providing a creative framework for exploration of internal and external influences on career decisions. In their study of college students within a university setting, Swank and Jahn provided students with a rectangular tray of sand, and miniature figurines and objects that included diverse people, mythical creatures, animals, buildings, vehicles, and more. Over four 50-minute sessions students were asked to use the sand and miniatures to "create your career world"; "create a world of things you like to do"; "create a world of things you are good at"; and finally, once again, "create your career world" (Swank & Jahn, 2018, p. 271). Swank and Jahn repeated the first prompt in the last session to provide an opportunity to consider change in views over the sessions. Practitioner and student reviewed each completed sand tray together and explored emergent themes. Students retained a photograph of the sand tray configuration for further reflection.

Based on interviews with students following the final sand tray session, Swank and Jahn (2018) found that students were initially skeptical regarding the sand tray process, but in the end, students recognized that the processes helped them refine ideas of what they might like to pursue as a career. Participants noted that they felt more confident about selecting jobs, they expanded awareness related to both internal and external influences and gained information on how their career fit into larger work/life constructs. Furthermore, students remarked that they benefited from the opportunity for self-expression, while others stated that the creative and reflective processes motivated them to continue their career exploration efforts. Participants credited the active and visual aspects of sand tray work with helping them explore themes without the pressure of talking, or with easing their ability to discuss job considerations. Notably, Swank and Jahn acknowledged that students were not finished with their career decision-making processes at the end of the study and that sand tray may be one several types of career interventions that would be offered to prepare college students for making satisfying career decisions.

Sangganjanavanich and Magnuson (2011) also suggested that sand tray sessions were effective in helping clients explore barriers to decision-making based on results from a particular case study and more informal career counseling experiences. To investigate clients' decision-making status, they invited clients to reflect on their current career decision-making situation and create a scene in the sand to represent career barriers or frustrations they had experienced. Sangganjanavanich and Magnuson contended that sand tray and miniature work helped clients move beyond literal conversations into deeper metaphoric exploration of work/life themes and advanced practitioner understanding of client concerns. Once meanings were discovered, the client and practitioner identified interventions to address career ambivalence or other barriers that were disclosed. Sangganjanavanich and Magnuson emphasized the importance of getting appropriate training for facilitation of sand tray work, and suggested that practitioners need to adopt a non-judgmental, supportive approach to addressing themes or tensions that may revealed in the clients' career scenes or stories.

Art-based interventions such as sand tray work may be regarded as informal assessment tools that support conceptualization of clients decision-making considerations or barriers. These processes can stand alone or be used in conjunction with formalized career decision-making assessments. A few examples of career development assessments which identify decision-making processes and concerns will be described below.

Formalized Decision-Making Assessments and Tools

Decision Space Worksheet

As noted in Chapter 4, the Decision Space Worksheet, created by Peterson, Lenz, and Osborn (2016), provides a visual means to identify, explore, and evaluate concerns that are present for the client as they embark on a decision-making process. Clients identify thoughts and considerations written as statements that are evaluated for positive, negative, or neutral status, and these statements in turn are depicted as spheres within a larger circle that represents the career concern being faced. Spheres representing each concern are sized to represent the importance of those concerns to the client, and therefore help the practitioner with identifying which concerns may be more important to address within the career counseling forum.

Career Decision-Making Difficulties Questionnaire (CDDQ)

Gati et al. (1996) designed the 34-item CDDQ to assess decision-making challenges a person may be facing. Gati and his research collaborators make this and other decision-making assessment and tools available to career practitioners and the public at: CDDQ. org. The CDDQ provides a global decision-making difficulty score but also provides means to evaluate subsections of decision-making concerns. Gati and Levin (2014) outlined ten difficulty categories which can be organized within three clusters of difficulties. These clusters include 1) difficulties that occur before decision-making; 2) difficulties that occur during decision-making; and 3) difficulties experienced in using career information. Challenges with motivation, overall indecisiveness, or dysfunctional beliefs about self or decision-making processes constitute the difficulties that occur before decision-making. Difficulties related to a lack of information about careers or decision-making processes form the second cluster. Challenges related to internal conflicts, external conflicts, and unreliability of information constitute the third cluster of decision-making difficulties. Following CDDQ assessment completion, practitioner and client can identify specific blocks to decision-making, so that interventions may be planned accordingly. Rochat (2019) advocated for even more specific consideration regarding CDDQ responses. Rochat examined clients' individual item responses to determine the most problematic career decision-making difficulty needing attention and intervention.

Career Thoughts Inventory (CTI)

The Career Thoughts Inventory (CTI; Sampson et al., 1996a, 1996b) assessment is based on cognitive information processing theory (CIP) and the CASVE Cycle which focuses on exploration and restructuring of negative thinking regarding career decision-making processes. Career practitioners use the CTI as a tool to identify and evaluate problems and to support learning about decision-making thought patterns. Constructs measured by the CTI include decision-making confusion, commitment anxiety, and external conflicts that contribute to career indecision. Decision-making confusion represents an overall "stuckness" on how to begin or move through the process of making a career decision. Commitment anxiety occurs when a person has successfully narrowed their options to a first choice with a backup, but fear prohibits them from acting on the choice. This fear could be fear of failure, fear of missing out on a better option, and other worries. External conflict happens when a person anticipates pushback for their career decision from significant others. The thoughts represented by the individual items on the CTI that a client endorses may or may not be grounded in reality. In other words, a client may *think* that a particular person is going to be very disappointed in them, but that may not be the reality. Asking a client to "tell me more about this item" on those that are rated highly can reveal the specific context and impact that thought is having on their career decision-making capability. For those with a number of negative career thoughts, the supplementary CTI Workbook (Sampson et al., 1996a), which contains readings and exercises to support cognitive restructuring, action planning, and examination of problem-solving and decision-making patterns may be recommended (Sargent & Lenz, 2017).

   A practitioner using the CTI might start with the overall scores. Norm scores are provided for high school, college students, and adults. Client norm scores are also reported in the manual (Sampson et al., 1996b). Elevated scores would suggest that the client is experiencing a high number of negative career thoughts that might be hampering the career decision-making process. Thus, a practitioner should focus the sessions on understanding the client's core negative beliefs, showing how negative thoughts can impede the other areas of decision-making, and help the client become aware of and learn how to address these beliefs. Cognitive restructuring is one tool that can be helpful. A common approach for restructuring is to ask the client for evidence for and against the belief being true and then creating an alternative thought that is less negative/maladaptive. Key words that suggest barriers include words like, "always," "never," "should," "must," and "ought." Restructuring could be verbal or written. An example of a verbal exchange is detailed here:

PRACTITIONER: You keep saying that you never make any good decisions.
CLIENT: It sure feels that way.
PRACTITIONER: I'm sure it does right now – but is it always the case that you never make good decisions?
CLIENT: I guess not.
PRACTITIONER: Can you think of a time when you made a good decision, or even an OK one?
CLIENT: I guess you could say coming here was a good decision.
PRACTITIONER: I appreciate that! So, would it be more accurate to say that you are able to make good decisions?
CLIENT: Some of the time, I guess.
PRACTITIONER: Some of the time, or more often than not?
CLIENT: I guess, when it matters, I am careful and make pretty good decisions.
PRACTITIONER: Do you see the difference between saying "I never make good decisions" and "When it matters, I am careful and able to make good decisions"?

In this case, the practitioner didn't confront the client the first time that a negative thought was mentioned, but waited until it had occurred several times. As the relationship grows, the practitioner will be able to confront more quickly and with fewer words, such as "*Always?*".

It is very important to help the client see how negative thoughts can impact decision-making rather than immediately suggesting a career assessment or showing occupational information, as pervading, unchallenged negative thoughts can impede both of those interventions, with statements such as "I'm not good at anything" or "I could never do this type of work." Clients with elevated negative thoughts can engage in these activities, but the practitioner should caution them to keep those negative thoughts at bay to avoid biasing the process and results.

Moderate or lower profiles should not be ignored. A single negative career thought can be so pervasive that it clouds the rest of the career decision-making process. Addressing the negative thought and exploring and challenging it fully is recommended. In addition to the overall score, the subscales can also be examined for elevation and discussion. For example, instead of keeping the focus on a general "external" who might be causing real or perceived conflict, a practitioner might say, "This scale suggests that there is a person or persons whose opinion you care about deeply, and you're concerned about how they might respond to your career decision. Can you tell me more about that?" It may turn out, especially with cultural differences, that the thought is not negative at all, but it is something a practitioner should be aware of so as not to impose values.

Career State Inventory (CSI)

Another career decision-making assessment is the CSI. Leierer et al. (2020) designed the CSI to assess career decision state and readiness for career problem-solving. The authors described the career decision state as "momentary consciousness regarding one's career goals or aspirations" (Leierer et al., 2020, p. 2). Career decision states encompass thoughts and feelings related to identity, direction, satisfaction, self-confidence, and self-efficacy. Career readiness relates to the effort one has applied to preparing for career problem-solving and decision-making. The brief questionnaire examines an individual's certainty and satisfaction with a career goal and experiences of clarity and confidence in their approach to career and life goals. This assessment aligns with the CASVE Cycle and the cognitive information processing theory (CIP) and has been used as a screening tool for individual career counseling. A practitioner can examine the three domains of the inventory to determine which aspect (decidedness, clarity, or satisfaction) is of greatest concern to the client.

My Vocational Situation (MVS)

The MVS was developed by John Holland (Holland et al., 1980) and consists of 18 true/false items measuring one's vocational identity such as "If I had to make an occupational choice right now, I'm afraid I would make a bad choice." Also on the MVS are two items that assess informational needs and perceived barriers. An open-ended prompt bookends the beginning and end of the MVS. The first asks the person to list all options they are currently considering, and the last simply prompts with "Anything else?" With the first prompt, a practitioner can have the individual talk through each of the options they are considering. A practitioner would listen for obvious excitement, misinformation, experiences, or skills related to the options, potential pressures, and might also encourage the client to examine across the options for common themes. The final prompt allows for identification of considerations not listed on the inventory that might be salient to the career discussion. The MVS has been used in multiple research studies, with strong psychometric properties, and is freely available.

Other Measures Related to Career Decision-Making

A plethora of inventories exist to measure variables related to career decision-making. For example, one of the best-known measures of career indecision was created by Osipow et al. (1997). The 18 items (plus one write-in option) represent 18 specific problems Osipow et al. saw that individuals had with career decision-making. Thus, while an overall score indicated higher indecision, an affirmative rating of any of the items merited more discussion with the client. Oftentimes, researchers will report on self-created measures of career decidedness, such as the CIP Skills Questionnaire (Osborn et al., 2020). That tool consists of four questions, related to each of the CIP domains, and asks individuals to rate their knowledge of self, options, decision-making skills, and ability to control self-talk. Studies have shown the four items to be both independent and interdependent (Osborn et al., 2020; Osborn et al., 2021). Sampson et al. (2013a) created a table comparing 49 different inventories measuring readiness for career decision-making. Once a better understanding of clients' decision-making concerns and barriers are ascertained through assessment processes, intervention strategies are proposed. Oftentimes, career counselors introduce decision-making models to help clients navigate complex decision-making processes.

Career Decision-Making Models

Career counselors have designed a broad array of career decision-making models to support client decision-making processes. Three categories of decision-making models include normative models, descriptive models, and prescriptive models (Gati & Kulcsar, 2021). Normative models focus on providing a logical and rational system of career selection to determine the most advantageous choice in a computational manner, which may be said to be ideal, but not attainable. Descriptive models reflect the idiosyncratic ways that individuals negotiate career decision-making outcomes based on subjective experiences and preferences. Gati and Kulsar asserted that prescriptive models combine logic and subjective components through systematic procedures that are compatible with intuitive processes. Such models break down decision-making processes into more manageable components that can be examined in reflective and logical ways to achieve a satisfying career outcome. Two examples of theory-informed prescriptive models of career decision-making are the PIC model (Gati, 1986; Gati & Levin, 2014) and the CASVE Cycle (Peterson et al., 1996; Sampson et al., 2020).

PIC Model

Gati's PIC model (Gati, 1986; Gati & Levin, 2014; Levin & Gati, 2015) describes the steps of decision-making as prescreening, in-depth exploration, and choice. In the prescreening process, a person identifies and thoughtfully considers a set of career possibilities that match their valued career factors. Factors they may examine during the prescreening process include financial considerations, prospects for advancement, location, and how the career matches their identified career aptitudes and values. At the end of this stage, suitable career alternatives are optimally narrowed to five to seven options. Next, the career explorer engages in in-depth exploration. Careers are thoroughly compared and evaluated to help the career explorer identify two to four career options that may satisfy them. Finally, during the choice stage, the career explorer weighs the advantages and disadvantages of each career, rank-orders the options based on desirability, and then makes a choice that they are interested in pursuing.

To extend this idea and to explore how the PIC model could be incorporated with art-making within career decisions and job choices, the authors invited art therapy graduate students to explore a broader set of available art therapy jobs, conduct an in-depth evaluation of those jobs, and then narrow the choices to two for a final decision-making process. The authors asked students to divide or fold their papers in half and choose from a variety of two-dimensional materials to complete their art process. Next, the authors invited students to creatively reflect on the two positions they had selected on the two halves of the paper. When images were completed, the authors asked the students to review the two halves of the artwork and consider them in the light of previously creating career vision boards and career value portraits. By comparing job choice reflections to earlier artworks noting career value systems, students could further examine which job might best satisfy their career and life goals.

Students responded positively to the art-infused decision-making process. Student 1 noted the value of the art and viewing processes related to her consideration of the job options. "Doing this reflection helped me better understand the pros and cons of each job. Through creating a sort of Venn diagram, I realized that the central state hospital didn't match the values I had in regard to having artmaking central to the therapeutic process." Student 1's job-choice art exploration and vision board are included in Figure 9.1.

Student 2 targeted her art therapy job search in a particular region of the country she deemed attractive and culturally supportive (Figure 9.2). She narrowed her choices to two positions and created art to reflect upon information she had gathered about them. See Figures 9.3 and 9.4.

Upon reflecting upon these artworks and her vision board (Figure 9.5) created at an earlier time, she noted that her vision board may have been overly idealistic, and that no job may measure up to the magically nurturing setting she envisioned. She also observed that Figure 9.2 emphasized the town where the job was located and didn't fully consider the job opportunity. She concluded that her reflection on the second job was more

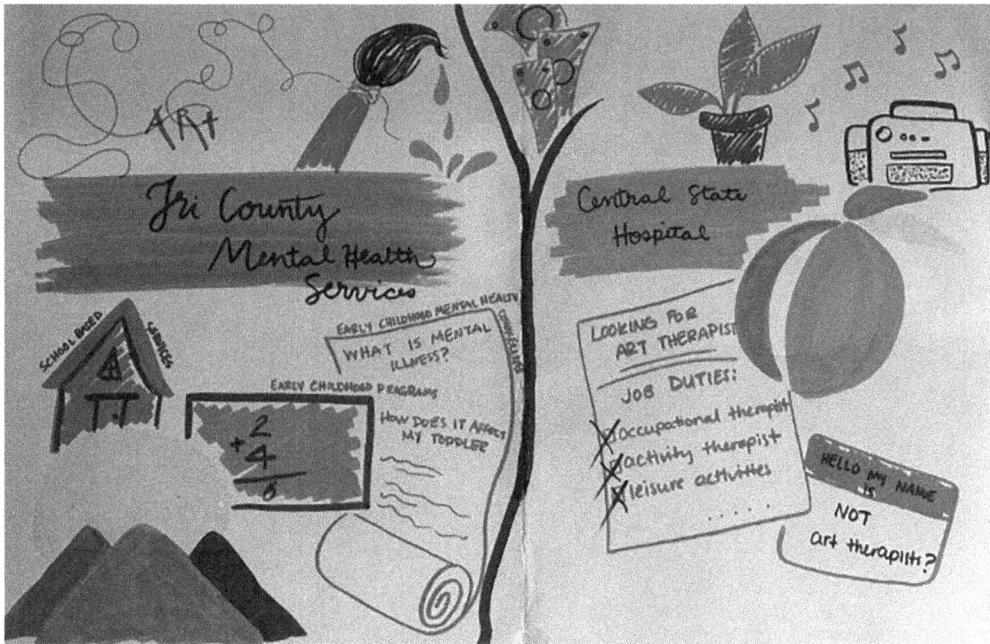

Figure 9.1 Student 1 Job-Choice Exploration

realistic but foreboding. At this stage, the student determined that she would not make a career decision based on these two options. While the art-based PIC process did not culminate in a job choice, it did help the student clarify her need for further job exploration and consideration of work setting characteristics that would be evaluated as satisfactory for her work and broader life goals.

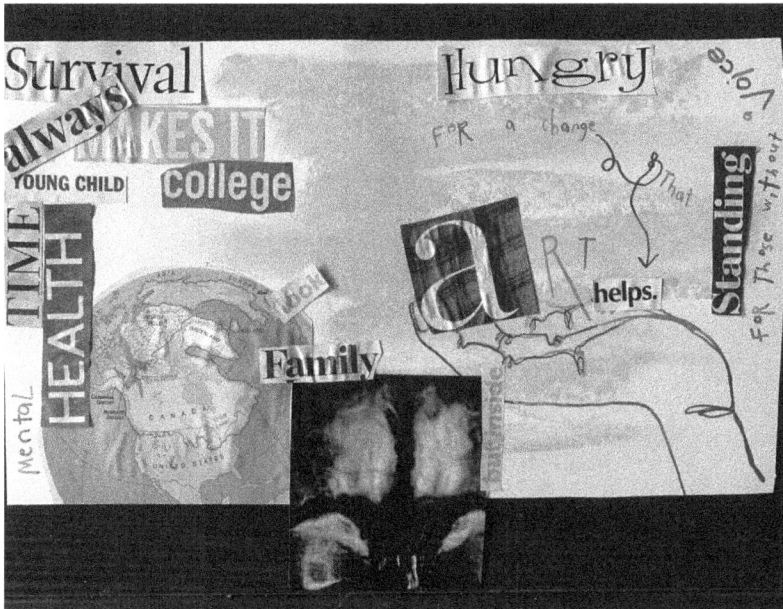

Figure 9.2 Student 1 Career-Life Vision Board

Figure 9.3 Student 2 Job Choice Option 1

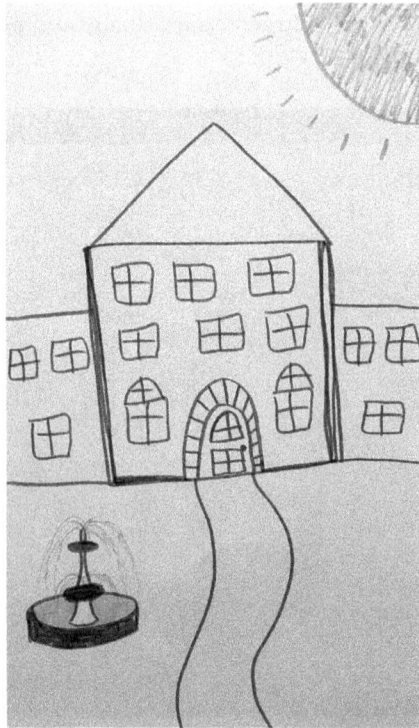

Figure 9.4 Student 2 Job Choice Option 2

Figure 9.5 Student 2 Vision Board

Other students found value in adding art to the PIC process and reflecting on their vision board. Student 3 stated, "While career decision-making might seem more straight-forward, the artwork helped me explore feelings surrounding both options." "I really enjoyed creating artwork to reflect on the two job options because it helped ease some of the anxiety I felt and gave me a more clear direction when making the final choice," said a fourth student. A fifth student emphasized the importance of consulting her vision board and her career values portrait as a part of her decision-making process as it reminded her of her career priorities.

CASVE Cycle

The CASVE Cycle is a second prescriptive decision-making model that supports positive career decision-making processes that will be addressed here. The CASVE Cycle first described in Chapter 2, includes moving through stages of Communication, Analysis, Synthesis, Valuing, Execution and back to Communication related to a career decision (Sampson et al., 2020). From a client's perspective, the first phase of communication would involve acknowledgment of the need to make a choice at the beginning of the cycle. In the analysis phase, the client would strive to understand both themselves and their career options, followed by the synthesis phase where they expand and narrow their choices. Within the valuing stage, the client would choose an occupation, job, or study or training focus to implement in the execution phase. At the end of the cycle, they would reflect and communicate perspectives on their satisfaction with an executed choice. Throughout the process, a client is encouraged to reflect on their thoughts and emotions. Clients can write their thoughts respective to each phase (e.g., for Valuing, "Here are my pro/con lists for each option I'm thinking of"). They could also represent the information using technology. Figure 9.6 shows an example of using Snapchat to demonstrate thoughts about the CASVE Cycle, and then inputting the pictures into a slide. It is

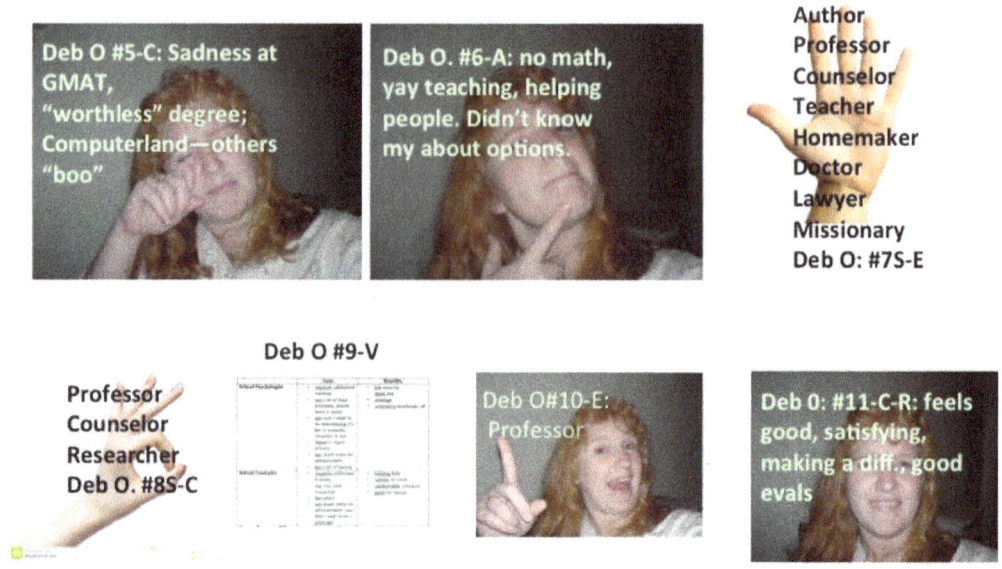

Figure 9.6 Sample CASVE Cycle via Snapchat

also possible to re-visit various phases. The Career Thoughts Inventory (Sampson et al., 1996a) and CTI workbook (Sampson et al., 1996b) identify negative career thoughts that may impact specific CASVE Cycle phases, that might need to be addressed, especially if a person is stuck in a particular phase.

Students or career explorers can self-identify or use support to identify their status within the cycle. If support is needed or requested, practitioners attune career decision-making interventions to assist with the stage of the cycle identified. CIP interventions that have been offered in FSU career courses include educating clients regarding the importance of active engagement in career planning, understanding of how their personal qualities may affect career decisions, supporting participants in learning practical job search and interview skills, and increasing awareness of economic trends that influence careers. Researchers have actively investigated the CASVE Cycle structure and found that advancing through the CASVE stages can enhance career decision-maker clarity, certainty, and confidence regarding choice-making (Osborn et al., 2020).

Related Art Process: Communication

Art-based processes can enhance exploration at each stage of the CASVE Cycle. During the initial communication phase, a practitioner may invite a client to create two artworks, one related to how they imagine their life in a year (or more) if they do not make a career-related decision at this time and a second artwork to reflect how they imagine their life in a year (or more) if they do make a career-related decision at this time. Similar art processes have been introduced to stimulate self-reflection and evaluation with those in treatment for substance use. Holt and Kaiser (2009) described the benefits of asking clients to depict themselves a year from now "if they made the changes that support recovery" (p. 9), as providing visual evidence related to choices that are under consideration and promoting awareness of potential consequences of action and inaction.

Figure 9.7 Collage: My Career In One year If I don't Consider a Work-Place Change

An example of this art process is represented by two collage artworks created by an attorney facing a career decision. The attorney reported that she had the unfortunate experience of being sexually harassed by a colleague at the prestigious law firm where she currently worked. She had filed a complaint with human resources department and the allegations were addressed by management. In the end, the attorney in question chose to resign from the firm in lieu of other sanctions. While she experienced relief and appreciation, she began to feel that others within the firm no longer trusted her and kept their distance. She had worked hard to advance in this firm but now felt unwelcomed by many. She came to career counseling to determine if she should stay with the firm or begin a search process for a more positive work climate. The first collage (Figure 9.7) represents the attorney's reflection on not making a work setting change within the next year.

The second collage (Figure 9.8) represents her situation if she would choose to seek other job opportunities outside of her current firm. After reflecting on both images and further evaluating her current situation and career values with support of career counseling, the attorney determined that she was willing to take the risk of seeking work elsewhere.

Related Art Process: Analysis

Creative processes can also be well aligned with the analysis phase of decision-making when individuals are exploring the fit between their skills and interests and possible career options. For example, Barba (2000) encouraged client use of creative processes such as art and writing, to explore personal values and limits that may inform career interests and choices. In one such process, Barba invited clients to recall experiences where they felt "lines had been crossed" and distress resulted. After recalling these events, clients were invited to draw emergent images and written narratives related to these experiences. Barba and clients reviewed the work together to identify the source

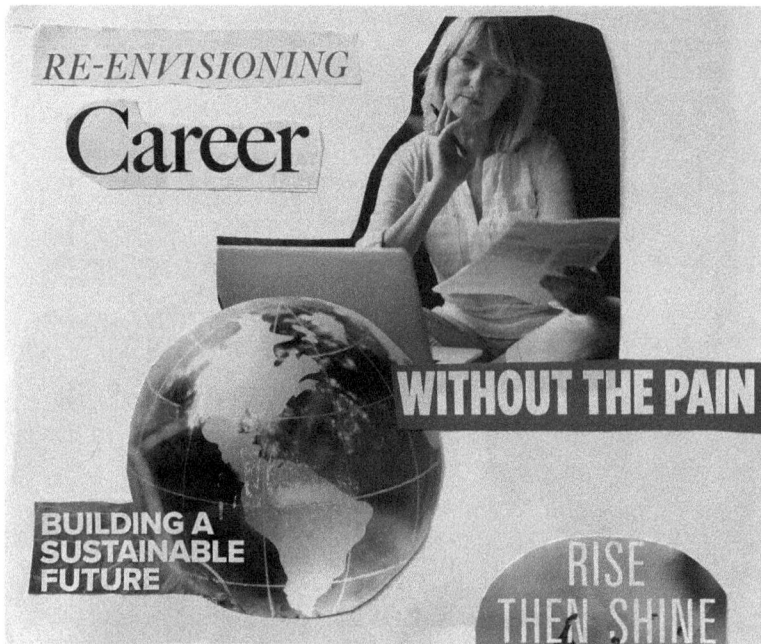

Figure 9.8 Collage: Reflection and Reinterpretation

of distress and implied values associated with the distress. Through the art, writing, and reflection process, clients increased their awareness of held beliefs that may inform satisfaction with career or work settings. Barba also facilitated guided imagery processes to stimulate imagination. Using guided imagery, she asked clients to imagine themselves on a magic carpet ride into their future. Images that emerged for the imaginal journey were created and reviewed for themes that may reveal interests and career and life goals.

In the synthesis phase, after more information about self and careers have been collected and examined, an art process inspired by Hayes' (2015) matchmaking model for career decision-making clients could be utilized. During this matchmaking process the client creates a series of artworks about what they have to offer a career focus or work environment, what they wish to receive from their work environment, and goals for growth and development within a chosen career. A manageable way to address this series of artworks would be to offer watercolor postcards that allow for drawing and painting on one side and written reflections on the opposite side. Next the client would create artworks related to career or work setting being considered related to expectations, conditions, opportunities, and future directions in the employment/career marketplace that may influence what may be available within that career or work setting in the coming years. Once characteristics of self and career or work setting have been depicted on the cards, the client can examine the matches and mismatches between their own qualities and wishes and the career or work setting expectations and offerings. This second set of cards could be made for a few final career options and be used to inform the valuing and execution stages of the CASVE Cycle. A synthesis-oriented series of artworks can provide a portfolio of visual information to be used for reflection and discussion between client and practitioner in support of a client's decision-making process.

In the final communication phase, a full review of CASVE-created artwork could be reviewed at the close of the client–practitioner relationship. Landgarten (1991) advocated for art task reviews at the closing of therapy, as a means of reflecting on themes that arose during the therapeutic experiences, to celebrate growth and decisions, and to prepare both client and practitioner for the appropriate goodbyes.

Understanding Personal Decision-Making Processes

Circles of Influence

Supporting client efforts to embrace the unknown and see potential in the unexpected events can prepare individuals for making necessary career decisions in difficult times. Pryor and Bright (2011) advocated for incorporating creative thinking strategies related to the chaos theory of career counseling into career decision-making counseling relationships. Creative thinking strategies encompass concepts and activities pertaining to challenges, probabilities, possibilities, and plans. Within these frameworks, clients explore their thoughts and perceptions regarding events, examine outcomes that could potentially occur, focus on possibilities instead of problems, and develop active strategies to move beyond current challenges.

Visually oriented tasks, such as the "Circles of Influence" technique created by Bright and Pryor (2003) and further described by Pryor and Bright (2011), can cultivate exploration regarding perceptions of career influences including unplanned events. Practitioners encourage clients to explore three circles of influence; 1) teachers, advisors, and media reflected in the inner circle; 2) family, friends, and colleagues represented in the middle circle; and 3) unplanned events that are represented within the third outermost circle. Clients are asked to list influences in each category to further their understanding of forces that have shaped their decisions in the past and to stimulate client considerations of probabilities for the future. Practitioners ask clients to reflect on one specific career decision they have made when they have completed the Circles of Influence form. In the case of adults, the practitioner may ask them to complete several forms to generate visual information that may reveal patterns of decision-making and influences. Additionally, reflecting on unplanned influences increases awareness of the role unexpected events may play in potentially positive ways.

Pryor and Bright (2011) recommended that the circle form be offered to clients for them to write their influences within the applicable circle. The finalized form would be reviewed with the practitioner. To extend this visual exploration, this author offers an art-based adaptation of the Circles of Influence task and provides a case example of how this adaptation may be used.

Case Example 1

The practitioner explained the Circles of Influence task and encouraged the participant to choose one career decision to explore. Instead of using a preset form, the practitioner provided the individual with a variety of circular forms for the client to select. In response, the individual elected to focus on her university and undergraduate major decisions. The client then selected the size of the circles of influences that represented teachers, advisors, and media, and the relative sizes of the second circle representing family, friends, and colleague influences, and the outer unplanned events circle. Next, the practitioner invited the individual to represent specific influencers in each circle and category using color. The individual chose watercolor crayons along with a brush and water to complete the art process (Figure 9.9).

When explaining her circle of influence to the practitioner, the individual observed that her high school teachers, reflected in the predominantly pink area, had a significant influence on her college major and the list of schools she considered. She remarked

Figure 9.9 Art-Based Circle of Influence, Watercolor Crayons on Paper

that she received good grades in her major and received encouragement and offers of references for her college applications. She also acknowledged the role of media in her college decision-making process. She noted that she had seen quite a bit of media about the status and reputation of the universities in her region and that the media was represented by the blue and yellow area. When she made her final decision, she selected the university that had the highest rankings in her state and significant recognition outside her state as well.

In terms of the family, friends, and colleagues circle, she stated that she was also strongly influenced by friends and family. Several of her high school classmates had selected the same school which eased some anxiety she had experienced about going away to school. However, she reported that the biggest influence on her was her family. Several family members on her mother's side of the family had experience with her major-related interests and were very encouraging of her pursuing a degree in this area. Additionally, her older sister had attended the same university and several great visits to her sister at the school in previous years, cemented her choice. She noted that all her family, friends, and influences were green because she felt that everyone was supporting her interests and growth.

When asked about the unplanned events circle, the individual became quiet, then slowly began to speak about the small dark triangle at its base. She noted that her father had unexpectedly passed away due to health issues four years before she was set to go to college. Given that her father had a "more practical" career and business, she wondered if he would have steered her towards a different career focus as she approached her college years. On a positive note, she was able to see the loss of her father as an experience that increased her sensitivity towards others and added additional motivation for her to pursue a psychology major. In subsequent conversations, the individual was able to identify her ability to move forward at that time as a sample of what she had the potential of doing in future difficult situations or unexpected career junctures.

Case Example 2

In this next example, an adult experiencing career transition was asked to review their "circles of influence" at four important career decision junctures. Provided with instructions that they may alter the size of the shapes that reflected each component (teachers, advisors, media; family, friends, colleagues; and unplanned events), the person elected to use their computer and word processing software to create the circles reflecting their undergraduate career decision, their graduate school and career change decision, and two job changes, where they had elected to move to new job opportunities. When reviewing the circles of influence side-by-side (Figure 9.10) they identified that teacher, advisor, and media influences had waned as they moved through their adult life.

They observed that family influences shifted from strong to moderate within the first three sets of circles, and then had a slightly increased during the fourth decision. The adult also noted that unplanned events played a consistent and significant positive role

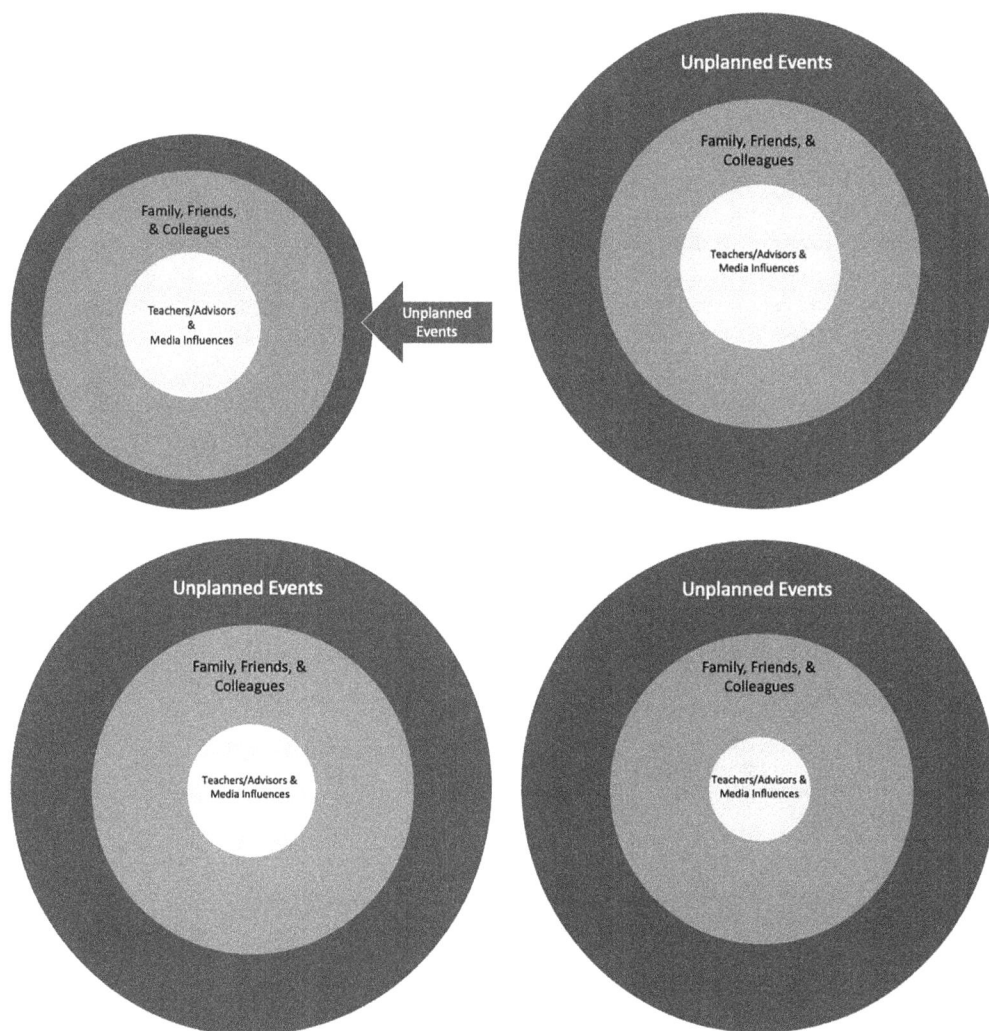

Figure 9.10 Circles of Influence: Pattern Exploration Related to Four Career Decision Junctures

in the last circumstances. When they experienced work setting climates as less satisfactory to them at past jobs, those conditions had made them curious about other options. Unexpectedly, attractive job opportunities had arisen at those times and motivated them to take a leap of faith in applying for and accepting options that would provide avenues for further career growth and improved work settings. Reflecting on their ability to embrace unplanned circumstances with success in several scenarios, they committed to an open-minded and curious approach to new opportunities that may appear. They began to work on action plans that would increase the prospects for unexpected positive events to be experienced.

Re-conceptualizing Unplanned Events and Exploration

Less structured art methods may also be used to explore one's responses to unplanned events or receptivity to new career investigations and decision-making. In this next example, see Figure 9.11, an individual used the art process to explore her attitude about her job search. As she approached her art process, she decided to relinquish control of the art medium and see what would come of it. She began by dropping watercolor on the paper and allowing it to run. She followed and expanded the drips with lines that represented potential new directions. After reviewing the multiple pathways, she developed some paths further and added footsteps to represent opportunities.

Upon reflection, she admitted that these options only vaguely represented job opportunities and that she was not ready to narrow her options. Still, she felt the experience opened her up to being more relaxed with career exploration versus prematurely narrowing her options to facilitate a quick conclusion to her career investigations. In this case, continued exploration of self-knowledge, options knowledge, and analysis would be important to complete prior to moving forward with synthesizing and executing career decisions.

Figure 9.11 Watercolor and Marker Unplanned Directions Exploration

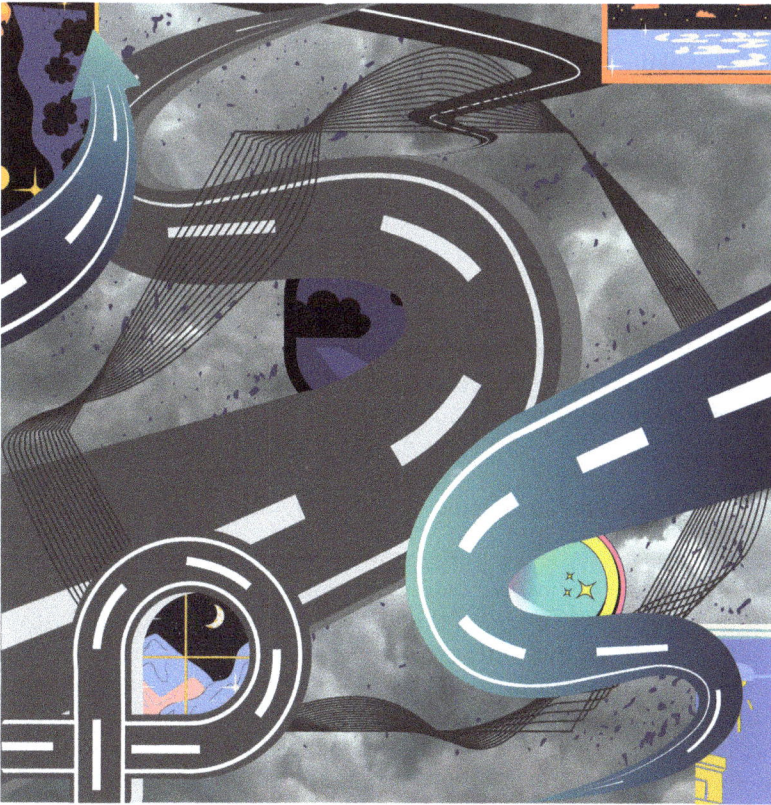

Figure 9.12 Tangle of Roads: Visual Consideration of Unplanned Events

A second student represented unplanned or unknown events that may influence their decision-making as a tangle of roads that could lead to various experiences or outcomes (See Figure 9.12). They described the overall feel of the artwork as stormy and that their initial response was to compare the construct of chance to a destructive tornado which destroys things and upsets plans. They noted they were uncomfortable with such negative feelings and were trying to consider the positive effects of unexpected changes and options that may come along. Therefore, they explained that the colorful sections within road loops or corners represented positive experiences that come from accidentally discovered opportunities. They concluded by observing that several of the roads appeared to extend off the page, representing pathways and options they have yet to imagine.

In this case, a practitioner subscribing to chaos theory-informed career interventions would support the client in embracing possibilities versus identifying and protecting a singular career outcome. The individual would be encouraged to make room for creativity, curiosity, risk-taking, and if necessary, learning from failure (Pryor, Amundson, & Bright, 2008). Given that the world is complex and subject to change, the unexpected should be expected, and this can be welcomed as means to new knowledge and growth. Individuals may be supported in identifying areas that could assist them in increasing their chances of making desired outcomes occur. Pryor et al. also noted that in the case of an indecisive client who has no problem generating possible pathways but has difficulty choosing a career starting place, the practitioner may need to steer the client to a more systematic manner of choosing from examined alternatives. Practitioner flexibility in responding to client needs is essential.

Summary

Career decision-making is a complex process that can feel unwieldy given the types and amount of information to be considered. Consequently, experience with career decision-making challenges is the most common reason people seek career-related support. Career decision-making problems encompass a broad spectrum of difficulties that occur before decision-making, during decision-making, and in the use of career information. As decision-making problems vary, many assessments have been designed to identify factors contributing to challenges. Once career challenges are illuminated, practitioners can fine-tune interventions to address specific concerns. Frequently, practitioners offer theory-based decision-making models to help clients manage career information and decision-making steps. Additionally, practitioners may provide creative art interventions to activate and bring attention to thoughts and feelings experienced related to career goals and decision-making processes.

Discussion Questions and Activities

1 Case exploration: Tina is an undergraduate student beginning her sophomore year in college. She began her studies at the university as an undeclared major and enrolled in a variety of general education classes during her first year to help refine her career goals and interest. This year, she has felt pressure from her parents to declare a major now, so as not to waste money on extra classes that may not count for a chosen major. While she has narrowed her interest to something in the visual arts, she still feels confused as there are many options at her school such as studio art, art history, museum studies, interior architecture to choose from. When looking at the majors' course requirements, she sees that there are fewer common classes among them during the sophomore year and is afraid she will make the wrong choice and waste her parents' money. She is also unsure if her parents will support her pursuit of a career in the arts and is now feeling anxious and frozen about which classes to take. She has come to the career services center to get some help with sorting out next steps. According to the CASVE Cycle, what stage of decision-making is Tina facing and what assessments or interventions would you offer?

2 What decision-making exploration processes or systematic models have you utilized to support your career decision-making? Which processes were most effective for you and how might your experiences influence the ways you would assist a client or student with a career decision-making process?

3 What are some creative ways that you could support a client's exploration and resolution of negative thinking regarding career decision-making?

4 What are some of the possible advantages of combining creative approaches with traditional prospective career decision-making model interventions?

5 Consider an everyday decision you need to make today, such as what to wear, what snack to get from the vending machine, what to eat for supper, which route you'll take home, and apply one of the career decision-making models to it. Then repeat the process with a different career decision-making model. Which worked better, if either? What contributed to that?

6 Think about the next major career decision you believe you will be making. Choosing one of the exercises described in this chapter, express that decision and factors impacting it in a creative manner. What does your art process and product reveal about your thoughts and feelings regarding this upcoming decision?

References

Barba, H. N. (2000). *Follow your bliss! A practical, soul centered guide to job-hunting and career planning.* Universal Publishers.

Bright, J. & Pryor, R. (2003). The exploring influences on career development technique. In M. McMahon & W. Patton (Eds.), *Celebrating excellence in Australian career practice: Ideas for career practitioners* (pp. 49–53). Australian Academic Press.

Forgeard, M., Silverman, A., Buchholz, J., et al. (2021). Changes in general self-efficacy and mindfulness are associated with short-term improvements in mood during art-making in a partial hospital program. *The Arts in Psychotherapy, 74,* 101799. https://doi.org/10.1016/j.aip.2021.101799

Gati, I. (1986). Making career decisions: A sequential elimination approach. *Journal of Counseling Psychology, 33*(4), 408–417. https://doi.org/10.1037/0022-0167.33.4.408

Gati, I., Krausz, M., & Osipow, S. H. (1996). A taxonomy of career decision making. *Journal of Counseling Psychology, 43,* 510–526. https://doi.org/10.1037/0022-0167.43.4.510

Gati, I., & Kulcsar, V. (2021). Making better career decisions: From challenges to opportunities. *Journal of Vocational Behavior, 126,* 103545. https://doi.org/10.1016/j.jvb.2021.103545

Gati, I., & Levin, N. (2014). Counseling for career decision-making difficulties: Measures and methods. *Career Development Quarterly, 62,* 99–113. https://doi.org/10.1002/j.2161-0045.2014.00073.x

Hayes, W. (2015). Matchmaking your career options. In M. McMahon & W. Patton (Eds.), *Ideas for career practitioners: Celebrating excellence in career practice* (pp. 103–105). Australian Academic Press eBook.

Holland, J. L., Daiger, D. C., & Powell, P. G. (1980). *My vocational situation.* Retrieved from https://career.fsu.edu/sites/g/files/imported/storage/original/application/f3dd4d17aeae2f581fb-9837fd16381f5.pdf

Holt, E., & Kaiser, D. H. (2009). The first step series: Art therapy for early substance abuse treatment. *The Arts in Psychotherapy, 36,* 245–250.

Kaimal, G., & Ray, K. (2017). Free art-making in an art therapy open studio: Changes in affect and self-efficacy. *Arts & Health, 9*(2), 154–166. https://doi.org/10.1080/17533015.2016.1217248

Landgarten, H. (1991). Termination theory and practice. In H. Landgarten, & D. Lubbers (Eds.). *Art psychotherapy: Issues and applications* (pp. 176–199). Brunner-Routledge.

Leierer, S. J., Peterson, G., Reardon, R. C., & Osborn, D. S. (2020). *The Career State Inventory (CSI) as a measure of the career decision state and readiness for career decision making: A manual for assessment, administration, and intervention* (2nd ed.). Florida State University. https://diginole.lib.fsu.edu/islandora/object/fsu%3A743264/datastream/PDF/view

Levin, N., & Gati, I. (2015). Facilitating the transition from school to work with a career decision-making approach: Process-related assessments and the PIC model. *Career Planning and Adult Development Journal, 30,* 127–143.

Osborn, D., Sides, R., Brown, C. A. (2020). Comparing career development outcomes among undergraduate students in cognitive information processing theory-based versus human relations course. *Career Development Quarterly, 69*(1), 32–47. https://doi.org/10.1002/cdq.1221

Osborn, D. S., Brown, C., & Morgan, M. (2021). Expectations, experiences and career-related outcomes of computer-assisted career guidance systems. *Journal of Employment Counseling, 58*(2), 74–90. doi:https://doi.org/10.1002/joec.12158

Osipow, S. H., Carney, C. G., Winer, J., et al. (1997). *Career Decision Scale.* Psychological Assessment Resources.

Peterson, G., Lenz, J., & Osborn, D. (2016). *Decision Space Worksheet (DSW) activity manual.* Florida State University Center for the Study of Technology in Counseling and Career Development. Retrieved from http://fsu.digital.flvc.org/islandora/object/fsu%3A540931

Peterson, G. W., Sampson, J. P., Jr., Reardon, R. C., & Lenz, J. G. (1996). A cognitive information processing approach to career problem solving and decision making. In D. Brown, L. Brooks, & Associates (Eds.), *Career choice and development* (3rd ed., pp. 423–476). Jossey-Bass.

Pryor, R., Amundson, N. E., Bright, J. E. H. (2008). Probabilities and possibilities: The strategic counseling implications of the chaos theory of careers. *Career Development Quarterly, 56*(4), 309–315.

Pryor, R., & Bright, J. (2011). *The chaos theory of careers: A new perspective on working in the twenty-first century.* Routledge.

Rochat, S. (2019). The Career Decision-Making Difficulties Questionnaire: A case for item-level interpretation. *The Career Development Quarterly, 67*, 205–218. https://doi.org/10.1002/cdq.12191

Sampson, J. P., Jr., McClain, M., Musch, E., & Reardon, R. C. (2013a). A partial listing of instruments that can be used as a component of readiness assessment. Center for the Study of Technology in Counseling and Career Development. Faculty publication. Retrieved from: https://fsu.digital.flvc.org/islandora/object/fsu%3A209960

Sampson, J. P., Jr., McClain, M., Musch, E., & Reardon, R. C. (2013b). Variables affecting readiness to benefit from career interventions. *The Career Development Quarterly, 61*, 98–108. https://doi.org//10.1002/j.2161-0045.2013.00040.x

Sampson, J. P., Jr., Osborn, D. S., & Bullock-Yowell, E. (2020). Promoting career choices. In S. D. Brown, & R. W. Lent (Eds.), *Career development and counseling: Putting theory and research to work* (pp. 675–702). John Wiley & Sons.

Sampson, J. P., Jr., Peterson, G. W., Lenz, J. G., et al. (1996a). *Career Thoughts Inventory: Professional manual.* Psychological Assessment Resources.

Sampson, J. P., Jr., Peterson, G. W., Lenz, J. G., et al. (1996b). *Career Thoughts Inventory workbook.* Psychological Assessment Resources.

Sangganjanavanich, V. F., & Magnuson, S. (2011). Using sand trays and miniature figures to facilitate career decision making. *The Career Development Quarterly, 59*, 264–273.

Santos, A., Wang, W., & Lewis, J. (2018). Emotional intelligence and career decision-making difficulties: The mediating role of career decision self-efficacy. *Journal of Vocational Behavior, 107*, 295–309. https://doi.org/10.1016/j.vb.2018.05.008

Sargent, A. C. & Lenz, J. G. (2017). The Career Thoughts Inventory (CTI) and CTI workbook: A purposeful integration of theory, research, and practice in career assessment and intervention. *Career Development Network Journal, 33*, 45–56.

Schwarzer, R., & Jerusalem, M. (1995). Generalized self-efficacy scale. In J. Weinman, S. Wright, & M. Johnston (Eds.), *Measures in health psychology: A user's portfolio. Causal and control beliefs* (pp. 35–37). NFER-Nelson.

Storme, M., & Celik, P. (2018). Career exploration and career decision-making difficulties: The moderating role of creative self-efficacy. *Journal of Career Assessment, 26*(3), 445–456. https://doi.org/10.1177/1069072717714540

Swank, J. M., & Jahn, S. A. B. (2018). Using sand tray to facilitate college students' career decision-making: A qualitative inquiry. *The Career Development Quarterly, 66*, 269–278.

Watson, D., Clark, L. A., & Tellegen, A. (1988). Development and validation of brief measures of positive and negative affect: The PANAS scales. *Journey of Personality and Social Psychology, 54*, 1063–1070.

Wong, C. S., & Law, K. S. (2002). The effects of leader and follower emotional intelligence on performance and attitude: An exploratory study. *The Leadership Quarterly, 13*(3), 243–274. http://dx.doi.org/10.1016/S1048-9843

10 Using Creativity to Support the Client Job Search Process

In this chapter, therapeutic and practical tasks related to the job search process of clients will be described. Art-based examination of clients' specific job search processes will be identified and illustrated through case examples and offered art-based exercises. Means for supporting development of résumé writing, interviewing skills, and social media management will also be included. Finally, challenges to job search processes, particularly related to discrimination, multicultural issues and contexts, and experienced career barriers will be examined.

Preparing for the Job Search

Importance of Self Knowledge

Preparing for a job search is a complex and often time-consuming task, especially if the need to launch a job search emerges suddenly or in an unexpected way, as with cutbacks or a need to relocate. Aside from addressing the technical elements of a job search (e.g., résumé writing, interviewing skills, job searching tactics, etc.), practitioners can support clients during a job search by helping answer the "What's next?" question in terms of their career plans. This may include a revisiting of the client's interests, values, and skills, or reviewing their job history to understand what was and was not fulfilling about their previous jobs. Many of the activities described in the earlier chapters might be helpful in clarifying the client's self-knowledge as a foundational step of successful job searching. Of key importance is clarifying needs. What does a client need their work to provide at this stage in their life? Are they looking for financial security, high salary, opportunity to progress, travel, flexible hours? Knowing and respecting what is of primary importance to the individual in their current context as they consider their options is key to designing an optimal job search. In addition, understanding the urgency for finding work is important. If a client does not have enough money to provide for shelter and food, the focus would need to potentially shift to stop-gap employment, or finding less-than-optimal work that will help provide for immediate needs, rather than exploring ideal options. Once primary needs are addressed, attention can then be shifted to longer-term employment goals.

Impact of Self-Talk on Job Searching

Exploring self-talk may also be important when working with a job searcher. What a person believes about themselves and the world of work may have an impact on how they approach the various aspects of job search. Asking how a client feels about the job search can be a useful place to begin. Emotions might range from dread to confusion to inadequacy or

DOI: 10.4324/9781003035756-10

excitedness. Exploring the thoughts behind the emotions can help a practitioner know where to focus. For example, if someone is feeling like they don't have much to offer a potential employer, a practitioner might spend time helping the client explore experiences and skills they have, and practice via mock interviewing answers to questions specific to skills. If the negative thoughts are intrusive, and the client is concerned about them impacting their ability during the interview, the practitioner can help them to develop cognitive reframes or simple mantras they can tell themselves in the moment.

Case of Dana

Dana is preparing for upcoming interviews, but shares with her practitioner that she is highly anxious about making a good impression. When the practitioner asks more about her concerns, she says she always gets nervous and starts talking really fast about irrelevant things. She can feel her face getting hot, and her hands feeling clammy. Mostly, she feels like a phony, that something she says will show to them that she really isn't qualified for the position. Then Dana said, "I'm getting worked up about it right now, just thinking about it!"

The practitioner asked Dana how she came to realize that she was experiencing the same emotions and physical reactions in that moment, and Dana said that she noticed she was the one doing most of the talking, and that she could feel the heat in her face and neck. Seeing this awareness as a positive sign, the practitioner worked with Dana to identify some coping strategies to use when in an actual interview and these symptoms occur. Some of these included taking a deep breath, coming with a water bottle and taking a sip, changing her body position to trigger a change in behavior, and putting her hand over her mouth as a physical reminder to speak less.

They then turned their attention to her negative self-talk. After exploring what core beliefs were undergirding her negative self-talk (e.g., "I'm not ____ (smart, skilled, savvy) enough" or "I don't deserve good things (like this job) to happen to me"), they came up with a list of evidence points to contradict those thoughts. For example, to address the knowledge and skills self-talk, their list included her degree, her grade point average, a recommendation letter from a faculty member, her internship, and an award she had received for a project. They then looked at the job description to identify further evidence points for specific required and desired skills, such as experience with specific software, which Dana had. They then brainstormed some cognitive reframes that would address this specific negative thought. Some of these included, "I have just what they are asking for, and more," or "I bring the whole package," or "Baby, you've got it." Dana practiced saying these out loud to the practitioner, and then into a mirror. She liked the last one best, because it came from a song she enjoyed. She decided she would play that song on the way to her interviews as a reminder and to reinforce the self-talk. In addition, the practitioner asked Dana to create or find a small 3D object that she could put in her pocket or hold in her hand prior to and throughout the interview that could serve as an in-the-moment reminder. Dana decided to create her own (see Figure 10.1). She said the character's name is Venus, after the song, and that the full body will remind her that she brings the full package, and that the fun design will remind her to smile and remember that she is uniquely qualified for their position.

If a client is truly lacking the skills for a specific occupation or job listing, the CP might focus the discussion on gaining those skills, highlighting other skills that are desired, or searching for opportunities that better match the client's skills. Job seekers are by nature involved in a potential transition, and thus discussing thoughts, emotions, and considerations related to this transition is also recommended. See Chapter 13 for recommendations for working with individuals in transitions.

Figure 10.1 Dana's 3D Object, "Venus"

Finding Job Opportunities

Once a client has clarified their employment preferences, the next step is to identify potential employers, openings, and opportunities. Some opportunities are obvious – they are posted on online job boards or via help-wanted ads, or on company websites. Others are not so obvious, and may not be advertised at all. These are part of "the hidden job market," and are most often accessed through networking. As an example, an employer may be thinking about expanding the business, or perhaps recently learned that an employee will need to relocate in the upcoming months. It's possible they aren't thinking about adding a position at all, but in conversation with a friend, or through reading an article about industry-specific trends, seeds for a future hire are planted. If a qualified job seeker emerges at the right place and time, the employer may make the hire without advertising the position, especially in smaller companies. A larger company may still need to advertise the position, but the job seeker in this case would have the advantage of knowing about the position ahead of time.

Career practitioners can help clients access the hidden job market by helping them become "findable" by employers, and by co-creating a plan for developing and strengthening their network and networking skills. In today's society, both of these are often best accomplished online. Although, job seekers should also include traditional means, such as mentioning they are looking for work to people they see on a regular basis, and especially those who interface with a wide range of people (e.g., a restaurant owner, barber, physician, etc.). Networking strategies will be covered more in depth later in this chapter.

Researching Employers

After a person identifies potential employers, the next essential step in the job search process is to learn about them. Common areas to explore include required education or training,

Table 10.1 Comparison of two job offers to individual preferences

What I want	Job A	Job B
Use my advertising degree	Smaller company – responsible for not only advertising, but also marketing, media productions, and graphic design.	Main focus is on creating advertising appropriate for clients.
Work in teams	Small advertising team within the company; work together and individually, depending on the project.	Larger team – may be opportunities to work in different teams.
Be a part of a company that actively gives back	Has multiple activities, scholarships, etc., that the company is involved with, as well as opportunities for employees' involvement.	Company donates 5% of its profits to charities determined by its employees.
International travel	Some – mainly for clientele that is specific to Ireland.	Limited, if at all – mostly US clientele.
Clear value of diversity and inclusion	Has an equal opportunity statement on their website; pictures on website show diversity – not so much clear diversity with upper management.	Has an equal opportunity statement on their website; provides a leadership training/mentorship focused on those from under-represented groups; leadership consists of clearly diverse people.
Voice in decisions	Smaller company – seems like everyone has a voice; employees say that they feel heard.	Advertising team has a leader who attends the larger meetings and voices ideas.
Salary around $40,000 with upward mobility	Stated starting salary is $35,000 with a $5,000 signing bonus, annual reviews, and bonuses for bringing on new clients.	Starting salary is $45,000, no signing bonus, annual reviews.

specific job tasks, salary, geographical location, travel (requirements or opportunities), and benefits. Other information that a person wants to learn is linked to their values (stemming from self-knowledge) – what do they want their work to provide? Examples of this might include stability, opportunity for advancement, working alone or in teams, dress expectations, commitment to diversity, flexibility in work hours, and so on. The client can then use this information as a plumbline against which opportunities and offers are evaluated.

Case of Elijah

Consider Elijah, who has been offered two positions, and is trying to determine which position will be the best one for him to pursue. Table 10.1 shows a brief comparison of what he knows about himself and jobs A and B. Because he knew what was most important to him, he was able to pinpoint his research of the companies and the positions, both in his online research and in his conversations with the employers and employees. While the final outcome is still undecided, he has more clarity about how each position may or may not fit him. The next step will be for him to consider what is essential to him, and what he is and is not willing to compromise.

How to Research Employers

Researching employers usually involves examining their website and social media accounts. A downside to just relying on these sources is that the information is biased – the employer is sharing what they want to share, which may be their ideal but not the reality. Searching other venues such as the name of the employer and the word "news" or searching within a news category can provide another perspective. Searching social media using the company's name as a hashtag will provide even more perspectives. Using negative words such as the company name plus "complaint" or "sucks" will highlight not just gripes, but specific areas for improvement. A job seeker wouldn't say "I noticed a common complaint about your company is ____, and I have just this answer," but instead might use this knowledge in a cover letter, résumé, or interview to highlight certain skills. For example, if a common complaint was customer service, clearly highlighting evidence of customer service would be a recommended step. Online job search sites such as glassdoor.com and even general online review companies such as Yelp may provide a job searcher with insight about the pros and cons of working for a specific company.

Researching Employers Builds Self and Options Knowledge

As indicated in the case of Elijah, as a person engages in the process of job searching and researching employers, they learn more about themselves and their options. Through exploring various options, whether online or through interviews, the client will begin to prioritize what is most important to them in making an employment decision. One strategy for helping a client prepare for a job search is to examine online résumés specific to the occupation(s) of interest. For example, use "accountant resume" as a key term and review the search results. By looking at several examples, the client can see what kinds of skills and experiences are common for individuals in that position, and then compare to their own résumé and skills. They can create a comparison table (Table 10.2) to see where they match and to provide specific examples they can then use in a cover letter or an interview. In this example, the client searched for accounting résumés, and created a list of recurring types of job tasks and skills in the first column. In the second column, they evaluated whether or not they had those experiences and skills, and in the final column, either wrote a specific example or identified a plan for developing the skill. A practitioner can also guide the individual to examine how they feel about the tasks and experiences listed on these samples. Looking at current résumés also provides the client with a knowledge of common résumé styles, what is and is not regularly included on résumés specific to that occupation, and ideas of how to present skills and experiences.

Table 10.2 Résumé versus reality comparison

Résumé	Have I done that?	Specific example or plan
Helped increased profits by implementing cost-cutting strategies	No	Plan: I will ask my internship supervisor if I can work with someone on this.
Performed financial analysis for new clients and evaluated potential risks	Sort of	Example: In my minor, we performed multiple analyses for different case examples. Plan: I will ask my internship supervisor if I can shadow or co-perform this task in the next month.
Reconciled monthly trust and control accounts, including group remuneration, principal on deposit, and accounts retrievable	Yes	Example: As treasurer of the accounting club, this was a regular part of my job.
Managed general ledgers	Yes	Example: I have had training on Excel Macro and other databases and used that in the accounting club.
Member of American Accounting Association	No	Plan: Join!

Accessing the Hidden Job Market

Job searching is no longer a one-way street, where a job searcher tries to locate potential employers, researches them, and then applies to selected positions. Headhunters, who are employed by companies to locate individuals who might be a good fit for their position, are an example of an employer who proactively is searching for potential quality employees before a position is even advertised, if it is advertised at all. This activity isn't limited to headhunters, and with online platforms, many small employers will use these tools in a similar way to find potential hires. Thus, job seekers need to be "findable" by these potential employers, and one key way to do this is through the development of an online professional identity.

Developing and Managing an Online Professional Identity

Individuals who have a virtual presence can provide tangible information and evidence to a potential employer about a candidate. The type of information that an individual provides online can critically impact impressions. Thus, prior to applying for jobs, it is advisable for applicants to complete an online audit of themselves, review their online presence, social media posts, images, and so forth and evaluate them from the perspective of an employer. What do these posts and pictures suggest? What assumptions might be made about how they might be in the work environment? At the same time, social media, handled professionally, can create a positive perspective. For example, creating a blog is relatively easy. A job seeker could begin a blog that focuses on a particular field, and could include posts about current events, summaries of recently published research, reviews of resources that might be useful, video demonstrations of specific skills, interviews with people and the field, and so forth. By creating a blog such as this, a person demonstrates their knowledge of the field, their connections, their knowledge of current issues and resources for their field, and their commitment to contributing to the profession's community and educating the community at large about the field. By including a link to their blog on their résumé and in their email signature, they create an opportunity for potential employers to see beyond the résumé and experience firsthand their knowledge and skills. Below, we highlight some of the more popular social media venues and describe how they might be used to support clients in the job search.

LinkedIn

While not all industries are represented online, many employers' go-to online source for finding potential professional employees is LinkedIn. LinkedIn is a professional networking site that is used for networking but also for job searching. Individuals can post their experiences, create blog entries, join professional groups, connect with other professionals and indicate they are job searching. Many books and guides (e.g., Dodaro, 2019; Wittman, 2019) have been written about how to maximize the benefits of LinkedIn. A practitioner should refer clients to these resources, but can also make some recommendations such as including a professional headshot, creating a professional summary that communicates their professional identity, including as many specific details as possible about employers, colleges and schools attended, joining relevant groups, include specific keywords in their headlines, and using the blog function to share professional information (Osborn et al., 2014). With a focus on networking, the client can best use LinkedIn by forming opportunities for other professionals to connect with their profile or via others who are connected with a desired employer. More details on networking are provided in an upcoming section.

Twitter

Not only does Twitter act as a social micro-blogging site, it is also an excellent source for networking and job searching. While many individuals use Twitter for their personal posts, the site is also home to thousands of employers who use Twitter as a venue for sharing insight into the company culture. Practitioners can help clients create a professional online presence on Twitter by helping them wordsmith their brief bio, linking to their LinkedIn profile, and considering what kinds of tweets and hashtags are likely to impress potential employers (Osborn et al., 2014). Practitioners can also teach clients how to search for employers, keywords specific to the industries they are interested in working in (to identify key players), and how to contribute meaningfully to those groups.

Instagram

As a visual social media platform, Instagram allows for users to post pictures and videos that demonstrate the individual's skills, experiences, and personality. Job seekers can post evidence of themselves demonstrating key skills required by a specific position. A person can be encouraged to continue posting evidence of work-related experience, awards, number of likes, and so forth, even after they've received a job, as it will then become evidence for future work. Similar to other social media websites, well chosen hashtags can increase the number of views. A search on #career yielded 6.4 million posts, while #hireme had 762,000 posts, and another on #resume tips resulted in 189,000 posts. Major companies also have Instagram accounts, and clients can be encouraged to post on topics of relevance to specific companies, join contests, and engage strategically in ways to get noticed in positive ways.

YouTube

Video résumés are a unique, warmer way of sharing skills, experiences, career goals, communication skills, and personality with potential employers. Videos should be brief, and well edited and produced. They can be targeted to a specific company or focus on a specific industry or skills set. The job searcher should seek professional feedback about how the video comes across before making it public. In addition, once the video is live, the job seeker can increase visibility by using hashtags, linking to it in other social media accounts, and adding a link to the email signature. Search "video resume" or "video CV" to see some current examples.

Facebook

Facebook has long been at the top of the social media sites. As such, employers also have a strong presence there, often posting information that won't be on their company website. Following a company's page can help a job seeker stay informed of company events and news (Osborn et al., 2014). Job seekers can also involve friends and family in their job search, but should be cautioned not to overdo it with requests for help, connections, and information. Letting friends and family know that they are looking for a specific type of work, in a specific location, and asking if anyone knows someone they might talk with is a recommended first step. If interested in a specific company, the job seeker can mention that as well. If the job seeker is currently employed and hasn't shared with their employer that they plan to leave, it would be advisable to not share that information on social media but instead to either ask more general questions to determine who might be helpful, ask via other means, or wait until the conversation has been had with the current employer.

Other Social Media

Clients should be encouraged to explore the social media sites they regularly use (a) to see if employers of interest have an account on that venue, and (b) to determine the message they are sending to potential employers. Companies with a marketing department or social media manager will be making their presence known on these sites as a way to engage with potential hires. TikTok, for example, is a social media platform that uses brief videos to communicate content. Clients can be coached to search for company names, to add hashtags. There are also sites that provide job searching advice on topics such as résumé writing and interviewing. Reddit is an example where everyday people comment on questions related to everyday concerns, including job search and career issues. As expected, not all of the advice and comments are ones that a practitioner might endorse. Still, there can be some information that is of value, such as learning from others' personal experiences. A practitioner might ask a client to bring examples of these sites into the session, or search for them together to evaluate the content and usefulness of what is being shared. This might also create ideas for unique self-marketing approaches for the individual.

Virtual Career Fairs

Career fairs traditionally are held in a large arena, with employers setting up tables and talking with prospective employees about the company/organization, available opportunities, and the job seeker's skills and experiences. If the conversation is positive, the job seeker might leave a résumé with the employer, and the employer might then follow up with an interview. Virtual career fairs follow the same idea, but differ in delivery, due to the online nature of the venue. A career fair could be hosted by one employer with various position openings or geographical opportunities, or it might be hosted by a larger group such as a university career center or a community center and include multiple employers. These employers might be focused on a specific career field, such as health-care jobs, or a geographical location, or type of work, such as part-time or contract work. In addition, virtual career fairs may also focus on specific populations, such as veterans or minority engineers (Osborn et al., 2014).

What actually happens at a fair varies as well. Employers might provide an overview of the company and positions and then take general questions, or they might have a sign-up sheet where prospective employees can chat for a short time, or both. When supporting a client who is preparing to attend a virtual career fair, a practitioner should encourage them to learn as much as possible about the fair, the employers of interest, and how the fair will be conducted. It may be that they will want the applicant to upload a résumé prior to talking with them; having that information is crucial to make a good impression. Knowing how to dress for an online interview, how to adjust sound and lighting to give off the best impression, are also important strategies.

Job Search Websites and Smartphone Apps

A common way of searching for jobs is to use websites and apps devoted to job searching. These tools allow a job seeker to create a general application or upload a résumé, and then send that résumé or application to employers of interest who have posted job openings on their site/app. Two examples of general job search sites/apps are indeed. com and glassdoor.com. Often these sites have information about the company, employer ratings, and other information such as common interview questions. Other job search websites might be specific to industry, such as higheredjobs.com, which focuses on positions within colleges and universities. Because these openings are viewable by the entire online population, employers will likely be inundated with applications. A client might need a practitioner's suggestions and guidance on how to make their application stand out from the rest. The strategies presented in this chapter that focus on how to demonstrate that connection between an employer's need and the job seeker's skills are likely the best way to accomplish this goal.

Professional Networking

A key aspect of all social media in the job search is developing and maintaining a professional network. While quantity is important, quality may be even more so. This translates into using social media as a tool in a precise way, consistently contributing to communities that will make an impression on potential employers, or on people who can connect the job seeker to potential employers. It's not enough to make a connection, that connection needs to be nurtured, through comments, hashtags, mentions, and contributions, such as "I saw this headline and thought of you/your company/your product."

To develop their professional network, a job seeker might start with their existing network, and see if any of those in the network are directly involved in the desired industry, work, geographical location, company, or agency of interest. In addition to reaching out to that person and asking for suggestions, they can also look at their contact's connections, and request an introduction. Groups or classes provide an excellent opportunity to practice networking. In Figure 10.2, we asked students to indicate on a map where they hoped to live after graduation. One person added New Zealand to our picture. We then chose specifically identified locations and asked students to indicate if they knew anyone in that state. We used that activity as an example of how closely connected we are, and that a contact linking to the desired position or place could be just one conversation away.

Some high schools and most colleges and universities have alumni clubs or groups that a graduate can join. LinkedIn (linkedin.com/alumni) can provide all kinds of work information on LinkedIn accounts from alumni from a specific university (Osborn et al., 2014). While requests for connecting are often automatic with many social networking

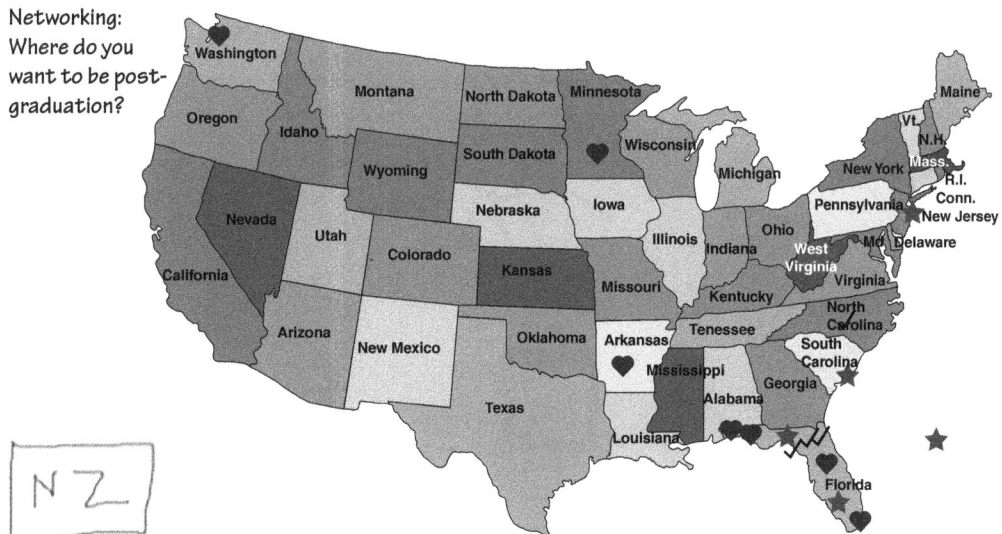

Figure 10.2 Sample Networking Map

sites, creating a more personalized introduction and request to connect is likely to yield more positive outcomes.

Art-Based Processes to Stimulate Ideas about Networks

While social media networks provide opportunities to extend networks, utilizing art-based means to conceptualize potential networks may be helpful. In this regard, Brown (2015) offered a simple visual form and network planning sheet for adult job seekers. The worksheet included circles with labels including friends, family, extracurricular contacts, work and study colleagues, and others. Job seekers are invited to fill these circles with brainstormed names of people that could be potential contacts and links to opportunities. Once the form was completed, the job seeker was prompted to select five people to contact, note the reason for contact, and then prepare questions for specific conversational inquiries.

This visual worksheet holds some resemblance to visual eco-maps that are utilized to examine social support systems available to clients. Baumgartner et al. (2012) described the eco-map as a graphic representation of an individual or family's links to formal and informal networks using lines, shapes, and colors that have been standardized to represent qualities of connections and relationships between the clients and their social resources. This form is completed by the individual or family and then reviewed together with the professional to enable the professional's increased understanding of client contexts and resources. Baumgartner et al. (2012) supported younger clients' use of utilized images or client photos to represent their social resources, finding that less abstract forms of images stimulated conversations. Similarly, an art-based network exploration in a career context can foster dialogues about potential networks and increase awareness regarding strengths and gaps in available resources.

Figure 10.3 represents a job seeker's initial depiction of networking options. These options included social media networks, fraternity, social engagements, fellow students,

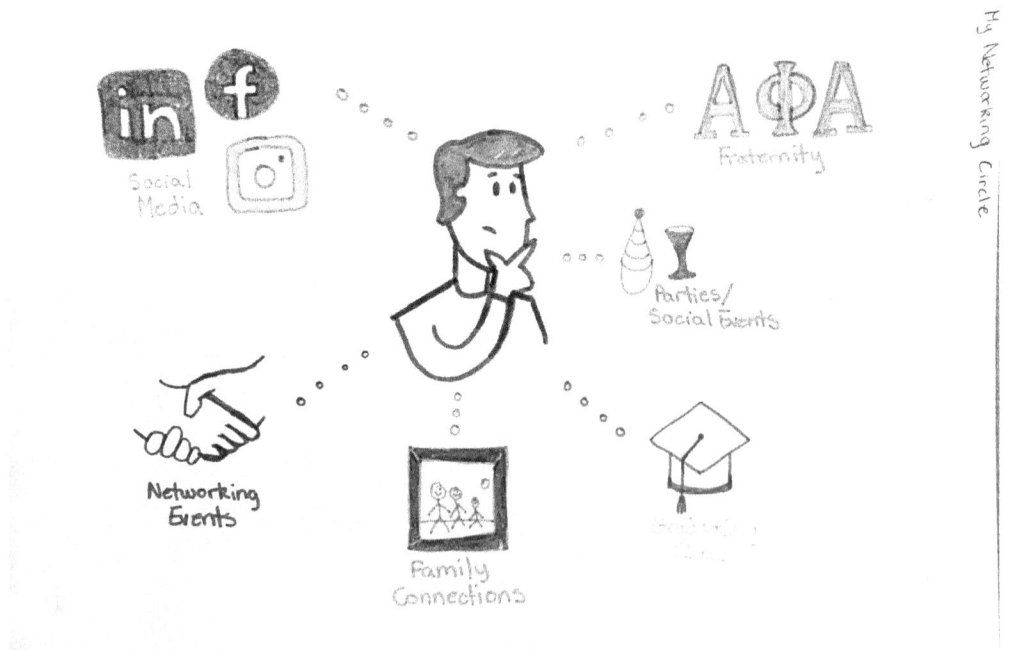

Figure 10.3 "My Networking Circles" Marker Drawing

Figure 10.4 "Networks Old and New", Gouache and Color Pencil on Paper

family members, and job fair networking events. During the exploration of the image the job seeker was encouraged to brainstorm more specifically regarding the contacts within those groups that may be most helpful to contact, so that more detailed strategies and plans for preferred inquiries could be made.

This second image (Figure 10.4) reflects a job seeker's creative depiction of her networks and her desire to extend her networks through social contacts. When reflecting on the image, she noted that she was the central figure in blue interacting with the woman in light orange and added that, at this very moment in this image, an important connection was being formed. She noted that taking time to visualize her networks and create a networking image helped her imagine possibilities that would help her meet her career objectives.

Résumé Writing

The traditional résumé has not become extinct. Having an up-to-date résumé is recommended for job seekers as well as those who are not yet seeking, as one never knows when opportunity may strike. The key purpose of a résumé is to interest the potential employer enough that they want to speak with the job seeker more. Thus, the goal for a résumé is to gain an interview. In the past, a job seeker would use the same résumé for multiple positions. This was because résumés were often typeset, so changing them was expensive. With the ease of word processing, tailoring a résumé to a specific type of work or even employer is now feasible and recommended. The résumé should demonstrate a clear connection between the job seeker and the qualifications the employer desires. A job seeker should be encouraged to use the same words the employer uses in the job description or on their website. For example, do they use the word teamwork or collaboration, lead or direct, vision or goal? Many guides and templates exist for résumé writing; a practitioner does not need to be an expert in this area but can refer clients to these guides. They can also provide general feedback on the overall look of the résumé and how well it communicates the desired message. Helping clients avoid common mistakes of typographical or grammar errors, providing too little or too much detail, is also recommended. Vitas are similar to résumés but are usually longer and for positions such as academia or research.

Some fields have definite preferences and traditions regarding résumés, what is and is not included on them, how they are formatted, the order of how items are listed, and so forth. To determine if the client's field is one of these, a career practitioner can help the client search online for the job title or occupation (e.g., mechanical engineer) and the word "resume." A quick review of the images posted can show general style, while a more detailed look can provide specific examples. Creative fields might be more open to unique types of résumés, such as the two in Figures 10.5 and 10.6.

Cover Letters

Cover letters can be seen as the introduction to a résumé or vita, thus, if a person is hand-delivering a résumé to the employer, one is not necessary. The letter is necessary when a job seeker is mailing a résumé, whether via traditional mail or email. Usually one page in length, the purpose of the cover letter is to convince the employer to take a close look at the résumé. The first paragraph is brief, introducing the person and clearly stating the purpose for writing. If a position number is known, that should be indicated as well. The second paragraph should highlight how the candidate matches the desired qualifications. This shouldn't be a repeat of what's on the résumé, but instead paint the bigger picture. If the person does not have a desired qualification, that can be pointed out with a caveat that the job seeker is willing and able to learn that particular skill. The final paragraph points the attention to the résumé and expresses a desire to talk more. A client might need a practitioner to help them identify the most salient points to include in a cover letter.

Interviewing

If the purpose of the résumé is to yield an interview, then the goal of the interview is to yield a job offer. Advice on interviewing is easily accessible online. Like the résumé, the focus should be on how to show a match between what the employer wants and the job seeker provides. It is not only the job seeker that is being evaluated; the job seeker should be evaluating how well the potential job fits their needs. A practitioner can help a job seeker by offering mock interviews, where they pose questions that the candidate is likely to be asked and allowing them to practice and refine their answers. While some general questions can be anticipated, such as "Why do you want to work for us?," or "What are your strengths and weaknesses in respect to this position," or "What questions do you have for us?" Job seekers can learn about specific questions the employer is likely to ask thanks to social media. Sites like glassdoor.com provide company reviews and often include current and past employee comments, ranging from interview questions that were asked to what the working environment is like.

Job applicants will most often be asked "What questions do you have for us?" This question requires preparation and is an opportunity for practitioners to help. While asking general questions about start dates and what a successful employer looks like can be helpful, asking more informed questions showcases the job seeker's resourcefulness and

Susan Smith

BOTANIST

EXECUTIVE SUMMARY

Result-oriented botany professional looking for a senior position in research industry where my experience of exploring all types of plants can help in research and find effective remedies for conservation, forestry, and horticulture

SKILLS AND EXPERTISE

Environmental assessment
Invasive plant management
Ability to conduct field surveys
Knowledge of state regulation
GPS mapping and data analysis

CONTACT ME AT:

Email: hello@reallygreatsite.com
Phone: (123) 456 7890
Website:
www.reallygreatsite.com
Office Address: 123 Anywhere St
Any City, State, Country 12345

WORK EXPERIENCE

BOTANIST

Zathrax ICF International, Cleveland, Ohio
November 2016 – Present

- Studying the life cycle of rare plant species from the samples of plant chromosomes, tissues and cells
- Working with other botanists to determine possible drugs, medicines and other products from plants
- Participating in on-field visits to identify new species of plants and determine their class of specimen

FIELD BOTANIST

Spanace Group Pvt. Ltd., Cleveland, Ohio
April 2013 – July 2015

- Performed on-field surveys for vascular plant species and prepared reports on advised control methods
- Coordinated with state resource specialists to update the surveys for rare plant and animal species
- Compiled a report on the status of affected botanical resources under renewable energy resource plan

SCHOOLS ATTENDED

OHIO STATE UNIVERSITY

Bachelor of Science in Botany 2011

Figure 10.5 Botanist Résumé

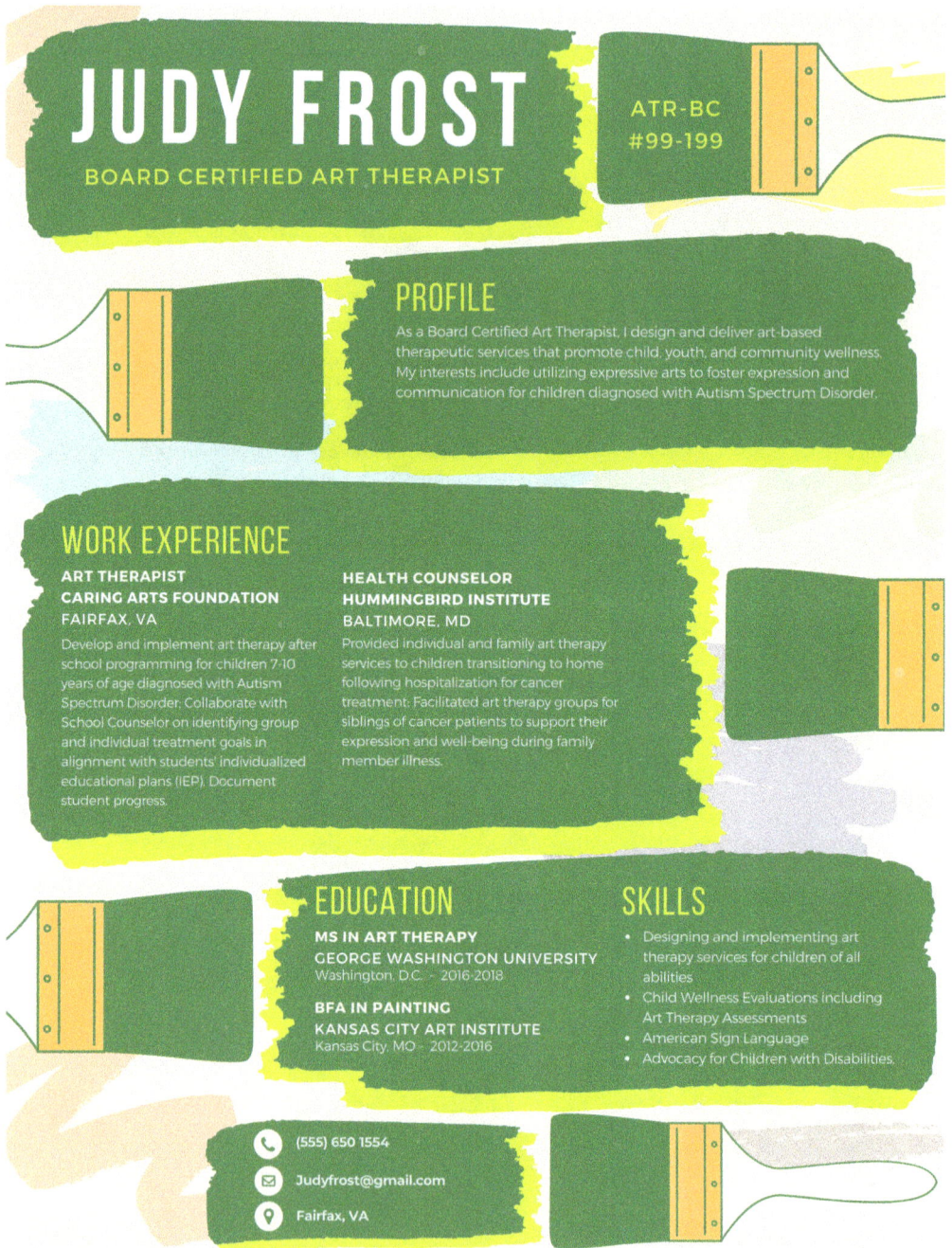

Figure 10.6 Art Therapist Résumé

interest. Thus, the applicant is encouraged to research the employer prior to the interview. Topics to research include what services or products the employer provides, which are the most and least sought after, who their competitors are, who their market is (and is not), news about the company (often posted on social media), where they are located, and so forth. Based on this information, a potential employee can ask targeted questions such as, "I saw the company is opening a branch in the Netherlands. Are there opportunities for transferring geographically?" Another question would be, "I read about this new product you have coming out. What are the plans for marketing it?"

One way practitioners can help clients prepare for the job search is through mock interviews, or an interview simulation. The practitioner can ask common interview questions, such as "tell me about yourself" or "what skills do you think you have that would be an asset to our work?" They can also use a job or position description or company website to create targeted questions and ask for informed responses, such as, "How do your personal career goals align with our company's mission?" or "As you know, we're looking for someone with knowledge and skills with specific software. What experiences have you had with those?" To increase the value of a mock interview, practitioners can record the practice interview and play it back in session, evaluating strengths and ways to improve collaboratively with the client.

General Job Searching Tips

Several specific job searching tips have been provided through this chapter. A focused job search requires organization, keeping track of whom has been contacted, how they were located (e.g., social media, company website, etc.), what actions have been taken, when the next action will occur, and important information gained at each step. This is especially important when a person is tracking multiple employers and opportunities.

A second recommendation is to use a multifaceted approach to job searching. When possible, clients should alert their network of friends and colleagues about their job search and ask for their help. Searching company websites as well as job search websites and apps can provide unique results, and sometimes, different types of information on the same position. Direct contact with a desired employer is another approach. Attending in-person or virtual career fairs is yet another. Relying on just one approach may result in a limited set of openings, while varying the approach may lead to more possibilities. With an online search, clients should be encouraged to use different keywords, as employers will not always use the same occupational title. For example, if searching for a counseling position, a client might be encouraged to use the words counselor, therapist, clinician, coach, advisor, and the like.

A final recommendation is to always keep the next job search in mind. Keeping the résumé and information on the professional networking sites up to date will save time in the long run, but also make one's credentials known to potential employers. Including a link to the LinkedIn account or professional blog is a strategy to keep sharing one's experiences and skills while simultaneously acting as a reminder to consistently update the profile. Proactively knowing what the next step may be and taking steps towards being ready is another strategy. This might involve taking on projects that are slightly out of the current skills base or engaging in professional development activities or extra trainings when offered. This also means maintaining a professional presence on social media, contributing to online communities, and maintaining or increasing one's credentials. Finally, keeping an eye on potential employers for the future, seeing who is doing the work that they desire to do, and following them on social media sites is also a strong strategy.

Challenges to Job Searching

Some clients, despite using all of the techniques shared thus far in the chapter, will face challenges when job searching. Discrimination, whether due to age, gender, sexual orientation, race, disability, offender status, or other issues, still occurs regularly. People who have been out of the job market for a sustained period of time will likely face questions about the currency of their knowledge and skills. People with arrest records may worry about how and when to disclose that information, and people who have hidden disabilities such as ADHD or depression, or people who are classified as sexual minorities, may wonder if, when and how they should disclose that information. Another challenge might be related to limited opportunities due to a partner's job or educational or military commitments, or their own commitment to providing care for a dependent. This might be exacerbated if that dependent requires multiple visits to doctors. International students often face difficulties because employers have to complete additional forms and offer assurances in order to hire them. Undocumented workers will likely have difficulty finding work. Single parents might face difficulties in negotiating a work schedule with demands of children. People who have never worked face an empty résumé and the task of convincing an employer to take a chance on them. People from rural counties or lower socioeconomic communities might also have few opportunities. A pregnant person who is not yet showing might consider if they need to disclose that information while on an interview, as might someone with a chronic or terminal illness, but who desires to work.

A practitioner should gain as much information as they can about the individual, their previous experiences with the issue, and specific concerns they have before strategizing possible responses. In addition, researching strategies and guidelines for working with someone with a particular issue is also recommended. In general, people obtain jobs based on their strengths and their skills, not their deficits or areas of their life that might be the source for bias. Helping clients to articulate their skills and the reasons an employer should consider hiring them is a primary step. If a client suspects that discrimination has occurred, the decision of what to do next should be discussed. The client needs to weigh whether lodging a complaint is the best move, especially if they are still in the process of job searching. Discussion points would include the purpose for lodging a complaint (i.e., what is the goal), how to go about expressing the concern, and the timing involved. In addition, the client might roleplay with the practitioner or discuss strategies going forward to hopefully proactively address concerns. For example, a person with an obvious disability (e.g., they are in a wheelchair or using visual aids) might proactively talk about their disability in an interview and how they have been successful in the past and plan to be in the future. Someone who has a criminal record might bring up the record and say something to the effect that, "I know that hiring someone with a record is a risk, but this is how I spent my time in prison, taking specific classes and job duties to build my knowledge and skills, so I can contribute to an employer." Or, they can ask employers if they have any specific questions or concerns about their backgrounds. The job seeker who directly and proactively brings up a likely concern will be addressing unspoken concerns that employers can't directly ask about due to legal constraints. It may not result in a job offer, discrimination may still occur, but at least the job seeker was able to state what they desired and did not leave the employer to jump to their own conclusions or remain biased without additional information.

Using Art Processes to Identify and Address Job Search Concerns and Challenges

Bringing concerns forward to the CP related to the job search process may be challenging for some job seekers. Consequently, the creative career professional may offer art-based structures to foster job seekers' exploration of job search concerns. Through art representation and discussions, known concerns can be presented, and concerns outside of current awareness may be revealed. Examples of artworks and art prompts related to résumé, interview, and discrimination concerns are presented for review.

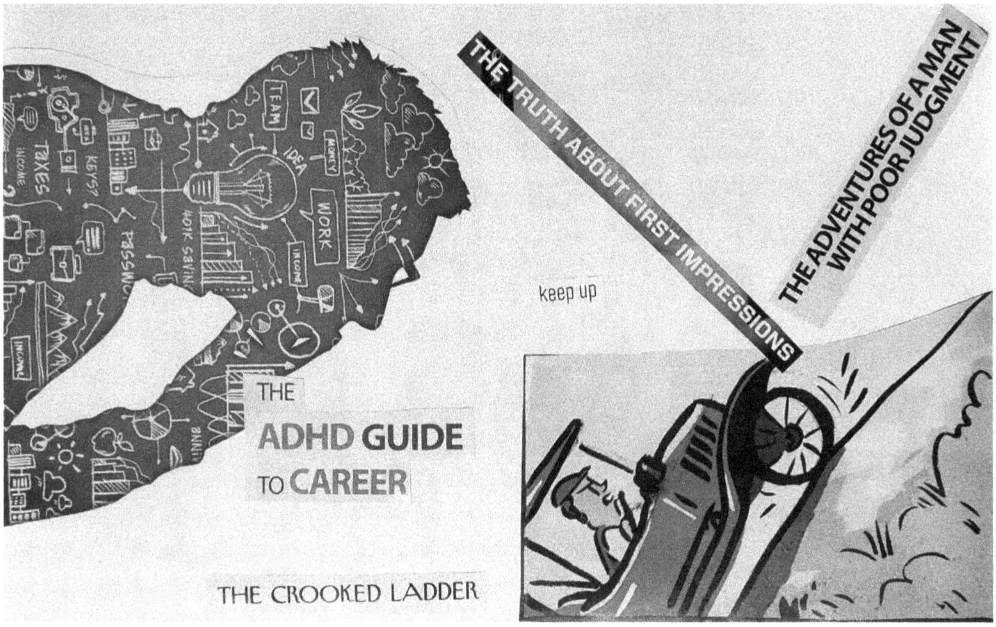

Figure 10.7 Rocky Road Résumé Collage

Rocky Road Résumé

The artwork shown in Figure 10.7 represents one job seeker's fears related to his job search process. Provided with drawing or collage options, the job seeker selected collage materials to reflect upon his concerns about his upcoming job search. In this case, the job seeker was concerned about how his diagnosis and experience with attention deficit hyperactivity disorder (ADHD) may impact his job search process. After completing the collage and viewing it with the CP, the job seeker reported that he was confident about his current strategies to manage ADHD symptoms and was happy about his current well-contemplated career choice, but also acknowledged that ADHD had influenced his past work history as he had held and left many different types of jobs over the past five years. His biggest fear was that he wouldn't get past an employer's first impression of his résumé as the résumé clearly documented the brevity of affiliation with several employers. The creation of the artwork within a career counseling session helped the job seeker raise these issues with the CP and opened opportunities for collaborative problem-solving.

Interview Anxiety

Job interview processes can be intimidating, no matter which career stage one is approaching. In this presented case, a recent graduate identified that she had "interview anxiety." To facilitate exploration, the art therapist invited the job seeker to represent her expectations for the interviewing process. Using markers and collage components, the job seeker depicted herself entering a room where many others were waiting for their interviews. She described seeing her competitors as having "stacks" more of experience and awards than she currently had (Figure 10.8). After exploring the image together, the job seeker and art therapist clarified the type of worries that the job seeker had about interview processes. The job seeker found that creating and viewing the artwork helped her identify that interviewing itself was not concerning, rather it was confidence in her ability to

Figure 10.8 Interview Anxiety Drawing and Collage

compete with others that was intimidating. Following this discussion, the job seeker and art therapist explored the job seekers' strengths and skills and compared them to the job description and work culture descriptions. These explorations supported the job seeker's development of a strategy for her upcoming interview. With the assistance of the artmaking, viewing, and discussion processes, specified job search concerns were brought to awareness so that appropriately focused interventions could be applied.

Endless Hurdles

At the beginning of a career counseling session, a job seeker expressed vague complaints about job search processes. They seemed hesitant to talk about specific obstacles they were experiencing, so the art therapist invited the job seeker to create an artwork related to experiences or concerns. Given the materials options such as markers, oil pastels, and watercolor paints and paper, or modeling clay, the job seeker selected watercolors and depicted the job search process as a series of hurdles on a track (Figure 10.9). Overall, the job seeker described the track as an endless loop of high-stake job search efforts. The job seeker labeled the track lanes charisma, résumé, and discrimination and identified each hurdle as a particular obstacle they were concerned about. They observed that the track did not include a finish line or an image of a successful job search outcome. Upon reflecting on the sky, the job seeker stated that they didn't want to present a sunny day which would be stereotypically happy or a stormy day which would be more foreboding. They had wanted to create clouds and described the clouds as fast moving and uncertain. After these symbolically represented concerns were viewed, the art therapist and the job seeker were able to begin a gentle process of exploring and acknowledging discriminatory practices the job seeker had experienced. At this stage in the art therapy process, it was important for the art therapist to demonstrate empathy and to accurately reflect the job seeker's experiences to confirm understanding.

Figure 10.9 Endless Hurdles Watercolor Painting

In each of these cases, offered art-based processes evolved from particular job seeker concerns and bridged communication challenges that existed within the professional relationship. Artmaking processes stimulated reflection and helped both the job seeker and the professional identify job search issues that required further exploration and strategizing.

Summary

This chapter reviewed multiple aspects of the job search and included specific strategies for helping clients with each of the components, including résumé writing, interviewing, and job searching. In addition, the role of social media was discussed with examples included on how to best utilize these in a job search. Barriers to job searching were identified, and suggestions provided for how practitioners might navigate these issues were presented. Additionally, the role of art-based strategies in expanding perceptions of job search strategies, concerns, and barriers was introduced.

Discussion Questions and Activities

1   Have your résumé and/or LinkedIn profile critiqued professionally or in class.
2   Complete a job history analysis using your résumé. What tasks did you enjoy most or least about each job? What aspects would you like in your next job?
3   Find two or three job announcements for current positions and compare them to your current résumé. What are common and unique requirements? How do you feel

about what you are reading in the job descriptions? What, if any, gaps, do you see? Create a plan for addressing the gaps.

4 Conduct an online audit of yourself. Look in images as well. Try to envision what a potential employer might assume about how you might be as a person and worker based on what you find. Ask an objective third party to do the same for you and share their opinions. What changes might you need to make?

5 Using photos, collage materials, and other two-dimensional materials, create a map of networks such as family, friends, organizations where you may find resources that could support your job search efforts. When the map is completed, identify one person from each category that you could connect with to explore job roles and opportunities. How would you begin the conversation with that person?

6 Using a popular social media site (e.g., Facebook, Instagram, Twitter, TikTok), search for career-related terms using hashtags or keywords, such as #jobopening, #resume, #art_therapist. What do you see? Are there ways you could market yourself in similar ways?

7 Choose a career barrier identified in the chapter, or another one you can imagine (e.g., someone who does not have reliable transportation). Suppose an individual wants help with their job search and is concerned about their ability to conduct the job search given that issue, or how an employer will respond if that issue is revealed. What recommendations might you make? How would you focus the session?

8 What creative methods would you utilize to get a better picture of clients' experiences with their job search? How would you explore job search problems such as negative self-talk or fears of discriminatory practices? What factors might influence your art medium choice for the creative exploration?

9 Critique the résumé in Box 10.1. Compare your critique with an online résumé critique guide.

References

Baumgartner, J., Burnett, L., DiCarlo, C. F., Buchanan, T. (2012). An inquiry of children's social support networks using eco-maps. *Child Youth Care Forum, 41*, 357–369. https://doi.org/10.1007/s10566-011-9166-2

Brown, C. (2015). A career development program for adult students. In M. McMahon & W. Patton, *Ideas for career practitioners: Celebrating excellence in career practice* (pp. 44–47). Australian Academic Press

Dodaro, M. (2019). *LinkedIn for students, graduates, and educators: How to use LinkedIn to land your dream job in 90 days: A career development handbook*. Author.

Osborn, D., Kronholz, J. F., Finklea, J. T., & Cantonis, A. M. (2014). Technology-savvy career counselling. *Canadian Psychology, 55*(4), 258–265.

Wittman, D. J. (2020). *Ignite your LinkedIn profile: Learn the secrets to how LinkedIn ranking really works*. Wittman Technology.

Box 10.1

Résumé with Multiple Errors

"Frisky" Loafer 813-264-2137, hotlips@yahoo.com, 1515 Merryview lane tampa fl
You Tube channel: FriskyGetsDown

Objective: to get a job. Real quick.

EXPERIENCE

from april 2008 worked in private practice for a while. Bought fone equipment and set up laptop.
Decorated my office real nice. Lots of warm, soothing colors. Still working there.

May 2005-jan 2006- worked at an agency. Saw clients and ran groups.

education

Master's degree from USF, graduated may 2007. Got along real well with my classmates and went to lots of
parties. Pledged a surority.

Practicum

spring 2006 volunteered at the life center and salvation army. Saw clients and ran gourps. Did whatever my
supervisor told me to do. Helped lots and lots of peoples.

Extra ciriciluar activites

- Won pink hair beer drinking contest 3 times in a row.
- Blew up baloons for orientation
- Spent
- Went to Italy spain Ireland over the summer with my family
- Work out A LOT. REALLY A LOT.

References

11 Exploring and Supporting Clients' Use of Resources and Information

Career practitioners use a variety of tools to help individuals with their career concerns, ranging from making an initial choice, to job search, to career transitions between work and through retirement. This chapter includes an introduction to how information and other resources fit into the overall career decision-making process, and how practitioners can teach clients to evaluate the integrity of information for their concern. Common types of resources and information tools used in practice to enhance career decision-making and helping clients with the job search process, including online resources, their applications, as well as benefits and drawbacks will be presented. Also included in this chapter is a demonstration of how to creatively integrate information and other resources into a session.

Role of Information in the Career Decision-Making and Job Search Process

Knowledge about options is a key element required for effective career decision-making. Frank Parsons (1909) described this knowledge as "conditions of success" for an occupation and argued that without knowing what was required for success in an occupation, there would be no way to evaluate if a person had the skills to perform the job accurately, and thus no way to evaluate the goodness of a fit of a person to an occupation. The conditions of success included content knowledge about the specific industry or occupation, specific skills required by the job, values of the organization (e.g., if pursuing a career with animals, Parsons listed "a sympathy for them and love for them" (p. 51) as a necessary condition for success), and knowledge of the larger field around a specific occupation.

While information is static in nature, when a person interacts with information, that process is anything but static. As a person reviews the information, especially for a career decision they are making, they are constantly comparing that information to what they know about themselves. For example, consider the conditions of success Parsons listed for social work:

- Love of the service, enthusiasm, character commanding respect.
- Power of expression.
- Organizing ability.
- Understanding of the people among whom the work is to be done.
- Knowledge of human nature in general.
- Knowledge of society, government, industry.
- Sympathy, tact, humor, cooperation.
- Patience, kindliness, high ideals.

DOI: 10.4324/9781003035756-11

- Good general education.
- Special training in social problems, organizations, research, etc.
- Attractive personality.

(Parsons, 1909, p. 62)

Someone considering the field of social work would take this list and inherently compare that to themselves. Do I have these skills? Do I have knowledge in these areas? Would I (and others) describe my personality in this way? Does this sound interesting to me? Do I share the value associated with this occupation? How do I feel as I reflect on what the occupation requires and who I am? The same type of cognitive–affective interaction occurs when job searching. As a person reads a job listing, reviews a company, or interviews for a position, an ongoing evaluation of the degree of fit between the job demands, company culture, and their own personal and professional values and goals occurs. Career and employment decisions are serious in nature, with consequences for self and significant others, such as financial, geographical, delaying or rejecting other goals in pursuit of the current one, and so forth. Given the seriousness of these decisions, practitioners need to make sure the information they share with clients is accurate, current, and addresses the client's needs. In addition, with the breadth of information available, and the quality sometimes questionable, part of our role is to teach clients how to evaluate the information they are obtaining before using it as a basis for their decisions.

Teaching Clients to Become Critical Consumers of Information

Information comes in many forms and runs the gamut in terms of objectivity, accuracy, and relevancy. Information that is provided by a company about itself is likely written in a way to highlight the positives and minimize or ignore any negatives. A person writing a blog about what it's like to be an electrical engineer is speaking from their perspective, about their specific job tasks, on a specific day, and thus the information can be incomplete, in that their job tasks might not be experienced by all electrical engineers, or biased, depending on whether their employer and colleagues are supportive, or on the kind of day they are having at the time of the writing. Bias could be intentional (e.g., for profit, or with a goal of painting an employer/field in a certain light) or unintentional (e.g., sharing from a restricted range of experience). In both the examples of the company and the blogger, the information can still be useful, as long as the individual using the material understands the potential bias, and does not rely solely on that source for information.

Given that individuals rely on information to make decisions about what major to study, career to enter, or job to take, practitioners need to model how to evaluate information for its validity and applicability (Hooley et al., 2010; Sampson et al., 2018; Zalaquett & Osborn, 2007), and this is considered an ethical responsibility as well (NCDA, 2015). Several aspects of information should be considered for determining its value for addressing a career concern or job search question, including:

- accuracy of information
- bias
- how current the information is
- comprehensiveness
- appropriateness for the user's capability (e.g., what a 4-year-old can understand and find useful differs greatly from what a 40-year-old can understand and find useful)
- authority of person(s) providing the information
- relevancy for the career concern (Sampson et al., 2018).

The term "information literacy" has been defined by the Association of College and Research Libraries (www.ala.org/acrl/standards/objectivesinformation) as including

> more than good information-seeking behavior. It incorporates the abilities to recognize when information is needed and then to phrase questions designed to gather the needed information. It includes evaluating and then using information appropriately and ethically once it is retrieved from any media, including electronic, human or print sources.

In other words, to be information-literate, individuals need to be able to find, evaluate and then apply or use the information to address their questions.

Practitioners can help clients become more critical consumers about information in a number of ways. A handout or online guide could be available that includes suggestions for how to find, evaluate, and apply career information related to common career concerns. As a practitioner is working with a client and searching for/reviewing online information, an intentional comment can be made about how the practitioner is evaluating the validity of the information. Given that social media is a common source for information, practitioners should not avoid using social media to help with career information, but proactively include it and describe how the information can be useful, but also potentially biased.

Types of Career Information

The type of career information a person needs varies, depending on the actual need, as well as information they already have. Common types of information that clients might need include information about an occupational field (e.g., the medical field), specific occupations (e.g., nurse practitioner), guides (e.g., career decision-making, job search strategies), linking majors or past experiences to occupational options, different training and educational pathways, job openings, ways to acquire work experience (e.g., volunteer, part-time and apprenticeship opportunities), and contact information for networking. A person might also want information and resources specific to their personal characteristics, such as employers who actively hire people from a specific demographic, like veteran, disability, or cultural status. Still others might be in a role of supporting the career decision-maker or job seeker, and the information they need includes not only resources already mentioned, but strategies of how to share that information and be supportive.

Common Sources of Career Information

People learn about careers from an early age. Children see people employed at various jobs, and form opinions about work tasks, specific careers, and about work in general. They engage in work-related tasks and environments such as school and extracurricular activities, which present expectations, assignments, deadlines, individual and teamwork, a "boss," and feedback. Part-time work, shadowing, and volunteer opportunities, memberships in clubs and organizations, and even discussions with friends' working siblings and parents expose individuals to information about the world of work and impact opinions. As work is a common experience among most people, and can take up a significant portion of a day, often people will share about work experiences and also search for work and career information via social media.

Other sources might be online searching by occupation or job title, talking to people who are in a specific job of interest or who know someone in that type of work, YouTube, books, newspapers, blogs, podcasts, television, computer-assisted career guidance systems, magazines, and the like. Practitioners utilize those resources to gauge what an individual knows about the options they are considering, and the variety of sources a person is using to access career information. In addition, practitioners share some common career resources that they routinely use with clients for career decision-making and job searching. The websites listed in the next section are all available in Spanish.

Informational Interviewing

One important source of career information is the informational interview, which differs from a traditional interview in that a person is seeking to obtain not a job offer but, as the name implies, information. The purpose of this information is to provide answers to questions the interviewer has that will help in the decision-making process for their career concern. Thus, the questions might focus on how to prepare for a specific career area, with questions like, "What major would you recommend?" or "What skills or software should I be focusing on?" If someone was trying to determine if the occupation might be a good fit, they might ask questions such as, "I really value the opportunity to ____ [be creative, work on my own, work in a team, etc.]. Is that something you think realistically happens in this type of work?" This question could be honed for someone who wants to explore whether the specific company might be a good fit, by adjusting it to "Do employees here have that opportunity?" The responses can help clear up any misperceptions of what the working environment might be like, provide clear indicators of how the client should focus their efforts to increase their attractiveness to that employer or field, and to help the client determine if the option is worth pursuing. Regardless of the outcome, thank-you notes should be encouraged following informational interviews, both as a courtesy for them taking their time to share, and as a way to strengthen the relationship.

With the exception of learning about a specific employer, clients should be encouraged to conduct at least two information interviews. This is to decrease the likelihood of bias, and to increase confidence in the information being gleaned. On any given day, the interviewee might be feeling more or less positive about their work, which might impact what they share and the filters they apply when sharing it. This might lead to them being overly positive about the work and opportunities and minimizing potential negatives, whereas someone who is having a bad day might share the opposite. Even if it is just a normal day, what the interviewee finds enjoyable or aggravating may not match the interviewer's preferences or values. For example, one entrepreneur may say a plus of their work is engaging with the public, while another may say that is the biggest drawback. One may say public engagement takes up the majority of the time, probably because it's the part of the work they enjoy most, whereas another might say it is takes up the least amount of their time, and again, probably by their design. If a client only interviews one person, they may formulate an inaccurate belief about the amount of public engagement that occupation requires. If the interviewee felt strongly about how much public engagement they desired, they might make a career decision based off of information from the interviewer that was either biased or reality for that one site. If, however, they interviewed both these individuals, they might come away with a more realistic understanding that there can be a great deal of variability on that topic. This might also give them confidence when talking with a potential employer to negotiate on that topic.

If possible, clients should try to conduct the interview in the actual place of the interviewee's employment. Being in the physical environment can provide additional information that might be of importance to the client. Clients can be coached to pay attention to the environment when on the information interview. What does the interviewee's office look like? Neat or cluttered? Individual or shared? Is it an office, or a cubicle? What does the overall office look and feel like? Busy? Quiet? Is there a buzz or energy in the air, multiple interruptions, people working in teams or individually? A sense of panic to meet deadlines or more relaxed conversations? What is everyone wearing? Does that differ between employees and administrators? The environment is likely to differ for each site, which is why going to at least two different sites is recommended for comparison purposes.

Websites Supporting Career Decision Making

Career decision-makers' career information needs will vary according to the type of decision being made and the type of decision-maker the person is. Someone who is more of a linear decision-maker may want to determine their ideal career first and then reverse engineer the steps to get there, identifying an ideal field of study, extracurricular activities, and other experiences, and plotting those to a timeline. Another person may have more of a "go with the flow" or happenstance approach to life and decisions, preferring not to have the future laid out in detail. The information that person needs may be along the lines of "what can I do with a major in ..." guide. Chapter 9 provided more details on types of decision-makers and how to support them. At some point, though, both types of personalities will have to identify which occupation(s) best fit their unique kaleidoscope of interests, values, skills, personality, needs, etc. To do this, they will need career information. When beginning to narrow down options, the career decision-maker won't need pages of detailed information, but instead could benefit most from a brief description of what the work entails. As their list of options is narrowed to a reasonable amount (around five to seven options), more detailed information becomes more helpful. In reviewing the sites in this section, overlap in terms of the most common information topics can be seen.

ONLINE OCCUPATIONAL OUTLOOK HANDBOOK

Maintained by the United States Bureau of Labor Statistics, the Online Occupational Outlook Handbook (OOH; www.bls.gov/ooh/) provides the following information about hundreds of occupations:

- summary of quick facts (such as basic description of the work, median pay, training, or education required, job outlook, and career videos)
- typical responsibilities of the occupation and specializations within it
- work environment (e.g., the number of jobs that were available, work setting, employment by the largest industries, work schedules)
- preparation or how to become employed in that occupation, including entry-level education requirements, qualities that are useful, licenses/certifications, how to advance in the field
- salary (median annual or hourly wages)
- job outlook, which provides job prospects based on a projection of how employment will change, shows growth or decline in the industry, and change in business patterns
- occupational information specific to states and areas
- similar occupations to the one being explored
- additional information which includes associations, organizations, and links to O*NET or career videos.

The projections on specific occupation projections are updated annually and show a decade's worth of patterns at a time. Information on the fastest growing, highest paying, and newest types of jobs is also available. Other information on the Bureau of Labor Statistics' website (bls.gov) that may be helpful for those engaging in career planning are the monthly labor review, career outlook which shows employment and field of degree connections (www.bls.gov/careeroutlook/), and section for K-12 students and teachers.

O*NET

Created by the United States Department of Labor, O*NET (onetonline.org) provides information for over 900 occupations and is updated annually. Users can search for occupations by bright outlook (i.e., employment projection is expected to grow greatly), STEM careers, industry, personal characteristics, or crosswalks such as military or standard occupational classification codes. Information provided includes:

- brief description of occupation
- sample of work titles associated with the researched job title
- tasks involved
- technology skills
- tools used
- knowledge
- skills
- abilities
- work activities
- detailed work activities
- work context
- job zone
- education
- credentials
- interests
- work styles
- work values
- related occupations
- wages and employment
- job openings
- additional information such as institutes, societies, and organizations specific to that occupation.

On the O*NET website are the career exploration tools (www.onetcenter.org/tools.html) which include an ability profiler, interest profiler, and a work importance locator that includes work value cards.

CAREER ONESTOP

Career Onestop (www.careeronestop.org) is sponsored by the United States Department of Labor, and houses multiple tools for learning more about occupations, finding training for specific occupations, job searching, a toolkit with multiple self-assessments that links back into occupations, as well as resources specific for targeted groups, such as young adults, self-employed, veterans, and so forth, that might be used in the job search. Occupational information includes a brief description, other job titles, career videos, outlook and projected employment, wages, training required, and knowledge and skills typically required for success in that occupation.

My Next Move www.mynextmove.org was developed by the National Center for O*NET Development, and sponsored by the US Department of Labor, Employment & Training Administration. Designed as an interactive tool, users can search for occupations in a variety of ways, such as keywords, browsing industries, or seeing occupations that match to an interest inventory's results. The presentation of information is more in an info-graphic style, with limited text and an engaging use of colors, with a link to O*NET for more details. There is also a section specific for veterans transitioning to civilian life.

Professional Organizations

One hallmark of a profession is a professional association comprised of members employed in that profession or closely related field. These associations often provide information about the field, trainings or conferences, newsletters and journals, and sometimes job openings. Someone who is deciding about whether that profession is of interest can scan presentation titles as well as other information to learn what is currently being discussed and evaluate their interest in and excitement for those topics.

Websites Supporting the Job Search Process

Committing to a job is the last step in a process that requires a great deal of information. Job seekers need access to all types of information. They need to know what jobs are available, what they entail, starting salaries, culture of a company, company reputation, diversity in the organization and also among leadership, financial health and outlook of an organization, competitors, what the company does well and where it needs improvement, and so forth. Job seekers also need to know information about the basics of job searching, such as how to write a résumé and cover letter, interviewing techniques, locating the hidden job market, networking, and negotiating offers. *These latter topics are addressed in Chapter 10.* Some of the sites listed in the previous section can provide clues for where to look for possible employers. Likewise, sites listed in this section can provide up-to-date information about occupations for career decision-makers. They can see specific expectations of what the job requires, and see desired experiences, training, and skills, and use that information in their own career planning.

Job Databases

Glassdoor, Indeed, Snagajob, SimplyHired, CareerArc, ZipRecruiter, and Monster are all examples of job databases, in which job seekers can input their information and be matched to job openings, or can browse job openings that employers list. In addition to identifying current job openings, these sites often contain useful information about the employer, including ratings, interview questions they often ask, and employee reviews. If a job searcher wants to know who is typically hiring for a certain position, a quick search for the job title can provide that information. Because these sites are openly advertising positions, competition for these job openings can be very strong. Job seekers should not rely on these sites as their only source for job openings.

Company Websites and Social Media

Companies often provide a wealth of information on their websites, and sometimes advertise directly on their site or invite submissions of résumés as opposed to using the large job search databases. Job seekers need to know which companies are hiring for the positions they desire. Clearly, a company that has the word "engineering" in their name will be interested in engineers, but they likely have a number of different positions that might be available, such as marketing/advertising, accounting, and human resources. A job seeker might need help in identifying companies that might offer positions that are less obvious, which is where some of the previously mentioned sites might be useful.

Company websites and their social media accounts provide other useful information to a job seeker, including their vision and mission statement, information about their products, who is in leadership, types of careers available at their site, company initiatives and accomplishments, and community involvement. Job seekers should also explore and follow and engage with social media sites of companies they are interested in working for. While this information will likely be written in positive terms about the company, an employer will expect a job seeker to be knowledgeable about this publicly available information. A job seeker can gain a more comprehensive view of a company by exploring competitors' websites and social media accounts, as well as searching for other online information about the company. Searching for recent news about a company and incorporating that information into an interview can be impressive to a potential employer.

Other Online Tools for Job Searching

In addition to identifying open positions, networking opportunities, and company information, job seekers may need additional information. When contemplating relocation for a job, understanding how cost of living expenses might be different in the new location might have a bearing on the salary needed. Thus, online salary and cost of living calculators will be valuable tools. Indicators of how a company is performing financially can paint a picture of their overall health, and so stock price information and annual reports can provide that information. LinkedIn is a professional networking site which, in addition to providing information about job openings, also has company pages, and one might find past or current employees who provide blog entries which might provide an insider's look at the company. Someone who is job searching and wanting to know about a specific company could reach out to members of their social media groups to ask for information. Setting up for news alerts about specific companies can also provide the job seeker with up-to-date information.

Creative Approaches for Using and Organizing Career Information

Providing world of work info has been identified via meta-analysis as one of five key ingredients of effective career interventions (Brown & Ryan Krane, 2000). In addition, NCDA (2009) listed delivery of information resources as one of the competency areas for practitioners. Notice it wasn't just knowledge of information resources, but skills in delivering these resources. Providing a list of resources for a specific topic such as using job searching can be helpful, especially for someone who is self-directed and doesn't need much support. But for someone who is overwhelmed, having a list may only add to the anxiety. A practitioner needs to be careful not to overload the person, but to be listening for and evaluating what type of information they need in light of the information they already have, how much they can handle, and what will best help them address their career decision. The remainder of this section provides examples of creative ways that individuals or groups can organize and apply career information.

Table 11.1 Occupational comparison table

	My preferences (for the items in the first column)	Option 1 Human service assistant	Option 2 Counselor	Option 3 Counseling psychologist
Work with people?	Yes	Yes	Yes	Yes
Creative	Yes	Maybe	No	Maybe
Training/education required	Bachelor's degree	Bachelor's	Master's	Doctorate
Salary	$30,000 to start	Around $35,000	Around $46,000	Around $78,000
Would I still consider it? (circle one)	——	Yes	Maybe	Maybe later

Options Comparison Table

An options comparison table is a means for organizing key information about options in one place. A blank template allows the table to be personalized. The first column can contain the priorities the individual is considering with respect to the options. The options could be occupations, majors, training paths, job opportunities, or any other options for a decision. Having the individual complete the first column provides a way to compare the information they find about their preferences. Additional columns can be added if the person is considering more than three. Table 11.1 is a completed sample for someone trying to choose a career.

In the example in Table 11.1, this person will have to weigh what they are willing to compromise on, educational level or salary. If the individual is still unsure, they might want to consider including more details like desired work tasks, opportunities for advancement, independence, ability to work from home, and so forth to help differentiate the occupations more.

Career Ladder

Career ladders provide a picture of not just the one occupation in question, but those that require less and more education, or provide lower or higher salaries. In doing so, they help the client see steps that lead to the identified occupation, but also, what might be required for the next step. Sometimes, this added information may lead to a person changing their plans. "With a little more education, I could have this type of position or that level of salary." In the occupational comparison above, it's apparent that increased education leads to increased salaries. The person will still need to decide if the time and costs associated with the different trainings are worth the differences in starting salaries.

Consider the example of this career ladder:

Judge	4+ years' education, law school, & experience	$136,910
Lawyer	4 years' education plus law school	$122,000
Paralegal	2 years' education	$51,740

Career Information Safari

Teams of students can learn about career information sources and gain experience evaluating them through a career information safari (Osborn, 2011). The activity can be enhanced by sharing the document online so they can paste images and links to it, and giving bonus points for unusual sources of information, such as a music video about the occupation, or a cartoon.

Mission: Your team must first identify an occupation to. Then, you are to find an example of the information types presented below and complete the table. You may divide up

Table 11.2 Career information safari

Information type	Title, reference or link	What's it about/ include?	Evaluation of source
O*NET (onetonline.org)			
Occupational Outlook Handbook (https://www.bls.gov/ooh/)			
Career Onestop (careeronestop.org)			
Social media: Facebook, Instagram, Twitter, Snapchat, TikTok			
My Next Move (https://www.mynextmove.org)			
LinkedIn			
Podcast			
Video of the person performing the occupation			
Professional organization for the occupation			
Blog about the occupation			
News article			
Internship opportunities for the occupation?			
Where can you get training for the occupation in your state?			
Study abroad options?			
Government jobs for that occupation?			
Military jobs for that occupation?			
Gender/diversity information for that occupation/field?			
Your choice of information site (not listed above)			

the task among your group members. In the final column, please evaluate the source, by stating whether you liked this source or not, and why. Your group will be researching online tools that are not commonly used by counselors. Be creative, use your investigative skills, and have fun! Table 11.2 shows a sample career information safari.

Converting Career Information into a Self-Assessment Table

If a person is deciding between one or two occupations or wants to better prepare for a specific career path, a counselor can help them use information about the occupation(s) to create a checklist that compares the individual's skills and experiences to the occupational requirements. In addition, the person could then create a plan for how to gain any skills or experiences that are lacking. This approach can also be used with individuals at the beginning of a training by using job notices to create the checklist. Table 11.3 is an example of a partial checklist based on an art therapist job opening.

Career Bingo Game

Designed for use in a group setting, career bingo increases learning about careers with a competitive element. Traditionally, bingo is played with five-by-five cards, but that can be adjusted for time and attention span. Prior to the game, the practitioner would prefill the cards with information such as specific job tasks, salaries, training requirements, and so forth. To make the game a little easier, the practitioner might survey the group prior to bingo day to identify the top five to ten occupations of interest, so as to narrow their search for information.

Career Crossword Puzzle

Using online tools such as https://puzzlemaker.discoveryeducation.com, practitioners can create an interactive activity that individuals can use either in a self-directed manner or with a partner or in teams. Puzzles can be created about general career fields, with the words being occupational titles and career clues being a description, or as in Figure 11.1, could be created for a specific occupational title with individuals being led to guess the

Table 11.3 Self-assessment table from career information

	I have it	I don't have it	Strategy for obtaining it
Master's degree in art therapy, approved by AATA		X	Enrolled now!
Experience working with veterans		X	Will aim for a practicum with veterans
Conduct, analyze, interpret, and report assessment data for functional domains	X		
Provides individual counseling	X		
Provides group counseling		X	Will talk with my advisor about opportunities
Incorporates the four-step process of assessment, planning, implementation, and evaluation of services delivered, and develops an appropriate and evidence-based art therapy treatment program	X	X Need to work on evaluation	Will be more diligent with evaluation

title upon completion. These can be useful as a stand-alone activities which individuals can use while waiting for an appointment, incorporated into workshops or classroom guidance activities, or placed on a program's website as an interactive way to educate about careers.

Guess the career clues

ACROSS

1. the general approach used to help clients express thoughts/feelings
4. term that combines visual arts, movement, drama, music, writing and other creative processes to foster deep personal growth and community development
7. type of counseling that involves more than one client
8. type of communication that does not use words
9. client-centered tool that encourages client art to express emotions/thoughts that is more open/abstract and without specific instructions
13. minimal education required to do this job
14. one of the Holland RIASEC types associated with this job
15. outlook expected for this field in terms of growth and number of openings
16. materials used for creating art
17. treatment of mental concerns by psychological means
20. annual median wage (in thousands, nationally)

DOWN

2. whether the art will be focused specifically on a topic or open
3. a strategy to help manage stress
5. goal of art as therapy through the creative process, with less discussion and more emphasis on helping client create a finished/satisfying product
6. "___" certified is the highest level credential for this profession
10. client-centered tool that encourages client art to express emotions/thoughts using specific instructions
11. type of communication that uses words
12. which ages this profession works with
18. type of art that focuses on the experience of making it, not the resulting art piece
19. name of professional association for this profession

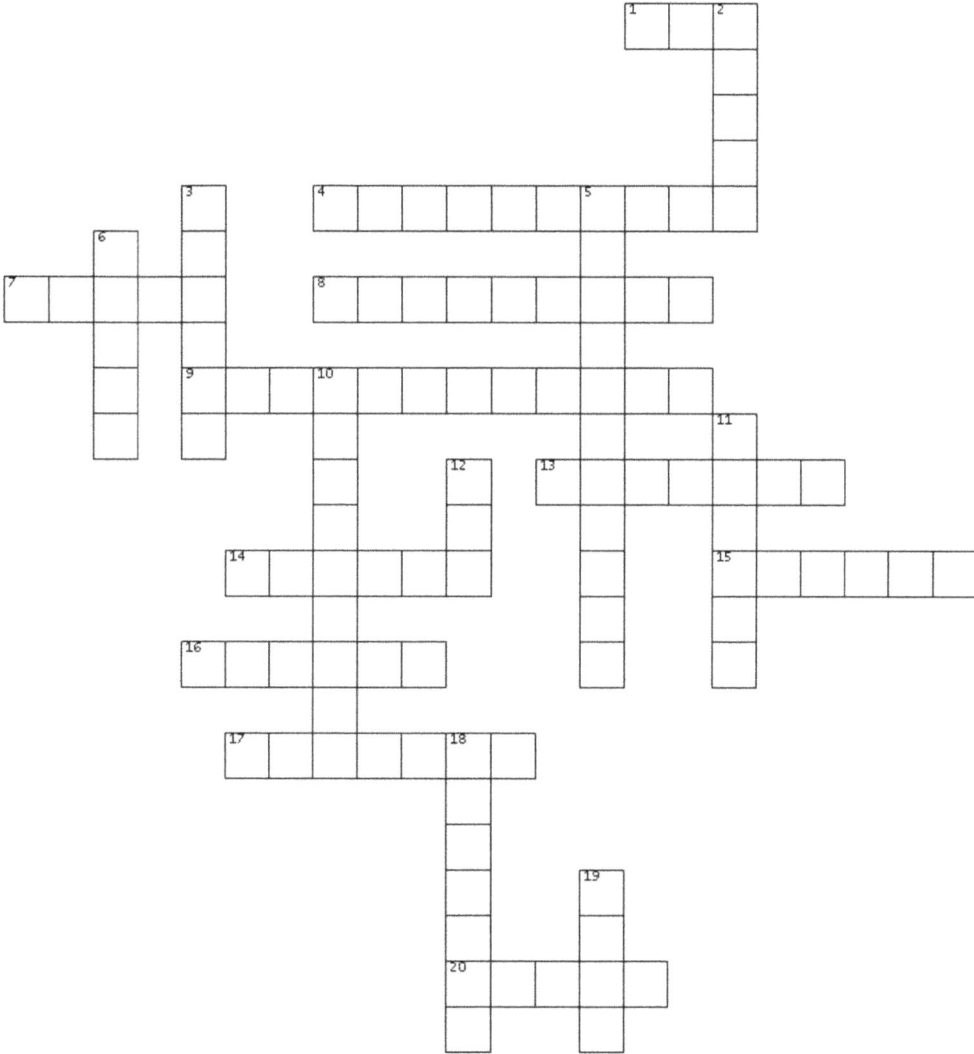

Figure 11.1 Guess the Career Crossword. Crossword Puzzle Created with https://puzzlemaker. discoveryeducation.com

Case Example of Integrating Career Information into a Career Conversation

Consider that someone is wanting to explore several occupational options that were generated with a career assessment. How should a practitioner proceed? Online assessments will have links to career descriptions via websites such as O*NET, but sorting through this information might be overwhelming. One option would be to have the individual rank-order the occupations in terms of initial level of interest, and then set a goal as to how many they read about. Or, the person could just go in the order they are listed. Another option would be for them to organize the occupations around certain themes, such as "analytical occupations" or "creative occupations." Prior to starting the exploration, it can be helpful to talk with clients about the criteria they are using to decide if the occupation is worth looking into more, or to have them clarify their work-related values, so they can focus on searching for information relative to those values.

This approach works well when the person is only looking at a handful of occupations. If they are trying to narrow down from a large number of occupations, it may be useful to have them read a brief overview of the occupation and ask them to pay attention to their thoughts and feelings as they read. Does this description sound interesting, exciting, awful, boring? Do they want to read more about it, leave it a "maybe" category, or remove it from consideration? Asking about the reasons why a person likes, dislikes, or is unsure about an occupation after reading about it can help clarify a person's self-knowledge. Consider the conversation following an initial exploration of occupations.

PRACTITIONER: So you've spent some time looking at what these occupations generally involve. I see you've got some stars by some, and you've crossed through others, and there are some that have some question marks. Tell me about that.

CLIENT: Well, the ones with stars are the ones that I felt really excited about as I started reading about them, and I definitely want to learn more about those. The ones that I crossed out were boring, or I just couldn't see myself doing those. The ones with question marks sounded OK, so I didn't want to cross them off completely, but they weren't as exciting as the ones with stars next to them.

PRACTITIONER: Great! That's a neat way to organize them. Let's start with the ones you starred. Can you tell me what stood out to you for each one of those?

CLIENT: Yeah. For firefighter, I really loved the idea of being in heat of the moment, literally [laughs], and the excitement and adrenaline that's there when you're trying to keep a fire from destroying something. I could never see myself behind a desk, dressed up everyday. That'd be the worst. For paramedic, you never know what you're going to get, so that's pretty exciting. Also you're jumping right into the problem. There's no lengthy debate about which way is the best way – you see a problem, and do the best you can to help. I also kinda liked the idea of being a detective.

PRACTITIONER: Why's that?

CLIENT: I can turn down jobs that I'm not interested in or don't think I can do well. And every case would be different. I also like the idea of figuring out something that isn't obvious.

PRACTITIONER: Thinking about these three options, what themes do you see that are similar across all of them? [clarifying self-knowledge]

CLIENT: Well, all three are outdoors, and all of them have this excitement or risk element to them.

PRACTITIONER: True. I also see that there is a lot of variety in each of them, and all of them involve fast problem-solving. Now tell me about some of the occupations you crossed off.

The client listed office manager, bank teller, and physician among the occupations he wouldn't consider. When the practitioner asked why, the client said that the jobs were indoors, stuffy, boring (because they were repetitive), and in the case of physician, required too much time in school. This information supported what he had said earlier about wanting a job with variety and some element of risk-taking, but added an element of how much schooling he was willing to pursue. Then the practitioner moved to the occupations that had question marks next to them, and asked the client to look at those and see if he could identify the kind of information he needed to help him make a decision about whether or not to keep considering them as options. He said that they seemed they seemed to have a mix of what he wanted, but not as much as the ones he starred, and he wasn't sure if that mix would be satisfying to him or not. Some of them seemed like exciting possibilities, but he wasn't sure if there were enough real jobs out there, or if they would pay enough. This conversation helped further his knowledge of what was important to him, with salary requirements entering the discussion, along with the idea of what was most important to him among the values he had stated.

Before taking a deeper dive into each of the options, the practitioner thought it would be helpful to engage in an art experience that would show what was most essential to him as he considered jobs. Given his preference for active engagement, the practitioner presented the client with paint, brushes, and a stack of 9″ × 12″ white paper. The client was offered a large palette for color mixing, and a review of color mixing options. The practitioner then invited the client to create lines, shapes, and colors which visually expressed the qualities that related to job characteristics such as: risk-taking and desk work; variety and repetition; high and low educational demands; moderate and high salary rewards; and outdoors work or desk work. The client moved quickly to representing risk-taking with yellow, orange, and red and remarked, "It looks exciting, like flares or fireworks. There are so many directions to follow and it's so bright." Figure 11.2 shows his initial

Figure 11.2 Risk

Figure 11.3 Variety

work. He continued with the series of work, and paused when he created the variety of images. He noted, this is "fun to look at. It has a lot of energy and colors. Variety is stimulating!" Figure 11.3 shows his continued work.

After moving through the tasks of representing outdoor work, and education and salary levels, the client used lines, shapes, and colors to depict controlled, repetitious, and desk work themes. When he stepped back to look at the desk job creation (Figures 11.4 and 11.5), he said, "this gives me a feeling of being trapped, kinda like a jail." Additionally, he remarked, "the repetition image was the worst to make, it seemed like it was going to take forever and I didn't enjoy it." Together the practitioner and client spread out all of the images created during the session, and looked to explore patterns and reactions. The client noted that he was drawn to the warmer colors and active strokes when they occurred in the works. On the other hand, he felt the blue and gray works were boring, and held little interest for him. Following the review, the practitioner and client discussed how the creations confirmed his preferences for particular job qualities. The practitioner encouraged the client to further reflect on his top career choices – fireman, paramedic, and detective – as homework between sessions.

At the beginning of the next session, the practitioner inquired about the client's homework, and asked if he wished to explore any other considerations regarding occupation options. He remarked, "Yeah, I thought about them a lot, and they all seemed like good possibilities. I'm not sure what to pick, exactly." To provide the client with further opportunity for reflection, the practitioner, once again, spread out the paintings from the last session on the table. One by one, they looked at the works named the associated work qualities. Next, the practitioner invited the client to paint three works using lines, shapes, and colors, depicting the qualities of his three top career options on larger sheets of paper (Figures 11.6, 11.7, and 11.8). The client energetically approached each work and announced, "I'm done" after a short period of time.

Figure 11.4 Desk

To help with the review, the practitioner displayed the three works amidst the career quality paintings, and the practitioner and client took time to look at the works as a group, then individually. The client made observations about the work such as feeling excited by the energy and risk-taking of the firefighter job and commented that the green in the image was connected to being outdoors. He definitely liked the risky exciting part of the work which was represented here. He then noted that he had looked more

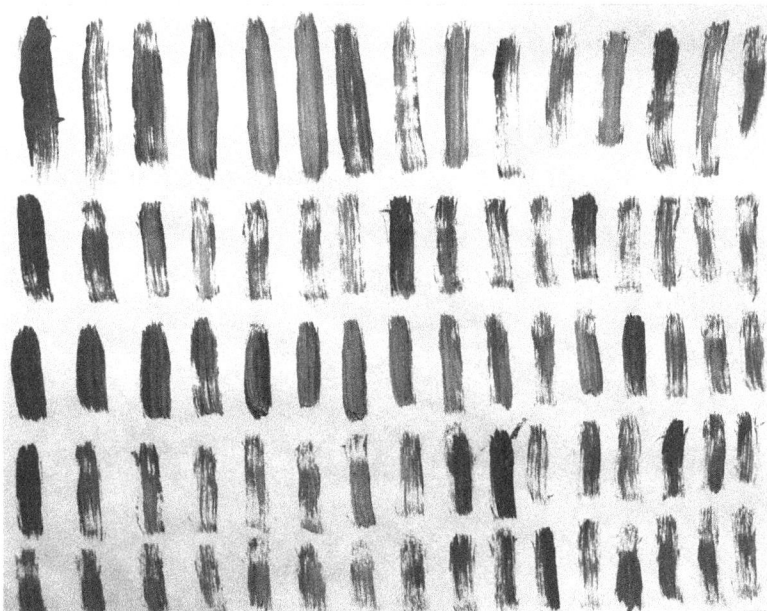

Figure 11.5 Repetitive

Figure 11.6 Detective

into firefighter responsibilities and understood that there could be a lot of downtime in between active firefighting tasks, so perhaps he would feel bored and stuck indoors during those times. In regard to the detective art, he remarked he liked the variety of colors and aspects that represented risk (yellow lines) and a city-like outdoors scene. However, he remarked that the big gray blocks represented the downside of detective

Figure 11.7 Paramedic

Figure 11.8 Firefighter

work such as completing paperwork and report writing related to sleuthing results. When he reviewed the paramedic painting, he stated that this time, the gray didn't represent something boring or tedious. He said the gray was an ambulance heading towards its important destination with urgency, surrounded with yellow representing risk and excitement. He expanded on this reflection reporting that he liked the idea of having a variety of situations to respond to and that of traveling through outdoor environments was attractive to him. He described feeling that paramedic work would provide more variety and less "waiting time" than a firefighter position, although there was some overlap of qualities and responsibilities. The practitioner and client devoted additional time to reviewing the career paintings side by side to stimulate conversations regarding preferences and clearer narrowing of choices. Following this activity, he stated he felt ready to move towards making an initial career decision and to begin the steps towards implementing his choice.

This scenario showed one example of how career information could be used to support a client in his career decision-making process. In addition, art therapy techniques can enhance the individual's experience of how information interfaces with their emotions and values.

Summary

Career information is a necessary component for effective career decision-making and problem-solving. Clients not only need to know what information is available, but where to find it, how to determine its value, and how to apply it to their career concern. While much of career information is available online, other sources of information can be valuable. How career information is introduced into the conversation can vary from providing links to more creative approaches, depending on the client(s), settings, and needs.

Discussion Questions and Activities

1   Choose an occupation of interest to you. Choose three of the sites in this chapter and create a comparison of information about that occupation. What do you notice about what the different sites provide? Which site would be of most use to the clients you typically serve? Based on the information provided, what next steps might be recommended for your career planning?

2   Choose three different occupations or job openings you are considering. Create and complete a comparison table or other visual that allows for comparison using your values for the basis of comparison. Does one option stand out above the others?

3   Using some of the job search sites, search for an opening specific to your career interests, to learn current information about what skills, experiences, and knowledge are required for that position. What are the gaps between your skills/experiences and what is required for the job? Based on what you find, what are some next steps you should take now to make yourself more marketable for the job search?

4   Locate a company or organization where you might consider working. Copy and paste information about their mission and values into a word cloud generator. What key words are indicated? How might this information be useful to a job searcher?

5   Anya is about to graduate with her degree in psychology. Graduate school is an option, but she would first like to get some work experience. She hasn't decided on a career path, but is very open to all possibilities. Her interests are in helping people, managing, directing, problem-solving, and so forth. She has come to you seeking help with her job search. Given this information and her questions, develop a plan with recommended resources. Try to use a different source per question. Finally, answer her questions. Her questions/concerns include:

   • What can I do with this degree (without a master's degree)?
   • Who are the top employers for psych majors?
   • I need to write a résumé. Should I include my picture on it? What about a list of my hobbies?
   • I also want to rock my interviews. What are the toughest interview questions out there?
   • I don't have any work experience – how can I get some experience in a hurry?
   • I'm also open to a career in business. Are there any magazines that are specific to Asian females in business?
   • How can I find out what salary to ask for if I get offered a job?
   • What do I do if employer #1 offers me a job and I'm still waiting to hear from employer #2?
   • How do I identify employers who are good employers for Asian females?
   • Where can I find job notices for entry level positions?

6   Create a poem or a visual that describes the tasks and requirements of a specific occupation. Have others guess the occupational title.

7   Identify two people who are in an occupation you might consider entering, or that are commonly identified as an interest among your clients, and conduct an informational interview with them. Ask questions about how they decided on their career path, the steps they took in terms of training/education and work experiences to prepare for the occupation, what they enjoy most/least about the work, and advice they would give to someone interested in entering the field today. Create other questions that reflect your values. For example, if you valued having your weekends and evenings to yourself or enjoy a high energy environment, you might ask questions

whether those are true in their experience. Compare your answers from the two informational interviews. Consider choosing individuals who share the same occupational title but in different work environments, such as profit and non-profit sectors. If several of your classmates are also interested in a given occupation, consider hosting a panel event where individuals can share about their work and field questions.

8 Search for current posts (e.g., news articles, association newsletters or periodicals, research, social media or blogs) that include recommendations for art therapists or career counselors. Compile these recommendations into a top ten list for your profession.

9 Find at least two local employers who hire for positions you might be interested in pursuing. Set up an appointment to conduct informational interviews. Compare your experiences at both places and consider how this information may shape your knowledge about yourself and future options you would consider.

10 Complete the crossword puzzle earlier in the chapter. Were you able to guess the profession? Across answers: 1) art; 4) expressive; 7) group; 8) nonverbal; 9) nondirective; 13) masters; 14) social; 15) bright; 16) medium; 17) therapy; 20) sixty. Down answers: 2) theme; 3) coping; 5) sublimation; 6) board; 10) directive; 11) verbal; 12) all; 18) process; 19) AATA.

References

Brown, S. D., & Ryan Krane, N. E. (2000). Four (or five) sessions and a cloud of dust: Old assumptions and new observations about career counseling. In S.D. Brown & R.W. Lent (Eds.), *Handbook of Counseling Psychology* (3rd ed., pp. 740–766). Wiley.

Hooley, T., Hutchinson, J., & Watts, A. G. (2010). Careering through the web: The potential of Web 2.0 and 3.0 technologies for career development and career support services. Retrieved from UK Commission for Employment and Skills website: http://derby.openrepository.com/derby/bitstream/10545/198269/1/careering-through-the-web.pdf

National Career Development Association. (2009). Career counseling competencies. Retrieved from www.ncda.org/aws/NCDA/pt/sd/news_article/37798/_self/layout_ccmsearch/true

National Career Development Association. (2015). NCDA code of ethics. Retrieved from www.ncda.org/aws/NCDA/asset_manager/get_file/339

Osborn, D. S. (2011). Information career safari. In T. M. Laura, M. Pope, & C. W. Minor (Eds.), *Experiential activities for teaching career counseling classes & facilitating career groups* (vol. 3, pp. 267–270). National Career Development Association.

Parsons, F. (1909). *Choosing a vocation.* Houghton Mifflin.

Sampson J. P., Jr., Osborn, D., Kettunen, J., et al. (2018). The validity of socially-constructed career information. *Career Development Quarterly, 66*(2), 121–134. Retrieved from http://purl.flvc.org/fsu/fd/FSU_libsubv1_scholarship_submission_1521225668_d3959a6c doi:10.1002/cdq.12127

Zalaquett, C. P., & Osborn, D. S. (2007). Fostering counseling students' career information literacy through a comprehensive career web site. *Counselor Education and Supervision, 46*, 162–171. doi:10.1002/j.1556-6978.2007.tb00022.x

12 Exploring and Supporting Career Development with People Living with Disabilities

People with disabilities experience similar but also more nuanced career needs, and practitioners need to be ready to support their career development, exploration, career navigation, problem-solving, and job search efforts. Consequently, this chapter will examine definitions and models of disability, disability identity, and disability culture that influence career-oriented service provision. As many types of mental and physical disabilities occur with broad ranges of presentation, severity levels, and functional implications too varied to address in one chapter, we highlight a few examples to demonstrate how career practitioners may understand, support, and facilitate appropriate career development interventions. The importance of practitioner sensitivity to disability identities, attitudes, and resources will be emphasized.

Disabilities and Employment

As the chapter topic is considered, it is important to examine the impact that disabilities may have on careers and employment. According to the US Department of Labor Bureau of Labor Statistics (2021), 19.1% of those with a disability are employed in comparison to 63.7% of people who do not identify as experiencing a disability. Additionally, 29% of workers with a disability worked part-time in comparison to 16% of those without a disability. Of the 19.1% of people with a disability who are employed, proportionately, more are self-employed relative to those who do not have a disability. People who are not currently employed or unemployed but looking for work are not considered to be a part of the US labor force. People living with disabilities constitute a significantly larger number of this group. However, it is important to note that over half of those identifying as disabled in some capacity, were over 65 years old.

Even when employed, people living with a disability experienced a variety of occupational disparities. The US Department of Labor Bureau of Labor Statistics (2021) reported, for example, that a person with a disability who has completed a bachelor's degree or higher, does not gain a greater chance of employment that is typically associated with higher educational levels. Statistics also showed the people living with a disability were less likely to work in management or other professional level occupations, and were more likely to work in service occupations, product production, transportation, or government work.

Disabilities Statistics, Definitions, and Models

According to the World Health Organization (2011) more than a billion of the world's people live with some form of disability, and approximately 200 million experience difficulties that significantly interfere with daily functioning. Notably, almost all people will experience a temporary or permanent disability within their life spans.

DOI: 10.4324/9781003035756-12

What is a disability? The US Census for the Bureau of Labor Statistics' (2021) Current Population Survey identified disabilities as being related to serious hearing difficulties, significant difficulties interfering with seeing (even with glasses), and serious difficulty with concentrating, remembering, or making decisions due to physical, mental, or emotional conditions. Other criteria for disability status were described as motor functioning challenges such as difficulty with walking or climbing stairs, or difficulty with activities of daily living such as bathing or dressing, and challenges with being able to independently complete life-sustaining errands such as grocery shopping and medical appointments.

These Bureau of Labor descriptions align with medical models of disability which focus on problems occurring within the body of an individual that cause impairment (Bogart et al., 2022). Practitioners viewing disability from a medical model lens focus on pathology, diagnosis, and treatment interventions aimed at reducing symptoms that interfere with a person's ability to function (Retief & Letsosa, 2018). Andrews et al. (2019) associated medical model influences with the use of dehumanizing language and emphasis on impairment, such as referring to a person as the paraplegic or the schizophrenic as opposed to considering the person's collective identities and capacities or considering the limitations of environments.

The World Health Organization (2011, p. 4) described disability as a "complex, dynamic, multidimensional, and contested" construct requiring discussions about barriers which limit access and optimal functioning for people who are differently abled. They defined disability as an interaction between individuals with impairments and attitudes and environments that hinder their equal and effective engagement in society. For example, disability occurs when an individual with a health condition, such as hearing impairment or motor impairment, interacts with environment that is not accessible or lacks social supports such as sign language interpretation that would enable translation and communication. These descriptions align with social models that emphasize the interaction between person and environment (Retief & Letsosa, 2018).

Not surprisingly, environmental demands have shaped how functional challenges are considered or categorized (Smart & Smart, 2006). For example, a person with a physical limitation regarding mobility may not experience any functional challenges related to work that focuses on cognitive skills or use of appropriate computer technologies, but would experience functional challenges in engaging with many tasks associated with construction labor. A person experiencing a severe reading disability may be considered functionally challenged for a law office role where significant reading was required, but may not experience any functional challenge in their role as a yoga instructor.

Smart and Smart (2006) articulated that people with different functioning abilities are frequently faced with physical inaccessibility of environments, negative attitudes, or lack of awareness by people in their environments who do not identify as having disabilities. While these factors do not cause the physical or mental health conditions that constitute a disability, they can exacerbate the range and severity of challenges that are experienced including participation restrictions and employment discrimination. Additionally, societal prejudices and stigmas attached to varied functional abilities may be intertwined with societal perceptions of the person's intersectional identities such as racial, cultural, ethnic, and gender identities, sexual orientation, or age, resulting in a complex system of barriers to fulfilling one's potential.

Retief and Letsosa (2018) described other ways that people frame disability based on an identity model. The identity model acknowledges that social forces create disability through environmental limits and attitudes but also affirms disability as a positive and collective identity. Disability identity concepts will be further explored in subsequent sections of this chapter.

Disability Identity in the Workplace

Creators of the Americans with Disabilities Act (ADA) of 1990, the ADA Amendments Acts of 2008, and other national legislation worked to set policies to extinguish discrimination in work settings. However, work discrimination, including harassment, remains a salient issue for people with disabilities (ADA National Network, 2022). Harassment can manifest in many ways. The United States Equal Employment Opportunity Commission (2022) defined harassment as offensive remarks expressed by coworkers or employers resulting in toxic work environments. Additionally, harassment can include negative worksite responses to the employee and their disability including unwarranted demotion or termination of employment.

Santuzzi and Waltz (2016) noted the complexity of disability identity as experienced and expressed in work settings. Complexities of disability identity may be revealed when a worker is responsible for coming forward to acknowledge a disability that requires accommodations and protection but does not identify themselves as disabled in other life contexts. Conversely, a person may identify as "disabled," but their condition or experience may not legally be considered a disability. A person also may not identify as disabled in the workplace to avoid stigma and other negative consequences.

To increase understanding of workplace disability identity complexity, Santuzzi and Waltz (2016) identified several factors that influence worker disability identities. These include intraindividual factors; interpersonal factors; organizational factors; and legal, medical, and cultural definitions of disability. These researchers described intraindividual factors as a person's internal interpretation of their physical or psychological states or experiences that may be considered a disability. For example, a person may not be aware of how their experiences constitute disability or impairment, while another may not identify as disabled to avoid labeling and associated stigma. Relationships and reactions of others were noted as interpersonal factors that affected workplace disability identity. For example, individuals with strong affiliation within the disability community may be more likely to assert their status as they have a network of valued relationships that support their concepts of meaning and worth outside of the work setting. Another person with a disability, may work to hide disability status out of concern that identifying as disabled may change others' perspectives regarding their skills or talents or shift established workplace relationships.

Organizational factors may contribute to workers' experiences of workplaces as positive or negative climates related to disability identification (Santuzzi & Waltz, 2016). For example, organizational policies that support or limit flexibility for workers with disability send messages to workers about organizational attitudes. Additionally, organizational policies and practices may connote sensitivity or insensitivity to work safety issues or ergonomic conditions that increase risks of disabling experiences. In terms of legal, medical, and cultural definition influences, as noted above, national legislation has been designed to protect employment rights and to ensure equal access to work. However, Santuzzi and Waltz posited that lack of uniform definitions of disabilities throughout various governmental agencies creates ambiguity that may lead to the confusion of individuals and organizations alike. Conflicts between legal and medical definitions can also be confusing as medical or mental health diagnoses do not necessarily constitute disability in the eyes of the law. Additionally, cultural and broader societal views on what constitutes disability may influence a person's or organization's conceptions of disability.

Disability Identity Development

On a broader level, Forber-Pratt and Zape (2017) developed a psychosocial identity development model for individuals with disabilities to aid understanding of how positive disabilities identities may be formed. They asserted that positive disability identity contributes to physical and psychological health, and a strong sense of self that fosters determination and resilience when faced with barriers. Bogart (2014) conducted a study with people experiencing congenital and acquired disabilities utilizing measures for satisfaction with life, self-esteem, and disability identity and disability self-efficacy scales. Study results supported hypotheses that affirming one's disability identity positively contributes to a person's sense of well-being. Bogart also found that people with congenital disabilities had higher rates of satisfaction with life when compared to those with acquired disabilities, even when disabilities had a greater effect on their daily living activities. Positive disability identity also predicted greater levels of disability self-efficacy, and subsequent satisfaction with life. Levels of self-esteem did not predict satisfaction with life.

To learn more about identity development factors, Forber-Pratt and Zape (2017) conducted and analyzed interviews with 17 college students who self-identified as having a disability. Participants in their study experienced a variety of predominantly physically based disabilities, some acquired and some experienced since birth. All participants had grown up since the enactment of the Americans with Disabilities Act. Based on their research findings, Forber-Pratt and Zape formulated four identity statuses: acceptance, relationship, adoption, and engagement. In brief, the Acceptance status pertains to individuals' various experiences of coming to terms with their disability and identifying with a disability status. These experiences differ in part due to age of onset and level of acceptance by friends and family. The Relationship status reflects experiences of building a network of others with disabilities, learning from that group, and reducing feelings of being alone. In the Adoption status, core values related to disability culture are incorporated and applied. Actions in this status included advancing knowledge of policy and regulations that may apply to their situation and navigating self-advocacy efforts. Forber-Pratt and Zape defined the Engagement status as times when a person continued their learning about the group but also contributed to the community, for example, serving as mentors for another person with a disability.

Forber-Pratt and Zape (2017) stressed that healthcare community members needed to increase their understanding of care recipients' disability identity statuses so that they may offer attuned interventions, such as sensitively listening and respecting a person's current views on how they may or may not wish to identify or engage with the disability community, or by providing information about community networks as they are ready to seek connections. Career and art therapy practitioners also need to be aware of how identity factors may shape views on career options and decision-making, career problems, problem-solving, and desired solutions within work settings.

Practitioner Considerations

Smart and Smart (2006) identified important factors for counseling practitioners to consider when approaching work with people identifying as disabled or experiencing disabilities. First and foremost, a practitioner must acknowledge and question assumptions regarding definitions and conceptualizations of disability, guard against potential overemphasis on physical aspects of disability, and align efforts with clients' articulation of their identities, aspirations, and experienced obstacles. Additionally, Smart and Smart described areas of contemplation and actions for counselors to pursue. These include, but are not limited to, examining their own emotional responses to the client's disability and how these responses and expectations may influence the working alliance; examining clients' feelings regarding their experience of a disability; appreciating clients' consideration of their disability as a valued part of their identity; emphasizing client agency in decision-making and actions that support their desired engagement and pursuit of goals; listening to experiences of prejudice and discrimination; expanding knowledge of agencies that people with disabilities often utilize to foster important collaborations; and engaging in institutional advocacy and policy change efforts on multiple levels, and more. Practitioners should anticipate the need for ongoing reflection, self-education, and training to provide a respectful and responsive space for client and practitioner collaboration.

Career Practitioner Considerations

Kwon (2019) stressed the importance of supporting self-determination in career development for young adults and noted that attainment of desired employment and a well-formulated career choice is influenced by the person's level of empowerment to choose their career pathways. Conversely, Kwan observed that well-meaning guardians, teachers, or professionals who steer clients to particular career choices as a means of care and protection, or direct them towards work the practitioner perceives as easiest for the individual, may reduce the person's confidence in themselves or their career decision-making skills. These acts also limit the person's pursuit of self-actualization goals and fulfillment of life meaning aspirations. Kwon identified these as oppressive practices that perpetuate constrained career options related to societal expectations.

To counter such dynamics, Kwon (2019) recommended career practitioners consider career frameworks that support clients' self-determination. For example, Kwon asserted that a career constructivist approach is well-suited to this work. Associated processes such as the exploration of career stories and the construction and deconstruction of these career stories provide structures to facilitate reflection on external and internal influences regarding career interest and choice.

Shogren et al. (2016) explored the Self-Determined Career Development Model (SDCDM: Wehmeyer et al., 2003) as a method for supporting self-determined career development with adults with disabilities. SDCDM interventions provided instruction regarding developing self-managed problem-solving skills designed for utilization during career exploration and employment goal-setting. Shogren et al. described the model as a three-phased instructional process where participants are presented with a career-related problem to be solved. During each of the instructional segments, the person with the disability identifies the presented career problem, brainstorms possible solutions to the problem, considers potential obstacles that may interfere with problem-solving, and then considers the possible results of proposed solutions. While self-determination is emphasized, facilitators play an important role in the process through providing a non-judgmental environment, supporting understanding of the model, valuing individual efforts, and advocating for client success as they move through problem-solving steps. In their study of adults with disabilities, Shogren et al. compared SDCDM experimental groups to equivalent control groups across provider organizations and found that experimental groups showed significantly greater scores related to the self-determination factor of autonomy as measured by the Arc's Self-Determination Scale–Adult Version (SDS-Adult; Wehmeyer, 1996). Since higher self-determination scores have been associated with positive career outcomes, it appears that career problem-solving instruction, rehearsal, and support may be beneficial strategies for practitioners to utilize when working with adults with disabilities. An excellent resource for working with clients who have disabilities and their career development needs, is Strauser's 2021 text, *Career Development, Employment, and Disability in Rehabilitation: From Theory to Practice.*

Art Therapist Considerations

Regarding art and art therapy practices, Solvang (2018) outlined a varied history of art therapy models and interactions that have been designed for people with disabilities. She reported that art therapy interventions have often centered on the process of art versus the product of art, as interventions were designed to support expression, personal development, and empowerment. Alternatively, some arts therapy practices have focused on providing opportunities for people with disabilities to access instruction and training as well as sales outlets so they may form artist identities and careers. Solvang noted that these approaches can be positive but may still perpetuate medical model views of people creating art as patients receiving services, or similarly, as outsider artists, a label that emphasizes artists' differences or separation from "mainstream" society. Solvang contrasted these models with disability art movements that have emerged from disability communities to advance cultural expression informed by disability experiences and struggles for equality.

Beck (2020), an art therapist who experiences a visible physical disability, asserted the importance of combating ableism within the helping professions. Beck described personally experienced situations where her perspectives were devalued and or explained to her by able-bodied practitioners. She observed others' discomfort with physical differences, assumptions of incompetence based on physical abilities, and lack of practitioner awareness of disability culture as a source of pride versus something that needs to be fixed. She advocated for practitioners to operate from a social disability model that acknowledges the limitations of the environments and prejudicial societal perspectives that marginalize and stigmatize people with disabilities. Beck found value in forming and participating within accessible disability community art spaces where disability stories and artwork were heard, valued, and exhibited. Beck emphasized that these environments reduced shame and promoted pride related to disability identity.

Accessible and Adaptive Tools and Materials

As in other contexts, practitioners may offer arts-based interventions as a part of career-focused explorations with people with physical disabilities and must have a good comprehension of art materials and their properties and how to make them accessible for their clients. Therefore, familiarity with low-tech art tool adaptations is essential for ensuring equal opportunity for expressive engagement (Coleman & Cramer, 2015; Schoonover & Schwind, 2018). Schoonover and Schwind (2018) created an adapted and repurposed tools (ART) kit that scaffolded independent art engagement and self-expression for youth with a variety of disabilities. They turned simple items such as pizza boxes into easels to help bring art to students' eye level and repurposed plastic milk jugs transforming handles into grips for paintbrushes. A few examples of art supply adaptations are provided in Figure 12.1, including a water bottle and a paint roller adapted to assist with grasp of paintbrushes. Tools that can be used to make art accessible, such as small, motorized toys with attached markers powered by touch, and paint rollers attached to wheelchairs inspired by Coleman (2012) are artistically depicted in Figure 12.2.

In addition to DIY art adaptations, practitioners may also utilize digital arts software and assistive technologies to make artmaking accessible for clients. Creed (2018) outlined a variety of assistive technology tools that artists with physical disabilities use such as Wacom tablets that can boost dexterity with digital artmaking applications. Coleman (2012) suggested computer drawing or painting programs that can be used with joysticks, track balls, or other adaptive input devices including head- or eye-controlled systems. Free art software programs are available for a variety of computer platforms and as phone/tablet applications to be used with or without such devices. Coleman identified Tux Paint (Tux Paint Development Team, 2002–2022) as one example of a free and easy to use program that features shape stamps and special effects in addition to various paintbrush styles, sizes and color options for creative expression. While originally

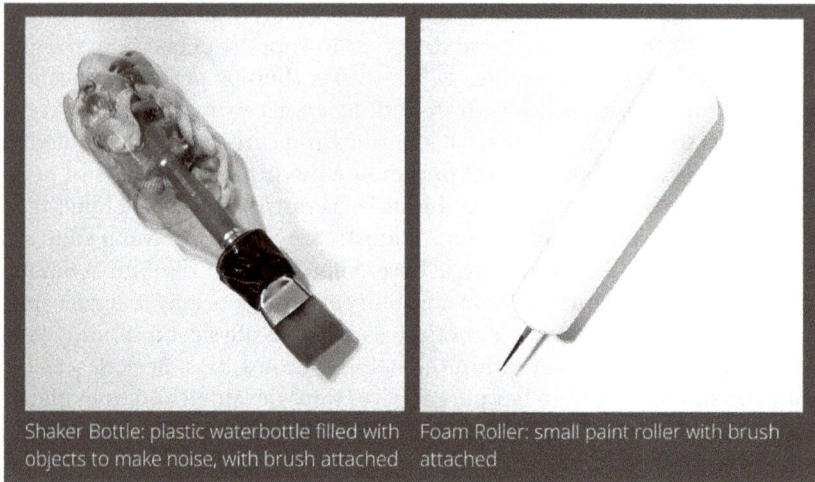

Shaker Bottle: plastic waterbottle filled with objects to make noise, with brush attached   Foam Roller: small paint roller with brush attached

Figure 12.1 Art Tool Adaptations a. Shaker Bottle. b. Frame Roller

designed with children in mind, Tux Paint software design is used by people of all ages, and provides adults with a very easy way to engage in digital artmaking processes that may use input devices or simple tablet touches. The artwork in Figure 12.3 is provided as an example of exploratory artwork created with Tux Paint.

Importantly, it is the responsibility of practitioners to match needs of clients and to remove barriers and ensure access to appropriate art therapy and counseling interventions and spaces. Such requirements have been outlined in professional codes and

Figure 12.2 Art Accessible Tool Example

Figure 12.3 Exploratory Artwork Using Tux Paint

competency documents. For example, the Art Therapy Credentials Board (2021) Code of Ethics, Conduct, and Disciplinary Procedures requires that art therapists provide functional environments and use practices in accordance with ability and identity statuses. The National Career Development Association Minimum Competencies for Multicultural Career Counseling Development (NCDA, 2009) also delineate that career counselors must have "knowledge of information, resources, and the use of technology to determine that these tools are sensitive to the needs of diverse populations amending and/or individualizing for each client as required" (p. 6). The NCDA ethics code (NCDA, 2015) also describes requirements for addressing technology-assisted services and for providing clients with information regarding resources that may help them access such options.

Knowing Resources

To provide informed career-focused services it is important to be knowledgeable regarding a broad range of topics regarding disabilities and employment. A select group of website resources will be outlined here to support reader knowledge of available resources.

Disability Resources

The Disability Resources website is available at www.disabilityresources.org and is a comprehensive website that serves as a gateway to information on a variety of disability topics. These topics include abuse, accessibility, advocacy and legal rights, assistive technology, caregiving, children, communication, culture, government disability benefits, disability issues, education, employment, healthcare, national disabilities organizations, rehabilitation treatments and therapy, and more. Following selection of a topic, the user is linked to information and provided additional websites and sources of information for further investigation into topic content. It is simply laid out and easy to navigate.

DO-IT

The DO-IT website available at www.washington.edu/doit/ is affiliated with Washington University in Seattle Washington and models how evidence-based practices are utilized to increase people with disabilities' opportunities in challenging academics and careers. DO-IT stands for Disabilities, Opportunities, Internetworking, and Technology, and the site provides guidelines for replicating DO-IT practices such as building mentoring communities, provides resources for exploring technologies and universal design in education to expand accessibility, and outlines strategies that promote institutional change.

EARN: Employer Assistance and Resource Network on Disability Inclusion

The EARN website is available at https://askearn.org. EARN aims to provide information and resources to employers so that they may recruit hire and retain people with disabilities. EARN offers resources that support development of positive workplace cultures and actions which help employers meet diversity equity, inclusion, and accessibility goals. A notable resource on the site is EARN's Mental Health Toolkit which can be found at https://askearn.org/page/mental-health-toolkit. This toolkit provides statistics on mental health concerns, impact on work, rationale for fostering mental health friendly workplaces, and ways that this can be accomplished. While this website is designed for employers, practitioners will value the site as it provides language to support advocacy efforts.

Job Accommodations Network (JAN)

The Job Accommodations Network (JAN) website is available at https://askjan.org. This website is provided as a service of the US Department of Labor's Office of Disability Employment Policy (ODEP, 2022). The website provides guidance on the Americans with Disabilities Act and offers accommodation options designed to benefit employees with disabilities and employers. JAN aims to stimulate recognition of values and talents of workers with disabilities. Sections of the website are devoted to employers, individuals, and others. Other targeted audiences include rehabilitation and medical professionals, union representatives, and attorney and legal representatives. Free webcasts and trainings are available through the site.

Office of Disability Employment Policy (ODEP)

The ODEP website is available at www.dol.gov/agencies/odep and is affiliated with the US Government Department of Labor. ODEP's mission is "to develop and influence policies and practices that increase the number and quality of employment opportunities for people with disabilities." The ODEP site provides a broader spectrum of topics when compared to the ODEP-affiliated site, JAN. The ODEP website covers broad categories of information for employers, employment support, information resources for individuals, and an "other" category, which highlights topics such as mental health and autism.

After building your awareness, knowledge, and competencies regarding career resources and applications you will be ready to apply this information in the practice setting.

Considering Career Counseling

A person with a disability may wish to explore, plan, or problem-solve an experience with a career problem at various stages of life and career development processes. Client and practitioner will work together to determine the specific goal that will be addressed during sessions. Hershenson (2005) highlighted the INCOME model (Beveridge et al., 2002) as a sensitively designed career framework that combined a variety of career constructs applicable to people with diverse backgrounds, ages, and abilities and provides accessible language to identify career concerns. The INCOME model includes six different statuses which can be experienced simultaneously or separately within the career exploration and decision-making process. The acronym INCOME stands for these six statuses: Imagining, iNforming, Choosing, Obtaining, Maintaining, and Exiting. The Imagining status includes expanding awareness of job types, fantasy imagining, and reality-based imagining of potential career options. The iNforming status relates to both an understanding of themselves, their skills and talents and knowledge of career options, and their requirements and qualities. Within the Choosing status, a person integrates their knowledge of self with the understanding of occupations and the world of work and selects an occupation. In the Obtaining status, the person searches for and optimally acquires a position in the preferred career areas. The Maintaining status involves the process of working and making adaptations that sustain positive engagement in the work roles and settings. The Exiting status relates to leaving a job or thinking about leaving a job and relates to work transitions.

Career counselors using this model plan interventions addressing problems that arise within the active status areas, starting with the most significant area of concern. However, it is also important to note that this is only one of many models that can be used to conceptualize career considerations for people with disabilities as evidenced by the number of theories presented in Chapter 2.

Invisible Disabilities

Not all disabilities are visible or readily detectible; consequently, some disabilities are known as invisible disabilities. Invisible disabilities include a broad spectrum of physical and mental conditions including depression or anxiety, traumatic brain injuries, autoimmune disorders, low vision or hearing loss, as well as many other types of challenges that are experienced but not necessarily seen (Prince, 2017; Santuzzi et al., 2014). Santuzzi et al. noted that people with invisible disabilities may have some observable symptoms such as slowed movement that can be misconstrued by others as having a transient nature, such as sleepiness, or another non-disability source. In both circumstances, if the disability is not visible or significantly apparent, a worker may choose to conceal their disability status. However, if an individual does not report an invisible disability that may affect their work performance, they may be vulnerable to poor reviews. If they do report their disability to the employer, they may have access to accommodation and other legal protections and could be more fairly evaluated. Other advantages of disclosure include reduction of stress related to holding on to a "secret"; greater ease in posing health insurance or other benefit questions to the employer; accommodations and individualized support that increase opportunities to succeed; a sense of agency when contributing to others' understanding and application of accommodations; and a more positive self-image as a result of self-advocacy efforts (Prince, 2017). Still, the majority of people with invisible disabilities do not disclose their conditions.

Rathbun-Grubb (2021) surveyed librarians that experienced chronic illnesses and conditions, to learn more about their experiences, coping strategies, and perspectives on disability, accommodations, disclosure, and consequences related to their careers. Of 616 respondents, 42% reported psychological disorders and 18% reported autoimmune disorders. Other conditions reported included migraines, cardiovascular disease, diabetes, digestive disorders, hearing and visual disorders, and more. Related to disclosure of conditions to employers, many had mixed views on revealing invisible disabilities. Some characterized disclosure as risky and articulated concerns about being judged or passed over for promotion as a result. Others noted they had experienced negative consequences such as discrimination and job loss following disclosure. Still others did not report their invisible disability due to worries they would not be believed. Some felt "forced" to disclose their disabilities when symptoms became more severe and that there was pressure to explain absences and to address coworker attitudes. On a more positive note, others who chose to disclose their disability helped them be more transparent and freed them to be a better advocate for what they needed.

When asked about accommodations, 35% of the surveyed librarians stated that they had requested accommodations and 79% reported receiving them (Rathbun-Grubb, 2021). Those that received accommodations described their libraries as supportive environments that valued equity, diversity, and inclusion. However, many surveyed librarians expressed wishes that administrators could be more proactive regarding learning and applying accommodations that would ensure worker success.

Librarians also designed their own strategies to navigate disabilities, outside of accommodations, to maintain their productivity (Rathbun-Grubb, 2021). Some of these strategies included taking time off for necessary appointments, adhering to the medication and dietary regimens, bringing their own assistive technology to work, prioritizing and scheduling demanding work tasks at higher energy times in their day, taking a short walk to increase energy, or finding a quieter space at work to re-group if necessary. Others noted that they took care of themselves at work and home by meditating, setting boundaries, and engaging in other practices that helped them manage their chronic conditions.

As noted from the survey examples, for those who experience invisible disabilities, making a decision to disclose and request accommodations can be quite complex. A career practitioner can begin to support this decision-making process by being informed about the disability rights and employment legislation, advocacy resources as well as an understanding of very real advantages and disadvantages of disclosure and its consequences. Additionally, a practitioner must cultivate a positive working alliance and a non-judgmental space within sessions to where the invisible experiences can be made visible to address. Art therapists have utilized art therapy practices with people with medical conditions for many years via many different forms (Anand, 2016; Rosner-David, 2016). Anand noted that art therapy goals with people with medical illness include but are not limited to decreasing isolation; improving socialization; supporting mastery of art materials to increase self-confidence; providing opportunities to express feelings regarding their illness; and fostering resilience through identification of strengths. Artmaking is uniquely situated to make internal experiences more visible and images of felt experiences can be jointly viewed, explored, and understood.

In this example (Figure 12.4), an individual used the forum of art therapy and artmaking to reveal the story of her autoimmune disorder and how her experiences differed from her work colleagues starting at the very beginning of her day. She titled her work *Hashimoto Morning Routine*.

In describing her image, she noted:

> Most people cannot tell by looking at me, but I have Hashimoto's thyroiditis, an autoimmune illness in which my immune system attacks my thyroid, impairing its ability to produce hormones that regulate metabolism, energy levels, anxiety, and mood. While most people would focus on showering and grabbing a quick bite in the morning, I wake up several hours before I have to leave for work just to get ready. To maintain a calm demeanor and competence among my colleagues, I incorporate

Figure 12.4 Hashimoto Morning Routine

activities that provide me with energy to prepare for the day, such as dancing and listening to mood-boosting music, invigorating shower additions such as eucalyptus leaves, and eating a proper breakfast with foods that do not aggravate my immune system further so I can take my thyroid hormone replacement medication. Then, before heading to work, I engage in soothing hobbies, such as lengthy walks while listening to music or a podcast, and keeping a few crafts on hand, such as drawing, crocheting, and beading materials, to use to alleviate my anxiety before starting work or during breaks.

Her descriptions demonstrate the numerous adaptations she has made in her home life to prepare herself for her work day, yet she has not requested any accommodations from her work setting. Goals for ongoing work with this client may focus on many of the aims outlined by Anand (2016) such as expressing feelings about her illness and fostering resilience. Additionally, a practitioner with knowledge about disability and disclosure issues could support her use of artwork to explore advantages and disadvantages of disclosure; facilitate rehearsal and problem-solving regarding work-related problems such as discrimination; provide resources to foster expansion of her community networks; and advance understanding of her options for accommodation and protection under the law.

Career Development and Disabilities Related to Mental Health

In regard to disability, mental health disorders are most frequently categorized as invisible disorders. While much of this chapter has focused on physical disabilities, it is equally important to address mental health concerns and career considerations as mental health symptoms may influence career development efforts and workplace experiences in a variety of ways. In this next section, considerations regarding career decision-making support for individuals diagnosed with attention deficit hyperactivity disorder (ADHD) and depression will be addressed.

Career Decision-Making and ADHD

Career decision making can be a daunting task given the amount of information that must be processed and evaluated to make a decision, and decision-making may be even more challenging for someone who has been diagnosed with attention deficit hyperactivity disorder (ADHD). The American Psychiatric Association (2022) described ADHD symptoms including inattention that contributes to difficulties with organizing a sequence of tasks, difficulty listening to instructions, and increased occurrences of being distracted or wandering off-task. Dipeolu et al. (2015) investigated the impact ADHD had on people's experience with career development tasks and found that people with ADHD had greater decision-making confusion than those who did not, and that people with ADHD may be prone to making premature career decisions. Following career decision-making, Dipeolu et al. (2013) noted that ADHD symptoms frequently interfere with work and employment functions, such as prioritizing, managing, or completing work-tasks, and inhibit career success. Consequently, they advocated for career practitioners to be well-versed in the symptoms of mental health disorders such as ADHD, to better individualize treatment strategies and facilitate positive transitions from school experiences to occupational success.

In her career sessions with young adults with ADHD, Brooks (2016) observed that clients with ADHD frequently appeared bored or restless, expressed concerns about having to commit to one type of job, and had doubts about their decision-making capacities. These situations can make career decision-making processes frustrating for both the practitioner and the client. Consequently, Brooks designed career decision-making goals and approaches that consider and accommodate for these experiences and concerns.

Brooks (2016) asserted that the first aim to cultivate with clients with ADHD is the generation of hope. To achieve this goal, Brooks stimulated clients' explorations of internal ideas about career options through short step-by-step tasks that build success and increase confidence and motivation. She also reported success with supportive cognitive behavioral approaches that challenge dysfunctional thinking about decision-making abilities. Statements such as "if my first job choice is not completely satisfying, it means I'll never find a job I like," which reflect irrational thoughts about career success and failure, get dismantled by exploring experiential evidence to broaden clients' career conceptualizations.

Brooks (2016) also adjusted career decision-making tasks to make them manageable, at times using visual and creative means. One such process is called Possible Lives Mapping. The specific purpose of the Possible Lives Map is to help people organize their ideas about potential careers and clarify career decisions. Brooks offered clients the following supplies to complete the mapping tasks: a blank piece of legal size paper, a marker, and adhesive notes. First, the person is instructed to write their name in the center of the page and create a circle around it. Once that is completed, the client is asked to think about careers they have considered since early childhood to the present. Each time a career is identified, the practitioner invites the client to write it on the paper and circle it with a target of ten identified career options by the time of completion. Brooks requested this number to prevent clients from becoming overwhelmed, but people can choose to note more or less. If a client has difficulty generating ideas, the practitioner can provide a prepared list of careers for review.

When all careers have been identified and written, the practitioner asks them to draw lines between the central circle with their name and each of the career options. Next, the practitioner asks to the client look at their map for career themes such as active careers, outdoor careers, service careers, and to write down what they find. After noting these themes, the client is asked to name three careers that currently appeal to them, centering the reflection process in the present. On the map, the client draws a stronger line between the central circle with the name and their primary career choices. After some reflective questions are facilitated by the practitioner, the client is asked to use the line to write the first three steps they would need to take towards these possible careers. Brooks noted that using the term *possible* instead career *choice* may reduce anxiety about commitment to job options. To help clients set intentions, Brooks might ask the client to write the themes of what they are looking for in a career on adhesive notes, starting with the statement, "I am looking for an opportunity to …" Brook explained that externalizing these intentions helps a client with ADHD focus on a selected item and may reduce internal confusion.

Testing the Process of Possible Lives Mapping

To test this process, the first chapter author, Barbara, created Figure 12.5 as a Possible Lives Map while musing on her own experiences of job interests since childhood. Her job options included portrait artist, violinist, teacher, artist, museum educator, gallery owner, coffee shop owner, and of course, art therapist. Barbara did appreciate that all of these options were contained in circles and did not feel overwhelming. In this sample, Barbara utilized the sticky notes to identify three themes that arose as she reviewed the job options. These themes included working with others, hands-on active work, and visual arts engagement. While not depicted in Figure 12.5, a next step in the process would be for Barbara to strengthen the line to the three current interest options, and list three first steps toward each option. For example, Barbara could have written the next

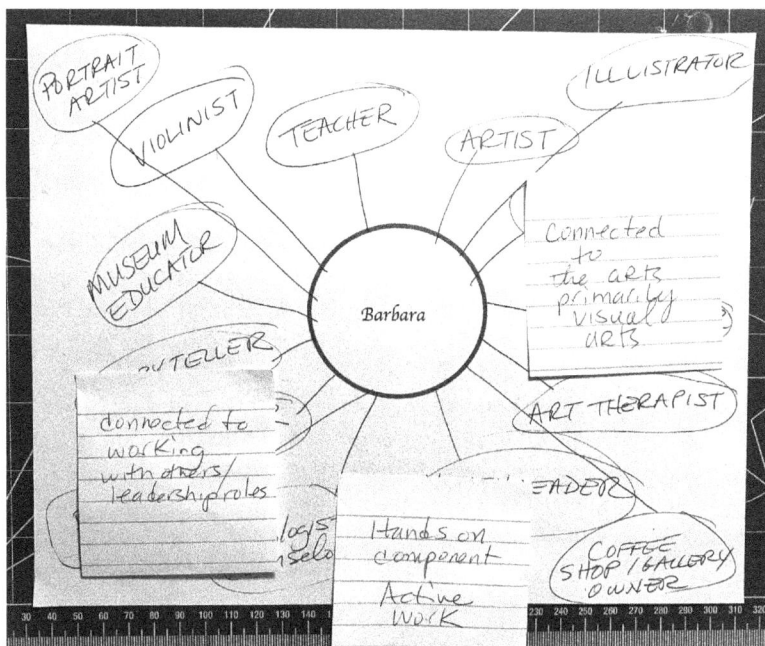

Figure 12.5 Barbara's Possible Lives Map

steps to pursuing a career in art therapy, such as finding out educational prerequisites, talking to an art therapist, and looking to see if a graduate art therapy program was available nearby. To set an intention, Barbara would use another sticky note to write what she was looking for in her career options, "I am looking for an opportunity to explore visual arts with other people."

Through the design and implementation of the described methods, Brooks modeled how practitioners can responsively adapt tasks and make career interventions more accessible for people experiencing ADHD. Her Possible Lives Mapping approach demonstrated how structured approaches can support career decision-making efforts using creative visual methods which help to externalize creative decision-making steps and increase organization and manageability of options being considered.

Career Decision-Making and Depression

Depression is a psychiatric disability according to the Americans with Disabilties Act, and clients with major depressive disorder might experience career barriers due in part to the symptoms they are experiencing (Hayden et al., 2016). Some specific symptoms are almost daily indecisiveness, feeling worthless, or slowed thought (American Psychiatric Association, 2022). These symptoms impact decision-making in general. For example, Muris and van der Heiden (2006) found that individuals with higher levels of depression are less positive in their beliefs about what the future will hold. Others (Blanco et al., 2013) have found that those with higher levels of depression are more likely to be uncertain, and will opt for simpler decision-making approaches. Still others (Lawlor et al., 2019; Murphy et al., 2001) have found those with higher depression levels take significantly longer to make decisions. With respect to career decision-making, Walker and Peterson (2012) found a relationship between depression, career indecision, and dysfunctional career thoughts (and especially decision-making confusion).

The case example below demonstrates how a client's depression might interact with their career concern, and how a career practitioner might navigate that conversation. The degree to which a CP might integrate mental health and career concerns should be determined by the CP's qualifications, boundaries of competence, employer policies, and ultimately, by the client's openness and agreement to discuss these issues.

When Career and Depression Intersect

Chelsea showed up to a drop-in career advising session to talk with a career practitioner (CP) about choosing a major. They noted a tone of hopelessness as she talked, evidenced in her tone and through statements such as "I guess the time has come for me to figure things out," and "none of these majors look really interesting to me." When the CP asked what options she was considering, she said she didn't have any, nor was she particularly curious about any majors – and when asked about her interests and skills, she said, "I don't know. I'm still trying to figure all that out." When asked why now, Chelsea said she wasn't allowed to register for any more classes until she declared a major. When asked what she thought might be making it difficult to make a decision, she commented about the lack of interesting options, not being sure of where to start, and that it seemed like the whole process was really involved and would take too much energy. Based on these comments, the CP asked if she would be willing to complete a short inventory (the Career Thoughts Inventory, Sampson et al., 1996) that might help them identify what might be getting in the way of her making a decision. Chelsea agreed, and her scores indicated highly elevated negative career thoughts, mostly in the decision-making confusion area. The CP also noted that she had endorsed several emotionally heavy items (e.g., "I get so depressed when," or "I get anxious," or "I am overwhelmed with"). As she began the review of the results, she stated, "Chelsea, it seems like you are feeling overwhelmed with starting this process. You also marked a lot of items about feeling depressed and anxious. Could you tell me more about that?"

Chelsea agreed with the general observation and shared that she is currently in counseling for depression and anxiety. She agreed to complete a release of information to allow her CP to talk to her counselor so they could coordinate efforts. The CP also shared how emotions and thoughts can impact career exploration and decision-making, and asked Chelsea what she had learned about how to be aware of and strategies for managing her depression and anxiety, as well as signs that it might not be the best time to make a major decision. Chelsea said she had mixed success at knowing when she "was in a funk in her head," but that sometimes she could hear the way she was talking to herself, or she paid attention to the number of shoulds and oughts in her self-talk. She said her therapist had been training her to also pay attention to her body, that if she was sleeping or eating a lot more, or just finding it hard to move her body, to check herself. She said she was still working on strategies, like using a thoughts app on her phone or reframing, and that she found that there was nothing that worked 100% of the time. On days when she had more energy, she might try several different strategies, but on other days, she would try to avoid making a decision or doing anything so she wouldn't make a choice she regretted. She also said her therapist had introduced her to scaling, so before a big decision, she would ask herself how much her anxiety and depression were influencing her in the moment, on a scale of one to ten. If it was below five, she felt like it was OK to proceed but with caution. A five or higher meant to put off the decision if possible for the time being.

The CP asked where she'd place herself now. Chelsea said, "When I first came in, honestly, I was at a six – but I was already here, and it took so much for me to get here, that I just decided I'd do something. I honestly didn't even care what major I chose – I'm just tired of the pressure of knowing I need to choose."

"That's when you first came in. Sounds like it's shifted a little?" the CP commented.

"Yeah," Chelsea said. "Sometimes when I talk about it, it lets the pressure off a bit. I'd say right now I'm at about a 4 – and I don't want you to just tell me what to do so I can be done with it. I would like to actually choose something that is nearer to who I actually am. I guess I'm feeling some energy about it now."

The CP responded, "We have tools that can help you organize information about yourself and then see how those might apply to different majors and careers. However, it is really easy to influence these by your self-talk, so you have to be in a headspace where you can honestly evaluate whether something interests you or not, and be sure it's not the depression speaking. Do you know what I mean?"

"I think so. I know I can talk myself out of things that I'd normally enjoy pretty quickly if I let myself. Like I might be thinking I want to go for a walk, but then the depression kicks in and I come up with a million reasons why it's not a good idea, and end up not going and feeling bad that I had such a stupid idea to begin with, and later feeling guilty that I listened to that voice. Sometimes, that voice is very loud."

"I get that. The issue with letting that self-talk run while doing these types of career exploration activities is that it can impact the results. You may end up with options that don't really fit you or even no options at all. So how will you make sure that you're holding that voice at bay while you're working on your career decision?"

Chelsea smiled, took out a notecard from her backpack that had a checkmark on it and placed it on the table. She said, I put this in front of me when I'm working on something and feel like I might slip and start listening to the depression. It reminds me to check my self-talk and do a scaling question."

As Chelsea affirmed that she'd like to continue with career exploration using her check-mark as a supportive strategy. The CP presented several options to Chelsea and asked which one she'd be interested in doing (e.g., card sort, interest inventory, collage), with a suggestion that they could do as many as she liked. They continued career counseling in this way, across multiple sessions, with the CP working with Chelsea's therapist to reinforce strategies she was using in therapy by applying them to the career concern, and giving Chelsea options about how to approach each step in the decision-making process, and control over which resources to use, and how much time/energy she felt like devoting towards the task.

In this example, we show how career and mental health concerns might be addressed in a way that respects the unique aspect of a person's mental health, and coordinate with other treatments being received. If the client is not receiving counseling, the CP might make a referral. If the client does not wish to pursue personal therapy, the CP can still share information about how self-talk impacts decision-making, and share resources related to mental health as the client is willing.

Summary

This chapter explored work disparities for people with disability, disability identity, disability models, and how disability identity may be considered in workplace settings. Additionally, practitioner responsibilities for understanding and addressing accessibility needs and resources that can support navigation of disability rights have been empha-sized and examples provided. Approaches and interventions to address various career concerns for people with visible and invisible physical and mental health disabilities were offered for review and consideration.

Discussion Questions and Activities

1 **Reflection**: At any stage of your life, have you, or someone close to you, experienced a temporary, permanent, or progressive physical disability? What experiences did you or this person have navigating within day-to-day work or school environments? How would you recommend organizations or institutions visited adapt their envi-ronments to be more accessible or shift attitudes to become more respectful or welcoming? What type of advocacy could you engage in to address unfair practices or inaccessible environments?

2 **Activity and Reflection**: Explore your current work, internship office, or studio. How accessible is this space to someone who may use a wheelchair, scooter, or walker? How could you change it to be more accessible?

3 **Activity**: Review referenced articles (Coleman, 2012; Coleman & Cramer, 2015, and Schoonover & Schwind; 2018) and create three to five low-tech art tool adaptions for pencil and paintbrush use from items in your home or work environment. Keep them in your studio or office workspace in the ready!

4 **Resource Exploration and Reflection**: Using the Internet to locate an organization that provides a community arts space or program for people with disabilities. Based on what you can find from their information, what type of model of disability do you believe informs their mission and practices? Who are involved in decisions related to the policies and practices of the organization? How do practices relate to partici-pants' vocational or occupational goals or engagement?

5 **Activity**: Review the other book chapters and pick one art prompt that you perceive as complex and/or potentially overwhelming. How might you adapt this prompt to make the art process more accessible or successful for a person with ADHD?

6 **Discussion and Activity**: Choose a visible or invisible physical disability that you know little about. What methods might you use to learn more about this particular disability and how this may be experienced in daily life in a variety of settings? After exploring three or more resources to learn about the disability and lived experiences, create a responsive artwork related to what you have learned. Reflect on the artwork and note your reactions and potential assumptions.

References

American Psychiatric Association. (2022). *Diagnostic and statistical manual of mental disorders* (5th ed.). American Psychiatric Association.

Americans with Disabilities Act National Network. (2022). An overview of the Americans with Disabilities Act. https://adata.org/factsheet/ADA-overview

Anand, S. A. (2016). Dimensions of art therapy in medical illness. In D. Gussak & M. Rosal (Eds.), *The Wiley handbook of art therapy* (pp. 409–420). John Wiley & Sons.

Andrews, E. E., Forber-Pratt. A. J., Mona, L. R., et al. (2019). #SaytheWord: A disability culture commentary on the erasure of "disability." *Rehabilitation, 64*(2), 111–118. https://doi.apa.org/doiLanding?doi=10.1037%2Frep0000258

Art Therapy Credentials Board. (2021). Code of ethics, conduct, and disciplinary procedures. www.atcb.org/wp-content/uploads/2020/07/ATCB-Code-of-Ethics-Conduct-DisciplinaryProcedures.pdf

Beck, B. (2020). Embodied practice: Reflections of a physically disabled art therapist in social and medical disability spaces. *Art Therapy: Journal of the American Art Therapy Association, 37*(2), 66–69.

Beveridge, S., Heller Craddock, S., Liesener, J., et al. (2002). INCOME: A framework for conceptualizing the career development of persons with disabilities. *Rehabilitation Counseling Bulletin, 45*, 195–206.

Blanco, N. J., Otto, A. R., Maddox, W. T., et al. (2013). The influence of depression symptoms on exploratory decision-making. *Cognition, 129*, 563–568.

Bogart, K. R. (2014). The role of disability self-concept in adaptation to congenital or acquired disability. *Rehabilitation Psychology, 59*(1), 107–115. https://doi.org/10.1037/a00035800

Bogart, K. R., Bonnett, A. K., Logan, S. W., & Kallem, C. (2022). Intervening on disability attitudes through disability models and contact in psychology education. *Scholarship of Teaching and Learning in Psychology, 8*(1), 15–26. http://dx.doi.org/10.1037/stl0000194

Brooks, K. S. (2016). Breaking through career indecision in clients with ADHD. *Career Planning and Adult Development Journal, 32*(1), 54–62.

Bureau of Labor Statistics US Department of Labor (2022). Persons with a disability: Labor force characteristics – 2021. www.bls.gov/news.release/pdf/disabl.pdf

Coleman, M. B. (2012). Technology spotlight: Art adaptations for students with physical disabilities. *Newsletter of the Division for Physical and Health Disabilities, 30*(2), 14–22.

Coleman, M. B. & Cramer, E. S. (2015). Creating meaningful art experiences with assistive technology for students with physical, visual, severe, and multiple disabilities. *Art Education, 68*(2), 6–13. http://dx.doi.org/10.1080/00043125.2015.11519308

Creed, C. (2018). Assistive technology for disabled visual artists: Exploring the impact of digital technologies on artistic practice. *Disability & Society, 33*(7), 1103–1119. https://doi.org.10.1080/09687599.2018.1469400

Dipeolu, A., Hargrave, S., & Storlie, C. A. (2015). Enhancing ADHD and LD diagnostic accuracy using career instruments. *Journal of Career Development, 42*(1), 19–32. https://doi.org/1177/0894845314521691

Dipeolu, A., Sniatecki, J. L., Storlie, C.A., & Hargrave, S. (2013). Dysfunctional career thoughts and attitudes as predictors of vocational identity among young adults with attention deficit hyperactivity disorder. *Journal of Vocational Behavior, 82*, 79–84. http://dx.doi.org/10.1016/j.jvb.2013.01.003

Forber-Pratt, A. J., Mueller, C. O., & Andrews, E. E. (2019). Disability identity and allyship in rehabilitation psychology: Sit, stand, sign, and show up. *Rehabilitation Psychology, 64*(2), 119–129. https://doi.org/10.1037/rep0000256

Forber-Pratt, A. J., & Zape, M. (2017). Disability identity developmental model: Voices from the ADA generation. *Disability and Health Journal, 10*, 350–355. http://dx.doi.org/10.1016/j.dhjo.2016.12.013

Hayden, S. C. W., Kronholz, J., Pawley, E., & Theall, K. (2016). Major depressive disorder and career development: Links and implications. *Career Planning and Adult Development Journal, 32*(1), 19–32.

Hershenson, D. B. (2005). INCOME: A culturally inclusive and disability-sensitive framework for career development concepts and interventions. *The Career Development Quarterly, 54*, 150–161.

Kwon, C. (2019). Career development of people with disabilities: Self-determination as a skill set or a mind-set? *Adult Learning, 30*(2), 78–83. https://doi.org/10.1177/1045159518817736

Lawlor, V. M., Webb, C. A., Wiecki, T. V., et al. (2019). Dissecting the impact of depression on decision-making. *Psychological Medicine, 50*, 1613–1622. https://doi.org/10.1017/S0033291719001570

Muris, P., & van der Heiden, S. (2006). Anxiety, depression, and judgments about the probability of future negative and positive events in children. *Journal of Anxiety Disorders, 20*, 252–261.

Murphy, F. C., Rubinsztein, J. S., Michael, A., et al. (2001). Decision-making cognition in anxiety and depression. *Psychological Medicine, 31*, 679–693.

National Career Development Association. (2009). Minimum competencies for career counseling and development. www.ncda.org/aws/NCDA/pt/sp/compentencies_multi_cultural

National Career Development Association. (2015). NCDA code of ethics. https://ncda.org/aws/NCDA/asset_manager/get_file/3395?ver=738700

Office of Disability Employment Policy (2022). Office of Disability Employment Policy website. www.dol.gov/agencies/odep.

Prince, M. J. (2017). Persons with invisible disabilities and workplace accommodation: Findings from a scoping literature review. *Journal of Vocational Rehabilitation, 46*, 75–86. https://doi.org/10.3233/JVR-160844

Rathbun-Grubb, S. (2021). Voices of strength: A survey of librarians working with chronic illnesses or conditions. *Journal of Library Administration, 61*(1), 42–57. https://doi.org/10.1080/01930826.2020.1845546

Retief, M. & Letsosa, R. (2018). Models of disability: A brief overview. *HTS Teologiese Studies/Theological Studies, 74*(1), a4738. https://doi.org/10.4102/hts.v74i1.4738

Rosner-David, I. (2016). Art therapy in medical settings. In D. Gussak & M. Rosal (Eds), *The Wiley handbook of art therapy* (pp. 441–450). John Wiley & Sons.

Sampson, J. P., Jr., Peterson, G. W., Lenz, J. G., et al. (1996). *Career Thoughts Inventory professional manual*. Psychological Assessment Resources.

Santuzzi, A. M. & Waltz, P. R. (2016). Disability in the workplace: A unique and variable identity. *Journal of Management, 42*(5), 1111–1135. https://doi.org//10.1177/0149206315626269

Santuzzi, A. M., & Waltz, P. R., & Finkelstein, L. M. (2014). Invisible disabilities: Unique challenges for employees and organizations. *Industrial and Organizational Psychology, 7*, 204–219. https://doi.org/10.1111/iops.1234

Schoonover, J., & Schwind, D. B. (2018). DIY Adapted Repurposed Tool (ART) kit: A recipe for success. *Journal of Occupational Therapy, Schools, & Early Intervention, 11*(1), 7–14. https://doi.org/10.1080/19411243.2018.1396016

Shogren, K. S., Gotto, G. S., Wehmeyer, M. L., et al. (2016). The impact of the Self-Determined Career Development Model on self-determination. *Journal of Vocational Rehabilitation, 45*, 337–350. https://doi.org/10.3233/JVR-160834

Smart, J. F., & Smart, D. W. (2006). Models of disability: Implications for the counseling profession. *Journal of Counseling & Development, 84*, 29–40.

Solvang, P. K. (2018). Between art therapy and disability aesthetics: A sociological approach for understanding the intersection between art practice and disability discourse. *Disability & Society, 33*(2), 238–253. https://doi.org/10.1080/09687599.2017.1392929

Strauser, D. R. (Ed.). (2021). *Career development, employment, and disability in rehabilitation: From theory to practice*. Springer.

Tux Paint Development Team (2002–2022). Tux Paint software. Available: https://tuxpaint.org

US Equal Employment Opportunity Commission. (2022). Disability discrimination. www.eeoc.gov/disability-discrimination

Walker, J. V., III, & Peterson, G. W. (2012). Career thoughts, indecision, and depression: Implications for mental health assessment in career counseling. *Journal of Career Assessment*, *20*, 497–506. https://doi.org/10.1177/1069072712450010

Wehmeyer, M. L. (1996). The Arc's Self-Determination Scale Adult Version. The Arc National Headquarters.

Wehmeyer, M. L., Lattimore, J., Jorgensen, J., et al. (2003). The Self-Determined Career Development Model: A pilot study. *Journal of Vocational Rehabilitation*, *19*, 79–87.

World Health Organization. (2011). World report on disability. PDF. Retrieved from www.who.int/publications/i/item/WHO-NMH-VIP-11.0

13 Using Creativity to Understand and Support Career Transitions

This chapter will explore how career opportunities and interests may change throughout the lifespan. Strategies that may be used by art therapist/career counselors to support renewed exploration and decision-making regarding careers will be provided. Specific transition themes related to career change will include work-setting conflicts, changes in workplace demands, as well as changes in family life roles and responsibilities. The chapter will highlight the chaos theory of career development and will provide creative and art-based means to exploring responses to changes while empowering clients to welcome opportunities to adapt and redefine career values and objectives.

The Nature of Career Transitions

Career transitions occur throughout the lifespan. Career transition has been defined as "any event, or non-event, that results in changed relationships, routines, assumptions, and roles" (Schlossberg, Waters, & Goodman, 1995, p. 27). The first career-related transition occurs when a child enters a working role as a student, in which they learn about performance expectations, deadlines, individual contributions, teamwork, and evaluation. Other career-related transitions occur when a person first engages in volunteer work or their first job, transitioning from high school into either post-secondary training or the world of work or military experience, movement from one position to another, or across different career fields, promotions, demotions, extended periods away from work, entry and re-entry, and finally, retirement. Some transitions may be planned, such as retirement or a relocation, whereas others might be unplanned, such as being fired or needing to quit a job due to unforeseen health concerns or as a result of a disaster such as the COVID-19 pandemic which saw many businesses permanently close.

   Times of transition are opportunities for reflection about self, and especially clarification of values (Brown, 1995). What was important prior to the transition might be less important at the time of transition, especially if these times are associated with shifts in developmental priorities. For example, Super (1957) identified five stages, and the transition between the first two stages, growth and exploration, occurs during the time Erikson (1963) identified as having a key task of identity development. The individual has to transition from who they've been told they are to discovering who they really are, and exploring how they can best function in the world. After a period of exploring, the person must then transition to making a commitment at the same time they are transitioning from dependency to independency and personal agency. It is the transition from being an adolescent to becoming an adult. This particular transition can be very difficult for those who "have an untested perception of self and only limited experience in the adult world" (Salomone & Mangicaro, 1991, p. 328). Others (Fouad & Bynner, 2008) identified four key types of career-related transitions, including to work from school,

DOI: 10.4324/9781003035756-13

from work experience to another work experience, to non-work (e.g., retirement, retraining, caretaking) from working, and from non-work to work (e.g., re-entry, or following maternity leave). Regardless of stage, transition implies movement. DeVos et al. (2021) describe the term "movement capital," which includes any factor that impacts a person's opportunity to be mobile. Transitions are beneficial for employees' employability.

When someone first starts out in their career, their main priority is establishing themselves as being knowledgeable and skilled in their chosen profession. After a period of time, the priority shifts away from gaining acknowledgment, to maintaining that position of expertness, and eventually, to letting go of that position as one moves towards retirement. At one point, moving up the ladder or gaining promotions and higher salary might be prioritized, but at another, working collaboratively with colleagues or having more flexibility in one's work schedule, perhaps to allow time for caregiver responsibilities, might be of greater importance. Erikson's stage of generativity versus stagnation led Bejian and Salomone (1995) to suggest a sixth stage of Super's model, namely, career renewal, which includes looking backwards about prior decisions, reflecting on accomplishments, realizing one's own mortality, and then consideration of what they would prefer to do next.

More recently, researchers have been examining *career shocks*, "a disruptive and extraordinary event that is, at least to some degree, caused by factors outside the focal individual's control and that triggers a deliberate thought process concerning one's career" (Akkermans et al., 2018, p. 4). Career shocks can also occur as a result of actively researching options, such as when a person stumbles across a previously unknown option or opportunity (Akkermans et al., 2021). Specific career shocks such as not receiving an expected promotion or feeling minimized at work, can move individuals to consider entrepreneurship. Career shocks may also come when an employee's health is significantly affected which causes them to reconsider their current work commitments. Another consideration is how a person's social identity and intergroup relations might be affected when a career shock occurs. In addition, "extra-organizational" shocks such as natural disasters that disrupt all aspects of a person's life can positively or negatively impact personal agency and lead to either desirable or undesirable career transitions (Wordsworth & Nilakant, 2021). Career shocks may or may not result in a career transition, but their presence is something practitioners should inquire about as leading to or resulting from a career transition.

Role of Career Adaptability

Career adaptability was originally defined as "readiness to cope with changing work and working conditions" (Super & Knasel, 1981, p. 195), with a greater emphasis on proactive behavior. Career adaptability has been strongly associated (.64, $p < .01$) with career transition readiness (Ghosh et al., 2019). Goodman (1994) suggested a "dental model" for helping individuals manage transitions and increase the likelihood of maintaining an adaptive perspective. As good dental hygiene includes regular checkups, and not only seeing a dentist in a time of crisis, she suggested that individuals have regular checkups on their career satisfaction. During these times, the person can examine whether the career is fulfilling, discuss possible or probable upcoming transitions, and begin planning for them.

Transitioning Styles

Bimrose and Mulvey (2015) identified four transitioning styles for mid-career adults, who were going through varied transitions, such as from education to first time employment, unemployed seeking to re-enter the workforce, and employed but seeking a change. The four styles included strategic, evaluative, aspirational, and opportunistic. The *strategic* style utilizes a cognitive approach, focusing on rational decision-making, and a strong belief that they can achieve their next goal. The *evaluative* style includes more emotions and reflection and a time of self-examination focused on needs and values. The *aspirational* style is characterized by having a more distant career or personal goal that may be somewhat vaguely described, with a mismatch between current level of skills or knowledge and the ideal goal, and work being seen as a means to that end. The *opportunistic* style focus on opportunities that present themselves in the moment, going with the flow of what is available and feels right in the moment, rather than considering how that immediate decision might impact longer-term career goals. The researchers suggest that individuals might use a combination of styles in making any given decision, or may alternate styles depending on the decision and its context. Regardless, a career practitioner can get a better understanding of how a person tends to approach transitions as well as how their conceptualization of and desire for how to proceed with the current transition may be similar/different. In addition, asking questions as to what are the positives and negatives associated with their preferred approach may be a useful conversation for augmenting with other strategies.

Conceptualizing Career Transitions via Chaos Theory

Chaos theory of careers (Bright & Pryor, 2012) is a constructivist theory of career development that is particularly useful for helping individuals in transition. Key components include that change is an inevitable part of life, certainty about what will happen is impossible, and that a focus on transferable skills is more important than planning towards a specific career. Uncertainty, creativity, risk-taking, and paradox are valued in this theory, as is paying attention to the individual situation as they are operating in a changing world (Amundson et al., 2013). In addition, helping clients to become aware of, open to and ready to act on opportunities as they arise are recommendations for practitioners (Pryor & Bright, 2011).

In 2014, the theorists (Pryor and Bright) provided a reflection on chaos theory as centered on five Cs: context, complexity, connection, change, and chance. They identified nine strategies to focus on with clients, including:

1 Work out what really matters now and how work fits into that;
2 Keep the mind open to opportunities;
3 Generate and try several possibilities;
4 Expect that some of them will fail;
5 Make failure survivable;
6 Seek and examine feedback to learn what works and what does not;
7 Utilize what works and examine what has emerged;
8 Combine and add as seems likely to improve career prospects;
9 Iterate the process starting back at 1.

(p. 8)

Other attitudes include a willingness to work "with incomplete knowledge and recognizing it will always be so," being optimistic, welcoming uncertainty, and following their curiosity (Pryor et al., 2008, p. 312).

Creative Approaches and Chaos Theory

Pryor and Bright (2014) identify several techniques, including mind-maps, a reality-checking checklist, archetypal narratives, card sorts, lattices, career education models such as the Butterfly Model, parables, films, collage, forensic interviews, visual arts, and

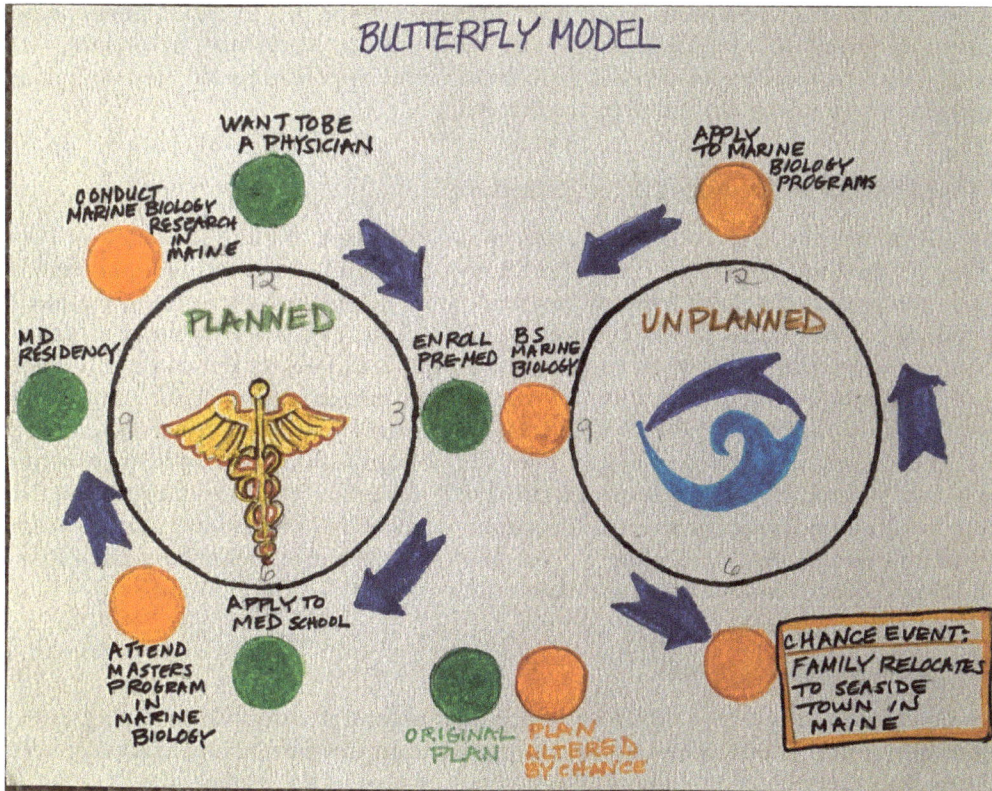

Figure 13.1 Butterfly Model

a signature exercise. For example, the Butterfly Model (Borg, Bright, & Pryor, 2006) provides a visual format for exploring how unplanned events may influence planned career trajectories, specifically exploring the development of skills specific to planning for the unplanned event, and skills in coping when an unplanned event occurs. Borg et al. utilized the Butterfly Model with secondary school students and asked them to project their long-term goals and 3-year, 6-year, and 9-year steps around the "planned" career objective circle. Next an "unplanned" event card is introduced and students are asked to imagine how that unplanned event may change their career development tasks and outcomes at the 3-, 6-, and 9-year increments. In the example provided in Figure 13.1, the student identified their long-term career aim was to become a physician. When the "unplanned" event was introduced, in this case a family move to coastal town in Maine, the student imagined her science interest shifting to marine biology and eventual engagement in research to preserve ocean wildlife. Exploring the interaction between planned and unplanned events can help students acclimate to expectations of change and future transitions.

Additionally, Pryor and Bright (2011) suggested clients review videos of sculptor Jean Tinguely's kinetic sculptures as a precursor to career exploration. Tinguely's artworks feature found objects, mechanical pulley systems, movement, and human or other environmental factors that interact in unexpected ways. (Several videos of Tinguely's work are available for viewing on youtube.com, museum sites, or other online forums.) After reviewing Tinguely's work, Pryor and Bright recommended clients consider the difference between traditional static sculptures and the kinetic sculptures and asked them to reflect on how these two sculptural forms represented their current strategies for career life design. Following these discussions, clients were encouraged to create kinetic sculptures with found objects. Their aim was to build clients' experiences of working with chance elements while simultaneously fostering their appreciation of the energy and beauty that welcoming chance elements may bring.

Using Objects to Enhance Client Reflection

Art therapists have also used found objects in art therapy to cultivate reflection. For example. Brooker (2010) and Camic (2010) encouraged clients to bring found objects into therapy and observed found-object work actively engaged clients on attentional, emotional, and cognitive levels. Inspired by these clinical findings, Camic et al. (2011) designed a qualitative study to further investigate found-object work in art therapy. Several themes emerged. Therapists felt the work promoted clients' active engagement therapy and encouraged reflective associations. Clients noted experiencing curiosity and enthusiasm when utilizing found objects in therapy. Additionally, clients perceived objects as stimuli for associations which aided self-understanding. Clients also noted that searches for found objects within their environments spurred them to look outside themselves for meaning and connections. These findings match nicely with the aims of Pryor and Bright's (2011) kinetic sculpture career interventions.

Case Study with Object Sculptures

To demonstrate how found object sculptures may assist a person with exploring career transition concerns, the below example is provided. In this case, the person completed the work as therapeutic homework. Using objects found in their home, the "Transition Mobile" (Figure 13.2) was created and brought to session. They described enjoying the search for items to create their sculpture and asserted that the discovered items influenced the final form of their work. Only when they completed the work did they begin to explore the meanings they attributed to their sculpture. For example, the bubble wrap seat and name tag-holder windshield were said to reflect a desire for protection from bumpy roads and potential hazards ahead. The steering wheel symbolized their feeling somewhat in control of next directions, and the heart and headlight stickers represented hope for future job hunt outcomes. On the other hand, they mused that the Transition Mobile resembled a chariot that may need to be pulled by a team of horses. In reflecting on this description, they admitted to relying on external sources of motivation to keep them on track with important job search tasks from time to time. As a result of these reflections, the practitioner and the client were able to address concerns and fine-tune career counseling next steps.

Sensitively used, found-object work may provide rich opportunities for activating client curiosity and imagination, revealing clients' concerns, and fostering creative problem-solving approaches that generate positive options for planned or unplanned career transition events and can deepen understandings of client considerations. To maximize the potential of found-object work, practitioners and clients benefit from examining the powerful meanings that may surface during the search, discovery, selection, and creative transformation of found objects (Brooker, 2010). Selected objects may have aesthetic or utilitarian appeal for a client or may reveal emotionally laden attachments and meanings. Additionally, examining the client's process of discovery, selection, and use of an object opens further opportunities to understand clients' associations with object engagement. For example, the experience of a client who "rescues" a discarded object from a public space may have a different experience or association with an object and

Figure 13.2 The Transition-Mobile: Kinetic Sculpture with Found and Created Objects

process than a client who chooses to utilize and transform a cherished object from their personal environment for art reflection or creation. Sensitive use of found objects within a career context requires practitioner attunement to the client object selection processes and associations as exploring the use of found objects can bridge client barriers to self-understanding.

Supporting Individuals in Their Career Transitions

4S Transition Model

Schlossberg (1984) identified four areas for practitioners to address when supporting clients making career transitions. Called the "4S Transition Model," the components for consideration include *Situation, Self, Supports,* and *Strategies.* Schlossberg recommends the individual to "take stock" of the resources and deficits a person has within each of these areas, and in the process of doing so, take some control of the transition. As with most therapy, the practitioner starts by exploring the *Situation* the individual is experiencing in terms of their current transition. Questions for each of the Ss are included in Table 13.1.

In exploring each of these areas, the practitioner can move into goal setting with the client. There may be specific action steps that need to be addressed in each area. The practitioner can work with the client to prioritize which to address first, or simultaneously. An art-based intervention can deepen the client's and practitioner's understanding of the situation, self, supports, and strategies.

Table 13.1 Schlossberg's 4S Model with sample questions

Situation	Self
• What is the context for this transition? • Where is the person in terms of the transition? Are they anticipating it in the middle of it, or moving out of the transition, also known as "Moving Into, Moving Through or Moving On" (Schlossberg et al., 1995; Anderson et al., 2012)? • Is the transition one that the individual is choosing or one that is being forced upon them? • What was the trigger for this transition? • How much control does the person have over organizing the terms of the transition? • How much time do they have before the transition occurs? • What does the current situation look like for the individual (and people in their lives who have been, may be, or are currently being affected by the transition)? • What are the ripple effects of this transition on other roles, events, plans? What roles are being left behind, taken on, or remaining the same? • What other stressors are going on simultaneously? • What experiences has the individual had with previous transitions that may be similar? • What needs are pressing in as they experience or consider this transition? • What barriers to a successful transition are they experiencing or anticipating having to face? • What emotions are being experienced? • How would they rate the difficulty of this transition and your current situation, on a scale of 1 to 10?	• How is the client feeling in the situation? • What are some personal characteristics that make this transition easier or harder to handle? • How do personal demographics (age, ethnicity, gender, health, etc.) impact how the client is experiencing the transition? • What values are coming into play as they reflect on this transitional experience? • How does the client feel about the likely outcome of this transition and their ability to manage this transition well? • How optimistic, resilient, and hopeful is the client? • How motivated is the client to work on understanding and navigating this transition? • How do they feel about their ability to handle the emotional and practical aspects of this transition experience?

Supports	Strategies
• Who and what supports does the client see as being most important to them during this time? • How are they supportive? • Which supports are most stable, and which are least stable? • What support needs are they experiencing, such as encouragement, information, practical help (Goodman & Hoppin, 1990)?	• What direct actions do they need to make to best manage this transition? • Do they know where to find the information they need? • Can they determine which step to take first? • How can they address barriers to their transition? • How can they mobilize their supports? • What other supports do they need and how might they acquire them? • How can they keep motivated and address negative self-talk?

The case of Mrs. L. demonstrates how offering collage art processes may be used to stimulate discussions on the 4S transition considerations. Mrs. L. sought career assistance due to an imminent and involuntary change that was happening with her current job. She had been notified that her bank was being taken over by another banking corporation six months ago, but she hadn't been sure if they would be keeping current employees to work at the branches. She hadn't considered looking for work until now, because she'd hoped that she would just be able to stay on with the new corporation in a

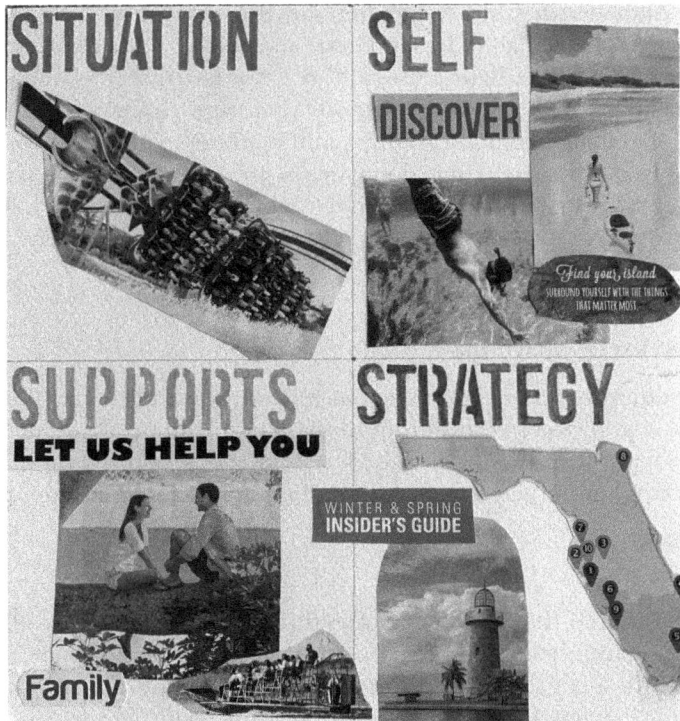

Figure 13.3 Sample Collage of 4S Model

similar capacity. Yet, in the previous week she received a two-month advance termination notice as the new corporation decided to bring their own loan officers to the region. Mrs. L noted she was the primary earner for her family, her husband and two children aged three and five. Mr. L. experienced a disabling construction work accident two years ago, uses a wheelchair, and currently serves as the primary caregiver for their children. She also reported that she lived several hours away from extended family many of whom lived on the west coast of Florida. Mrs. L. stated that the job transition brought up more than just job questions for her but potential relocation questions and more.

After reviewing the 4S transition concepts of Situation, Self, Supports and Strategy with Mrs. L., the practitioner invited her to create a collage that would reflect the most salient considerations of each concept, utilizing one to five images or words she found in the magazines. The practitioner explained that the collage work may help identify concerns, resources, and aspects of the transition that could use more consideration and support. In response, Mrs. L. used markers, stencils, and magazine images to compile the 4S image (see Figure 13.3). Mrs. L. described the *Situation* as topsy turvy and a bit out of control as represented by a water roller coaster ride where people were hanging upside down. In regard to *Self,* Mrs. L. stated she had to "do a deep dive" and consider things differently. She reported being confident in her qualifications and preparation for future work, but had a lot on her mind about relocation options, such as where might the best opportunities be for her career and financial goals, and where might she have the most support for addressing family educational and medical needs? She reflected that she had taken on a lot since her husband's accident and now was considering being closer to family to extend her system of support. In terms of *Support,* Mrs. L. described hesitance in seeking her husband's emotional support due to his situation, but affirmed that he was available and supportive when she sought him out. She also felt she had a lot of extended family support and she just had to lean on everyone a little bit more. Her *Strategy* images included a map of Florida, a lighthouse, and the words "Insider's Guide." Mrs. L. said she would systematically review work locations that were closer to her family and rely on contacts she had made from her training and banking experiences to identify stable banking systems in those areas. After "doing her homework" she expected to consult with her husband on how to narrow the search and establish timelines. Mrs. L. stated that she found the structured art process helpful in reducing her feelings of being overwhelmed with the many transition tasks.

Transitions for Various Groups

In addition to examining career transitions in general, researchers have focused on transitions for specific groups, often resulting in the identification of unique recommendations for that group, which may be of use for practitioners focusing on that population. Some of the groups and targeted recommendations are included in this section.

Athlete Retirement

Erpič et al. (2004) found that the quality of ending a sports career was dependent upon whether the termination was voluntary, the athlete's perception of their athletic accomplishments, how prevalent their athletic identity was, their educational status (i.e., ranging from finishing elementary school to finishing a university degree), and co-occurring negative non-athletic transitions that were happening at the same time. Negative non-athletic transitions were defined as career, family life, education, economic status, interpersonal relations, or other important life events that were perceived as having a negative impact. Discussing how much control an athlete has over their decision to retire, and giving them as much control as possible in planning their next steps is recommended, as is focusing on both the athletic and non-athletic aspects of their lives.

Career and Technical Education Graduates

These individuals focus on learning skills for a specific trade while in high school, as they work for specific companies to apply the knowledge and build competency. However, after graduation, the co-op position ends, as does the formal support offered by the high school. In one study looking at post-graduation outcomes, Packard et al. (2012) found that those who lost their job changed their career plans, those with limited access to college had fewer options while those with access had more options, and those who had a relevant job in high school that continued after graduation continued in that career path. Also, for many, CTE served as a backup plan or allowed them to pursue higher education while working. In addition to discussing the role of CTE, practitioners are encouraged to help CTE students connect with alumni, identify places of work that will increase their chances of ongoing employment after graduation, and provide support for determining their next steps, whether in job searching or additional training.

College to Work

Career practitioners are encouraged to explore compromises the student is willing to make, especially between interests and aptitudes (Ryu & Jeong, 2020). Wendlandt and Rochlen (2008) identified three areas where college graduates report feeling challenged with respect to this transition. First, is the cultural change between college life and professional work life. For example, college offers structure, specific expectations or rubrics for assignments, and regular feedback about performance, whereas a working environment may have less structure, less specific directions or expectations, and performance evaluations once or twice a year. Other shifts are from individual performance and personal accomplishment to teamwork and prioritizing company success over individual success. Second is the lack of skills and experience employers desire or expect, and third are expectations about what work life will be like that are not accurate. They suggest using a transition model focused on socialization, comprised of anticipation (planning prior to the transition), adjustment (the process of fitting in once the transition occurs), and achievement (actions that increase the likelihood of staying in that position).

First Generation College Students

These students may need support for learning how to be academically successful in college, especially focusing on existing and developing supports, addressing perceptions of barriers in learning about self and options (such as skills), and building self-efficacy in career decision-making (Toyokawa & DeWald, 2019).

High School Students

Helping high school students identify satisfying work environments prior to graduation, as well as opportunities to be involved in meaningful activities, and exploring self-talk were recommended by Borgen et al. (1996) from their study of 172 transitioning high school students. Savickas (1999) suggested that to help with this particular transition, high school students need to "look ahead and look around" (p. 327) by developing skills in self-knowledge, occupational knowledge, decision-making, planning and problem-solving. Others (Yang & Gysbers, 2007) have found that seniors with lower psychological resources such as readiness, confidence, and support in the transition also had lower career search self-efficacy and increased distress. A second group was identified as those feeling ready to make a career decision but lacking confidence to cope with the transition and being resistant to that transition.

Immigrants

Immigrants might be facing multiple transitions, including the adjustment to a new country, and in some cases, finding that the credentials they had in their home country are not valued in their new country. Cultural rules and beliefs, such as appropriateness of sharing personal matters, need to be examined and respected. Discussions about experiences with racism, discrimination, and stereotypes, as well as providing resources that specifically describe technical expectations such as clothing, social etiquette, and interviewing approaches may be useful (Kennedy & Chen, 2012). A qualitative study (Koert et al., 2011) specific to female immigrants identified the following as positively and negatively impacting a successful transition and, therefore, useful to discuss with this population: internal beliefs/resilience; taking action such as setting goals, taking a course, networking; lack of skills or education; personal challenges such as homesickness, depression, age, pregnancy, and dealing with expectations; self-care; relationships and supports; government/community resources; and work environment. Finally, they identified contextual challenges such as balancing work and family.

Individuals Going through a Midcareer Crisis

Perosa and Perosa (1983) examined 134 individuals who had either changed careers, were in the process of changing, or who desired to change but were choosing to remain in their current vocation. The majority of those in the first two groups reported a "serious psychological risk" (p. 77) if they stayed in their current career, as opposed to those who decided to stay, who minimized that risk if they stayed. Questions they suggest asking to midcareer individuals experiencing a career crisis include: "Are the risks serious if I do or don't change my career?"; "Is it realistic to hope to find a better solution?"; and "Is there sufficient time to search?" (p. 78). Other points of exploration include feelings of self-doubt, search for and importance of finding meaning in their work, and the degree to which they feel immobilized. Others (Barclay et al., 2011) suggest exploring the positives and negatives associated with changing careers, identifying life themes, motivational interviewing, and redefining self.

Individuals Transitioning from Incarceration

Bennett and Amundson (2016) suggest emphasizing aspects of chaos theory (e.g., flexibility, change, curiosity, chance, and hope) with this specific group. Advocating for these clients with employers, building career preparedness, résumé building, and linking with community resources are recommended. In addition, Amundson (2009) offers practical strategies practitioners can use. For example, one way to increase flexibility in thinking would be to encourage clients to create roadmaps to their career goal, including potential roadblocks and alternate routes. Designing a circle of strength is a way to build hope. The intervention begins with a person sharing a story in which they overcame a challenge, and then reflecting on their strengths that were demonstrated in that story. Juvenile offenders who are transitioning might have additional information needs, mental health concerns, discussion of how their record might impact options, and how to find and maintain training and employment (Osborn & Belle, 2019).

Involuntary Job Loss

Eby and Buch (1995) found that family flexibility was the most predictable variable for career growth in women who had been fired, as well as avoiding long-term financial outcomes, and not being satisfied prior to being fired. For men, avoiding long-term financial outcomes was the most important predictor for career growth, with other important predictors being emotional acceptance, not being unemployed for too long, and receiving support from friends and coworkers.

Job Loss due to Downsizing

Amundson et al. (2004) found that individuals wanted to be informed about the process of downsizing, and to be involved in how the business was restructured. Transparency from leadership was seen as an issue of trust, and lack of transparency constituted betrayal. Coworker relationships during and after the process of downsizing and the uncertainty of job security were seen as important. Attending to emotional grief of losing coworkers, whether they had adequate time to say goodbye, and encouraging attempts to stay connected after downsizing are recommended.

Midlife Male Scientists and Engineers

One set of researchers (Liu et al., 2012) looked at this specific group through a qualitative lens and found career transitions had positive and/or negative outcomes psychologically, such as growth and autonomy or emotional distress and decreased self-esteem. Similarly, their reflections on transitioning included positive (e.g., changing career fields to what was previously an avocation, moving into consultation, or becoming an entrepreneur) and negative experiences, such as failed entrepreneurship attempts, decline in mental health, substance abuse, and loss of relationships. Coping strategies included focusing on positivity and optimism and staying adaptable, flexible, and resilient. In addition to exploring the issues these men identified, it appears teaching cognitive strategies such as reframing and working from a positive psychology perspective would be recommended for career practitioners.

Military Spouses

Due to frequent moves, this group can experience difficulties gaining sufficient education, developing skills, and building seniority in a position (McBride and Cleymans, 2014). They are often required to take any job they can find with each move, and oftentimes, these jobs don't coincide with their interests, and thus can be very dissatisfying. McBride and Cleymans (2014) suggest helping spouses create a career lattice instead of a career ladder to include both lateral and vertical career moves, emphasizing how their diverse experiences can lend to a well-rounded career path. They also suggest focusing on résumé building, marketing skills, interview preparation, utilizing non-traditional education and training opportunities, volunteering, and encouraging them to document their accomplishments along the way.

Transitioning to Retirement

Consider health, financial issues, desire for post-retirement work, and work values as related to next steps (Wöhrmann et al., 2014). Discussions might also focus on options: no retirement, bridge employment, full retirement, encore career (Boveda & Metz, 2016), or cycling between work and leisure. Carter and Cook (1995) suggest that the transition involves "role expansion, redefinition, and change" (p. 68). In addition to discussing roles, they suggest that locus of control and "retirement self-efficacy" (p. 68) are two important areas for discussion for this group.

Veterans Transitioning to Civilian Work

Engage in discussion of how to translate military skills to non-military work (Hayden et al., 2014), as well as their experiences in the military and linking to military specific resources (Clemens & Milsom, 2008). Practitioners should also examine negative career thoughts and, when elevated, examine for depressive symptoms, which were found to be correlated for student veterans (Buzzetta et al., 2020). Women warriors who experienced military sexual trauma had the most difficulty re-integrating into society, and experience career-related issues such as feeling pressured or unmotivated to work, feeling unable to work but wanting to, lack of clarity for next career steps, and difficulty finding work (Stein-McCormick et al., 2013). These authors also suggest that National Guard members often have difficulty maintaining work, especially when the military interferes with their civilian work schedule and can be unpredictable.

Youth with Significant Disabilities Transitioning out of High School

In most cases, this special group will have parents or guardians involved in the discussion of what happens after high school. Ideally, this discussion will occur far enough ahead of this time to allow for transition planning. Lo and Bui (2020) suggest several strategies, such as ongoing conversations with the teen about their life after high school, assessing functional skills, teaching life skills such as self-care, self-management, banking, as well as career management skills such as how to fill out an application or interview skills. As with other teens, gaining experience in the world of work is vital to building skills, confidence, and networks. Helping caregivers learn about community supports for adults with disabilities is also a recommended strategy. McCormick et al. (2021) found that youth with disabilities who had more regular case management meetings and who were employed earlier on were more likely to be employed post-high school. They also emphasized the need for a comprehensive approach that integrates independent living, education, and employment.

Perceptions of Situation and Self: The Lattice as an Art-Based Exploratory Structure

As noted above, McBride and Cleymans (2014) explored career transitions of military spouses and advocated for reducing perceived barriers to career success related to histories of work role changes necessitated by family moves. The lattice framework was emphasized as a multidirectional but strong structure for career development which incorporates skills and experiences gained at work and volunteer positions as opposed to the unidirectional pathway represented by the ladder. Comparing one's career trajectory to the ladder can lead to negative or restrictive conceptualization of positive career movement directionality. Using the lattice metaphor and visual structure in art therapy processes can stimulate exploration and identification of experiences that may have been minimized and overlooked. Additionally, this process can support reconceptualization of strengths and skills that can be applied to career search tasks including résumé writing and interviewing.

When introducing the lattice art process to clients, visual examples of lattices that exist in natural phenomena such as cells, crystals, and bone, or those that exist in engineered and designed environments, can be shown to demonstrate how overlapping networks create solid forms and building blocks for larger structures. Figure 13.4 shows a sample

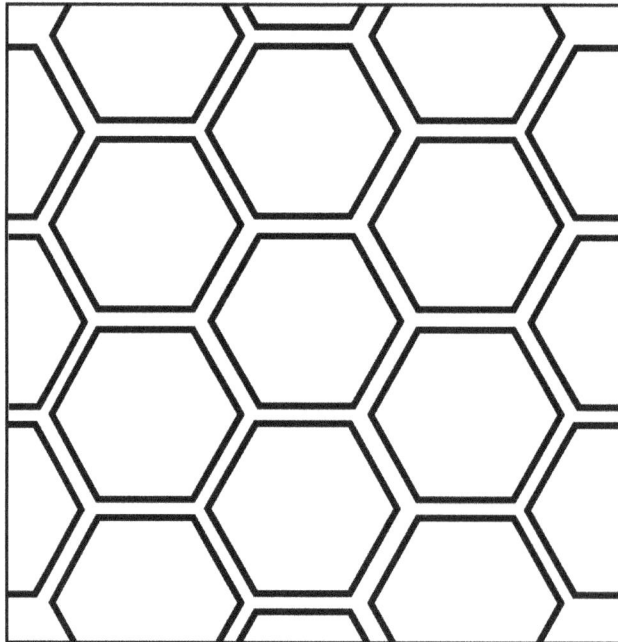

Figure 13.4 Sample Lattice Template

Figure 13.5 Lattice of Life and Work, Marker and Collage

lattice template. The CP can then provide the client with a lattice template as a base for artwork or may invite them to design their own lattice structure as they explore and depict their experiences. Next, the CP invites the client to fill their lattice with strengths, skills, qualities, work experience(s) value, volunteer experience(s) value, other life role experience(s) value, that reflect all the assets they may bring to future work setting. In the below example, Figure 13.5, the individual represented their educational experiences, volunteer experiences, parenting, caregiving experiences, engagement in hobbies and interests, and flexibility learned from several moves throughout the country as well as international travel to represent the richness she would bring to a new work setting.

Interventions for Managing Career Transitions

In addition to considering the unique contexts of individuals and exploring the issues identified in the previous section specific to certain groups, general strategies have been identified for supporting clients going through a career transition.

Attend to Emotions, Beliefs, and Overall Mental Health

Practitioners can support individuals moving through a career transition in a variety of ways. First, attending to the emotional aspects of the client during the transition is important, as is realizing that the individual might be experiencing multiple emotions in ranging intensities. While preparing for and managing the transition are highly cognitive, as practitioners, we need to attend to feelings of worry, fear, and anger as well as positive feelings of curiosity, hope, and excitement. Negative thoughts about the transition and potential outcomes should be identified, challenged, and reframed when appropriate. Someone who believes things will never work out for them, or that the outcome will be nothing short of awful, will likely have a hard time engaging in proactive steps to make the transition successful. In addition, practitioners should regularly scan for when the emotions have escalated to the point where the person is experiencing extreme difficulty in making career and life decisions, and in those cases, share the observation, focus on mental health (if the practitioner has the credentials to do so), or refer to a mental health practitioner. One specific inventory, the Career Transitions Inventory (Heppner et al., 1998) has been designed to identify supports and barriers for career transitions, focusing on readiness, confidence, control, perceived support, and decision independence.

Explore Values, Interests, Skills

Practitioners can lead clients to examine what is important to them as part of the transition discussion. Brown (1995) suggested several creative approaches to help individuals identify their values, such as exploring daydreams peak experiences as well as the worst experiences the person has had in their lives, using imagery to create their future, or describing people the person admires most or least. In addition to clarifying values, it may be a time to identify what skills might be needed for successful transitioning, and identifying a plan to gain that knowledge or competency. It may also be a time for a client to explore working in a different area of their interests. Thus, career assessments or art-based interventions that focus on a client's current interests, values, and skills might be valuable.

Provide Targeted Information

Linking individuals with information about the "landing spot" of the transition, as well as the process of transitioning, can help relieve anxiety and lead to decreased "fears of the unknown," and better preparedness. In the case of a new position, helping the client find out more about the employer, as well as the culture of the organization or geographical region might help them feel more at ease. Wendlandt and Rochlen (2008) suggest three steps to support clients as they transition into an organization. First, practitioners can help the new employee form realistic, accurate perceptions about their employer. Talking with alumni who are employed by that employer, looking at reviews of the company by current and past employees, or coaching clients to ask specific questions about the culture and how individuals acclimate to the new environment, or asking if they might talk with a newer employee about their transition, are all recommended. Second, practitioners can increase the likelihood of successful adjustment by encouraging engagement in part-time work, job shadowing, volunteering, or interning to help the individual acquire basic knowledge and skills relevant to the job. Third, practitioners can increase achievement in the new position by helping the client learn how the workplace differs from other environments such as school, along with issues of professionalism, understanding the workplace culture, and how to navigate office politics.

In the case of someone who is transitioning to the world of work for the first time, or after a long period of being out of the labor force, focusing on job search resources such as résumé and cover letter writing, interviewing, networking, and locating employers might help. If they are moving to a different geographical area, learning how to calculate cost of living adjustments can be useful. During these discussions, practitioners might not only focus on the current aim of locating a position, but how to maintain employment, establish themselves, and plan for the next step (Super, 1957).

Address Practical Concerns

Ebberwein et al. (2004) found that financial resources (or the lack thereof) at the time of transition had the strongest impact on how individuals in their qualitative study coped with their transition. The perception of having some type of financial buffer helped offset feelings of anger and anxiety, as well as impacting other decisions, such as whether to pursue further training or take a stop-gap job (i.e., a temporary job to meet financial needs while waiting on/searching for the desired position). In addition to finances, exploring the interaction between work and family life was also recommended, as shifts in roles were likely to happen during the transition period. Because of shifting roles, various feelings, and the impact that a transition often has on others in the person's immediate family, counselors should explore the ripple effect and, when possible, offer to include or refuse those being affected in the conversation, as they are part of the client's context. A final practical concern is employability at the time of transition, in that if the person has not been keeping their skills and knowledge up-to-date, they may not be as competitive for career options.

Co-create a Plan Optimizing Their Control

Krumboltz et al. (2013) stated that the perceived loss of control that occurs especially with an unplanned transition is one of the most difficult challenges a person faces, in that it undermines their belief in personal agency as related to their career decisions. Happenstance learning theory would suggest that practitioners can help clients re-gain control by working with the client to create opportunities where unplanned, positive, work-related events might occur. These opportunities might be volunteering, joining a job club, or informational interviews with potential employers. Building off of Schlossberg's model, a 3M model suggests practitioners might discuss with clients how they can modify their current situation, reframe the meanings they are applying to themselves due to the transition, and monitor and manage their stress. Exploring previous transitions and discussing thoughts about what went well and what they wish they might have done differently as they reflect back can provide a foundation for approaching the current transition. Teaching a career decision-making process, incorporating decision-making and coping skills, as well as offering guidance are recommended as part of this plan (Lipshits-Braziler & Gati, 2019). Model of decision-making are presented in Chapter 9.

Preparing for Future Transitions

Part of supporting a client as they move into and through a career transition is helping them prepare for inevitable future transitions. Tasks they are engaging in for the current transition are made lighter when they need to be polished, not created. For example, keeping a résumé or online presence current and purposely planning for ongoing trainings to ensure one is up-to-date will better position the client for a transition, whether it is self-initiated or imposed on them. Those are examples of how to prepare the self; other strategies might focus on the other Ss. For example, with supports, the client can be encouraged to continuously develop new and purposely invest in personal and professional relationships as well as networking. These post-transition efforts increase a person's readiness for the next transition.

Summary

Transitions are a part of everyone's lives, and yet, depending on the type and timing of transition, as well as other considerations such as amount of control one has over the transition, the experience of career-related transitions may be quite unique to the individual. This chapter presented general questions and approaches to supporting clients as they prepare for, move through, and move past career transitions, as well as raising concerns and providing strategies and interventions for specific types of transitions.

Discussion Questions and Activities

1 Examine at least three important transitions you've undergone through the lens of the 4S model. What themes do you see? What was different about each? What do you think you've learned about yourself as you prepare for your next transition?

2 What are some unplanned transitions that you've been through? Looking back, what was helpful/unhelpful to you during those times? If you could go back and give yourself some advice, what would you say?

3 What is the next transition you anticipate having to go through? How might the 4S model apply to this transition? What steps might you need to take now to prepare? What is your current movement capital?

4 Create a timeline along with markings for your associated career and family milestones. Think about the time just prior and just after those marks. What helped you adapt to these changes? Is there anything you wish you had known, or done differently? How might this inform your next transition?

5 List out your unique identities and roles. How might these individually, and interactively, add stress or support to you during a time of transition?

6 Choose a group that may have special issues related to transition, and create an infographic with information, strategies, and resources that might be helpful to them.

7 How have you successfully welcomed unexpected results in your own artmaking process? How can these experiences of adaptation be applied to a transition in your career life or inform art interventions that you may use to support others undergoing career transitions?

References

Akkermans, J., Collings, D. G., da Motta Veiga, S., et al. (2021). Toward a broader understanding of career shocks: Exploring interdisciplinary connections with research on job search, human resource management, entrepreneurship, and diversity. *Journal of Vocational Behavior, 126*, Article 103563. https://doi.org/10.1016/j.jvb.2021.103563

Akkermans, J., Seibert, S. E., & Mol, S. T. (2018). Tales of the unexpected: Integrating career shocks in the contemporary careers literature. *SA Journal of Industrial Psychology, 44*, Article e1503, 1–10. https://doi.org/10.4102/sajip.v44i0.1503.

Amundson, N. E. (2009). *Active engagement: The being and doing of career counseling* (3rd ed.). Ergon Communications.

Amundson, N. E., Borgen, W. A., Jordan, S., & Erlebach, A. C. (2004). Survivors of downsizing: Helpful and hindering experiences. *Career Development Quarterly, 53*, 256–271.

Amundson, N. E., Mils, M. E., & Smith, B. A. (2013). Incorporating chaos and paradox into career development. *Australian Journal of Career Development, 23*(1), 13–21. https://doi.org/10.1177/1038416213496760

Anderson, M. L., Goodman, J., & Schlossberg, N. K. (2012). *Counseling adults in transition: Linking Schlossberg's theory with practice in a diverse world* (4th ed.). Springer.

Barclay, S. R., Stoltz, K. B., & Chung, Y. B. (2011). Voluntary midlife career change: Integrating the transtheoretical model and the life-span, life-space approach. *Career Development Quarterly, 59*(5), 386–399. https://doi.org/10.1002/j.2161-0045.2011.tb00966.x

Bejian, D. V., & Salomone, P. R. (1995). Understanding mid-life career renewal: Implications for counseling. *The Career Development Quarterly, 44*, 52–63.

Bennett, A., & Amundson, N. (2016). The need for dynamic models of career development for transitioning offenders. *Journal of Employment Counseling, 53*(2), 60–70. https://doi.org/10.1002/joec.12028

Bimrose, J., & Mulvey, R. (2015). Exploring career decision-making styles across three European countries. *British Journal of Guidance & Counselling, 43*(3), 337–350. https://doi.org/10.1080/03069885.2015.1017803

Borg, T., Bright, J., Pryor, R. (2006). The Butterfly Model of Careers: Illustrating how planning and change can be integrated in the careers of secondary school students. *Australian Journal of Career Development, 15*(3), 54–59.

Borgen, W. A., Amundson, N. E., & Tench, E. (1996). Psychological well-being throughout the transition from adolescence to adulthood. *The Career Development Quarterly, 45*(2), 189–199.

Boveda, I., & Metz, A. J. (2016). Predicting end-of-career transitions for baby boomers nearing retirement age. *The Career Development Quarterly, 64*(2), 153–168.

Bright, J., & Pryor, R. (2012). The chaos theory of careers in career education. *Journal of the National Institute for Career Education and Counseling, 28*, 10–20.

Brooker, J. (2010). Found objects in art therapy. *International Journal of Art Therapy, 15*(1), 25–35. https://doi.org/10.1080/17454831003752386

Brown, D. (1995). A values-based approach to facilitating career transitions. *Career Development Quarterly, 44*, 4–11.

Buzzetta, M. E., Lenz, J. G., Hayden, S. C. W., & Osborn, D. S. (2020). Student veterans: Meaning of life, negative career thoughts, and depression. *Career Development Quarterly, 68*(4), 361–373. https://doi.org/10.1002/cdq.12242

Camic, P. M., Brooker, J., Neal, A. (2011). Found objects in clinical practice. *The Arts in Psychotherapy, 38*, 151–159. https://doi.org/10.1016/j.aip.2011.04.002

Camic, P. M., Kaufman, J. C., Smith, J. K. & Smith, L. F. (2010). From trashed to treasured: A grounded theory analysis of the found object. *Psychology of Aesthetics, Creativity, and the Arts, 4*(2), 81–92. https://doi.org/10.1037/a0018429

Carter, M. A. T., & Cook, K. (1995). Adaptation to retirement: Role changes and psychological resources. *Career Development Quarterly, 44*, 67–82.

Clemens, E. V., & Milsom, A. S. (2008). Enlisted service members' transition into the civilian world of work: A cognitive information processing approach. *Career Development Quarterly, 56*(3), 246–256. https://doi.org/10.1002/j.2161-0045.2008.tb00039.x

DeVos, A., Jacobs, S., & Verbruggen, M. (2021). Career transitions and employability. *Journal of Vocational Behavior, 126*, 103475. https://doi.org/10.1016/j.jvb.2020.103475

Ebberwein, C. A., Krieshok, T. S., Ulven, J. C., & Prosser, E. C. (2004). Voices in transition: Lessons on career adaptability. *Career Development Quartery, 52*, 292–308.

Eby, L. T., & Buch, K. (1995). Job loss as career growth: Responses to involuntary career transitions. *Career Development Quarterly, 44*(1), 26–42.

Erikson, E. H. (1963). *Childhood and society* (2nd ed.). Norton.

Erpič, C., Wylleman, P., & Zupančič, M. (2004). The effect of athletic and non-athletic factors on the sports career termination process. *Psychology of Sport and Exercise, 5*(1), 45–59. https://doi.org/10.1016/S1469-0292(02)00046-8

Fouad, N. A., & Bynner, J. (2008). Work transitions. *American Psychologist, 63*(4), 241–251.

Ghosh, A., Kessler, M., Heyrman, K., et al. (2019). Student veteran career transition readiness, career adaptability, and academic and life satisfaction. *Career Development Quarterly, 67*, 365–371.

Goodman, J. (1994). Career adaptability in adults: A construct whose time has come. *Career Development Quarterly, 43*, 74–84.

Goodman, J., & Hoppin, J. (1990). *Opening doors: A practical guide for job hunting* (2nd ed.). Oakland University, Continuum Center.

Hayden, S. C. W., Ledwith, K., Dong, S., & Buzzetta, M. (2014). Assessing the career-development needs of student veterans: A proposal for career interventions. *The Professional Counselor, 32*, 129–138.

Heppner, M. J. (1998). The Career Transitions Inventory: Measuring internal resources in adulthood. *Journal of Career Assessment, 6*(2), 135–145. https://doi.org/10.1177/106907279800600202

Kennedy, T., & Chen, C. P. (2012). Career counselling new and professional immigrants: Theories into practice. *Australian Journal of Career Development, 21*(2), 36–45.

Koert, E., Borgen, W. A., & Amundson, N. E. (2011). Educated immigrant women workers doing well with change: Helping and hindering factors. *The Career Development Quarterly, 59*(3), 194–207. https://doi.org/10.1002/j.2161-0045.2011.tb00063.x

Krumboltz, J. D., Foley, P. F., & Cotter, E. W. (2013). Applying the happenstance learning theory to involuntary career transitions. *The Career Development Quarterly, 61*(1), 15–26. https://doi.org/10.1002/j.2161-0045.2013.00032.x

Lipshits-Braziler, Y., & Gati, I. (2019). Facilitating career transitions with coping and decision-making approaches. In J. G. Maree (Ed.), *Handbook of Innovative Career Counseling* (pp. 139–156). Springer. https://doi.org/10.1007/978-3-030-22799-9_9

Liu, Y., Englar-Carlson, M., & Minichiello, V. (2012). Midlife career transitions of men who are scientists and engineers: A narrative study. *Career Development Quarterly, 60*(3), 273–288. https://doi.org/10.1002/j.2161-0045.2012.00023.x

Lo, L., & Bui, O. (2020). Transition planning: Voices of Chinese and Vietnamese parents of youth with autism and intellectual disabilities. *Career Development and Transition for Exceptional Individuals, 43*(2), 89–100. https://doi.org/10.1177/2165143419899938

McBride, P., & Cleymans, L. (2014). Strategies for assisting military spouses in obtaining a successful career path. *Career Planning and Adult Development Journal, 30*(3), 92–102.

McCormick, S. T., Kurth, N. K., Chambliss, C. E., et al. (2021). Career management strategies to promote employment for transition-age youth with disabilities. *Career Development and Transition for Exceptional Individuals, 43*(2), 120–131. https://doi.org/10.1177/2165143421991826

Osborn, D. S., & Belle, J. G. (2019). Preparing juvenile offenders for college and career readiness: A cognitive information processing approach. *Journal of Educational and Psychological Consultation, 29*(3), 283–313.

Packard, B. W.-L., Leah, M., Ruiz, Y., et al. (2012). School-to-work transition of career and technical education graduates. *The Career Development Quarterly, 60*(2), 134–144. https://doi.org/10.1002/j.2161-0045.2012.00011.x

Perosa, S. L., & Perosa, L. M. (1983). The midcareer crisis: A description of the psychological dynamics of transition and adaptation. *The Vocational Guidance Quarterly, 32*(2), 69–79. https://doi.org/10.1002/j.2164-585X.1983.tb01561.x

Pryor, R. G. L., Amundson, N. E., & Bright, J. E. H. (2008). Probabilities and possibilities: The strategic counseling implications of the chaos theory of careers. *The Career Development Quarterly, 56*(4), 309–318. https://doi.org/10.1002/j.2161-0045.2008.tb00096.x

Pryor, R. G. L., & Bright, J. E. H. (2011). *The chaos theory of careers: A new perspective on working in the twenty-first century*. Routledge.

Pryor, R. G. L., & Bright, J. E. H. (2014). The chaos theory of careers (CTC): Ten years on and only just begun. *Australian Journal of Career Development, 23*(1), 4–12.

Ryu, J., & Jeong, J. (2020). Career compromise types among university graduates during the school-to-work transition. *Career Development Quarterly, 69*, 19–33.

Salomone, P.R., & Mangicaro, L. L. (1991). Difficult cases in career counseling: IV – floundering and occupational moratorium. *Career Development Quarterly, 39*(4), 325–336.

Savickas, M. (1999). The transition from school to work: A developmental perspective. *Career Development Quarterly, 47*, 326–336.

Schlossberg, N. K. (1984). *Counseling adults in transition*. Springer.

Schlossberg, N. K., Waters, E., & Goodman, J. (1995). *Counseling adults in transition*. Springer.

Stein-McCormick, C., Osborn, D. S., Hayden, S., & Van Hoose, D. (2013). *Career development for transitioning veterans*. National Career Development Association. Retrieved from http://associationdatabase.com/aws/NCDA/pt/sd/product/1132/_self/layout_details/false

Super, D. E. (1957). *The psychology of careers*. Harper & Bros.

Super, D. E., & Knasel, E. G. (1981). Career development in adulthood: Some theoretical problems and a possible solution. *British Journal of Guidance and Counselling, 9*, 194–201. https://doi.org/10.1080/03069888108258214

Toyokawa, T., & DeWald, C. (2019). Perceived career barriers and career decidedness of first-generation college students. *Career Development Quarterly, 68*(4), 332–347. https://doi.org/10.1002/cdq.12240

Wendlandt, N. M., & Rochlen, A. B. (2008). Addressing the college-to-work transition: Implications for university career counselors. *Journal of Career Development, 35*(2), 151–165. https://doi.org/10.1177/0894845308325646

Wöhrmann, A., Deller, J., & Wang, M. (2014). A mixed-method approach to post-retirement career planning. *Journal of Vocational Behavior, 84*(3), 307–317.

Wordsworth, R., & Nilakant, V. (2021). Unexpected change: Career transitions following a significant extra-organizational shock. *Journal of Vocational Behavior, 127*(6), Article 103555. https://doi.org/10.1016/j.jvb.2021.103555

Yang, E., & Gysbers, N. C. (2007). Career transitions of college seniors. *Career Development Quarterly, 56*(2), 157–170. https://doi.org/10.1002/j.2161-0045.2007.tb00028.x

14 Art Therapy and Career Counseling Program Design and Evaluation

The goal of this chapter is to describe how to create, implement, manage, and evaluate comprehensive programs that integrate art therapy and career counseling. Beginning with needs assessments and culminating in program evaluation, this chapter will outline specific steps to program planning and delivery.

The Process of Career Program Design

Career counseling can be delivered in multiple formats, such as brief advising, individual or group counseling, seminars, workshops. When a specific career concern becomes voiced by several clients, or when a career counseling need is perceived in the community, developing and providing a career-focused program might be desirable. While it is possible that a career program will be developed as a stand-alone center, it is more likely for it to emerge from an existing site that recognizes a need and determines to meet that need. For example, consider the two case scenarios below.

Angela is an art therapist in an agency that provides services for foster group homes. A main focus of her work is to help the older youth build social skills and to prepare them to transition out of the group home and into society through individual and group activities. Through this work, she became aware that many of the youth felt unprepared for the transition, and seemed to be lacking in both knowledge and skills about how to enter into a career path. Based on this information, Angela decided to pitch the idea of having a career-focused program that integrated art therapy and career counseling components to the agency's board. The board stated that they would be supportive if she could provide evidence of a need, and create a comprehensive career program plan.

Jordy is a career counselor at a university career center. In his role, he is a liaison to the College of Fine Arts. As part of that work, he meets individually with students from those majors to talk about career directions and job searching, and also identifies employers who are interested in hiring students from those majors. He regularly provides career workshops for the college on topics such as choosing a career, résumé writing, and job seeking, but given the artistic and creative interests of many of the students, he would like to begin infusing more creative activities in the services he is providing. He talks with the career center director, who is supportive of his ideas, but want some more information about the student demand or interest for this type of program and wants to make sure that he builds the program using best practices.

In the scenarios above, both programs were conceived based on scanning the environment and becoming aware of clients' common concerns. The process of designing

DOI: 10.4324/9781003035756-14

a program can be both exciting and overwhelming. General steps to program design include:

1 establishing the need for program
2 designing the program
3 resourcing the program (finding space, staff, funding, materials)
4 marketing and advertising the program
5 delivering the program
6 managing and maintaining the program
7 evaluating the program (formative and summative)
8 adjusting the program.

To begin, Angela and Jordy both need to conduct a needs assessment to provide evidence that would justify the time, effort, and resources that would be needed to develop and sustain the program. In addition, this might mean that other currently existing programs would need to be reduced or eliminated in order to support a new program.

Needs Assessments

The process of assessing and understanding the comprehensive needs of a population is complex and involves many steps. The needs of today may not be the needs of tomorrow, and thus building a program based solely on needs assessment may not be sustainable. At the same time, beginning a program without understanding the needs of the population may result in a solution no one asked for and that was not needed. Three main purposes for needs assessment exist. First, and primarily, it is vital to understand specific needs of current and potential clients, business partners, and the community in order to determine if a need exists. Second, the results of needs assessments feed into, shape, and define the rationale for program design and development. Third, needs assessments provide proof of program effectiveness.

Designing the Needs Assessment

To begin the needs assessment process, a review of the mission, values, and goals of the overall organization (if the program is an extension of the organization) is recommended. The more the proposed program is in line with and contributes to achieving the organization's mission, the greater the likelihood that the program will be supported. If this is a start-up program, mission, values, goals, and objectives will need to be established. While the information gained from asking others about needs, wants, and preferences is important, having a clear vision of these program characteristics is foundational for building the program. In reviewing the needs and determining potential solutions, the program designer can use these foundational elements as a plumbline for determining priorities.

A second step in the process is to identify who would most likely be interested in your proposed program. Hopefully, the specific population you're interested in will be. But who else? Other people (e.g., family, teachers, health providers) who interact with the identified population might be excited about knowing a program existed and refer to it. Individuals or groups who have a financial interest in the program, such as a governing board or your employer will certainly be interested. Identifying key players who might utilize, refer to, or otherwise benefit from your program is important. First, they may have very specific needs or interests related to your program, and thus require their own type of needs assessment.

Second, they are critical to your program's success, and having their buy-in to the program increases the likelihood that they will help in marketing or getting the word out about your program, and perhaps even direct resources towards your program.

After identifying the key players, the next step is to identify the likely needs or concerns for each group. These will likely differ across the groups. The group of primary concern, though, is your specific population of interest. Consider not only the content of the need (e.g., "I wish knew how to show employers the value of my art skills," or "I need help finding a job"), but also on how, when, and where they would prefer these needs to be met (e.g., an online or printed guide, workshop format, webinar, individual meetings, during the regular day, in the evenings, etc.). There could also be other issues beyond the specific need that should be examined, such as transportation, cost of the service, caregiving responsibilities, technological capabilities, literacy, physical and mental health, and so forth. This is why asking a question about "what might impact your ability to attend a program such as this" and "what other concerns [about the issue] do you have that I haven't asked about?" would be useful and informative.

The initial list of needs will probably emerge from conversations with current clients, or frustrations of therapists not having adequate resources or referrals for specific clients' needs. The list shouldn't end there, however. You will probably want to generate several possible questions, and then narrow down to a reasonable amount. Other ways to identify needs include:

- Examining the scholarly literature for research about the characteristics of the specific population of interest. This might include needs, but also values, priorities, strengths, preferred ways of learning, and so forth. If that literature is non-existent or minimal, expand the search. Also explore outcome research on effective programs for the population of interest. This might provide factors that are useful to measure during program evaluation. Finally, consider professional organizations and national task forces that often identify best practices as a way to inform program design. Be sure that the materials being researched address individual and cultural differences (Calley, 2009).
- Conducting a focus group or open-ended survey of individuals in the specific population of interest.
- Identifying priorities of the overall organization and creating questions that reflect those. For example, if one of the priorities of the organization is innovation, consider how your current and proposed program could better meet that initiative, and at least one question might address innovation.
- Market analysis. Exploring local and online resources that exist to meet the needs, and evaluating what they do well, what they don't do at all, and what could be improved upon. Also, take note of practical issues, such as location, operating hours, childcare, costs of services, limits of services (e.g., ten sessions), acceptance of insurance, credentials of staff, length of time in existence, and so on. This will identify gaps as well as opportunities for a new program to address.
- Creating a satisfaction survey to determine how happy individuals from this group are with current services. Also include questions about usability and access. There may be a fantastic resource in the community, but because of specific operating hours, it is inaccessible to certain segments of that population.

As you review the expanded list of possible questions, keep in mind the overarching question, "What is most important for me to learn?" The answer to this question may differ for the different key players you've identified and should help in prioritizing and selecting the most important questions. It may be tempting to ask questions beyond the scope of what the program can provide; try to avoid the temptation. Your survey takers may get tired and either not answer all the questions, or start answering haphazardly, resulting in poor data – data upon which you are making decisions! To help ensure that the survey is the right length and asking the best questions to provide you with the information you need, pilot test the survey on a few individuals. In addition to answering the survey items, ask these individuals to give you feedback on the survey itself. Was it too short or too long? Confusing or clear? Too many open-ended items? Too many Likert options? Did they wish you had asked about something else? Other recommendations? As you review the survey results from the pilot study, evaluate how helpful they are. Are they answering your key questions? If you received 20 more responses similar to these, would you be able to move forward in designing your program, or is the information too specific or too vague? Do you need to revise your questions?

Multiple sources are available on how to format and administer needs assessments and surveys. While open-ended questions and telephone interviews can provide great depth in terms of responses, they take a great deal of time to complete and to analyze. Relying solely on Likert-scale or numerical/ranking approaches provide a quick but sometimes shallow analysis, so finding the right balance is important. An additional challenge is asking the question in the best way to get the most useful information. For example, in the case of Angela, she wants to know which career workshops would be of greatest interest and help to the group home residents. She could ask an open-ended question, or give them a list of options to check off, rank-order, or rate/prioritize. The open-ended question could yield rich data or very little. Another challenge with using an open-ended question for this example is that potential clients may not know what types of career workshops exist or are even possible, so might have difficulty answering that question. Check-off boxes provide a picture of all the possible workshops, but run the risk of someone checking off all of them. This challenge could be addressed by limiting the number they can check off – although there is no way to know what their main preference is. Another question could be added to have them identify their top choice. While rank-ordering does answer the question of most important workshops, it could be that after the first few workshops, there isn't a clear preference among the rest, which could then result in misleading data. Finally, rating scales provide a way to see how much interest there is for each workshop, but again, may not clearly identify their prioritized needs or preferences. So, each type of question has positives and potential negatives, which is why it is necessary to think through and then pilot test the questions.

Needs assessment questions should be designed in the way that will allow the desired analysis once the data has been collected. If Likert-scale data is collected, then mean scores can be compared. But compared for whom? Current clients versus potential clients? Across different demographics? Those with other characteristics, such as those who have higher levels of anxiety or career indecision, or those in an arts-related major versus those in other majors? To be able to compare across any of these groups, specific questions in the needs assessment must identify those aspects.

Collecting and Analyzing the Needs Assessment Results

Once the questions have been finalized, the data needs to be collected. Collecting from current clients or program users is relatively straightforward, but their completion of the needs assessment shouldn't be linked to their ability to continue their current involvement in the program. Ideally, the client can fill out the needs assessment anonymously, and won't feel pressured to do so by the counselor. Asking key players to share the needs assessments will increase the likelihood of individuals from varied backgrounds who might benefit from the program completing the needs assessment. This leads into the question of an

Table 14.1 List of career concerns and preferred workshops

	Top career needs	*Top preferred workshops*
Lower division	Choosing a career	Beyond the Major: Designing My Career
	Finding an internship	Matching Majors to Occupations
	Business etiquette	Dress to Success and Act to Impress
Upper division	Résumé writing	Résumé Writing/Cover Letters
	Finding employers	Personal Branding
	Applying to graduate schools	Creative Job Searching

online versus paper needs assessment. While providing a link to a survey makes it easier for the assessor, because the data is immediately stored into a database, is it more likely that a person will complete the online version or a paper version that is in front of them? A link is easier to distribute through social media, posting on a website, or sharing through email. Another consideration is how many times the assessment will be shared or sent, and how long the needs assessment will stay open before moving into analyzing the data.

Ideally, the needs assessment results will be organized around the questions that were identified and responses received. Open-ended questions can be explored for key themes and, once identified, can be coded for number of times a theme is noted. Themes could also be analyzed according to participant characteristics. Quantitative data can be presented in terms of frequencies, means, medians, and modes (Hammond, 2001). More sophisticated analyses can be incorporated as the number of respondents increases. In most cases of program design, these advanced approaches will not be necessary. In the case of Jordy, knowing that career development needs are very different for most entering students as compared to graduating students, he decides to examine prioritized workshops and career needs across levels. In doing so, he noticed that there was a clearer divide between upper and lower divisions, and so decided to present the data to his administrators in that manner. He gave a list of career concerns and workshops as well as options for open-ended responses. The results are in Table 14.1.

Once the data is in hand and the answers to the questions identified, initial decisions about the program are made. The results may confirm or be contradictory to assumptions held about the needs. The design of the program should respond to clearly identified needs, but not rely completely on the results of the needs assessment. Effective program design will involve more complexity, pulling in considerations of other programs, available resources, overall organizational goals, and staff strengths. For Jordy's program, he was surprised to see how many lower division students identified business etiquette as a career need. Consistent with his expectations, most lower division students wanted workshops related to career exploration and planning, while upper division students wanted job search and life-after-college career planning. Some of the write-in options yielded interesting results such as dealing with discrimination, workshops specific to art majors, and finding the hidden job market. He decided to create workshops with those titles, and also decided to regularly ask attendees about ideas for other workshops.

Designing the Program

Common Components and Services

Career-related programs share some common components, in terms of content and services provided, regardless of the setting. Content-wise, career programs typically focus on helping clients build self-knowledge, learn about their options, career decision-making, and job search. Other content might emerge from clientele specifics. For example, if working in an area where there is a military base, content might focus on transitions from military to civilian life, or career counseling specific to military members' significant others. Transitions might be a focus for other groups, such as adolescents, ex-offenders, and those moving into or out of group homes. Individuals from different sexual orientations or those with disabilities might need focused programming on if, how, and when to disclose this information to current or potential employers. Practitioners working with low-income or homeless populations might offer a professional clothes closet. Another consideration is the intersection of other issues or characteristics with career concerns, such as mental illness, physical health, or spirituality.

In addition to the aforementioned population characteristics and work-related needs, art therapy programs need to factor in developmental, personal, and social context and systemic considerations which influence program space requirements and design, materials offered, art safety protocols, storage of materials, and management of completed artwork in compliance with confidentiality requirements (Partridge, 2016). For example, in the context of a prison-based career preparation and release program, security requirements limit the type of art supplies tools that may be used, or if and when a program participant could keep their artwork for further reflection without penalty. When designing a career program and selecting materials for program art experiences for young adults on the autism spectrum, the practitioner must consider information processing styles and possible sensory aversions to materials experienced by clients and rely more on digital artmaking options (Darewych, 2021). With any population, art program choices can lead to the necessity of securing a program space with higher functioning ventilation, electrical, and plumbing systems to enable safe practices and adherence to health and safety codes (McCann & Babin, 2008). Program developers must estimate costs and identify resources that can support their ongoing materials and equipment needs as they may not be sufficiently funded by client fees or insurance reimbursement alone. Consequently, art therapists may consider applying for community grants and/or collaborating with existing arts organizations or institutions to make art-based career programs affordable, accessible, and attractive to particular communities (Partridge, 2016).

As such, practitioners designing art-based career program designs may be inspired by community-based art therapy practices. Ottemiller and Awais (2016) advocated for community-based art therapy programs which extend beyond medical models for mental health and set goals related to "social inclusion, empowerment, and stigma reduction" (p. 144). These programs include collaborative development of programs that rely on community input and affirmation of identities. Accordingly, Ottemiller and Awais articulated a five-component model they considered essential to community program building. These components include: collaborative development of program goals; building of trust and relationships within the community by getting to know community members and leaders and their experiences; cultivating open communication regarding roles of providers and the strengths and limitations of art-based services; sharing decision-making throughout program implementation; and fostering collaborative conversations regarding how people involved in the program wish to be referred to, for example, member, collaborator, participant, or artist, and how they wish to refer to program facilitators.

An example of a community arts-based program that bridges mental health recovery with artmaking, occupational preparation, and engagement in social citizenship is THE ARTS STUDIOS program (Damiano & Backman, 2019). The program, which has been in operation in Vancouver, Canada since 2003, has been built upon mental health service consumers' conceptual contributions to program development and professionally supported program activities which include psychoeducational groups, a pottery group, and arts and crafts instruction. Program components foster individual recovery and transformation of community roles as participants often move from client to volunteer assistant or peer mentor, and then to paid art instructors within the program.

Cultivating Program Development Skills

At Florida State University master's level art therapy program, art therapy students are required to take a program development course where they identify a community-based need and design an art-based program to address that need. Within a semester, small teams of students plan strategies for conducting needs assessments, explore literature to increase understanding of needs and intervention approaches to aid program design; identify resources required and available; establish budgets; and consider program evaluation tools. At the semester's conclusion, students present a formal proposal and receive feedback regarding the quality and feasibility of their programs. Additionally, team presentations give students experience with marketing their ideas and help them refine their communications skills.

One student, M., who completed the program development class, noted the importance of practicing individual and group brainstorming processes within program design efforts. They stated:

> As different ideas come to mind, the brain begins to make connections and form new thoughts based on the material. While "in the zone," these connections start to interact with each other, and create a fluid whirlpool of realization.

She provided the following images (Figures 14.1 and 14.2) to expand upon the brainstorming they experienced within the class format.

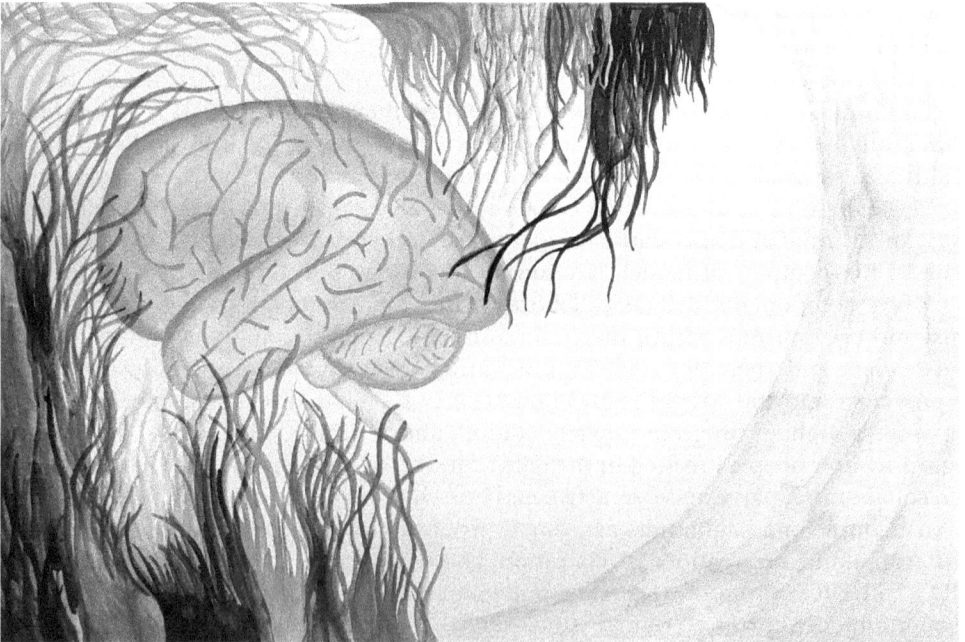

Figure 14.1 Program Development Brainstorm

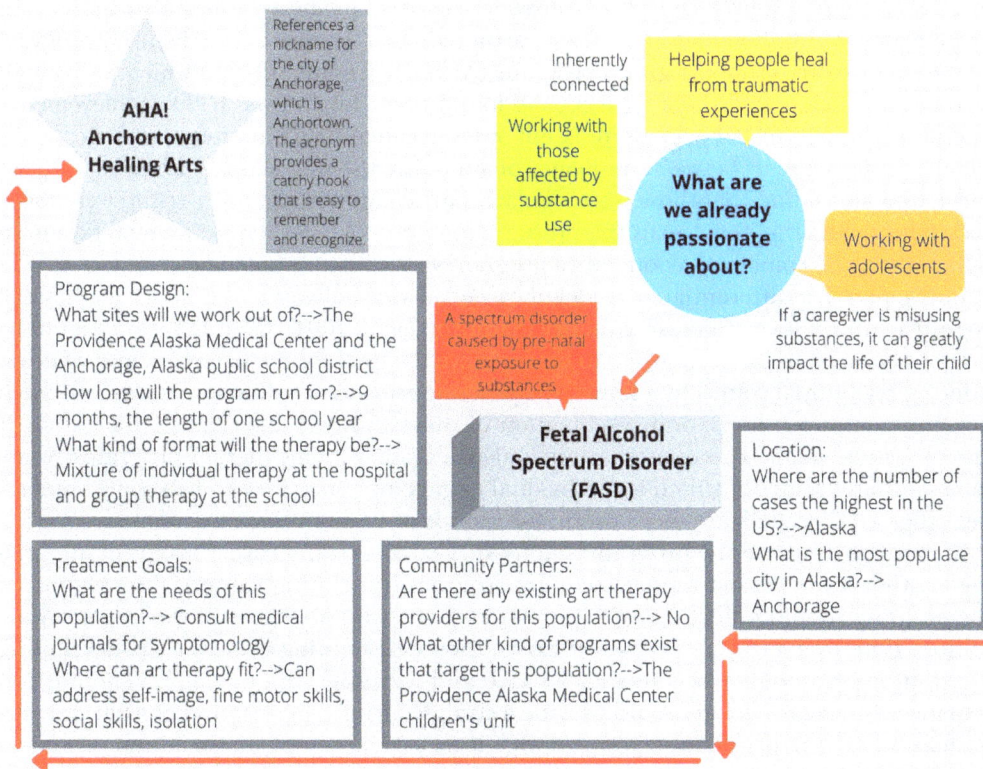

Figure 14.2 Program Development Brainstorm Chart

M. remarked that the first image reflected internal processes that they experienced as brain processes were stimulated by consideration of program development factors. The second image depicts results of group brainstorming processes related to their particular team project. They noted, "working with my group facilitated a much more comprehensive understanding of the population as well as the program created." They particularly valued brainstorming out loud and exchanging feedback in real time. Since program development frequently requires group efforts, team development activities such as the practice of brainstorming, communication, and leadership skills provide a preparatory base for the complex tasks of identifying, navigating, and serving community needs.

Career Programs

Career programs share commonality in the types of services that are provided. Of course, these may vary in terms of resource availability and the goals for the program. Common services include individual or group career counseling, career-related workshops (live or pre-recorded), infographics, tweetchats, mock or practice interviews, drop-in advising hours, webinars, and self-help guides (available in person and/or online). Lindo and Ceballos (2020) described their development of an eight-week group intervention that included an adaptation of a career counseling tool, the Career Construction Interview (CCI; Savickas, 2015) integrating expressive arts such as sand tray, but also using art tools to create expressions of their answers to specific CCI questions. Another example that combines art therapy with career concerns is described by Griffith et al. (2015), which utilized an open studio in a community resource center that provides services, including job skills training, for those experiencing homelessness. They partnered their psychosocially focused program (Art Corner) with a support group program (Artifacts Cooperative) in which individuals who were homeless sold their artwork, and found overall increases in "life achievement," operationalized as reaching goals in six out of seven categories. They found statistically significant improvements between frequency of attending the workshop and finding employment, and also found that those who regularly participated in the partnership were more successful in meeting their goals than those who were solely in the psychosocial group. In other words, the combined, cooperative program yielded better outcomes.

In Chapter 2, a differentiated model of career service delivery was described as part of cognitive information processing theory (Sampson et al., 2004). Consideration should be given of how services are delivered to best achieve the goals of the program, and whether offering traditional counseling hours, drop-in opportunities, self-help options, outreach presentations/workshops, or a combination of these will best meet the clientele's needs and programs' goals. This consideration is also necessary for art therapy programs. Some interventions are better suited for individual engagement in a face-to-face environment, but other art directives are more useful for groups or in an online environment.

Regardless of where the program is housed (i.e., an existing career program integrating art therapy or an existing art therapy program integrating career), the creation of the program should reflect the values, mission, goals, and objectives of the larger organization. If no overseeing organization exists, then determining these for the developing program is paramount for consistency's sake and for program evaluation. The mission statement for the program should provide a straightforward description of what the program is, whom the program serves, and what it seeks to accomplish. Goals and objectives should reflect the program values and tie into the program mission. Goals and objectives can change over time, either as they are achieved, or more pressing ones come into play. Needs assessment results often inform goals and objectives. While it is possible that the program's specific mission, values, goals, and objectives will differ from those of the larger organization, these should not directly conflict with each other. Finally, whenever possible, services and interventions should be evidence-based.

The two examples provided in this chapter were both at the initial stages of development. Both Angela and Jordy decided to keep goals for their projects fewer and focused. Jordy decided on primary goals: (1) integrate and provide expressive arts into currently existing career-related workshops; (2) work with an art therapist to develop resources that can be used in one-on-one sessions for career exploration and career planning; (3) offer at least one art-enhanced career workshop weekly; (4) collect and analyze workshop evaluations; and (5) collaborate at least once a month with current faculty and student groups within the College of Fine Arts to identify needs and opportunities. Angela, in trying to create a career-focused art therapy program for foster group homes, decided upon these goals: (1) talk with existing career services providers to learn of opportunities, resources, and opportunities for collaboration; (2) identify and invite local employers to talk about how to interview, what they are looking for on résumés, and opportunities to gain experience; (3) collaborate with a local career center to co-create career-related workshops that include an expressive arts activity; and (4) collect and review evaluative feedback from surveys, attendance, and presenters.

Strategic Planning

Strategic planning is the process through which the program is designed or evaluated. Typically, this would involve the key players who have an emotional or financial investment in the program's success, as well as those who will be involved in directly delivering the program. Multiple approaches or models can be applied in this process. One approach to strategic planning would be to use a "SWOT" analysis, to examine strengths, weaknesses, opportunities, and threats to the existing program, competing programs, or a proposed program. The program should build from existing strengths and resources. Another approach would be to apply a decision-making model, such as the CASVE Cycle (Sampson et al., 2004) in planning the program. Applying this model, questions would examine the gap between what exists and what is needed, exploring current programs in depth, expanding and narrowing options for content, services, and delivery, prioritizing the options, trying out the best option, and then evaluating the degree to which the gap was narrowed.

In strategic planning, both the content of the program, and the process (i.e., how the content will be delivered) should be addressed. In addition to providing a service, consider whether the program will also provide training and/or research opportunities for art therapy or career counseling. An example of this is Lister et al. (2009) and the Florida State University Career Center, both of which created settings, the former for art therapy, and the latter for career advising and counseling, with intentional goals for service delivery, training of graduate students, and collecting and contributing to research. A final aspect of strategic planning involves the creation of an action plan, including evaluation, with timelines delineated.

Policies and Procedures

If the program being designed is under the umbrella of a larger organization, it might be possible to simply adopt the policies and procedures that are in existence. More likely, the program will need to create or adjust policies. Policies are guiding principles that tend to remain over time, and might include values/goals of the program, who is and is not served, what the services are, limitations of services, roles of partners, social media, and so forth. Separate policies might exist for employees of the program, such as equal opportunity, harassment, pay and benefits, dress code, disciplinary procedures, and attendance/punctuality expectations. Procedures are detailed steps to address the operational needs of the program, and tend to flex with the ongoing demands of the program, such as operation hours, who opens and closes the program and how, how complaints and requests are handled, how decision are made, how proposals for additional services are handled, how often the program is evaluated, and so forth.

Resourcing the Program

Once the key components and desired services of the program have been identified, the practical task of translating the ideal into the real becomes necessary. Initial questions to consider include: Where will the program be housed? Will there be a physical location? Will it be a stand-alone building or within an existing building? Is there no physical space reserved for it, but a space created for it when needed (e.g., workshop space, or partner meeting)? Is it completely virtual? What other resources are needed? Handouts? Web design and delivery? Printed and online guides? Furniture? Phones? Computers? Projection devices? Copier? Internet?

Staffing requirements must also be considered. What skills and credentials are required to provide the program? What different roles must be covered? If the operation is small enough, it could be that one or two people can handle all aspects of the work, ranging from design to delivery, marketing the program, posting regularly to social media, scheduling requests, and so forth. If the program is part of a larger organization, it may be possible for staff of the whole to assist in functions such as managing a webpage or technical issues for the program, or handling scheduling. If a goal of the program is also to provide training for paraprofessionals, skills in supervision are necessary. The need for specific training will become apparent as the needs of the program and the skills of the staff are examined from a holistic perspective.

Budgeting for the program ensures that resources for the primary services are available. If part of a larger organization, a specific amount of funds (staff, and staff time) may have been allocated. If this is the case, clearly knowing what the program will cost will help ensure that the budget is not exceeded, and that the program doesn't overpromise what it is able to deliver. If the program is not part of a larger organization, funding sources will need to be identified. Sources might include grants for non-profit organizations, grants, loans, business partnerships, or donations.

Collaboration

Collaborative partners can provide a rich avenue for strategic planning with respect to program development, delivery, and evaluation. However, partners should be considered carefully. Ideally, a partner will have a shared interest in and passion for the program that is being developed and the population being served, while simultaneously bringing a unique set of experiences, perspectives, network, and so on to the table. Having a partner that is a mirror-image of someone else on the team is redundant and unnecessary. In both of the program design examples provided at the beginning of the chapter, finding a career counseling or art therapy partner, respectively, will be essential to accomplishing the program design goals. Additional partners may also be desired, given the program needs. For example, if the plan for the program is for it to be delivered mainly online, having someone on the team who has online program design and delivery experience will be valuable. If the aim is to reach a certain demographic, having representation from that demographic would be important.

What are the expectations of and for partners? What should they be contributing? How often will they be tapped for meetings and consultations? How are they involved in decision-making? How much power do they have? For example, do they have an equal voice in the program content and delivery, or on how funds are spent? Who has the final say on these decisions – the collective, or the program director? Are decisions made based on a simple majority, or consensus, or is a unanimous decision required? What are the benefits of partnership for the partners? What is the duration of the partnership? Lister et al. (2009) emphasize the importance of finding committed partners:

> Tap into the resources of an established program, such as theater or other department within a university where other people may be mobilized to create an initial vehicle for public outreach like a play. The success of these events can motivate and catalyze the people involved to further pursue their ideas.
>
> (p. 36)

Marketing and Advertising the Program

Once the program has been designed, it needs to be advertised to potential clients. Through partnerships and discussions in the strategic planning process, hopefully some key players are invested in sharing the news about the new program being launched. Prior to advertising, everything should be set up to make it easy for a potential client to learn about and engage with the program. For example, an easy-to-find working website should be available that outlines services, office hours, and a calendar of events, with a contact form or email. A consistent brand with a logo, program title, and catchphrase should be evident across all platforms. Social media accounts should be created for the program. An ongoing marketing plan should be developed. For example, how often are social media posts made, who makes them, what do they consist of, when do they go out, and who evaluates their impact? Other types of advertising might include posters, flyers, inserts in magazines, business cards, or on partners' websites. While some marketing and advertising costs are free in terms of dollars, someone is having to take the time to create them. Therefore, learning how the majority of people are learning of the program is vital to cost effectiveness when it comes to marketing and advertising.

For Jordy's career program activities within the College of Fine Arts, he decided to create flyers specific for the different majors. He talked with the different groups to learn of their social media groups, and partnered with "influencers" within the different groups to share upcoming workshops and events. Due to the residential aspect of participants, Angela did not need to market the program to the residents. Instead, she focused marketing efforts to potential speakers and investors.

Delivering, Evaluating, and Revising the Program

Program delivery is the ongoing practical provision of the program's identified services, operating from the program mission, goals, and procedural framework. While delivery of the program begins when the physical or virtual doors of the program open, plans for evaluation of the program begin prior to this moment, as part of the strategic planning process. Evaluation should include both formative (ongoing) and summative (final) reviews. A formative review occurs along the way to the summative reviews, with a main objective being the ability to pivot and correct approaches, services, and the like, if the evaluation is negative. The evaluation plan should include a re-visiting of how well the mission, values, and goals of the program are being accomplished.

Clearly, it is helpful to know what will be evaluated prior to the evaluation. These metrics or benchmarks might include questions of how people learn about the program, the number of workshops or specific services provided, the focus of these interventions, the number of people who engaged in the different services, representation of diversity, and satisfaction surveys. This information can provide valuable information on the accomplishments of the program, areas that need improvement, areas of redundancy or underutilization, and goals that are and are not being met. Much of this information needs to be collected along the way. Sign-in sheets that collect data such as demographics of the individual, the service or needs they have related to the program, and how they learned of the service provide an overall picture of who is (and is not) being served, for what needs, as well as useful marketing information. This information, collected and organized on a schedule, such as daily or weekly, can also indicate trends, as well as provide data for determining if the financial costs are merited (Hammond, 2001). Surveys that occur immediately following service delivery can focus not only on satisfaction, but changes in knowledge, skills, and attitudes (e.g., confidence about their ability to perform a specific task), as well as interest to engage in future services.

Even the evaluation process needs to be evaluated. Sometimes, responses to questions will be unclear, unhelpful, and need to be honed or deleted. For example, Feen-Calligan and Nevedal (2008) found in their program evaluation that 73% of their participants said they liked the art materials, making art, and self-expression through art, but that led the researchers to wonder why the artmaking was liked so they could better understand the "process and efficacy of art therapy" (p. 181). At the same time, there were 8% who indicated they didn't like a specific process or art medium, and the researchers wished they had asked a question about the reasons. Another follow-up question would be what the impact is of liking or not liking the art medium or process on other outcomes, such as perceived value of the workshop, client growth, and so on. Based on the responses to their program, Feen-Calligan and Nevedal decided to change their evaluation instrument and process, by asking participants to identify workshop goals prior to the beginning, and then evaluating how well they had accomplished their goal(s) at the conclusion of the workshop. They also decided to ask for more specific information on art therapy aspects they liked and disliked.

Based on the evaluation results, a program is likely to be revised. Data is rarely static. What may be effective for one group and one month may not be for another group the next month. That being said, implementing change based on evaluation data is an important step of the process, which then re-starts the process of delivering the augmented program and ongoing evaluation. Ongoing evaluation increases accountability for a program, provides the data needed to show the program's effectiveness, ensures program relevancy to not only the overall mission and goals, but also to the clients being served, and ultimately establishes/supports the need for continuing the program.

Both Jordy and Angela decided early on to collect information that was important to their administrators in determining whether the program should continue, and if so, in the same manner as before, or if adjustments needed to be made. They kept records of days and times workshops were provided and from that information were able to identify the best times to provide workshops. They asked for feedback on each of the workshops and presented overall means. They also regularly reviewed the evaluations and shifted the focus based on comments. They identified the most preferred workshops and decided to offer more opportunities for students to attend. They sought out feedback in individual conversations. Because they regularly collected and examined their evaluation information, they were able to attend early on to under-represented groups, and pivot their plans to try and better reach those groups.

Summary

Program development requires both comprehensive and creative components. The ability to prove a program exists and that it is meeting an important need requires technical skills of connecting and tracking goals, objectives, products, and outcomes. Collaboration among key players is an essential key to program success, and ongoing evaluations increase the likelihood that the program is sufficiently meeting the needs of the people it is intended to help.

Discussion Questions and Activities

1   Create a needs assessment specific to a population of interest to you. Include questions based on personal experience or from research. Be sure to include different types of questions (e.g., open-ended, closed-ended, focused on content as well as practical needs). Administer the survey to three to five peers, and include some questions about the survey itself. Was it easy to complete/understand? Too short, too long, or just right? Missing anything? Based on the responses to the survey itself (i.e., how useful is the information you received) and the peers' evaluation, make adjustments.

2   Choosing a population of interest, design an art-infused career development workshop. The focus should be on addressing a common career need of that population. Possible general career topics might be choosing a major or career, job searching, résumé writing, interviewing, and so forth. The workshop outline should include

goals related to client characteristics, ice breakers and active learning strategies, and desired outcomes of the workshop.

3 Design a website that reflects an integrated art therapy and career development program. Include the mission, goals, values, and objectives. Include a list of services provided, appropriate materials and directives to accompany these services, and demonstrate how the program imbeds the levels of the Expressive Therapies Continuum.

4 Examine three career centers or career programs (could be in person, online, via phone, or any combination, etc.) and identify key elements such as services provided, the mission statement, goals, outcome objectives, and policies. Identify the three centers, and briefly summarize your findings. Then, write a rough draft of the key elements you want to have in your program, a mission statement, goals, and outcome objectives, being sure they reflect ethical standards.

5 Identify and research five "top" national companies (perhaps, Fortune 500). What is it that makes them a top company, and what are the implications for program development? Also, identify their mission statements.

6 Using social media and company specific hashtags (e.g., #apple, #NFL) of your favorite companies whom you purchase from, explore the different marketing techniques. Then, identify competing companies and do the same, making comparisons about the impact of their advertising/marketing approaches on your decision to engage or not to engage.

7 Identify three to five companies/stores that you frequent. Do a search on their mission statements. What observations can be made? Is it clear what their purpose is? What is the message that is being sent? Are there similarities across these statements? Now try to locate mission statements for career and/or art therapy programs that are serving a population similar to yours, or providing content similar to yours. What is being/not being communicated? Try developing a brief mission statement for your proposed program.

8 Consider that you have a set amount (e.g., $1000) to purchase resources for your program. Create a priority list of items, including costs as well as a link to the publisher, and match these resources to your program objectives.

9 Identify the staff needed for your program. Using the NCDA guidelines, as well as sample job notices, develop position descriptions for each of your professional staff. (Note: do this for the main positions, such as director, associate director, assistant director, and career advisor – not every office assistant, every advisor, etc.). It might be helpful to view job descriptions that are available at naceweb, chronicle and higheredjobs.com. Create a plan for continued training and supervision for your staff.

10 Create a budget for your career program. You can start with a set of assumptions – that is, that this is not your first-year start-up costs and that you already have furniture, computers, some set of resources, etc. Just make a note of that. The goal of this activity is to estimate how much it will cost to run your operation on a yearly basis.

11 Identify four potential funding sources for your career program or a component of your career program.

12 Do an online search for marketing strategies. Start with a general search, then look for strategies specific to your population of interest. Consider marketing in traditional ways as well as through more current approaches (e.g., social media). Use this information to complete the next activity.

13 Outline your marketing strategies for your program. Consider the population of interest in your strategies, but also others who might be in positions to refer people to your program. How can you best reach them?

14 Create an advertisement brochure or infographic for your career program.
15 Learn more about what your community offers to the clientele you serve, with respect to career counseling and art therapy. If you were to create a program, who would be your competitors? What is already being done? Is it being done well? What are they not doing or not doing well? How might your program differentiate itself?
16 Create a framework for evaluating your career program. Include plans for regular monitoring of your career program.

References

Calley, N. G. (2009). Comprehensive program development in mental health counseling: Design, implementation, and evaluation. *Journal of Mental Health Counseling, 31*(1), 9–11.

Damiano, N. & Backman, C.L. (2019). More than art, less than work: The paradoxes of citizenship and artmaking in community mental health. *BC Studies, 202*(2), 41–63.

Darewych, O. (2021). The future is now: Group digital art therapy for adults with autism spectrum disorder. *Canadian Journal of Art Therapy, 34*(1), 26–32. https://doi.org/10.1080/26907240.2021.1907940

Feen-Calligan, H. & Nevedal, D. (2008). Evaluation of an art therapy program: Client perceptions and future directions. *Art Therapy: Journal of the American Art Therapy Association, 25*(4), 177–182.

Griffith, F. J., Seymour, L., & Goldberg, M. (2015). Reframing art therapy to meet psychosocial and financial needs in homelessness. *The Arts in Psychotherapy, 46*, 33–40.

Hammond, M. S. (2001). Career centers and needs assessments: Getting the information you need to increase your success. *Journal of Career Development, 27*(3), 187–197.

Lindo, N. A., & Ceballos, P. (2020). Child and adolescent career construction: An expressive arts group intervention. *Journal of Creativity in Mental Health, 15*(3), 364–377. https:/doi.org/10.1080/15401383.2019.1685923

Lister, S., Tanguay, D., Snow, S., & D'Amico, M. (2009). Development of a creative arts therapies center for people with developmental disabilities. *Art Therapy: Journal of the American Art Therapy Association, 26*(1), 34–47.

McCann, M., & Babin, A. (2008). *Health hazards manual for artists.* (6th ed.). Lyons Press.

Ottemiller, D. D., & Awais, Y. (2016). A model for art therapists in community-based practice. *Art Therapy: Journal of the American Art Therapy Association, 33*(3), 144–150. https://doi.org/10.1080/07421656.2016.1199245

Partridge, E. E. (2016). Access to art materials: Considerations for art therapists. *Canadian Art Therapy Assocation Journal, 39*(2), 100–104. http://dx.doi.org/10.1080/08322473.2016.1252996

Sampson, J. P., Jr., Reardon, R. C., Peterson, G. W., & Lenz, J. G. (2004). *Career counseling and services: A cognitive information processing approach.* Brooks/Cole.

Savickas, M. L. (2015). *Life design counseling manual.* Retrieved from vocopher.com

15 Art Therapist/Career Counselor Self-Assessment

Am I Ready for Practice?

This chapter will provide a summary of art therapy and career development topics and learning outcomes. Art-based processes for self-reflection will be provided to readers as a means for them to understand their career counseling skills, knowledge, strengths, and weaknesses. Additionally, skill and concept checklists related to learning outcomes will be provided. Finally, an art therapy career development goal sheet will be provided to support students in identifying areas that they may further study and practice. Accessing career development resources and supervision regarding client career development issues will be emphasized.

Art Therapy and Career Development Topics and Learning Outcomes

Both the fields of art therapy and career development have their own requisite knowledge bases, theoretical orientations, necessary skills, and evidence-based interventions that are specific to their respective professions. Overlap exists between the two, such as the ability to establish and maintain a counseling relationship, set counseling goals, and treatment planning and monitoring. Throughout this book, we have sought to demonstrate how art therapy and career counseling can be integrated with respect to the various topics covered. Some of these include skills for building a working alliance with a client, knowledge of resources specific to the client concerns, sensitivity to diversity, administering and interpreting assessments (qualitative and/or quantitative), and understanding of and capability in applying ethical standards. Despite these many shared components, art therapy and career counseling also have their specific areas of expertise.

Art Therapy Required Skills

When considering required art therapy skills, two guiding documents are important to review for those who are practicing in the United States, the Standards and Guidelines for the Accreditation of Educational Programs in Art Therapy, which identifies curriculum competency requirements and student learning outcomes expected for students graduating from art therapy programs accredited by Commission on Accreditation of Allied Health Education Programs (CAAHEP, 2016), and the Art Therapy Credentials Board Registration Standards (ATCB, 2022), which note the educational, practicum training experiences, and supervisor endorsement of skills required for professional practice. For the purposes of this chapter, the focus will be on specific areas of knowledge, skills, and experiences that focus on the centrality of art-based concepts and processes not typically addressed in professional standards or competencies established for related helping professional fields.

DOI: 10.4324/9781003035756-15

Knowledge, Skill, and Practice with Art Materials and Processes

The ATCB (2022) Registration Standards highlight the importance of preparatory experiences and familiarity with two- and three-dimensional art materials as a foundation for graduate level studies in art therapy. Specifically, The ATCB identifies 18 semester or 27 quarter credits or documented equivalent experiences as sufficient for forming a baseline of understanding of art materials and processes. Adding to this base, art therapy graduate students are engaged in art processes that expand their knowledge of materials' therapeutic properties, including non-traditional materials, and understand research-informed models regarding art media use, such as the Expressive Therapies Continuum (CAAHEP, 2016). Additionally, art therapists must be aware of art materials safety and consider the importance of artmaking space design and maintenance when offering art-based interventions to clients.

As you reflect on your competencies with art materials including an ability to teach these methods to others, note the range of your art media skills including traditional, technology-based, and other non-traditional materials, such as found-object art, and identify any gaps of experience or understanding that you may have.

Reflection Questions

1 Which art materials and processes do you consider to be outside of your competency?
2 How might your areas of comfort with materials differ from those who you may serve?
3 What are the specific benefits or limitations of materials you plan to use?
4 What art materials and methods do you believe you understand sufficiently to utilize to explore or enhance career development?

Action Items

1 Identify ways that you can expand your art media understanding, through continuing education, art classes, and personal art experimentation.
2 Engage a qualified supervisor trained to address media properties and application questions and evaluate competency. Collaboratively develop media learning strategies and plans.

Art Materials and Processes within Helping Relationships

Knowing materials is a first step but knowing how to offer and apply them within helping relationships is ethically essential. In this regard, CAAHEP (2016) outlines several guidelines that encompass necessary learning outcomes indicative of being competent in using art materials within a helping relationship. First, practitioners must be knowledgeable of evidence-based practices that inform effective art therapy interventions with people of various ages, developmental capacities, cultural backgrounds, needs, and treatment concerns and goals. Additionally, practitioners must understand how the offering of art materials, art interventions, and potential discussions regarding art products, or the presence of practitioner artmaking during sessions may influence the therapeutic alliance and treatment outcomes. In group treatment settings, art therapists must understand how art materials and processes influence group dynamics and how to apply this knowledge to the development and implementation of art interventions. Furthermore, therapist artmaking outside sessions may be used as a way of gaining reflective understanding of clients' or groups' responses to the person of the therapist and/or the art materials and experiences offered.

Reflective Questions

1 Consider a setting and a particular population and/or age group with whom you would like to integrate art-based methods within career counseling. What is your level of familiarity with evidence-based art therapy practices related to that setting and group?
2 What types of client behavior and responses do you imagine may indicate that an art-based intervention is well aligned with the clients' characteristics and treatment goals?
3 What types of client behavior and responses do you imagine may indicate that an art-based intervention that you offered did not match client needs and goals, or was diminishing the therapeutic alliance? How might you respond in that moment?

Action Items

1 Identify two scholarly resources that will expand your knowledge of evidence-based art therapy practices for a population with whom you would like to work. Then read them! Check your understanding.
2 Before planning to use an art-based intervention provided in this book, complete the art process yourself. Note your personal responses to the process and reflect on how art prompts may be received by clients you wish to serve.
3 Refer to Chapter 5 for materials on building, maintaining, and closing art therapy and career counseling relationships.

Understanding Creativity, Symbolism, and Metaphor

As examples in the book have demonstrated, artmaking adds rich visual communication into the art therapy or counseling space. Art-based interventions provide clients an opportunity to explore and understand emotions, values, and beliefs that may escape awareness, may be closed off from verbal, or may be more clearly articulated in visual form. Artworks also provide an opportunity for both client and practitioner to step back and look together at artistic outcomes to enhance understanding of concerns and aims. CAAHEP (2016) guidelines outline learning outcomes that lead to competency regarding the use of creativity, symbolism, and metaphor within art therapy practices. These include describing understanding of theories and models related to creativity, symbolism, metaphor, and artistic language, and the application of these models. CAAHEP standards also recognize that symbols and metaphors and artistic language are not the same for each individual and that cultural and systemic experiences influence materials' associations and meanings attributed to symbols and metaphors. Accordingly, practitioners must be able to demonstrate sensitivity and awareness of differences in experiences and expression, and continually expand their own understanding of diverse creative and symbolic frameworks. Understanding clients' symbolic work also requires practitioner humility as the client is the ultimate expert on their symbolic expressions.

Reflective Questions

1 What types of experiences have you had looking at artwork outside of therapeutic contexts?
2 Consider one artwork that you have seen recently. What observations, materials, or conversations helped you gain understanding about the artwork's meaning? How did you confirm, if at all, that your understanding was in alignment with the artist's intentions?
3 What symbols, materials use, or art activities do you associate with your family or cultural traditions? How would you recommend that a practitioner engage you to learn more about your art, symbols, and traditions?

Action Items

1 Go to a museum, gallery, or a museum or artist's website. Choose an artwork to view, preferably by an artist with a different cultural background than yourself. Before reading about the artwork, take time to notice visual qualities, materials, and symbols used. Next, identify what you believe the artist wished to express and/or the meanings they attributed to the work. Now, read available materials. Explore how your interpretation differed from the materials provided.

2 Review artworks that you created in conjunction with your learning art therapy and career development through this text and/or a related course. Following this review, write an artist statement that reflects the major themes and ideas that were represented in your artworks. Title your body of work.

Art Therapy, Career Development, and Art Assessment Tools

The CAAHEP standards for accredited art therapy educational programs state that career development content is recommended, not required, and the inclusion of career development content within art therapy educational programs is often influenced by certification or state licensure requirements within the program's region. The standards provide a broad description of content and competency expectations:

> The curriculum should provide students with the opportunity to understand knowledge and skills considered essential in enabling individuals and organizations to positively affect career development and aptitude. Additional areas of coverage include methods of assessment and strategies to facilitate career development with diverse clients.
>
> (CAAHEP, 2016, p. 29)

CAAHEP also provides a set of detailed student learning outcomes including knowledge, skills, affective experiences, and behaviors that should be accomplished related to career development concepts to establish competency. These learning outcomes emphasize knowledge of theories and models of career planning and decision-making; understanding assessment tools and techniques; skills related to applying information resources to support client choice and assessing career and lifestyle matches, along with mental health factors; and valuing multicultural and ethical strategies for facilitating career development goals. It is noteworthy that CAAHEP specifically identifies knowledge of "assessment tools and techniques including art therapy assessments relevant to career counseling" (CAAHEP, 2016, p.29) as essential to competency in the career development domain. When using assessments, art therapists must be able to identify the purposes of the art-based assessment, and to apply best practices for administration. Additionally, art therapists must understand different types of assessments, such as standardized and non-standardized assessments, and appropriate interpretation methods that may be ethically used.

Reflective Questions

1 How would you explain the advantages of adding informal art-based assessment processes to an initial evaluation of clients' career interests and influences?

2 How would you describe the advantages and limitations of art-based assessment processes to a client?

Action Items

1 From the chapters in the book, pick one informal art-based assessment process that you had not previously engaged in. Complete the art experience. Identify two career development contexts and populations for which the assessment would be well-matched.

2 Explore art therapy and career counseling resources in your area including career service centers, career counselors, and art therapists. Identify centers or practitioners to whom you would refer clients for assessments, administration, and interpretation outside of your competency areas.

Combining Art Therapy Competencies with Career Competencies

In this text, we believe we have demonstrated how work/life roles impact quality of life for people and communities throughout their lifespans and that integrated art therapy assessment and interventions can expand pathways used to support positive career development. As you consider your competencies and readiness for assisting those you serve with career development process, it is recommended that you review the NCDA checklist of competencies for career counselors. We invite you to examine your current competencies and to identify next steps for career counseling related learning and application.

Career Counseling Required Knowledge and Skills

Career Counseling Knowledge

The Council for the Accreditation of Counseling and Related Educational Programs (CACREP) program standards (2016) require sixty credit hours of graduate training for those in training to be counselors, regardless of specialization. Career development is a core competency area for all counselors in training. For those desiring to be career counselors, additional specialized coursework and clinical experiences focused on the foundations, contextual dimensions, and practice of career counseling are required. Table 15.1 outlines the CACREP standards current at the time of this publication date (see cacrep.org for updates).

Not all individuals who provide career assistance are counselors with graduate level training. The National Career Development Association also provides training and credentialling for those with a bachelor's degree who desire to become a Certified Career Services Provider. The training required covers similar content and demonstration of skills, but with less commitment and cost. These knowledge areas include: helping skills, labor market information and resources, diverse populations, ethical and legal issues, career development models, employability skills, training clients and peers, program management/implementation, promotion and public relations, technology, and consultation.

Reflection Questions

1 Which career-related questions have your clients shared or expressed that you have been unable to answer?

2 Considering the required content knowledge outlined in Table 15.1, what are the gaps in your knowledge?

Table 15.1 CACREP standards for career development for all counselors and for those specializing in career counseling

---

Career development standards for all counselors

Theories and models of career development, counseling, and decision-making.

Approaches for conceptualizing the interrelationships among and between work, mental well-being, relationships, and other life roles and factors.

Processes for identifying and using career, avocational, educational, occupational and labor market information resources, technology, and information systems.

Approaches for assessing the conditions of the work environment on clients' life experiences.

Strategies for assessing abilities, interests, values, personality and other factors that contribute to career development.

Strategies for career development program planning, organization, implementation, administration, and evaluation.

Strategies for advocating for diverse clients' career and educational development and employment opportunities in a global economy.

Strategies for facilitating client skill development for career, educational, and life–work planning and management.

Methods of identifying and using assessment tools and techniques relevant to career planning and decision-making.

Ethical and culturally relevant strategies for addressing career development.

Career development standards for those in career counseling specialization

---

Foundations

History and development of career counseling

Emergent theories of career development and counseling

Principles of career development and decision-making over the lifespan

Formal and informal career- and work-related tests and assessments

Contextual dimensions

Roles and settings of career counselors in private and public sector agencies and institutions

Role of career counselors in advocating for the importance of career counseling, career development, life–work planning, and workforce planning to policymakers and the general public

The unique needs and characteristics of multicultural and diverse populations with regard to career exploration, employment expectations, and socioeconomic issues

Factors that affect clients' attitudes toward work and their career decision-making processes

Impact of globalization on careers and the workplace

Implications of gender roles and responsibilities for employment, education, family, and leisure

Education, training, employment trends, and labor market information and resources that provide information about job tasks, functions, salaries, requirements, and future outlooks related to broad occupational fields and individual occupations

Resources available to assist clients in career planning, job search, and job creation

Professional organizations, preparation standards, and credentials relevant to the practice of career counseling

Legal and ethical considerations specific to career counseling

Practice

Intake interview and comprehensive career assessment

Strategies to help clients develop skills needed to make life–work role transitions

Approaches to help clients acquire a set of employability, job search, and job creation skills

Strategies to assist clients in the appropriate use of technology for career information and planning

Approaches to market and promote career counseling activities and services

Identification, acquisition, and evaluation of career information resources relevant for diverse populations

Planning, implementing, and administering career counseling programs and services

Action Items

1 Prioritize which areas of career counseling and development knowledge would best help you in your work with your clients.
2 Create a plan for addressing specific knowledge gaps. Consider readings, webinars, conferences, and workshops as possible avenues for learning.
3 Explore whether credentialing as a career services provider or career coach might enhance the services you deliver or help you to better support the clients you see and their career issues.

In addition to specific career counseling knowledge domains, career counseling requires specific skills for effective practice. Table 15.2 provides a checklist of competencies required for career counselors, as described in NCDA's (n.d.) Career Counseling Competency statements. In addition to the specific list of competencies, Table 15.2 includes a self-check for comparison purposes. While the list of competencies is lengthy, the purpose is to cover the multiple roles a career practitioner might find themselves playing. A recommended step would be to start by examining which roles might be most pertinent and then examining the specific competencies listed for that area.

Table 15.2 Career counseling competencies

Competency	I have limited skills and/or knowledge in this area	I have moderate skills and/or knowledge in this area	I am very skilled and/or knowledgeable in this area
I want to help others learn about themselves, their options, and how to help them make their dreams come true.			
Career counseling roles – I can effectively:			
Help individuals clarify life/career goals.			
Conduct group counseling sessions focusing on career issues.			
Administer inventories to assess abilities, interests, and other factors to identify career options.			
Interpret inventories to assess abilities, interests, and other factors to identify career options.			
Utilize career-planning systems and occupational information systems to help individuals better understand the world of work.			
Help clients improve their decision-making skills.			
Assist clients in developing individualized career plans.			
Understand and effectively teach job-hunting strategies and skills.			
Provide appropriate résumé writing critiques.			
Help clients resolve personal conflicts on the job through practice in human relations skills.			
Assist in understanding the integration of work and other life roles.			
Provide support for persons experiencing job stress, job loss, and career transition.			

(Continued)

Table 15.2 Career counseling competencies (*Continued*)

Competency	I have limited skills and/or knowledge in this area	I have moderate skills and/or knowledge in this area	I am very skilled and/or knowledgeable in this area
Integrate career theory into the practice of career counseling.			
Utilize various career counseling resources, including books, assessments, and online tools.			
Apply the ethical standards specific to career counseling.			
Demonstrate sensitivity to the role that various personal issues, such as race, age, disability, culture, sexual orientation, religious beliefs, etc., may play in the career decision-making process, and discuss these issues with clients.			
Establish and maintain a productive consultation relationship with people who can influence my clients' careers.			
Create, organize, lead, and critique career workshops.			
Collaborate with other professionals to plan for client success.			
Use technology specific to career counseling.			
Locate and utilize funding sources for career counseling activities and programs.			
Career development theory – I have knowledge of:			
Counseling theories and associated techniques.			
Theories and models of career development.			
Individual differences related to gender, sexual orientation, race, ethnicity, and physical and mental capacities.			
Theoretical models for career development and associated counseling and information-delivery techniques and resources.			
Human growth and development throughout the lifespan.			
Role relationships which facilitate life–work planning.			
Information, techniques, and models related to career planning and placement.			
Individual and group counseling skills – I can effectively:			
Establish and maintain productive personal relationships with individuals.			
Establish and maintain a productive group climate.			
Collaborate with clients in identifying personal goals.			
Identify and select techniques appropriate to client or group goals and client needs, psychological states, and developmental tasks.			
Identify and understand clients' personal characteristics related to career.			
Identify and understand social contextual conditions affecting clients' careers.			

(*Continued*)

Table 15.2 Career counseling competencies (*Continued*)

Competency	I have limited skills and/or knowledge in this area	I have moderate skills and/or knowledge in this area	I am very skilled and/or knowledgeable in this area
Identify and understand familial, subcultural and cultural structures and functions as they are related to clients' careers.			
Identify and understand clients' career decision-making processes.			
Identify and understand clients' attitudes toward work and workers.			
Identify and understand clients' biases toward work and workers based on gender, race, and cultural stereotypes.			
Challenge and encourage clients to take action to prepare for and initiate role transitions by:			
• locating sources of relevant information and experience,			
• obtaining and interpreting information and experiences, and			
• acquiring skills needed to make role transitions.			
Assist the client to acquire a set of employability and job search skills.			
Support and challenge clients to examine life–work roles, including the balance of work, leisure, family, and community in their careers.			
Individual/group assessment – I can effectively:			
Assess personal characteristics such as aptitude, achievement, interests, values, and personality traits.			
Assess leisure interests, learning style, life roles, self-concept, career maturity, vocational identity, career indecision, work environment preference (e.g., work satisfaction), and other related lifestyle/ development issues.			
Assess conditions of the work environment (such as tasks, expectations, norms, and qualities of the physical and social settings).			
Evaluate and select valid and reliable instruments appropriate to the client's gender, sexual orientation, race, ethnicity, and physical and mental capacities.			
Use computer-delivered assessment measures effectively and appropriately.			
Select assessment techniques appropriate for group administration and those appropriate for individual administration.			
Administer, score, and report findings from career assessment instruments appropriately.			
Interpret data from assessment instruments and present the results to clients and to others.			

(*Continued*)

Table 15.2 Career counseling competencies (*Continued*)

Competency	I have limited skills and/or knowledge in this area	I have moderate skills and/or knowledge in this area	I am very skilled and/or knowledgeable in this area
Assist the client and others designated by the client to interpret data from assessment instruments.			
Write an accurate report of assessment results.			
Information/resources – I have knowledge of:			
Education, training, and employment trends; labor market information and resources that provide information about job tasks, functions, salaries, requirements, and future outlooks related to broad occupational fields and individual occupations.			
Resources and skills that clients utilize in life–work planning and management.			
Community/professional resources available to assist clients in career planning, including job search.			
Changing roles of women and men and the implications that this has for education, family, and leisure.			
Methods of good use of computer-based career information delivery systems (CIDS) and computer-assisted career guidance systems (CACGS) to assist with career planning.			
Program promotion, management, and implementation – I have knowledge of:			
Designs that can be used in the organization of career development programs.			
Needs assessment and evaluation techniques and practices.			
Organizational theories, including diagnosis, behavior, planning, organizational communication, and management useful in implementing and administering career development programs.			
Methods of forecasting, budgeting, planning, costing, policy analysis, resource allocation, and quality control.			
Leadership theories and approaches for evaluation and feedback, organizational change, decision-making, and conflict resolution.			
Professional standards and criteria for career development programs.			
Societal trends and state and federal legislation that influence the development and implementation of career development programs.			
I can effectively:			
Implement individual and group programs in career development for specified populations.			
Train others about the appropriate use of computer-based systems for career information and planning.			

(*Continued*)

Table 15.2 Career counseling competencies (*Continued*)

Competency	I have limited skills and/or knowledge in this area	I have moderate skills and/or knowledge in this area	I am very skilled and/or knowledgeable in this area
Plan, organize, and manage a comprehensive career resource center.			
Implement career development programs in collaboration with others.			
Identify and evaluate staff competencies.			
Mount a marketing and public relations campaign on behalf of career development activities and services.			
Coaching, consultation, and performance improvement – I can effectively:			
Use consultation theories, strategies, and models.			
Establish and maintain a productive consultative relationship with people who can influence a client's career.			
Help the general public and legislators to understand the importance of career counseling, career development, and life–work planning.			
Impact public policy as it relates to career development and workforce planning.			
Analyze future organizational needs and current level of employee skills and develop performance improvement training.			
Mentor and coach employees.			
Diverse populations – I can effectively:			
Identify development models and multicultural counseling competencies.			
Identify developmental needs unique to various diverse populations, including those of different gender, sexual orientation, ethnic group, race, and physical or mental capacity.			
Define career development programs to accommodate needs unique to various diverse populations.			
Find appropriate methods or resources to communicate with limited-English-proficient individuals.			
Identify alternative approaches to meet career planning needs for individuals of various diverse populations.			
Identify community resources and establish linkages to assist clients with specific needs.			
Assist other staff members, professionals, and community members in understanding the unique needs/characteristics of diverse populations with regard to career exploration, employment expectations, and economic/social issues.			
Advocate for the career development and employment of diverse populations.			

(*Continued*)

Table 15.2 Career counseling competencies (*Continued*)

Competency	I have limited skills and/or knowledge in this area	I have moderate skills and/or knowledge in this area	I am very skilled and/or knowledgeable in this area
Design and deliver career development programs and materials to hard-to-reach populations.			
Supervision – I can demonstrate:			
Ability to recognize own limitations as a career counselor and to seek supervision or refer clients when appropriate.			
Ability to utilize supervision on a regular basis to maintain and improve counselor skills.			
Ability to consult with supervisors and colleagues regarding client and counseling issues and issues related to one's own professional development as a career counselor.			
Knowledge of supervision models and theories.			
Ability to provide effective supervision to career counselors and career development facilitators at different levels of experience.			
Ability to provide effective supervision to career development facilitators at different levels of experience by:			
• knowledge of their roles, competencies, and ethical standards			
• determining their competence in each of the areas included in their certification			
• further training them in competencies, including interpretation of assessment instruments			
• monitoring and mentoring their activities in support of the professional career counselor			
• scheduling regular consultations for the purpose of reviewing their activities.			
Ethical/legal issues – I have knowledge of:			
Adherence to ethical codes and standards relevant to the profession of career counseling (e.g. NBCC, NCDA, and ACA).			
Current ethical and legal issues which affect the practice of career counseling with all populations.			
Current ethical/legal issues with regard to the use of computer-assisted career guidance systems.			
Ethical standards relating to consultation issues.			
State and federal statutes relating to client confidentiality.			
Research/evaluation – I can effectively:			
Write a research proposal.			
Use types of research and research designs appropriate to career counseling and development research.			

(*Continued*)

Table 15.2 Career counseling competencies (*Continued*)

Competency	I have limited skills and/or knowledge in this area	I have moderate skills and/or knowledge in this area	I am very skilled and/or knowledgeable in this area
Convey research findings related to the effectiveness of career counseling programs.			
Design, conduct, and use the results of evaluation programs.			
Design evaluation programs which take into account the need of various diverse populations, including persons of both genders, differing sexual orientations, different ethnic and racial backgrounds, and differing physical and mental capacities.			
Apply appropriate statistical procedures to career development research.			
Technology – I have knowledge of:			
Various computer-based guidance and information systems as well as services available on the Internet.			
Standards by which such systems and services are evaluated (e.g. NCDA and ACSCI).			
Ways in which to use computer-based systems and Internet services to assist individuals with career planning that are consistent with ethical standards.			
Characteristics of clients which make them profit more or less from use of technology-driven systems.			
Methods to evaluate and select a system to meet local needs.			

(adapted from NCDA's Career Counseling Competency Statements, www.ncda.org)

Art-Based Processes for Self-Reflection

In the following section, art-based processes for self-reflection and evaluation of your knowledge, skills, and comfort level with integrated career and art-based services will be offered. To begin your learning review, self-evaluation, and ongoing training goals choose from the following art-based explorations.

Symbol of Art Therapy and Career Development

Based on your experiences with readings and related assignments and reflections, create a symbol or logo that integrates art therapy and career counseling and represents your vision of that potential relationship. Symbols may be created via digital art methods, drawing and painting materials, or other media of your choice. Following your creation of the symbol or logo, explore how the image components reveal your conceptualization of art-informed career counseling and the aspects of this integration that may be salient for your current or future professional work. A few samples, one using a readily available web-based design program (Figure 15.1) and another with traditional materials completed by a graduate art therapy student following a career development art therapy course are provided here.

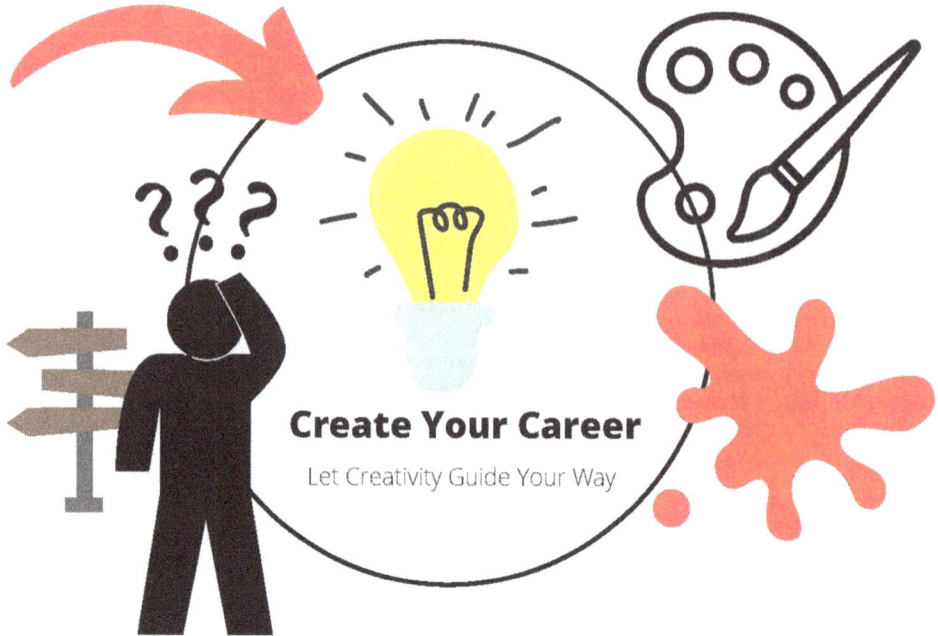

Figure 15.1 Symbolic Representation of Art Therapy and Career Counseling Integration #1

After reviewing their image, Figure 15.2, the graduate student summarized their experience of the potential of career counseling and art therapy integration:

> Art therapy and career counseling work together to merge a client's internal world with external realities. It allows the client to express their beliefs, values, and feelings, which are then able to be translated to real-world applications. The left side of the image depicts the person's internal world, an interaction between genetics and developed sense of self. The right side of the image depicts the external world, the influences felt from others as well as societal structures and norms. Those two sides meet in the middle, sending signals across to each other, and equally exchanging information. What results is a beautiful amalgamation of the two, a conclusion that is achieved through the guidance of the counselor.

What does your creation say about your current understanding and perspectives? Discuss your creation with a professional colleague or peer? What ideas stand out or call for further exploration and development?

Career Counseling and Art Therapy Toolbox

It has been the authors' intention to provide you with many ideas and methods for implementing theory-informed art therapy and career counseling processes. As you consider the chapter topics and content and your expanded knowledge, what ideas, interventions, strategies, or approaches will you place in your toolbox to inform your professional work with others? Depending on your background as a student or professional in art therapy, career counseling, or another related field, your toolbox may be filled with quite different items. In the Career Counseling and Art Therapy course at Florida State University we have frequently closed the semester by having students contribute to a digital whiteboard

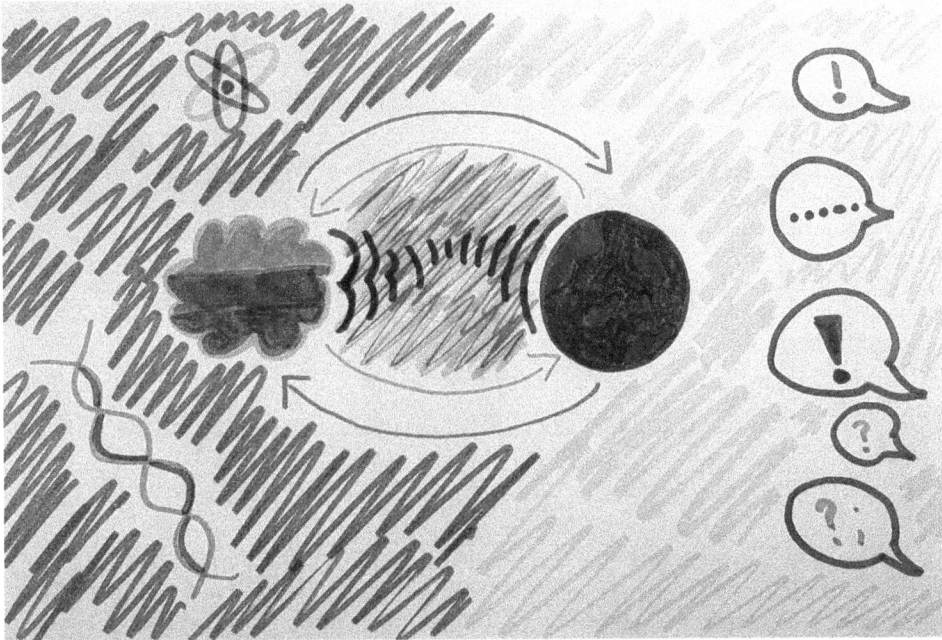

Figure 15.2 Symbolic Representation of Art Therapy and Career Counseling Integration #2

toolbox, filling it with course ideas and practices they felt ready to carry forward into future practical contexts. Figure 15.3 shows one such end of semester career counseling and art therapy toolbox.

What's in Your Toolbox?

Figure 15.4 provides a template for designing your own toolbox and space for representing the knowledge, strategies, and skills that you have gained regarding art therapy and career counseling after completing this text and/or a related course. In addition to utilizing the template, or a digital whiteboard, consider creating your own toolbox design

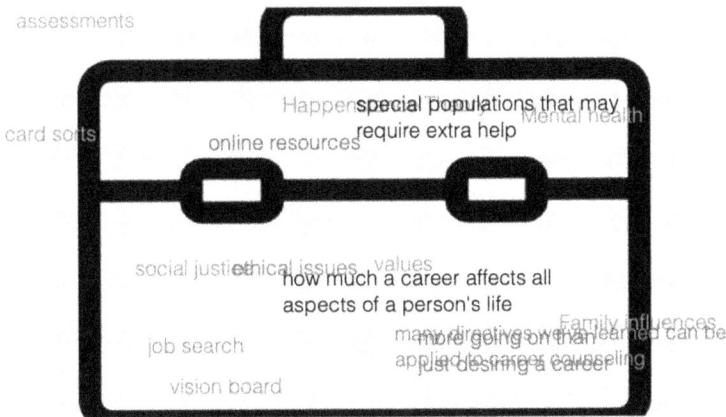

Figure 15.3 Career Counseling and Art Therapy Toolbox

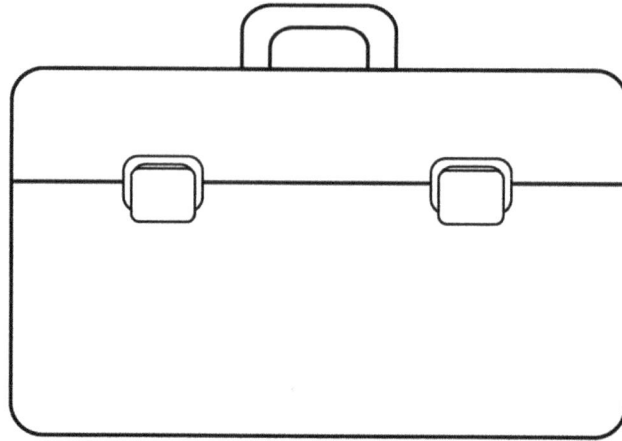

Figure 15.4 Toolbox Template

on a 12″ × 18″ paper and utilizing magazine and other collage materials, add images, words, or a combination of images and words to your Art Therapy and Career Counseling toolbox. Once you have completed your toolbox, step back, take an inventory of tools represented, and celebrate the presence of these tools? Secondly, review the contents of your toolbox and consider what additional tools might support your service to those who seeing assistance with career development concerns. What plans can you implement to add tools to your box? Identify reliable sources of information and additional training available to you.

Confidence Level Evaluation

Noting components of knowledge and skills held is one step in a comprehensive self-evaluation process (see Figure 15.5). Another step in the process, is assessing your confidence level in applying the ideas, strategies, and skills that you have learned. For example, O'Brien et al. (1997) developed the Career Counseling Self-Efficacy Scale to explore student levels of confidence in their ability to understand, organize, and perform a variety of career counseling interventions, tasks, and skills including navigating therapeutic alliance considerations; assessment selection, interpretation, and outcome

Figure 15.5 Confidence Meter Template

reporting; applying multicultural competency frameworks to practice; and knowledge of and ability to apply current ethical standards, research, and job market trends to the practice of career counseling. O'Brien et al. recommended using the measure to explore areas where additional training and preparation may be supportive or necessary. For each activity presented in the scale, individuals reported their current level of confidence on a scale from 0 to 4, 0 representing not confident, 2 representing moderately confident, and 4 representing highly confident.

As this is an art therapy and career counseling text, we are inviting readers to explore their confidence levels using a visual form. Figure 15.5 provides a visual Confidence Meter template for your use. Although not a validated measure, it may be helpful in revealing areas where you may wish to have more support or training to advance your confidence and competency in art therapy and career counseling. For this process, review each book chapter and identify the primary learning goals and topics for that chapter. Next, using the confidence meter form, fill in the form with marker or color pencil to show your level of confidence regarding your ability to utilize the learning concepts and skills presented. If you experience no confidence, leave the form blank. If you experience lower confidence, fill in a small portion of the scale. If you have a moderate level of confidence, fill in the form half-way. If you have very high confidence in the chapter topics and skills, fill in all of the form. Of course, you may fill in the form to the visual level that seems right for you. Be sure to label the form with the chapter name or number. Once you have completed the form for each chapter, note topics and trends regarding areas of lower and higher confidence. Here are some questions to consider. If you have low confidence, ask yourself, what chapters would be helpful to review? What available scholarly resources are available to extend learning in a particular area? What training or supervision might assist you in gaining confidence in navigating the therapeutic alliance or material qualities and processes?

Art Therapy and Career Counseling Brochure: Two Options

The final creative evaluative processes are presented in the form of a brochure designs with two different foci. Option 1 invites you to utilize a visual format for summarizing your text and/or course-related learning. Option 2 invites you to envision your "dream" career art therapy practice and a "vision-brochure" that would represent your ideas about services you may offer.

Option 1: Review of Art Therapy and Career Counseling Learning

To begin, refer to Figure 15.6 for a visual model of a tri-fold brochure. Using a 12″ × 18″ fold the paper in three. You will have up to six surfaces to cover. Alternatively, use any

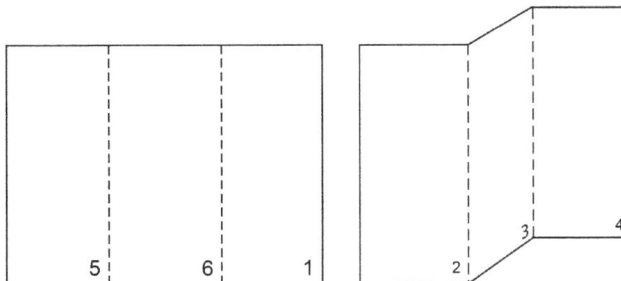

Figure 15.6 Visual Model of a Tri-Fold Brochure

digital art or web-based program with brochure design, graphics, and text options. If you are using paper, select drawing or painting materials of your choice, such as markers, color pencils, watercolors, or a combination of them. If you are using a water-based medium be sure to use a heavier stock paper that can absorb the fluid nature of the medium. Review the topics and directions for the pages, then plan and create your design.

1 Top Cover Page: On the cover of your brochure include your name and a symbol or image that represents your perspective and approach to career development/life counseling. Add a motto or quote that amplifies these ideas. Such as "The best way to predict the future is to create it" – Abraham Lincoln.
2 Inside Left Page: On this page, list and/or visually represent your learning accomplishments. Review the chapter topics to stimulate your ideas as necessary.
3 Inside Center Page: On this page, list or represent any specific areas of career development that interest you, or alternatively, a population you would be interested in working with related to their career development needs.
4 Inside Right Page: On this page, list and/or represent approaches and activities that you'd most like to use in the future. If you wish, match these approaches and activities to the area of population of interest.
5 Outside Right Page: On this page, list and/or represent how you wish to advance your career learning in the future and the next steps towards your learning goals.
6 Back Center Page: On this optional page, use images or words to reflect anything left unsaid, or questions you wish to have answered regarding career counseling and art therapy.

When finished with your brochure, show and discuss your work with a classmate, peer, colleague, or supervisor. Celebrate accomplishments and support each other in brainstorming ways to achieve identified next steps towards advancing learning goals.

Option 2: Your Art Therapy and Career Counseling "Vision-Brochure"

1 Top Cover Page: On the cover of your brochure include your name and a symbol or image that represents your population focus and philosophical or theoretical approach to work with that population. Add a motto or quote that amplifies these ideas.
2 Inside Left Page: On this page, list and/or visually represent career concerns and goals frequently experienced or set by people within the chosen group.
3 Inside Center Page: On this page, describe and/or represent your personal approach to working with clients to identify personal goals and how this approach may support them on their career journeys
4 Inside Right Page: On this page, list and/or represent assessment or intervention strategies that you may use with this population
5 Outside Right Page: On this page, imagine a client's or group's testimony regarding your high-quality work and success with this client group. Add an image and at least one "quote" that reflects the success you are aiming for.
6 Back Center Page: Visualize your long-term accomplishments related to your professional achievements and work with this population. Then, on this page, use images to represent credentials earned, awards received, or other items that demonstrate recognition of your positive work with this population.

When finished with your vision-brochure, show and discuss your work with a classmate, peer, colleague, or supervisor. After describing your vision for an ideal future practice, brainstorm options for making that vision, or a component of that vision a reality. Identify the first steps that you could take to move towards that goal.

Developing and Maintaining Knowledge and Skills

One is probably best equipped for practice immediately following graduation from one's master's program. Armed with the most up-to-date knowledge on the areas other professionals have deemed most critical for effective practice, coupled with highly supervised therapeutic experiences, and versed in the most current ethical guidelines, the recent graduate is well prepared, albeit likely somewhat nervous, to launch into providing services as a professional. Time and experience will further hone skills, but research continues to emerge, theories develop, new techniques are discovered and older ones honed. Legislative priorities that impact the profession and/or our clients shift with changing administrations. Staying aware of the ever-shifting landscape requires purposeful planning on the part of the ethical practitioner.

Proactive planning for continued professional development is likely to include a commitment to continued education. What type of continuing education is needed may be influenced to some degree by the clientele the therapist is seeing, and is also restricted by what a licensure or certification board will approve. For example, a therapist may find themselves working in an area with a certain population, such as military, veterans, retirees, or a specific ethnic group. In this case, obtaining additional information specific to their population would likely enhance their understanding of their client's population, including challenges that group faces as well as resources they prefer and that are specifically targeted for them.

Professional organizations are an excellent resource for providing continuing education topics on specific populations, research outcomes, and new approaches or assessments. These workshops and presentations are often approved by boards. In addition, many professional organizations have an advocacy component or group that will keep members aware of legislation that might impact the profession. National organizations will have greater offerings in terms of content and presentations, and advocacy efforts at the national level, while state organizations offer the targeting of legislation that will impact the state directly.

Other ways to stay informed include signing up for alerts about key topics, regularly visiting information sites, blogs, and newsfeeds specific to the profession, and following social media accounts of people who are informed about the field. The practitioner will need to evaluate for the presence of bias. Another way to stay informed on legislative issues is to visit the House of Representatives' and Senate's pages and follow relevant bills, committees, and legislators.

Sharing Your Knowledge and Experiences

Practitioners learn from their clients with every interaction. As practitioners put the science they have learned into practice, they weave in their own personalities and creativity. Research and theory provide guides for what might be impacting a client, and strategies for how to support a client, but it's the experience that happens with a client that brings research and theory to life. Practitioners can serve a vital role in informing theorists, researchers, and other practitioners, in that they can share how they implemented these in practice, roadblocks they encounter, unique nuances they experienced with a particular population or in a given setting, additional areas of concern voiced by their clientele, and strategies they found useful as they worked with their clients. This feedback can help inform researchers on what areas need further research, and challenge theorists on how to expand or deepen their theories. Some ways practitioners can share their knowledge include submitting workshop proposals for conference presentations, writing a blog, joining and contributing to professional social media sites such as LinkedIn or an association's social media venue, or writing for journals or magazines of professional associations. A benefit of sharing your passion and knowledge with others is that they might be inspired and equipped to apply your experiences and, in doing so, further expand your impact. Through sharing, you just might be helping individuals, colleagues, and the field in ways you never imagined possible.

Art Therapy and Career Development Goal Sheet

As noted above, learning and expanding skills regarding art therapy and career counseling is a career-long endeavor. Where does one begin? As each reader brings different skills and art therapy and career counseling practice, each reader will have a different next-step learning goal to strive towards. Begin the next learning journey by using the Art Therapy & Career Development Goal Sheet provided in Figure 15.7. Identify a SMART (Specific, Measurable, Attainable, Relevant, and Timely) art therapy and career development goal and list four action or reflection steps and dates for completion. Next, complete your action and reflection steps and celebrate achievements. Repeat as often as desired!

Summary

The pages of this chapter and the book in its entirety have described requisite knowledge and skills for integrating art therapy and career counseling. This final chapter provided several checklists and art processes for identifying strengths as well as areas for further growth and personal plan development. Committing to a goal of continued growth, along with regular evaluation of skills and engagement in learning activities, will lead to an enhanced understanding of how these two fields can intersect to provide powerful support for our clients and their career concerns.

Discussion Questions and Activities

1 Complete chapter checklists, reflection questions, and art processes provided throughout this chapter. Also consider the chapter headings within this book. Note which areas are your particular strengths, and which areas need shoring up. Create a plan for your continued professional development.

2 Based on your self-evaluation, in what circumstances would you be most likely to refer your patient, client, or student to a career counselor (if you are an art therapist) or to an art therapist (if you are a career counselor)?

3 Commit to evaluating your current level of skills on an annual basis. Identify a date and mark it on a calendar.

4 Review offerings for continued professional development by professional organizations and see if any will address your noted areas of growth or deepen current understandings.

5 Consider areas of professional interest, skills, populations, and experiences that you have. See if you can locate possible avenues for sharing from these areas with others, whether through professional associations, their conferences and publications, or

through less formal routes such as social media and blogs. Commit to sharing at least once a year something you've learned in your practice.

6 Collaborative challenge: Meet with a colleague (art therapist or career counselor) or (art therapy student or career counseling student), discuss your ideas and visions on how the two fields can collaborate to best serve clients and create a work of art that reflects this collaboration. For inspiration, refer to the authors' co-created artistic collaboration in Chapter 1 (Figure 1.5).

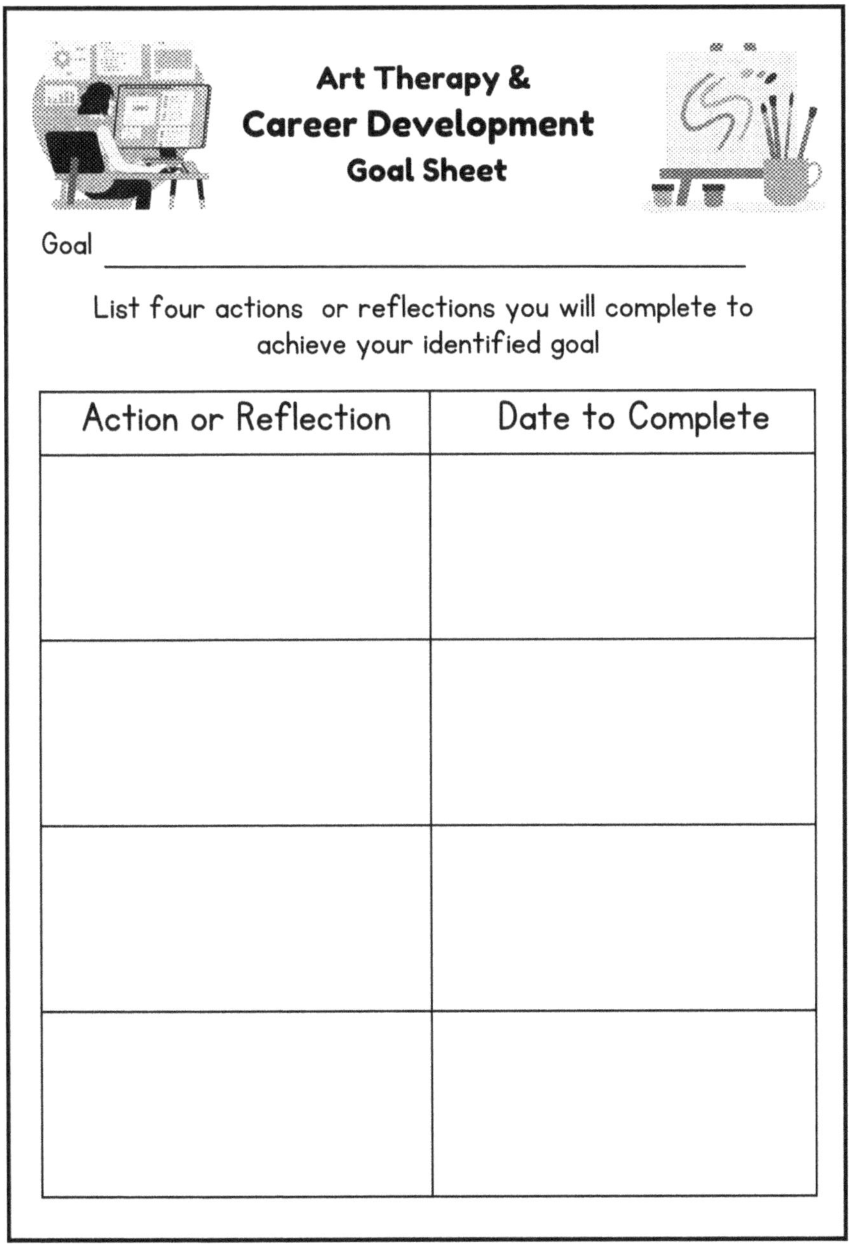

Art Therapy &
Career Development
Goal Sheet

Goal ______________________________

List four actions or reflections you will complete to achieve your identified goal

Action or Reflection	Date to Complete

Figure 15.7 Art Therapy and Career Development Goal Sheet. Copyright Parker-Bell 2022

References

Art Therapy Credentials Board (2022). Registration standards. www.atcb.org/registration-standards/

Commission on Accreditation of Allied Health Education Programs (2016). Standards and guidelines for the accreditation of educational programs in art therapy. www.caahep.org/CAAHEP/media/CAAHEP-Documents/ArtTherapyStandards.pdf

Council for Accreditation of Counseling and Related Educational Programs. (2016). 2016 CACREP standards. Retrieved from https://www.cacrep.org/for-programs/2016-cacrep-standards/

National Career Development Association. (n.d.). Multicultural career counseling competencies. www.ncda.org/aws/NCDA/pt/sp/compentencies_multi_cultural

O'Brien, K. M., Heppner, M. J., Flores, L. Y., & Bikos, L. H. (1997). The Career Counseling Self Efficacy Scale: Instrument development and training. *Journal of Counseling Psychology, 44*(1), 20–31.

Appendix
Career Counseling Art-Based Interventions

Dr. Barbara Parker-Bell and Dr. Debra Osborn

IMPORTANT NOTE: Utilization of these art-based interventions requires competency in career counseling and art therapy concepts and skills. Developments in the working alliance between therapist and client, goal agreement, and an awareness of client contexts and abilities also inform how art-based career interventions and counseling processes are best implemented.

Table A.1 Career counseling art-based interventions

Chapter #	Art-based intervention	Purpose	General directions	Materials/ETC considerations	Discussion focus process questions	Sources/citations
Chapter 1	Career Journey Line Group Activity	Explore various paths towards career interests/expand concept of career journeys	• Preformed central circle represents major or career choice • From edge of paper towards the central circle create a line that represents your journey to that major or career choice • Discuss as group	• Computer whiteboard screen with central circle • Craft paper mural with center circle • Broad markers	• What does your line say about your journey? • What did you notice about others' lines and journey descriptions? • What are you taking away from this group experience?	Parker-Bell, 2018
Chapter 2	Work/Life Role Meaning Life Review/Plan Accordion Book	Identify meaningful activities, roles, accomplishments identify areas to resolve and preferences/interests/meaning for future planning such as retirement	• Create a simple accordion book • Create a page per decade or other predetermined time span • For each decade artistically/symbolically represent: significant role(s), significant achievements, significant motivations, significant meaning • Reflect on themes • Create a page for the next decade with symbols that represent projected aspirations	• Self-made accordion book at least ten pages • Card stock, paper • Collage/variety of drawing media, scissors, glue	• What themes did you discover? • How have your roles, motivation, and meaning changed over your life span? • How might this history inform your future aspirations?	Parker-Bell, inspired by Kuo, 2018 Gibson, 2018
Chapter 2	RIASEC Collage and Self-Symbol Exploration: Where Do I Fit?	Further self-knowledge of person–work environment fit	• Create a series of collages or environments that reflect your associations, thoughts, and feelings regarding the Holland Code career types, related activities, and possible occupations • Create a self-symbol • Situate the self-symbol in each Holland Code career environment • Next, imagine yourself in each environment • Following reflection, take the parts of each environment that you would like to include in the ideal career environment • Construct a collage bringing these qualities together • Place the self-symbol into the ideal setting and reflect upon careers that combine these elements	• Seven 8" × 11" blank pages • Color papers • Tissue paper • Magazine images • Scissors • Ruler • Pencils • Glue sticks • Blank figure cut-out or photo cut-out or self-symbol to be mounted on cardstock • Reference materials and descriptions of the six types: Realistic, Investigative, Artistic, Social, Enterprising, Conventional	• In which career types or environments did you feel most comfortable? • In which career types or environment did you feel most uncomfortable? • How might your final collage creation and reflection experiences guide you in narrowing down your career options? • What career options do you wish to investigate further? • How may some of your preferences be satisfied in other areas of your life, such as leisure pursuits or hobbies?	Parker-Bell Holland, 1997

(Continued)

Table A.1 Career counseling art-based interventions (*Continued*)

Chapter #	Art-based intervention	Purpose	General directions	Materials/ETC considerations	Discussion focus process questions	Sources/citations
Chapter 2	**Building on Layers of Resources to Support Positive Career Outcomes**	Support identification of resources, positive experiences, and optimal career outcomes	• Identify career problem/create artwork that represents the problem • Create an artwork that represents resources that may assist you addressing the problem/barrier • Create artwork that represents positive ways/successes navigating concerns in the past • Create an artwork that reflects optimal career outcomes	• Watercolor paints • 12″ × 18″ thick white or watercolor paper	• What resources have you identified to assist you with this career concern? • What successes or positive experiences did you uncover that may be applied to your career goals? • Describe how images reflect resources, experiences, and optimal outcomes	Parker-Bell, 2017, inspired by Bannink, 2014
Chapter 2	**Career Story/ Pictorial Narratives**	Understand personal themes and values that inform career narratives and direction	• Use upward arrow questioning techniques • Career story exploration: three people admired, favorite movie/book, favorite motto • Problem picture • Preferred outcome picture • When finished with pictures provide a "catchy title" for each • Juxtapose problem and preferred outcome pictures	• Color pencils • Paper	• As we review your career story, what themes do you notice? • How well do the career themes characterize your desired career journey? • What aspects of this career story would you like to modify? • How might these career themes help you address the identified career problem and/or attain the preferred outcome?	Taylor & Savickas, 2016
Chapter 3	**Bubble Self-Portrait**	Explore the overlap of skills and responsibilities between career counselors and art therapists Identify areas within and outside of your preparation and competency Identify areas for further professional training and supervision related to professional roles and goals	• Create two different "bubble figures" to explore the roles and responsibilities of art therapists and career counselors and examine where those roles may overlap • Explore your own training and levels experience and create the "bubble self-portrait"	• Paper • Variety of 2D drawing materials	• What are the boundaries of my expertise? • What do clients need to know about my expertise and limitations to help clients make an informed decision about selecting me as a care provider? • What statements can I ethically make about my career and art therapy skills on my résumé or professional advertisements?	Art process inspired by ethical decision-making models, such as Hartel & Hartel, 1997

(*Continued*)

Table A.1 Career counseling art-based interventions *(Continued)*

Chapter #	Art-based intervention	Purpose	General directions	Materials/ETC considerations	Discussion focus process questions	Sources/ citations
Chapter 4	**Creative Career Genogram**	Increase awareness of external influences on career interest, knowledge, and decision-making Explore family career patterns and values	• Client gathers pertinent career information from family members • Explain purpose • Create chart of family members to support beginning of genogram creation • Chart is transformed into genogram symbols • Genogram symbols can be depicted in creative forms using a variety of media less traditional than genogram structures	• Traditional career genogram example • Variety of 2D/3D materials • Collage materials • Paper	• What family patterns exist? • What family members had a clearly formed work identity? • Which family member did you most admire? • Whom did you identify with? • What family traditions or legends existed? • How did these affect you?	Chope, 2005 Storlie et al., 2019
Chapter 4	**"Strengthened" Career Genogram**	Increase self-knowledge Empower to reconstruct family messages/ influence to construct new career/life narrative	• Career genogram • Jewel box • Mirror • Letter • Parchment • Review/discuss • Construct life/career narrative	• Paper • Variety of 2D drawing material • Parchment paper, or create your own parchment paper • 3D materials optional for jewel box and jewel box items, such as pre-existing boxes, clay, or more	• Client reflects on series of artworks and answers: • What do I take away from my work genogram? • What caught your attention the most? • What has impressed them as regards their professional life and future • Focus on meaning-making	Di Fabio, 2010
Chapter 5	**Career Concept Form**	Explore client status regarding career goal setting and decision-making Explore related factors such as client resources, talents and interests, steps necessary for goal achievement, and rewards that contribute to career decisions	• Fill in as much as you know about your career goals, career qualities, rewards of pursuing such a career, supports and resources that would enable you to pursue your goal, and skills, talents, or interests that will help you be successful and/or satisfied with the career • Also, list or fill in steps you believe you would need to take to move towards your career goal	• Paper • Variety of 2D materials • Collage material	• What do you notice first about this image? • What steps towards your career goals are you excited about? • What steps towards your career goals feel worrisome? • What gaps in information, if any exist in your image? • What actions could you take to fill in those gaps?	Parker-Bell, 2022

(Continued)

Table A.1 Career counseling art-based interventions (*Continued*)

Chapter #	Art-based intervention	Purpose	General directions	Materials/ETC considerations	Discussion focus process questions	Sources/ citations
Chapter 5	**Career Bridge Drawing**	Support visualization of career goals, pathways to achievement, and current progress on that path Explore identified supports (internal and external) that may assist in goal attainment	• Guided imagery regarding ideal career • Draw bridge to ideal career • Place self on bridge • Draw career on other side of bridge • Write/create steps towards career on bridge path • Draw/write career supports into the bridge support	• Paper 12″ × 18″ • Drawing/painting materials	• How would you describe your current career goal? • How would you describe your current progress towards this goal? • What types of experiences and resources support your career path and goals?	Casado-Keho, 2016
Chapter 5	**Career Collage Story and Headline**	To facilitate engagement in career counseling and to elicit motivational and affective reflection	• Create a collage that reflects your current career development interests and concerns • Provide a headline for the collage as if it was the illustration for a featured newspaper story about your career interests, concerns, or status	• Paper • Variety of 2D materials • Collage material	• Explore the who, what, when, where, and how of the story as it may be described to readers	Parker-Bell
Chapter 5	**Values Portrait**	Identify/explore most important work/life values Support decision-making/action	• Complete values card sort • Create a portrait of top work/life values identified	• Variety of 2D materials • Collage material • Paper	• How does your artwork reflect or enhance or change your understanding of your career values?	Parker-Bell Card sort: VCU Career Services, 2019
Chapter 5	**Exploration of Dominant Qualities**	Explore personal traits client perceives may interfere with their career satisfaction, career effectiveness, or desired goals Externalize the trait and examine it dimensionally	• Think about a personal trait that you have defined as a weakness • Externalize the thing and give it substance – that is, draw it, shape it in a lump of clay, write a poem that captures its different aspects • Take some time to reflect upon your creation	• Paper • Variety of 2D drawing materials • Clay	• What is it? • How did it originate • How does it serve you? • What challenges, opportunities, or dangers does it present? • How do you, or can you, compensate for its other side, its shadow? • If it could speak, what might it say? • What does it have to teach? • What does it have that you need?	Barba, 2000

(*Continued*)

Table A.1 Career counseling art-based interventions (*Continued*)

(*Continued*)

Chapter #	Art-based intervention	Purpose	General directions	Materials/ETC considerations	Discussion focus process questions	Sources/ citations
Chapter 6	**Inclusive Career Genogram**	Explore career influences beyond family to include broader societal, community, and "non-traditional" relations Appreciate cultural contexts	• Career interview/gathering of information about career "influencers" and reflection • Create self-symbol in middle of the page • Symbols of influencers are created and placed on the page. • Lines between self and influencers indicate the perceived significance of each influencer	• Posterboard • Markers • Whiteboard and whiteboard markers • Surface should be large enough to allow room for all necessary components	• What role models, heroes, influencers, and career themes appeared in your inclusive genogram? • What can you learn from each influence? • Which influences do you feel most connected with or strengthened by? • Which influences would you wish to discard, if any?	Buxbaum & Hill, 2013
Chapter 6	**Cultural Vessel Art Process**	Address cultural humility creatively, using a creative process and product to express, hold, examine, and discard beliefs and assumptions	• Create a bag, toolkit, or vessel out of paper, a metaphorical holding of biases assumptions, beliefs, skills as you examine prejudicial systems, oppression, and concepts of "colonialism, racism, classism, sexism, heteronormativism, and ableism" • Add to your creation and review and replace components with new perceptions, thoughts, and understanding	• Paper bag • Variety of 2D drawing materials • Collage materials	• What biases or assumptions do I carry with me? • How do these biases or assumptions influence the art materials or processes I offer? • How do these biases or assumptions influence the career aptitudes, interests, or pathways that I explore with clients? • How do these biases or assumptions influence the art materials or processes I offer? • How do these biases or assumptions influence or interfere with my working alliance with the client? • What are some ways can challenge a bias or an assumption I have and learn more about the systems influencing my clients' experiences? • How can I advocate for change of oppressive systems that impact client opportunities?	Bodlovic & Jackson, 2019

Table A.1 Career counseling art-based interventions (*Continued*)

Chapter #	Art-based intervention	Purpose	General directions	Materials/ETC considerations	Discussion focus process questions	Sources/ citations
Chapter 6	**Similarities and Differences**	Cultivating conversations regarding cultural values and customs to increase awareness and acknowledgment of practitioner and client experiences related to career and work concepts	• Both practitioner and client participate in process • Divide paper into three columns, the first marked "Similarities" and the second and third column "Differences" • Consider work/career concepts • The first column provides a space to identify what concepts/ideas and practices are shared • The second and third columns provide spaces for practitioner and client to identify/ depict perceived differences in identities, experiences, concepts, and practices	• Large piece of paper, post board • Markers, paint, collage	• What similarities and/or differences did you find noteworthy? • Which work and career values identified need further attention and discussion to advance understanding and goal alignment? • What cultural values and practices would you like to incorporate and/or leave behind as you explore this current work/career journey?	Dye, 2017
Chapter 7	**When I Grow Up**	Fostering career curiosity and imagination about career options in children	• Read or listen to a reading of the book *When I Grow Up* by Yankovic and Hargis • Create at least one fantastical career option using drawing and painting materials	• Paper • Variety of 2D materials	• During this past week, how many people did you see working at their jobs? • How many types of jobs can you name? • What do you imagine people do in those jobs? • If you could make up any kind of job, what might that be? • What would you do in that job?	Parker-Bell, inspired by the book by Yankovic & Hargis, 2011
Chapter 7	**Career Haiku and Photo**	Increase students' creative exploration of talents and interests and support development of long-term career goals	• Students are encouraged to begin the career exploration by capturing digital photographs of hobbies, interests, places, or things that represent their skills or strengths • After reviewing these images in small groups and learning about the haiku poetry process, the students use the stimulus of a selected photograph to write their poem about the career interest	• Disposable camera/ digital camera/ camera on phone • Printer/printer paper/ink • Writing paper and utensils	• Completed haikus are read and discussed in the small groups • What does your photo and/or haiku say about your hobbies or interests? • How might your hobbies or interests connect to a career interest? • What more do you want to know about that career interest?	Parker-Bell art adaptation of Hermann & Hasha, 2015

(Continued)

Table A.1 Career counseling art-based interventions (*Continued*)

Chapter #	Art-based intervention	Purpose	General directions	Materials/ETC considerations	Discussion focus process questions	Sources/ citations
Chapter 8	**Strengths Collage**	Gain awareness of your strengths and how they may be applied to your everyday life	• Complete the VIA-IS • Create a "My Strengths" collage based on the strengths identified and/or those that resonate with you	• Paper, magazines, markers, paint, and other drawing material	• Which strengths did you choose to represent? • How do your strengths support your career pursuits? • How could you best utilize your strengths within your current career roles? • What other careers, work roles, or work settings provide a greater fit for your strengths?	Darewych & Bowers, 2018
Chapter 8	**Photo Voice: Exploring Barriers and Assets**	Consideration of cultural contexts of client barriers and assets regarding career choice and opportunities Empower and support development of hope and relevant career planning	• Career barrier/asset map • 12 photos of barriers/assets • Two photos selected • SHOWED process used for reflective writing	• Disposable camera/ digital camera/ camera on phone • Printer/printer paper/ink • Writing paper and utensils	• Use SHOWED method • Support identification and exploration of assets, and identification of resilience regarding barriers	Smit, Wood, & Neethling, 2015
Chapter 8	**Vision Board**	Identify career goals/aspirations Motivate action towards career goals	• Encourages client to list goals for career/ life and to think about images that go with those goals • Select goals to focus on for vision board • Use collage images and words to represent goals • After completion and reflection on it, have client place vision board where it can be seen by client • Encourage client to look at vision board daily	• Posterboard/blank mask, flowerpot, bulletin board, etc. • Collage materials • Scissors • Glue/glue stick	• Support client's reflections regarding items included on the vision board and ask clarifying questions as needed • Explore ways the vision board may be utilized to support efforts towards career goals • Support client in identifying place where vision board will serve as a reminder of goals	Burton & Lent, 2016
Chapter 9	**PIC Review with Art Investigation**	Decision-making support/checking compatibility between career/ job option and self	• Have vision board and values portrait available for viewing • After narrowing five to seven career job choices to two, investigate the two preferred options • Create response art regarding two career/ job options that have been investigated to assist with choice • View response art along with vision board and values portrait to explore themes	• 12″ 18″ paper • Collage/variety of 2D materials • Oil pastels, markers	• After reviewing your response art, vision board, and values portrait, explore how your choices agree with or contrast with your vision and values • What do you see? • How may your observations shape your choice?	Gati & Asher, 2001 Rochat, 2019 Parker-Bell art investigation

(Continued)

Table A.1 Career counseling art-based interventions (Continued)

Chapter #	Art-based intervention	Purpose	General directions	Materials/ETC considerations	Discussion focus process questions	Sources/citations
Chapter 9	**Possible Lives Map/Art Adaptations**	Explore and identify themes of career interests Examine and identify possible, probable, and intended career paths depending on level of readiness	• Create circle/self-symbol in center of page • Write careers that you have considered during your lifetime • Circle each career option • Connect circled careers to self with line • Review for themes • Identify three to put on sticky notes • Note steps to three careers on line from self to career	• Legal size paper • Pencils, markers • Sticky notes • Additional materials for creative adaptations	• What three career themes did you identify in this process? • Describe the steps that you would need to take for each career • Considering the themes and the steps, which of these options seems most interesting and manageable? • Identify the first step towards that option	Brooks, 2016
Chapter 9	**Circles of Influence**	Cultivate exploration regarding perceptions of career influences including unplanned events	• Reflect on a career decision you have made in the past • Consider the three circles of influence described below • Determine the size of each circle based on their degree of influence on your career choice: The inner circle represents teachers, advisors, and media influences on the identified career choice The middle circle represents the family, friends, and colleagues that influenced this career choice The outermost circle represents unplanned events that influenced the career choice • Create the three-circle form to reflect the degree of influence each circle had on your choice • Within each circle, represent specific influences related to each category using line, shape, color, symbol, and/or words • Repeat for two other job choice experiences • Compare similarities and differences of influences on career decision-making at different junctions	• Variety of circles in different sizes • Variety of 2D materials Paper • Or; digital art programs and computer/tablet	• As you review your circles of influences, which influences stand out? • Which influences increased or decreased in importance related to most recent choices? • How did unplanned events influence your career choices? • Describe three positive aspects of one or more unplanned influences on career choice	Parker-Bell adaptation of Pryor & Bright, 2011

(Continued)

Table A.1 Career counseling art-based interventions (*Continued*)

Chapter #	Art-based intervention	Purpose	General directions	Materials/ETC considerations	Discussion focus process questions	Sources/citations
Chapter 13	**Career Lattice**	Support positive transitions Identify strengths and experiences that are applicable to work goals/circumstances Value experiences that are not hierarchical in nature (lattice vs. ladder)	• Introduce lattice vs. ladder concepts • Show a variety of lattice images • Using desired lattice form, depict strengths and experiences that you have had that could be drawn upon for career pursuits	• Choice of 2D or 3D materials	• As your review your lattice of experiences and strengths, what themes do you notice? • How might these themes inform future work interests • How might you translate these themes to a potential employer?	McBride & Cleymans, 2014 Parker-Bell, 2020, art adaptation
Chapter 13	**Career Mobile**	Address ambivalence Support readiness for change	• Create or find small objects that represent reasons to make career change and reasons not to make career change • Attach to mobile structure (created with sticks, hanger) • Explore balance or lack of balance of elements • Explore visual, physical, and emotional weight of the pros and cons	• Craft sticks • Hangers • Variety of paper • String/yarn • Found/created objects • Scissors	• What did you notice/learn from the process of creating the mobile? • Which elements visually or physically weigh the heaviest or lightest or need more attention? • Based on what you see, what next step may be most important for you?	Parker-Bell
Chapter 15	**Art Therapy Vision Brochure**	Utilize a visual format for summarizing your text- and/or course-related learning	• Fold paper in three • Top Cover Page: include your name and a symbol or image that represents your perspective and approach to career development/life counseling; add a motto or quote that amplifies these ideas • Inside Left Page: list and/or visually represent your learning accomplishments • Inside Center Page: list or represent any specific areas of career development that interest you, or alternatively, a population you would be interested in working with • Inside Right Page: list and/or represent approaches and activities that you'd most like to use in the future	• 12″ × 18″ paper • Variety of 2D materials • If you are using water-based medium, be sure to use a heavier stock paper that can absorb the fluid nature of the medium	• When finished with your brochure, show and discuss your work with a classmate, peer, colleague, or supervisor • Celebrate accomplishments and support each other in brainstorming ways to achieve identified next steps towards advancing learning goals	Parker-Bell

(*Continued*)

Table A.1 Career counseling art-based interventions (Continued)

Chapter #	Art-based intervention	Purpose	General directions	Materials/ETC considerations	Discussion focus process questions	Sources/citations
			• Outside Right Page: list and/or represent how you wish to advance your career learning in the future and the next steps towards your learning goals • Back Center Page: use images or words to reflect anything left unsaid, or questions you wish to have answered regarding career counseling and art therapy		• What are three things you are taking away from your career counseling and art therapy experience? • How would you like to utilize these tools in the future?	Parker-Bell
Chapter 15	Career Toolbox	Career skills/self-efficacy exploration Closure of career counseling and art therapy	• Provide preformed toolbox • Encourage client to symbolize career knowledge, skills, strategies, and outcomes of career counseling and art therapy	• Preformed toolbox (either outlined drawing or small box) • Markers, collage, colored paper, card stock, scissors, glue sticks		
Extra	Mandala of Inner/Outer Career Influences	Increase self-knowledge/awareness of career interest influences	• Provide circle shapes of various sizes for tracing • Ask to reflect on inner and outer influences regarding career choice • Select size of circle that will hold/contain the inner influences and trace in center of the page • With 2D materials, create line, shape, colors, or symbols of inner influences within the circle, outer influences outside the circle	• Circle shapes for tracing • Markers/other 2D drawing materials, collage optional • 18" × 24" paper	• Describe the circle size you selected to represent your inner influences • Describe the relationship between your inner and outer influences • What do you notice?	Parker-Bell, 2018
Extra	Career Constellation	Exploring career influences and reflecting upon primary influences regarding career decision-making	• Identify work influences • Place symbol of self in center of page • Place influences in constellation stars based on closeness/importance of influences • Sketch and name your career constellation • Describe your constellation's story	• Worksheet • Can be adapted to traditional art materials/paper on a larger scale • Markers, pencils, and color pencil pens	• Describe your constellation's visual qualities? • What do you notice about your constellation content? • What themes do you notice in your constellation story?	Falco et al., 2011

References

Bannink, F. P. (2014). Positive CBT: From reducing distress to building success. *Journal of Contemporary Psychotherapy, 44*(1), 1–8.

Barba, H. N. (2000). *Follow your bliss! A practical, soul-centered guide to job-hunting and career life planning.* Universal Publishers.

Bodlovic, A., & Jackson, L. (2019). A cultural humility approach to art therapy multicultural pedagogy: Barriers to compassion. *The International Journal of Diversity in Education, 19*(1). https://doi.org/10.18848/2327-0020/CGP/v19i01/1-9

Brooks, K. S. (2016). Breaking through career indecision in clients with ADHD. *Career Planning and Adult Development Journal, 32*(1), 54–62.

Burton, L., & Lent, J. (2016). The use of vision boards as a therapeutic intervention. *Journal of Creativity in Mental Health, 11*(1), 52–65. http://dx.doi.org/10.1080/15401383.2015.1092901

Buxbaum, E. H., & Hill, J. C. (2013). Inclusive career genogram activity: Working with clients facing forced career transitions to broaden the mind and encourage possibility. *Career Planning and Adult Development Journal, 29*(4), 45–59.

Casado-Keho, M. (2016). Bridge of life: Creating a career path. In W. K. Killam, S. Degges-White, & R. E. Michel (Eds.), *Career counseling interventions: Practice with diverse clients* (pp. 166–168). Springer.

Chope, R. (2005). Qualitatively assessing family influence in career decision making. *Journal of Career Assessment, 13*(4), 395–414. https://doi.org/10.1177/1069072705277913

Darewych, O. H., & Bowers, N. R. (2018). Positive arts interventions: Creative clinical tools promoting psychological well-being. *International Journal of Art Therapy, 23*(2), 62–69. https://doi.org/10.1080/17454832.2017.1378241

Di Fabio, A. (2010). Life designing in 21st century: Using a new, strengthened career genogram, *Journal of Psychology in Africa, 20*(3), 381–384. https://doi.org/10.1080/14330237.2010.10820389

Dye, L. (2017). *Using art techniques across cultural and race boundaries: Working with identity.* Jessica Kingsley.

Falco, L. D., Hatfield, A., Hirdes, C., & Tatum, T. (2011). Career constellation worksheet. In T. M. Lara, M. Pope, & C. W. Minor (Eds.), *Experiential activities for teaching career counseling classes and for facilitating career groups* (pp. 158–159). National Career Development Association

Gati, I., & Asher, I. (2001). Prescreening, in-depth exploration, and choice: From decision theory to career counseling practice. *The Career Development Quarterly, 50*, 140–157. https://doi.org/10.1002/j.2161-0045.2001.tb00979.x

Gibson, F. (Ed.) (2018). *International perspectives on reminiscence, life review and life story work.* Jessica Kingsley.

Hartel, C., & Hartel, G. (1997). Assisted intuitive decision making and problem solving: Information-processing-based training for conditions of cognitive busyness. *Group Dynamics: Theory, Research, and Practice, 1*(3), 187–199.

Hermann, K. M., & Hasha, L. R. (2015). Career story haiku. In S. Degges-White & B. Colon, *Expressive arts interventions for school counselors* (pp. 227–229). Springer.

Holland, J. L. (1997). *Making vocational choices: A theory of vocational personalities and work environments.* PAR.

Kuo, T. (2018). Reminiscence and life review work in Taiwan. In F. Gibson (Eds.), *International perspectives on reminiscence, life review and life story work* (pp. 125–144). Jessica Kingsley.

McBride, P., & Cleymans, L. (2014). A paradigm shift: Strategies for assisting military spouses in obtaining a successful career path. *Career Planning and Adult Development Journal, 30*(3), 92–101.

Pryor, R., & Bright, J. (2011). *The chaos theory of careers: A new perspective on working in the twenty-first century.* Routledge.

Rochat, S. (2019). The Career Decision-Making Difficulties Questionnaire: A case for item-level interpretation. *The Career Development Quarterly, 67*, 205–219. https://doi.org/10.1002/cdq.12191

Smit, S., Wood, L., & Neethling, M. (2015). Helping learners think more hopefully about life after school: The usefulness of participatory visual strategies to make career education more contextually relevant. *Perspectives in Education, 33*(3), 121–140.

Storlie, C.A., Hilton, T. M. L., McKinney, R., & Unger, D. (2019). Family career genograms: Beginning life design with exploratory students. *The Family Journal: Counseling and Therapy for Couples and Families, 27*(1), 84–91. https://doi.org/10.1177/1066480718819866

Taylor, J. M., & Savickas, S. (2016). Narrative career counseling: My Career Story and pictorial narratives. *Journal of Vocational Behavior, 97*, 68–77.

Virginia Commonwealth University Career Services. (2019). Values card sort. Retrieved from https://careers.vcu.edu/media/career-services/career-documents/ValuesCardSort_19.pdf

Yankovic, A., & Hargis, W. (2011). *When I grow up*. Harper.

Index

For Product Safety Concerns and Information please contact our EU
representative GPSR@taylorandfrancis.com
Taylor & Francis Verlag GmbH, Kaufingerstraße 24, 80331 München, Germany

www.ingramcontent.com/pod-product-compliance
Lightning Source LLC
Chambersburg PA
CBHW080129270326
41926CB00021B/4405

9 7 8 0 3 6 7 4 7 6 6 5 6